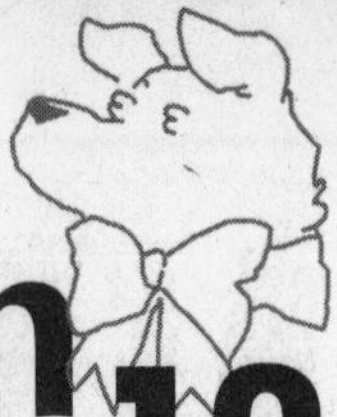

maison ikkoku 12

STORY AND ART BY RUMIKO TAKAHASHI

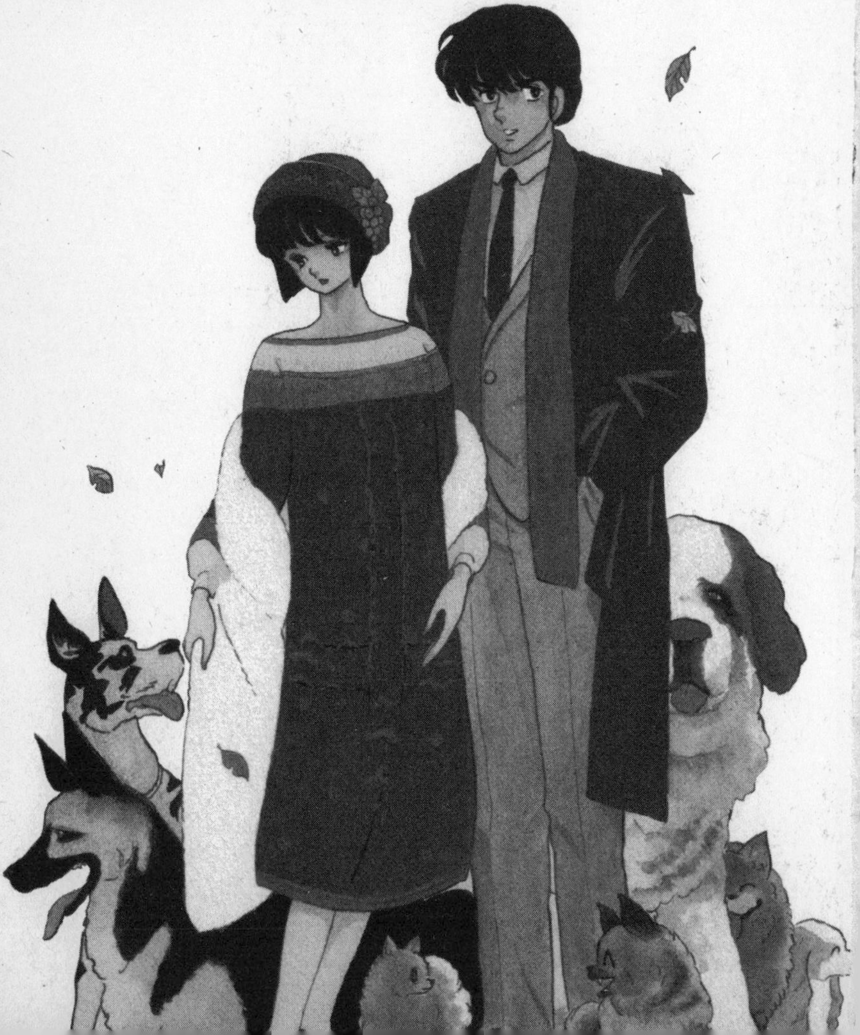

TABLE OF CONTENTS

Part One: Hair o' the Dog---------------------------------3

Part Two: Oh, You Lucky Dog----------------------------21

Part Three: Like Bubbles on the Breeze-------------43

Part Four: The Sun Will Shine---------------------------63

Part Five: Silence Is Golden
              (Or at Least Very Expensive)-----------83

Part Six: Coming Clean-------------------------------103

Part Seven: Mr. Godai Regrets
              (He Is Unable to Lunch Today)-------123

Part Eight: Good Mourning---------------------------141

Part Nine: The Chrysanthemum and the
              Building Block-----------------------------159

Part Ten: Back from the Grave-------------------177

Part Eleven: Never Let You Go---------------------------195

Part Twelve: The Age of Innocence----------------------211

PART ONE

HAIR O' THE DOG

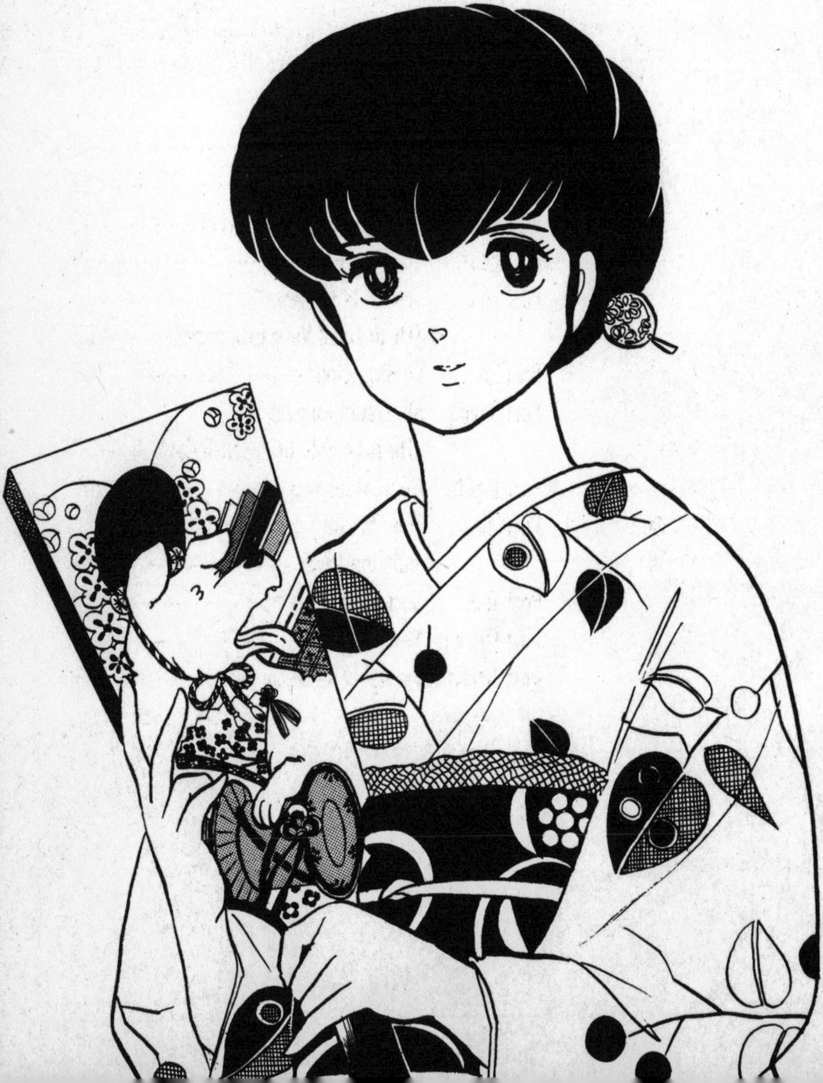

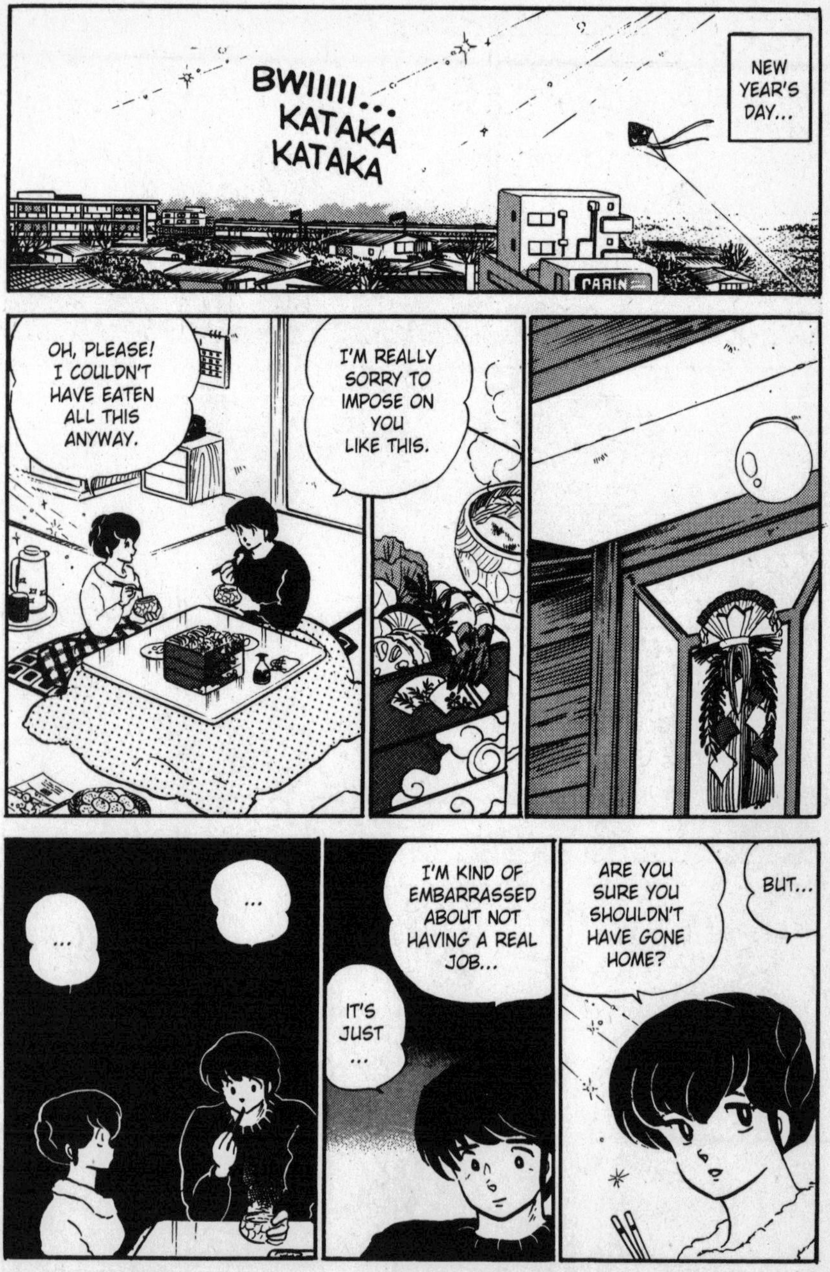
NEW YEAR'S DAY...
BWIIIII... KATAKA KATAKA
CABIN
I'M REALLY SORRY TO IMPOSE ON YOU LIKE THIS.
OH, PLEASE! I COULDN'T HAVE EATEN ALL THIS ANYWAY.
BUT...
ARE YOU SURE YOU SHOULDN'T HAVE GONE HOME?
I'M KIND OF EMBARRASSED ABOUT NOT HAVING A REAL JOB...
IT'S JUST ...
...
...

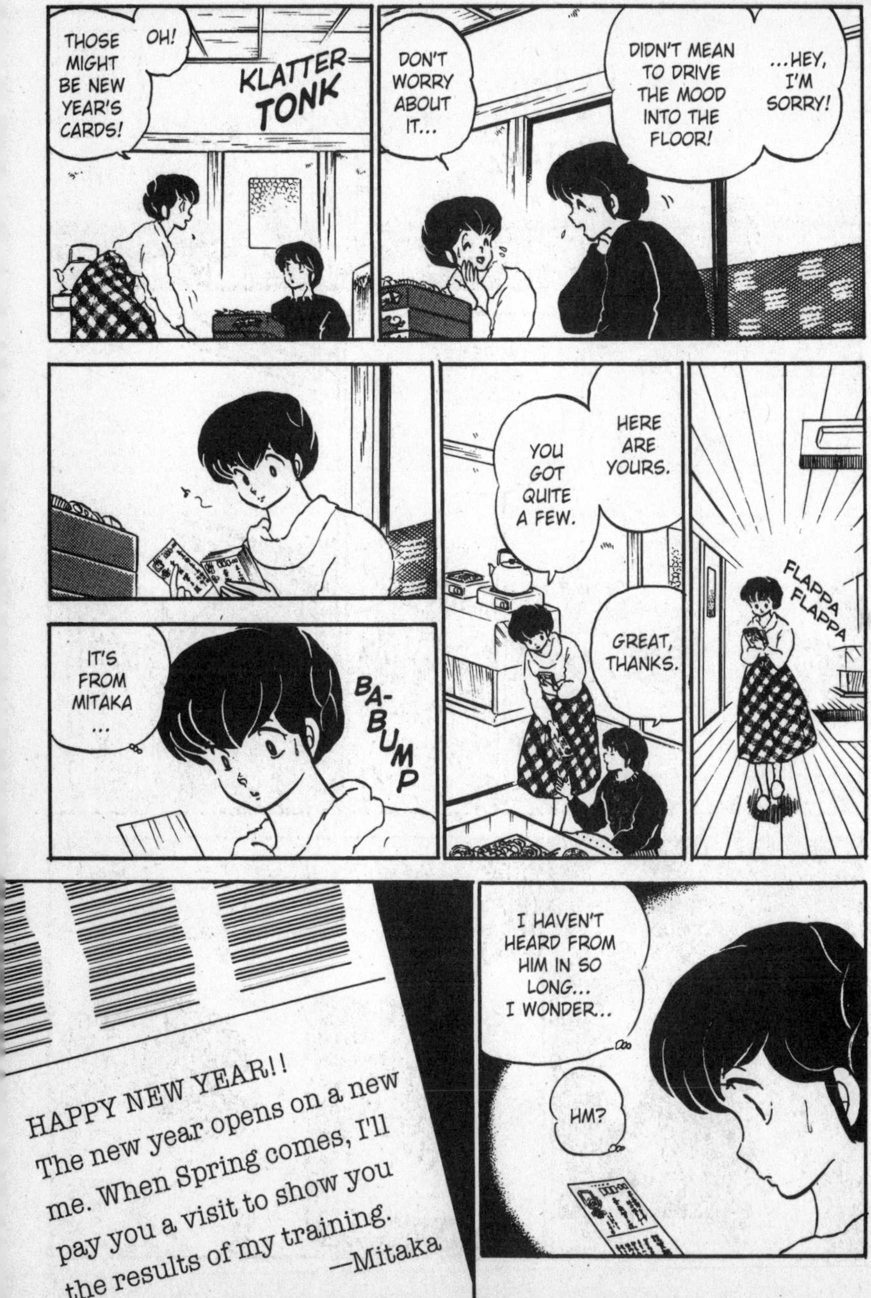
...HEY, I'M SORRY!
DIDN'T MEAN TO DRIVE THE MOOD INTO THE FLOOR!
DON'T WORRY ABOUT IT...
OH!
THOSE MIGHT BE NEW YEAR'S CARDS!
KLATTER TONK
FLAPPA FLAPPA
HERE ARE YOURS.
YOU GOT QUITE A FEW.
GREAT, THANKS.
IT'S FROM MITAKA ...
BA-BUMP
I HAVEN'T HEARD FROM HIM IN SO LONG... I WONDER...
HM?
HAPPY NEW YEAR!!
The new year opens on a new me. When Spring comes, I'll pay you a visit to show you the results of my training.
—Mitaka

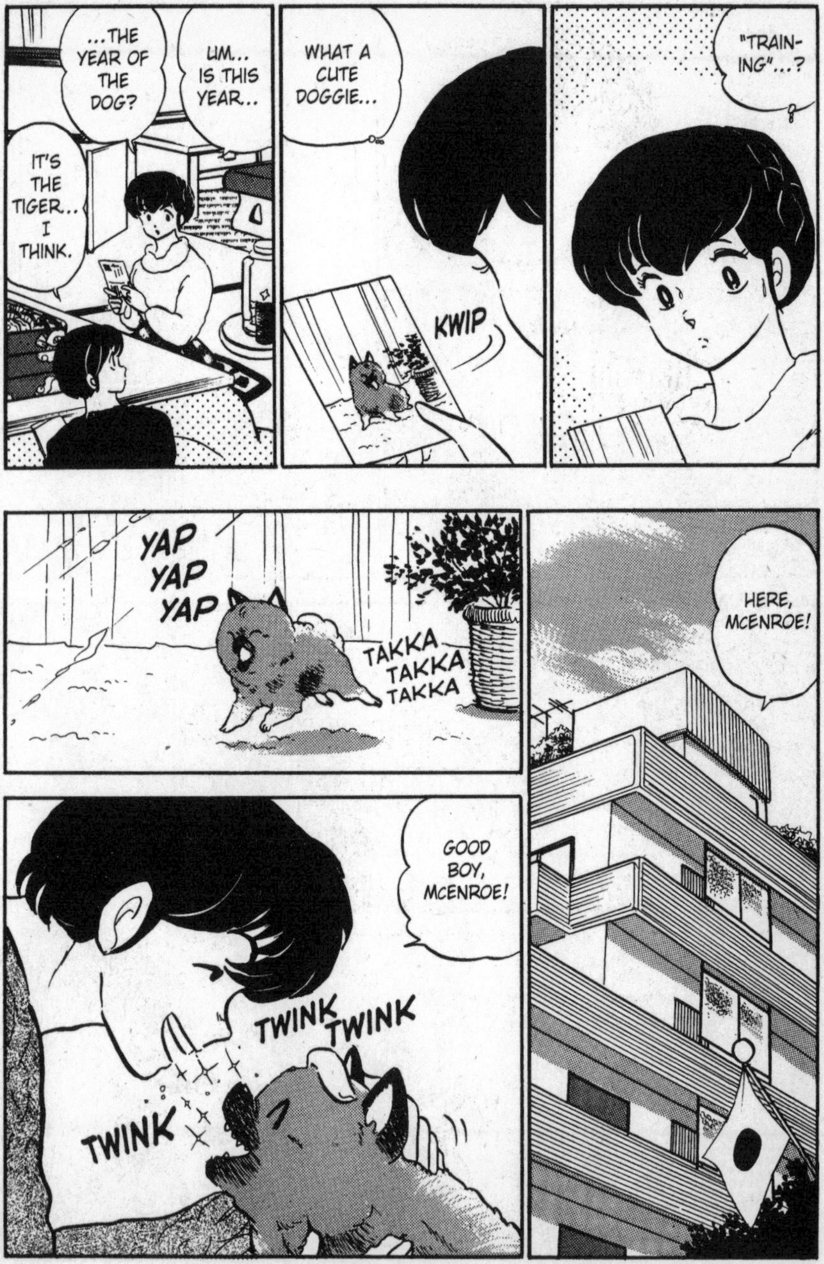
"TRAIN-ING"...?
WHAT A CUTE DOGGIE...
KWIP
UM... IS THIS YEAR...
...THE YEAR OF THE DOG?
IT'S THE TIGER... I THINK.
HERE, MCENROE!
YAP YAP YAP
TAKKA TAKKA TAKKA
GOOD BOY, MCENROE!
TWINK TWINK
TWINK

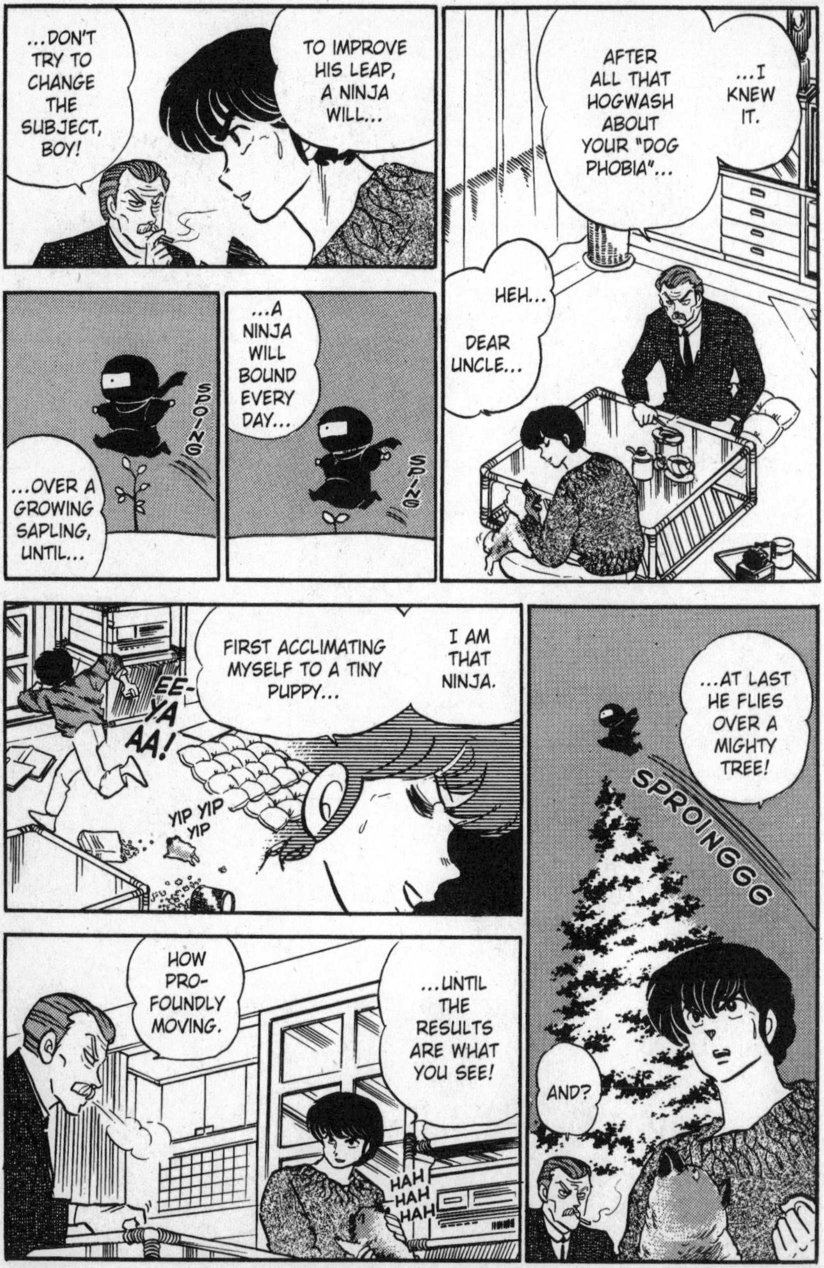
...I KNEW IT.
AFTER ALL THAT HOGWASH ABOUT YOUR "DOG PHOBIA"...
HEH...
DEAR UNCLE...
TO IMPROVE HIS LEAP, A NINJA WILL...
...DON'T TRY TO CHANGE THE SUBJECT, BOY!
...A NINJA WILL BOUND EVERY DAY...
SPING
SPOING
...OVER A GROWING SAPLING, UNTIL...
...AT LAST HE FLIES OVER A MIGHTY TREE!
SPROINGGG
AND?
I AM THAT NINJA.
FIRST ACCLIMATING MYSELF TO A TINY PUPPY...
EE-YAAA!
YIP YIP YIP
...UNTIL THE RESULTS ARE WHAT YOU SEE!
HOW PRO-FOUNDLY MOVING.
HAH HAH HAH

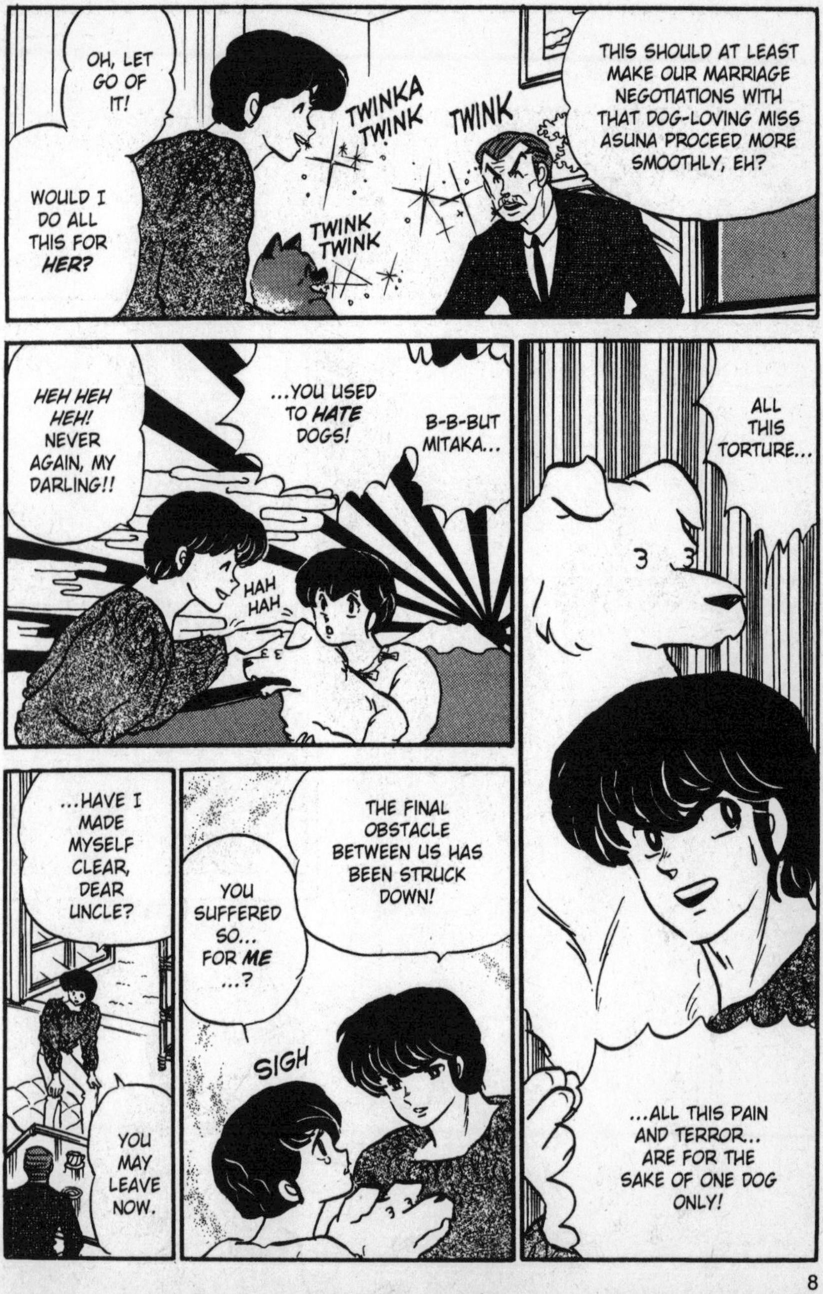
THIS SHOULD AT LEAST MAKE OUR MARRIAGE NEGOTIATIONS WITH THAT DOG-LOVING MISS ASUNA PROCEED MORE SMOOTHLY, EH?
TWINK
TWINKA TWINK
TWINK TWINK
OH, LET GO OF IT!
WOULD I DO ALL THIS FOR *HER?*
ALL THIS TORTURE...
...ALL THIS PAIN AND TERROR.. ARE FOR THE SAKE OF ONE DOG ONLY!
B-B-BUT MITAKA...
...YOU USED TO *HATE* DOGS!
HEH HEH HEH! NEVER AGAIN, MY DARLING!!
HAH HAH
THE FINAL OBSTACLE BETWEEN US HAS BEEN STRUCK DOWN!
YOU SUFFERED SO... FOR *ME* ...?
SIGH
...HAVE I MADE MYSELF CLEAR, DEAR UNCLE?
YOU MAY LEAVE NOW.

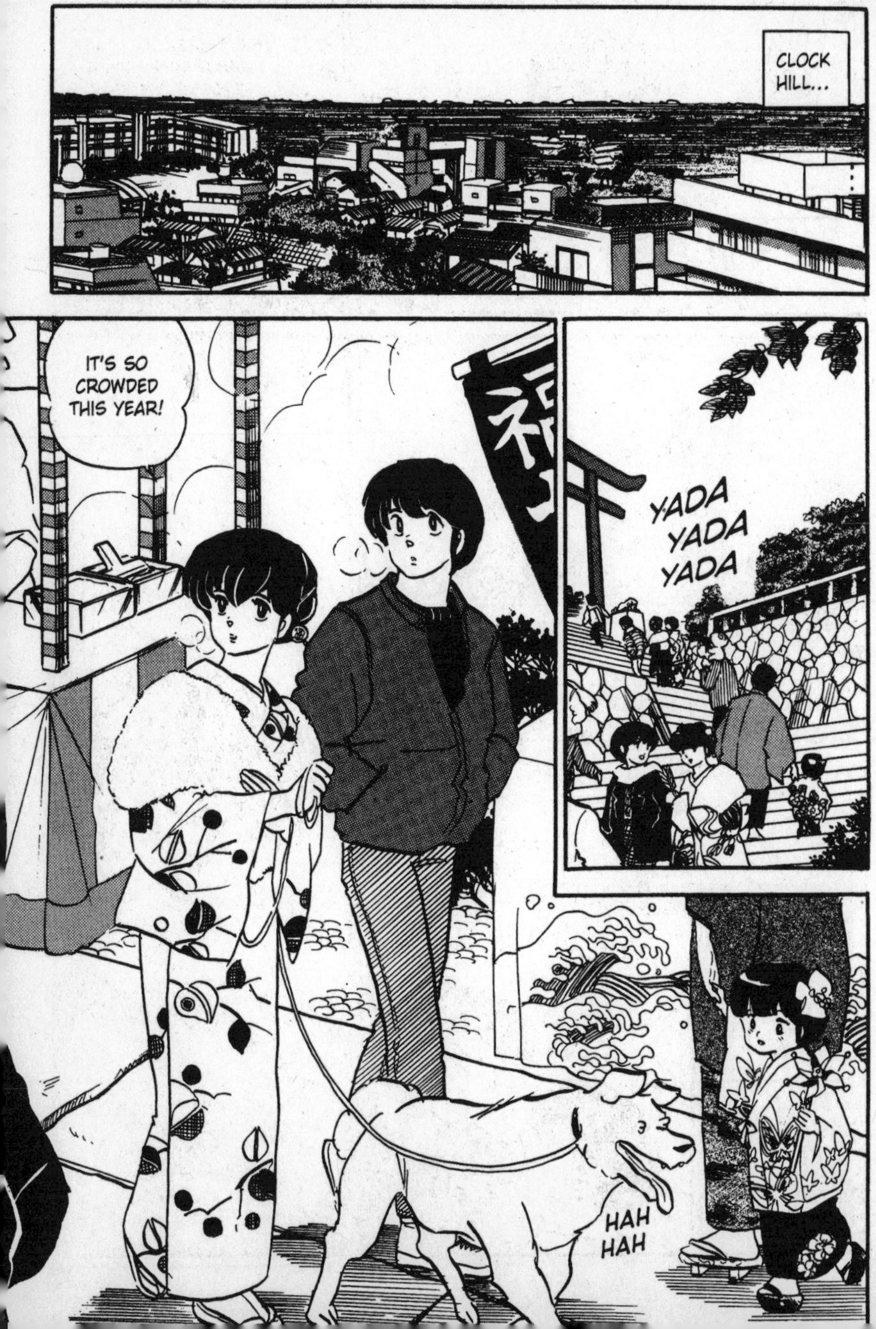
CLOCK HILL...
YADA YADA YADA
IT'S SO CROWDED THIS YEAR!
HAH HAH

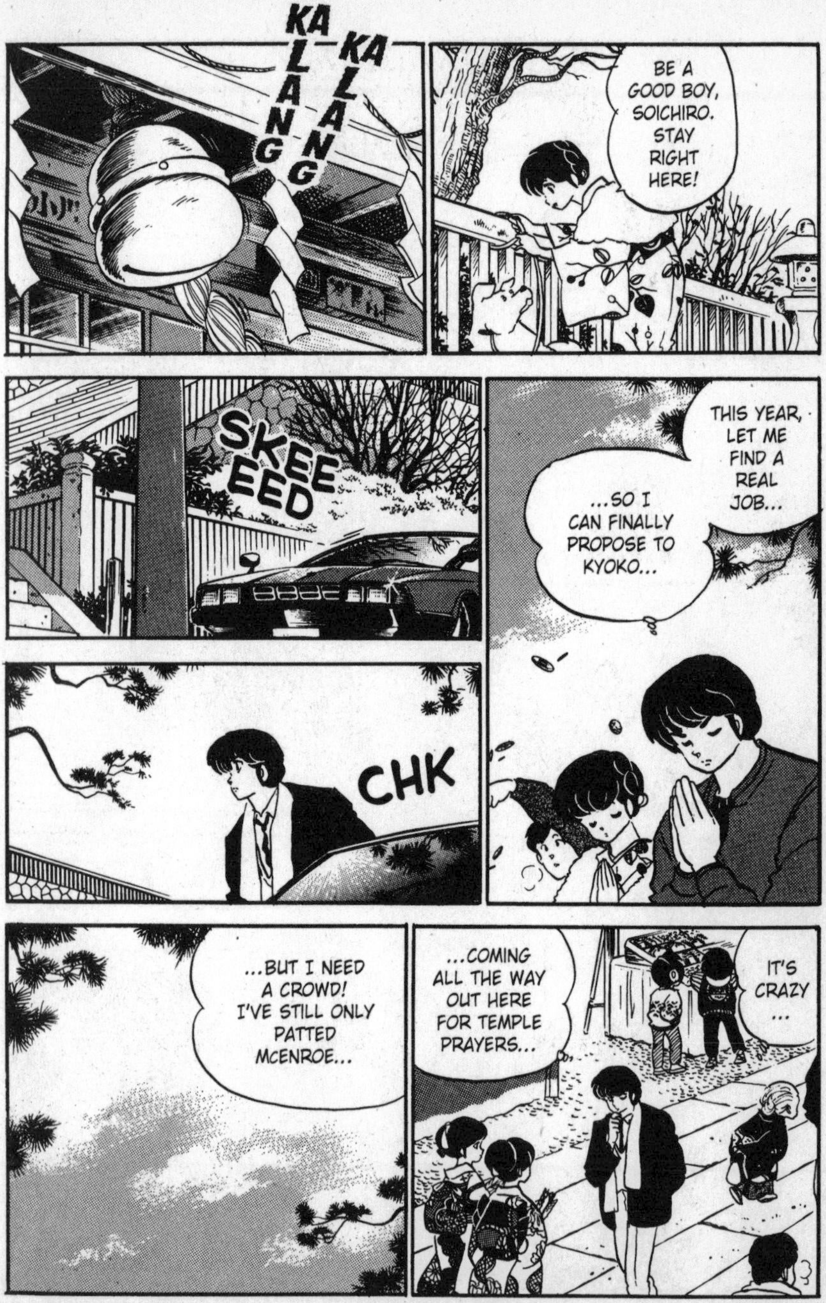
BE A GOOD BOY, SOICHIRO. STAY RIGHT HERE!
KA-LANG
KA-LANG
THIS YEAR, LET ME FIND A REAL JOB...
...SO I CAN FINALLY PROPOSE TO KYOKO...
SKEEEED
CHK
IT'S CRAZY ...
...COMING ALL THE WAY OUT HERE FOR TEMPLE PRAYERS...
...BUT I NEED A CROWD! I'VE STILL ONLY PATTED McENROE...

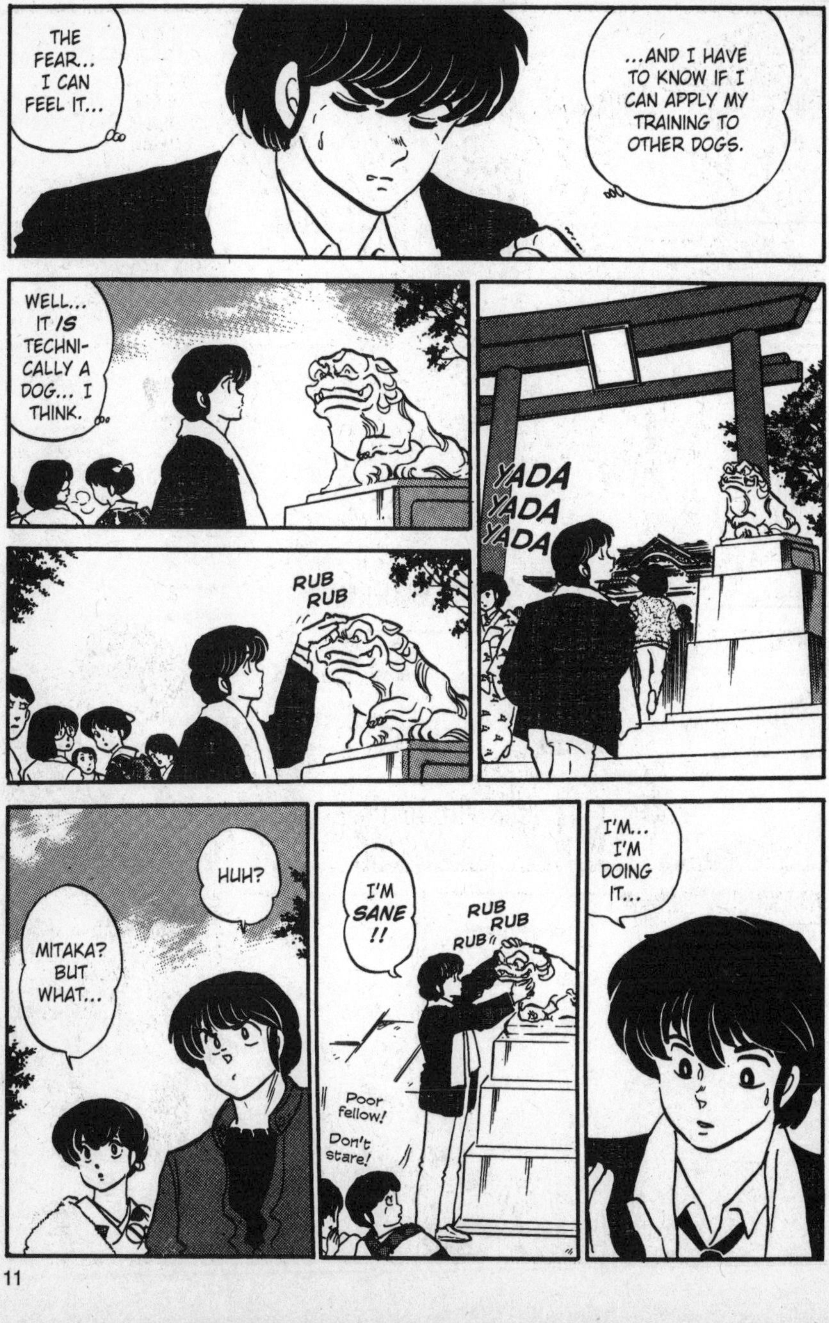

THE FEAR... I CAN FEEL IT...
...AND I HAVE TO KNOW IF I CAN APPLY MY TRAINING TO OTHER DOGS.
YADA YADA YADA
WELL... IT *IS* TECHNICALLY A DOG... I THINK.
RUB RUB
I'M... I'M DOING IT...
I'M *SANE* !!
RUB RUB RUB
Poor fellow!
Don't stare!
HUH?
MITAKA? BUT WHAT...

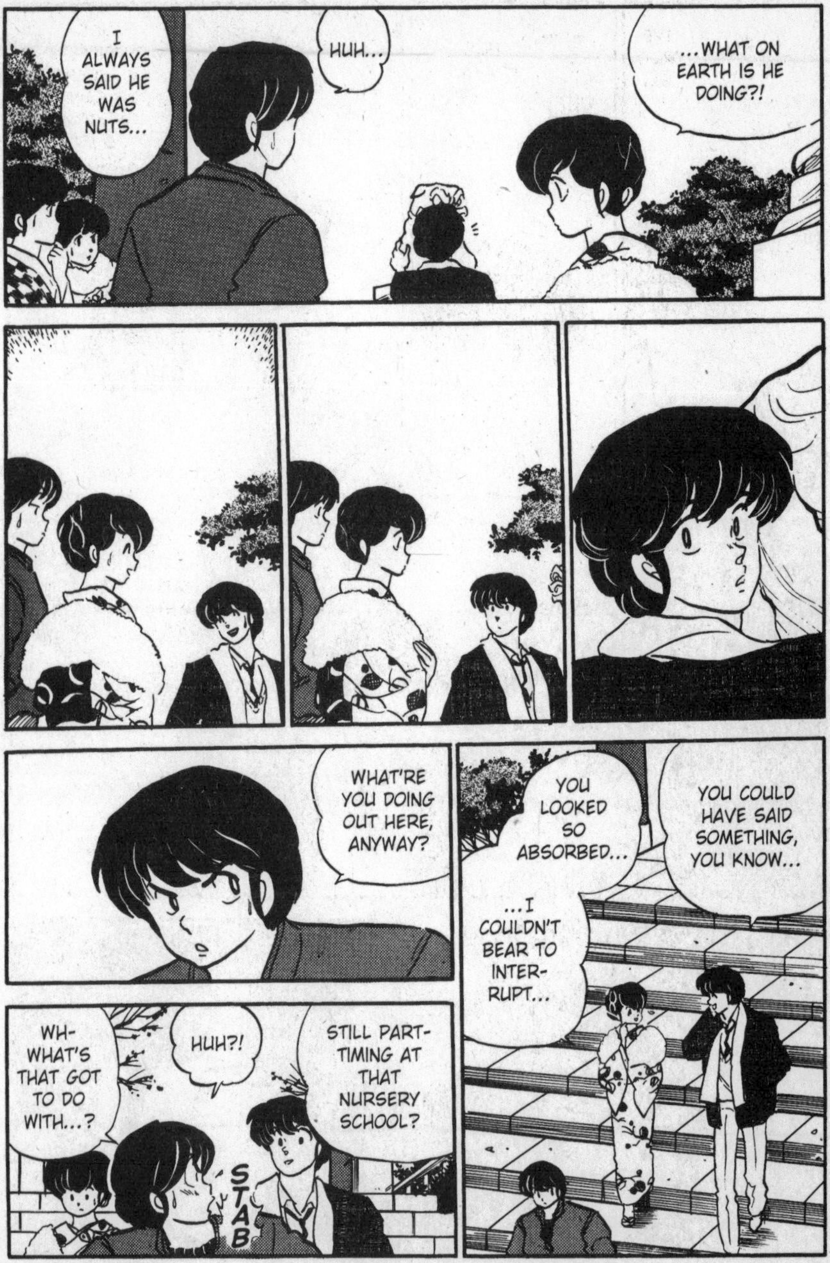
...WHAT ON EARTH IS HE DOING?!
HUH...
I ALWAYS SAID HE WAS NUTS...
YOU COULD HAVE SAID SOMETHING, YOU KNOW...
YOU LOOKED SO ABSORBED...
...I COULDN'T BEAR TO INTER-RUPT...
WHAT'RE YOU DOING OUT HERE, ANYWAY?
STILL PART-TIMING AT THAT NURSERY SCHOOL?
HUH?!
WH- WHAT'S THAT GOT TO DO WITH...?
STAB

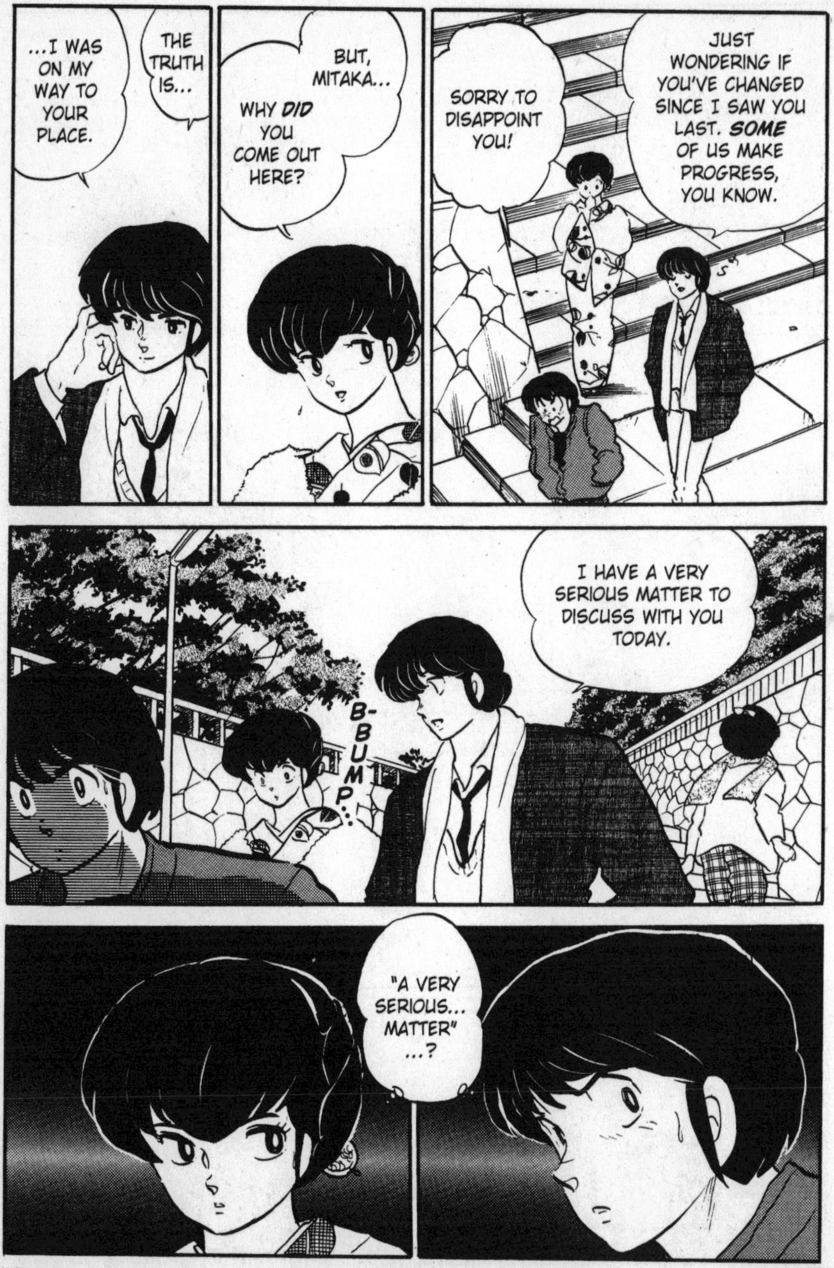
JUST WONDERING IF YOU'VE CHANGED SINCE I SAW YOU LAST. *SOME* OF US MAKE PROGRESS, YOU KNOW.
SORRY TO DISAPPOINT YOU!
BUT, MITAKA...
WHY *DID* YOU COME OUT HERE?
THE TRUTH IS...
...I WAS ON MY WAY TO YOUR PLACE.
I HAVE A VERY SERIOUS MATTER TO DISCUSS WITH YOU TODAY.
B-BBUMP...
"A VERY SERIOUS... MATTER" ...?

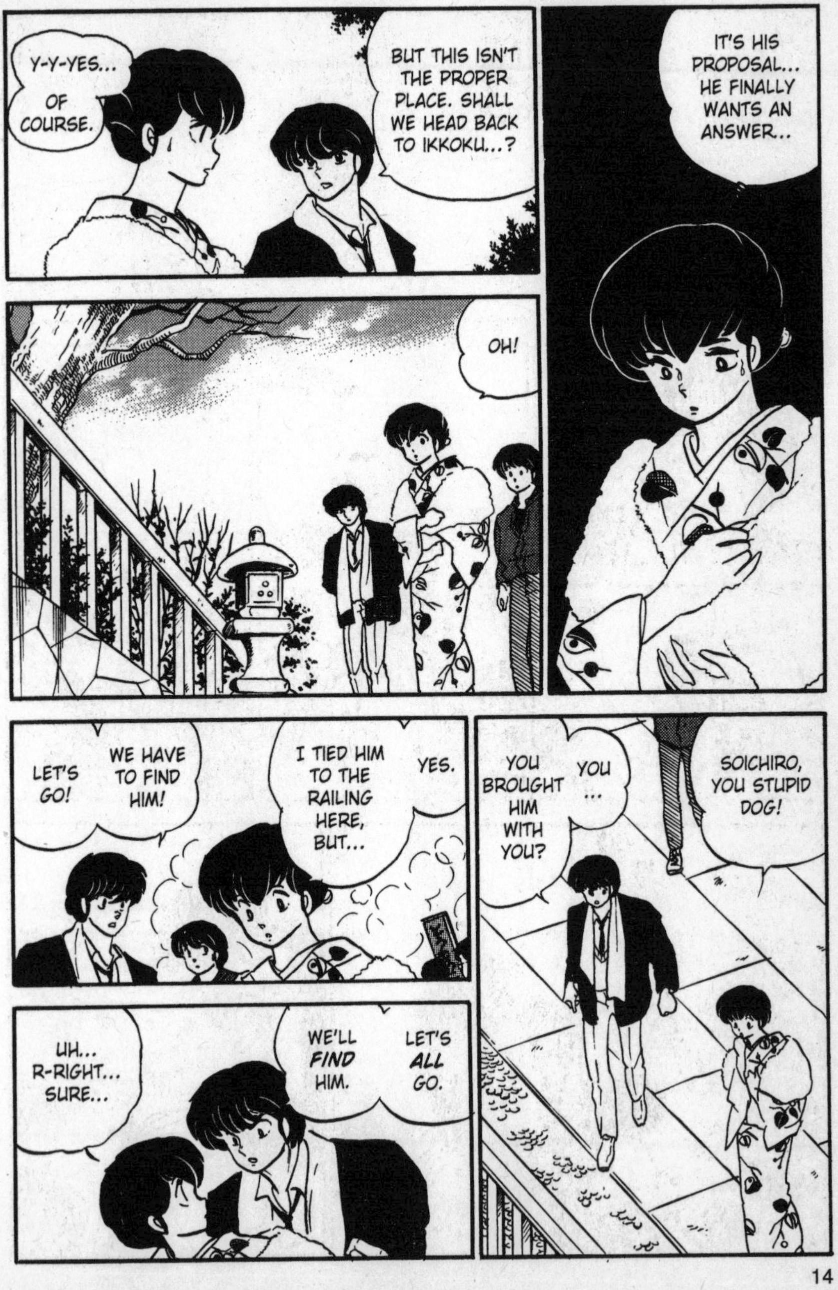
IT'S HIS PROPOSAL... HE FINALLY WANTS AN ANSWER..
BUT THIS ISN'T THE PROPER PLACE. SHALL WE HEAD BACK TO IKKOKU...?
Y-Y-YES... OF COURSE.
OH!
SOICHIRO, YOU STUPID DOG!
YOU ...
YOU BROUGHT HIM WITH YOU?
YES.
I TIED HIM TO THE RAILING HERE, BUT...
WE HAVE TO FIND HIM!
LET'S GO!
LET'S ALL GO.
WE'LL FIND HIM.
UH... R-RIGHT... SURE...

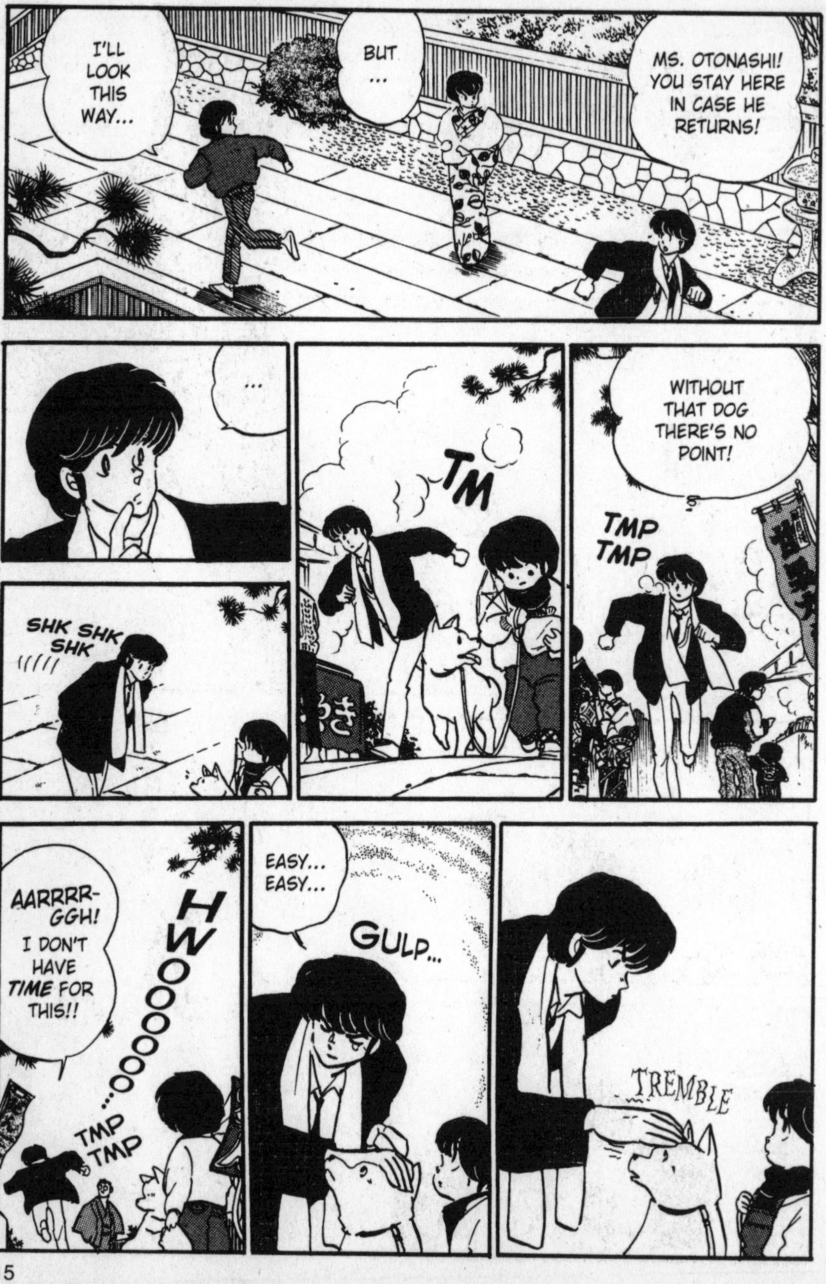
MS. OTONASHI! YOU STAY HERE IN CASE HE RETURNS!
BUT ...
I'LL LOOK THIS WAY...
WITHOUT THAT DOG THERE'S NO POINT!
TMP TMP
TM
...
SHK SHK SHK
TREMBLE
EASY... EASY...
GULP...
AARRRR-GGH! I DON'T HAVE *TIME* FOR THIS!!
HWOOOOOOO...
TMP TMP

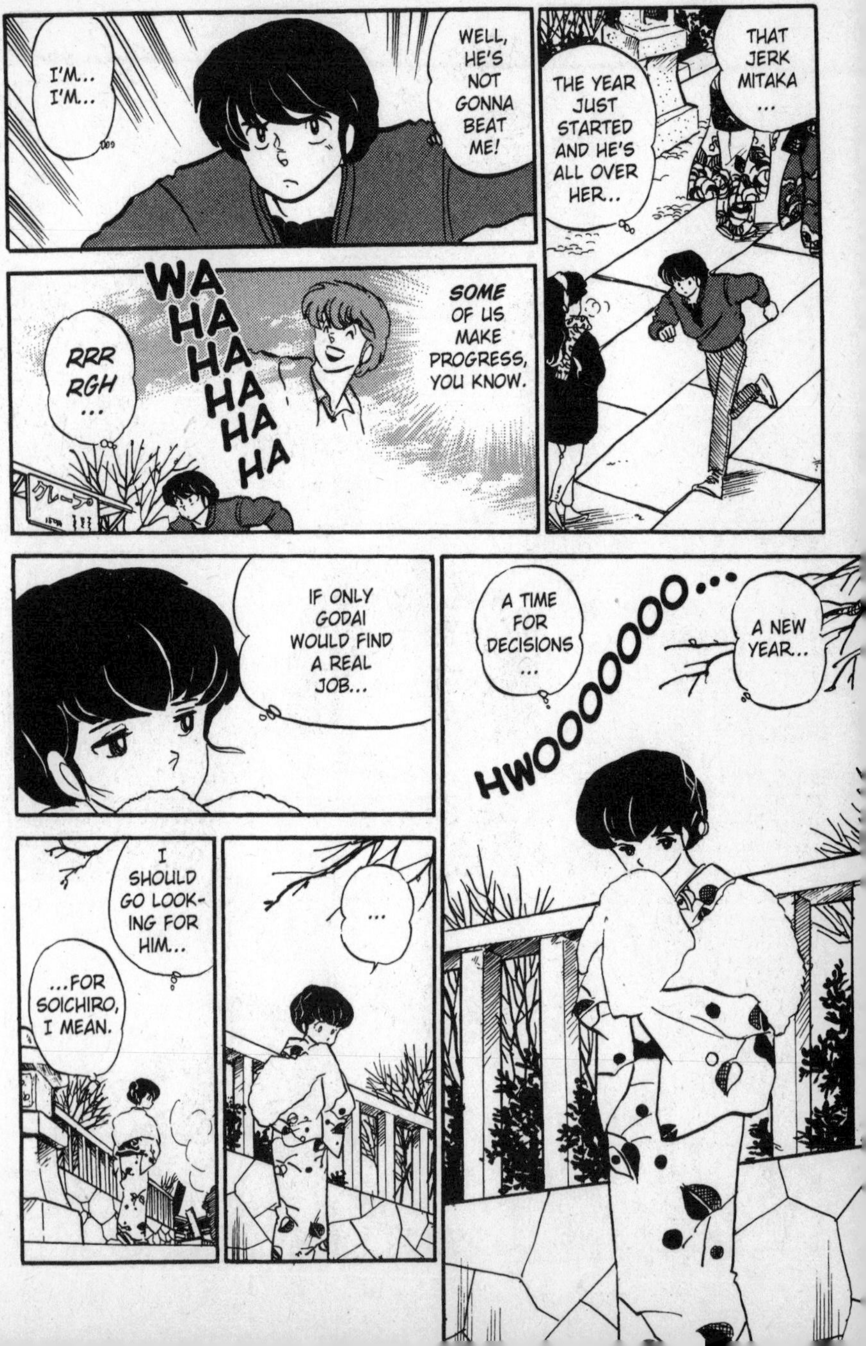
THAT JERK MITAKA...
THE YEAR JUST STARTED AND HE'S ALL OVER HER...
WELL, HE'S NOT GONNA BEAT ME!
I'M... I'M...
SOME OF US MAKE PROGRESS, YOU KNOW.
WA HA HA HA HA HA HA
RRR RGH...
A NEW YEAR...
HWOOOOOOO...
A TIME FOR DECISIONS...
IF ONLY GODAI WOULD FIND A REAL JOB...
...
I SHOULD GO LOOKING FOR HIM...
...FOR SOICHIRO, I MEAN.

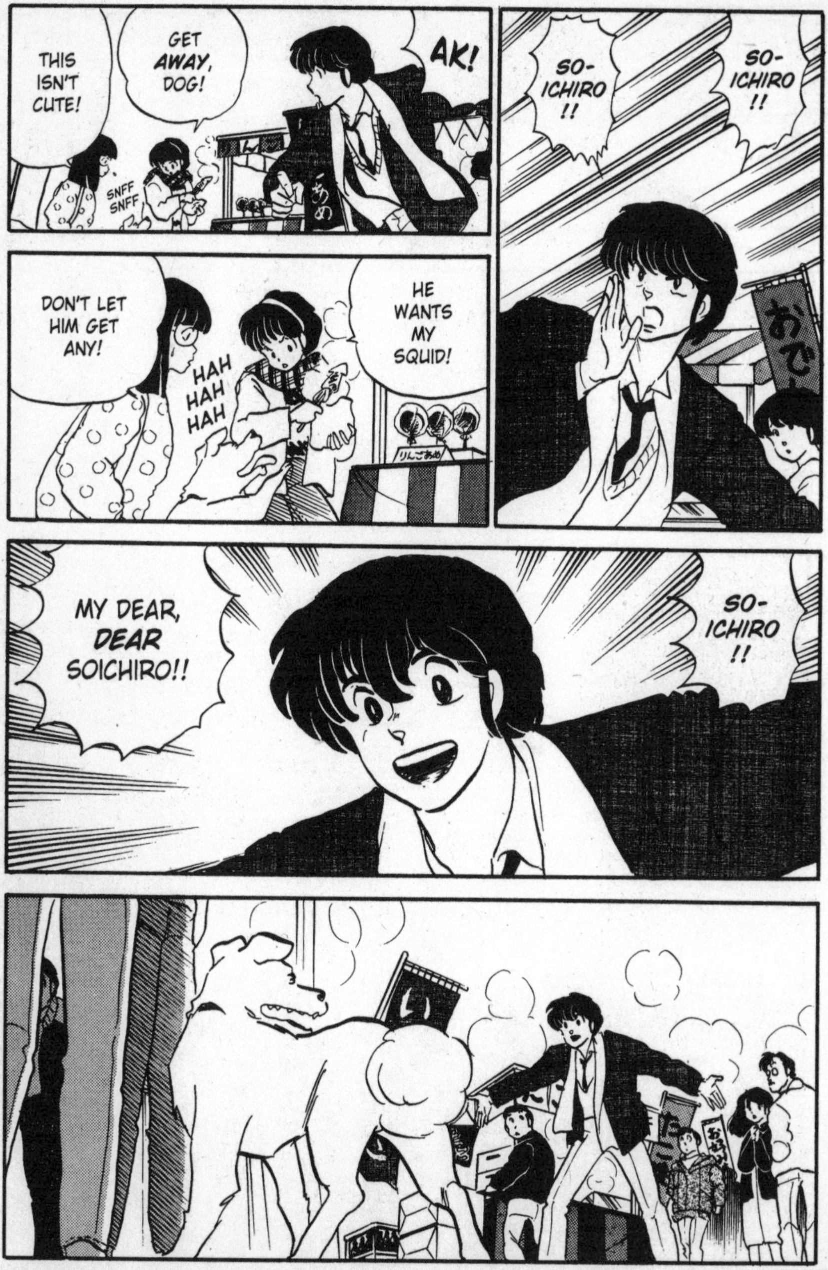
SO-ICHIRO!!
SO-ICHIRO!!
AK!
GET AWAY, DOG!
THIS ISN'T CUTE!
SNFF SNFF
HE WANTS MY SQUID!
HAH HAH HAH
DON'T LET HIM GET ANY!
SO-ICHIRO!!
MY DEAR, DEAR SOICHIRO!!

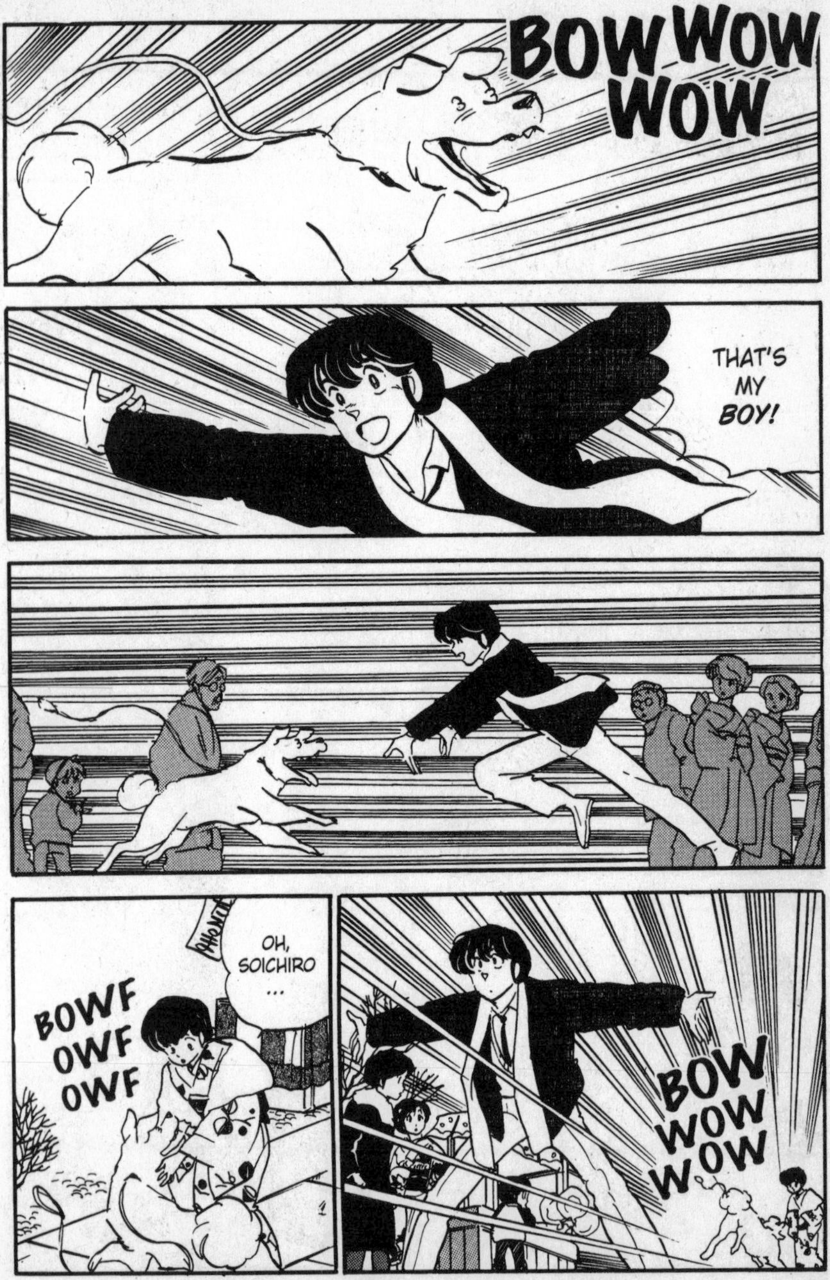
BOW WOW WOW
THAT'S MY BOY!
BOW WOW WOW
OH, SOICHIRO ...
BOWF OWF OWF

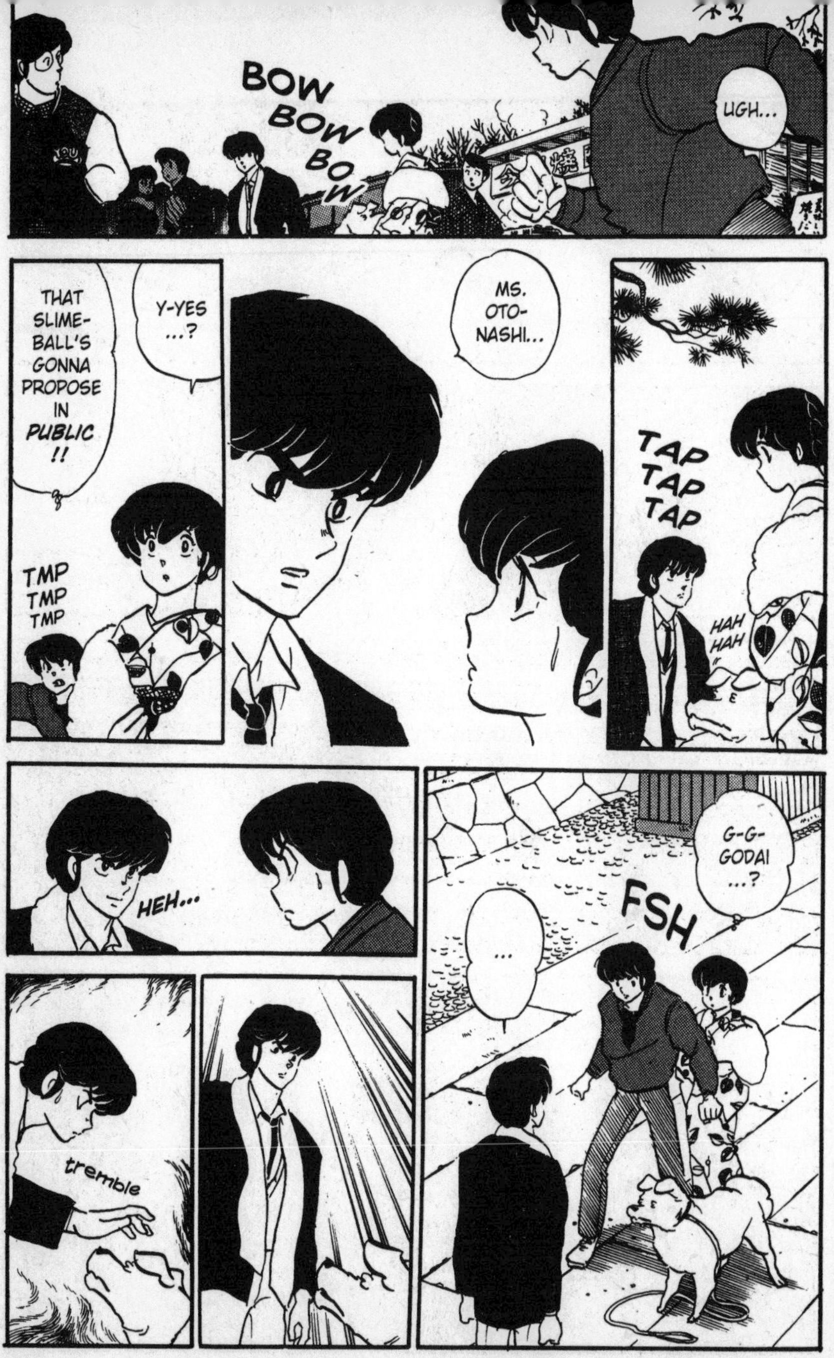
UGH...
BOW BOW BOW
TAP TAP TAP
HAH HAH
MS. OTO-NASHI...
Y-YES ...?
THAT SLIME-BALL'S GONNA PROPOSE IN PUBLIC !!
TMP TMP TMP
G-G-GODAI ...?
FSH
...
HEH...
tremble

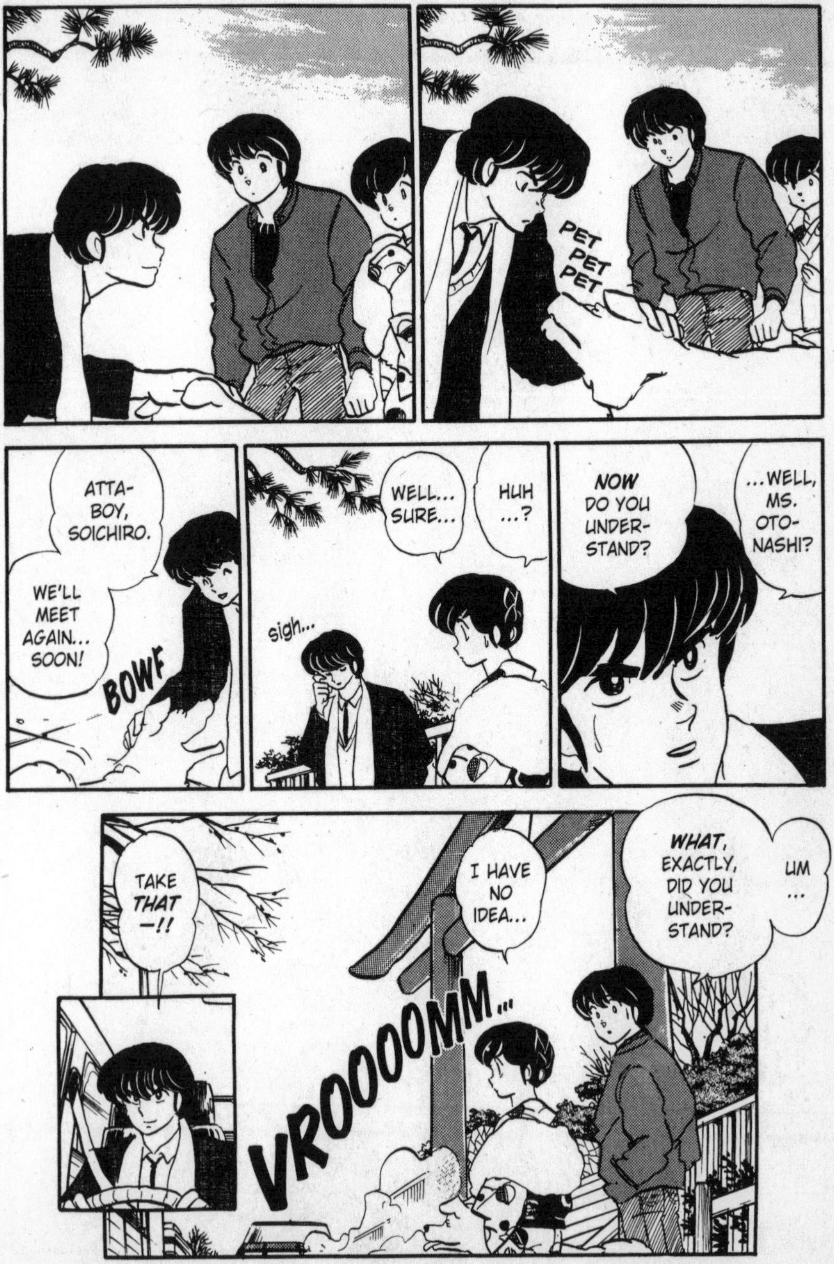
PET PET PET
...WELL, MS. OTO-NASHI?
NOW DO YOU UNDER-STAND?
HUH ...?
WELL... SURE...
sigh...
ATTA-BOY, SOICHIRO.
WE'LL MEET AGAIN... SOON!
BOWF
UM ...
WHAT, EXACTLY, DID YOU UNDER-STAND?
I HAVE NO IDEA...
TAKE THAT—!!
VROOOOMM...

PART TWO

OH, YOU LUCKY DOG

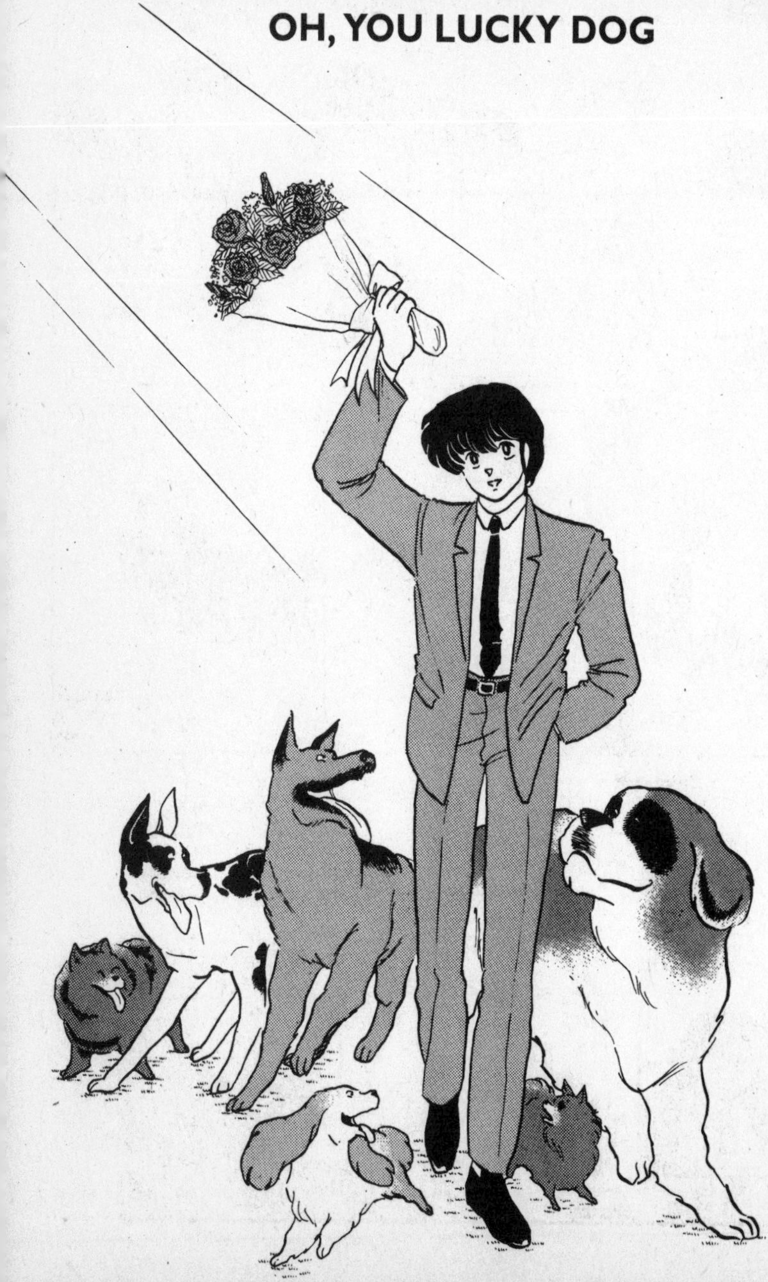

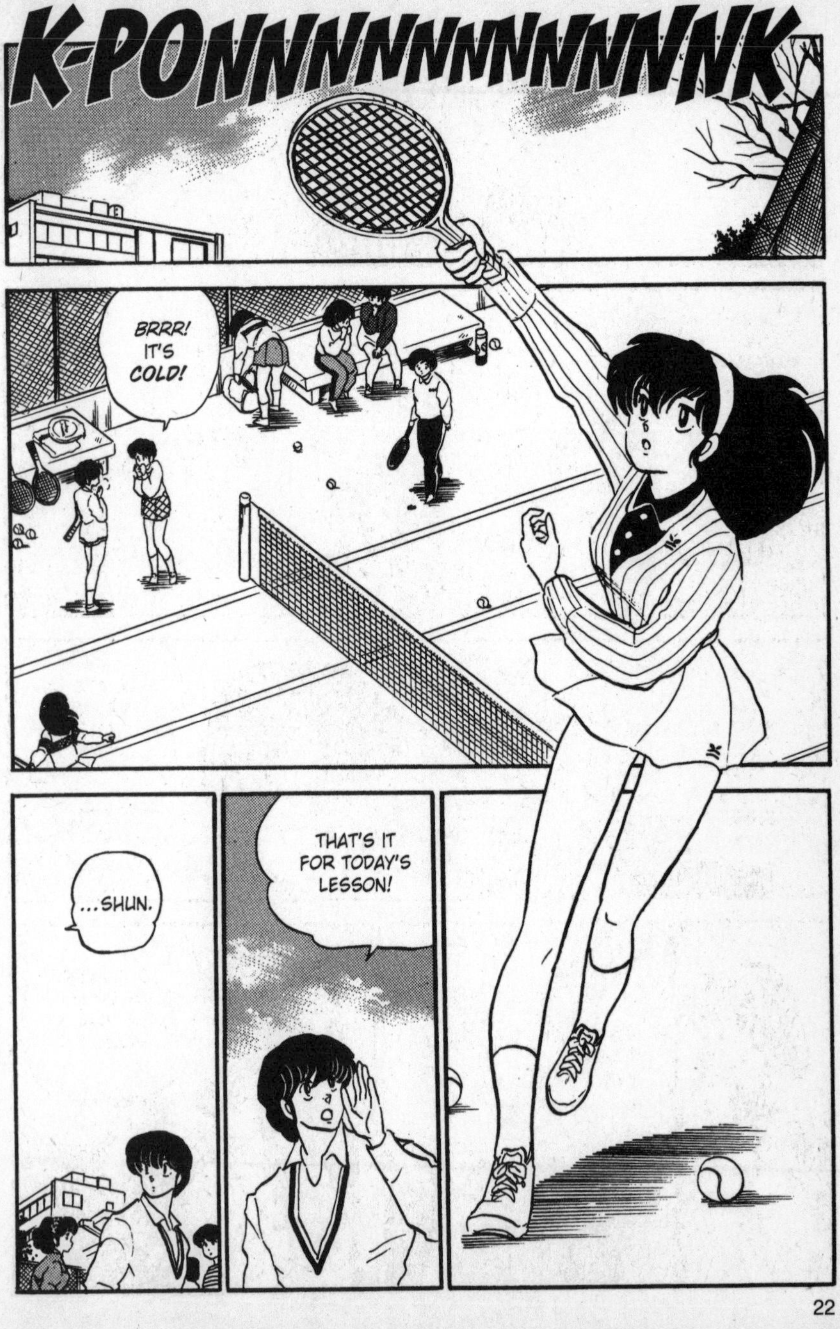
K-PONNNNNNNNNNNNK
BRRR! IT'S COLD!
THAT'S IT FOR TODAY'S LESSON!
...SHUN.

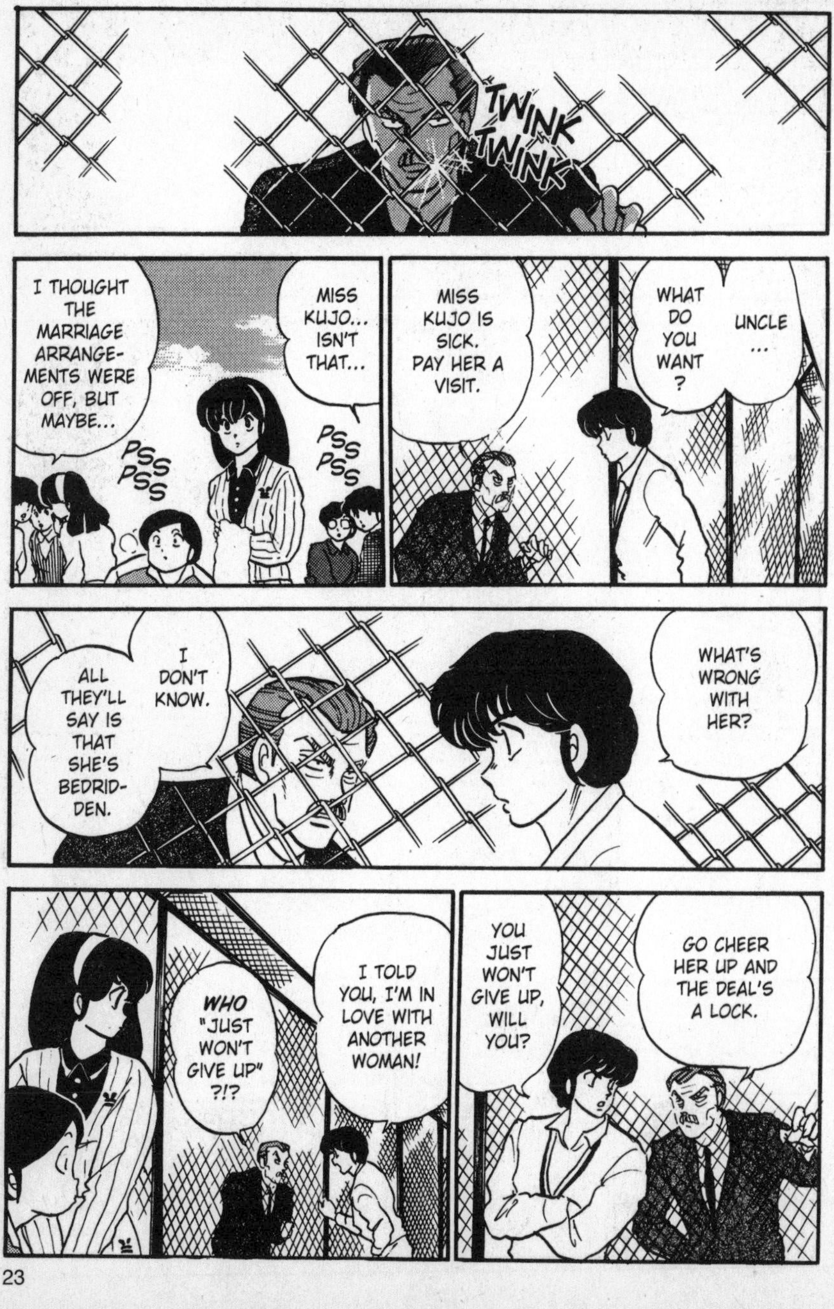
TWINK TWINK
UNCLE ...
WHAT DO YOU WANT ?
MISS KUJO IS SICK. PAY HER A VISIT.
MISS KUJO... ISN'T THAT...
PSS PSS
I THOUGHT THE MARRIAGE ARRANGEMENTS WERE OFF, BUT MAYBE...
PSS PSS
WHAT'S WRONG WITH HER?
I DON'T KNOW.
ALL THEY'LL SAY IS THAT SHE'S BEDRIDDEN.
GO CHEER HER UP AND THE DEAL'S A LOCK.
YOU JUST WON'T GIVE UP, WILL YOU?
I TOLD YOU, I'M IN LOVE WITH ANOTHER WOMAN!
WHO "JUST WON'T GIVE UP" ?!?

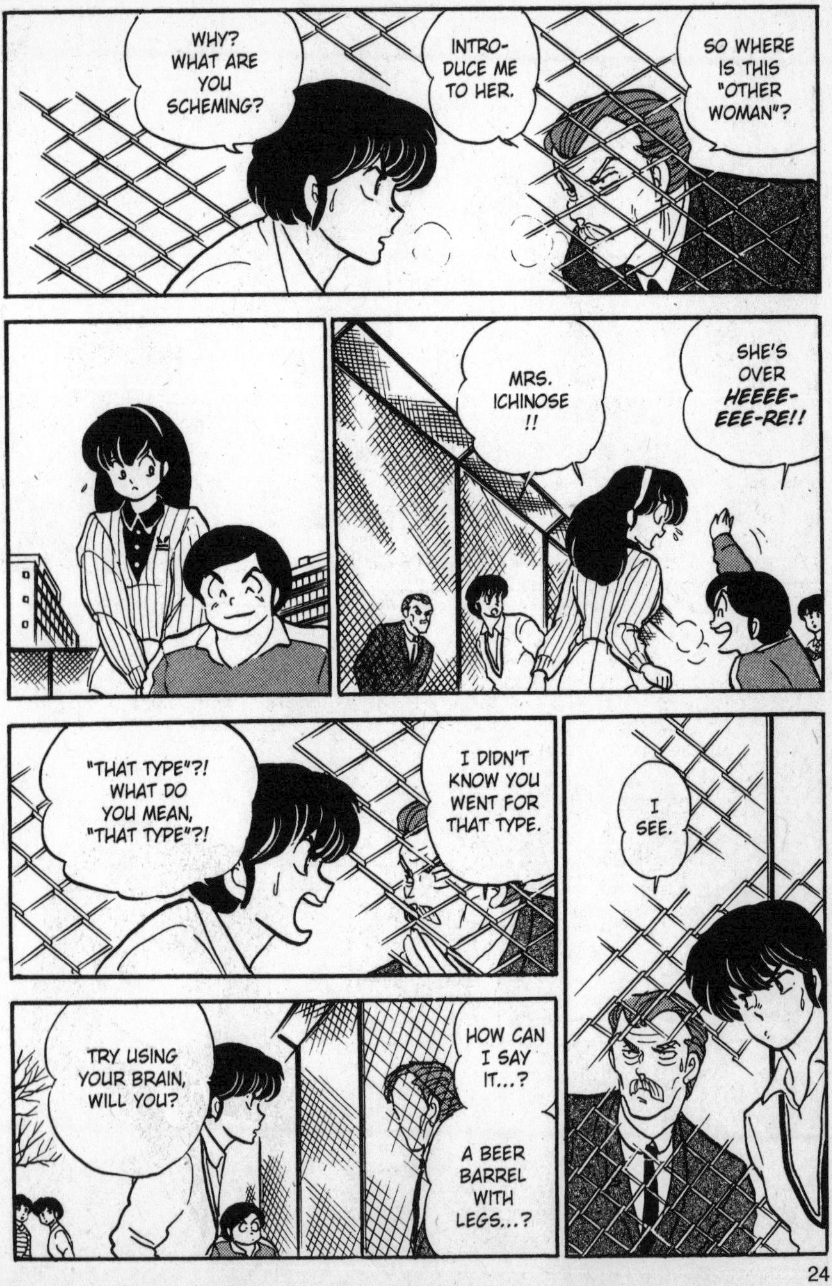
SO WHERE IS THIS "OTHER WOMAN"?
INTRO-DUCE ME TO HER.
WHY? WHAT ARE YOU SCHEMING?
SHE'S OVER ***HEEEE-EEE-RE!!***
MRS. ICHINOSE !!
I SEE.
I DIDN'T KNOW YOU WENT FOR THAT TYPE.
"THAT TYPE"?! WHAT DO YOU MEAN, "THAT TYPE"?!
HOW CAN I SAY IT...?
A BEER BARREL WITH LEGS...?
TRY USING YOUR BRAIN, WILL YOU?

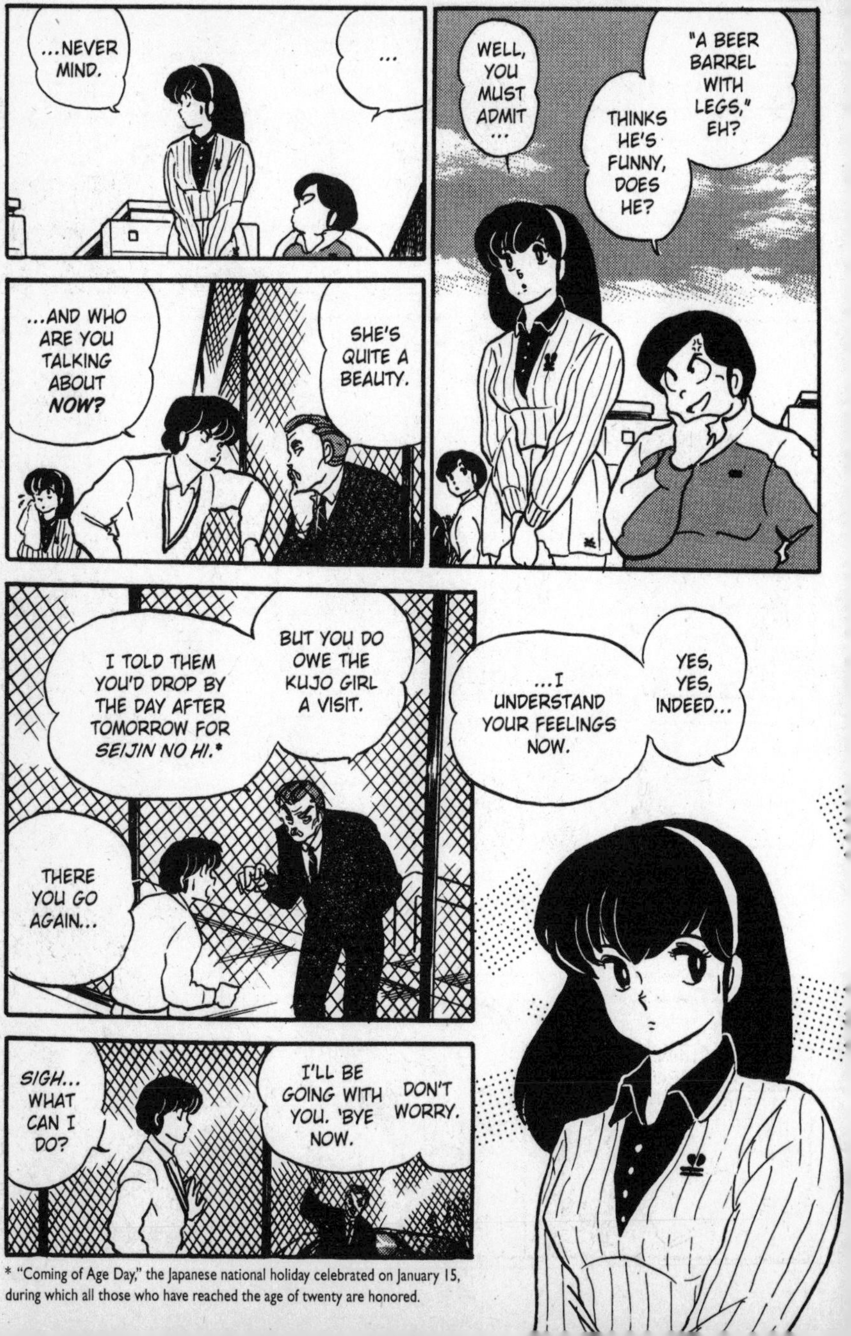
"A BEER BARREL WITH LEGS," EH?
THINKS HE'S FUNNY, DOES HE?
WELL, YOU MUST ADMIT ...
...
...NEVER MIND.
SHE'S QUITE A BEAUTY.
...AND WHO ARE YOU TALKING ABOUT *NOW?*
YES, YES, INDEED...
...I UNDERSTAND YOUR FEELINGS NOW.
BUT YOU DO OWE THE KUJO GIRL A VISIT.
I TOLD THEM YOU'D DROP BY THE DAY AFTER TOMORROW FOR *SEIJIN NO HI.**
THERE YOU GO AGAIN...
DON'T WORRY.
I'LL BE GOING WITH YOU. 'BYE NOW.
SIGH... WHAT CAN I DO?

* "Coming of Age Day," the Japanese national holiday celebrated on January 15, during which all those who have reached the age of twenty are honored.

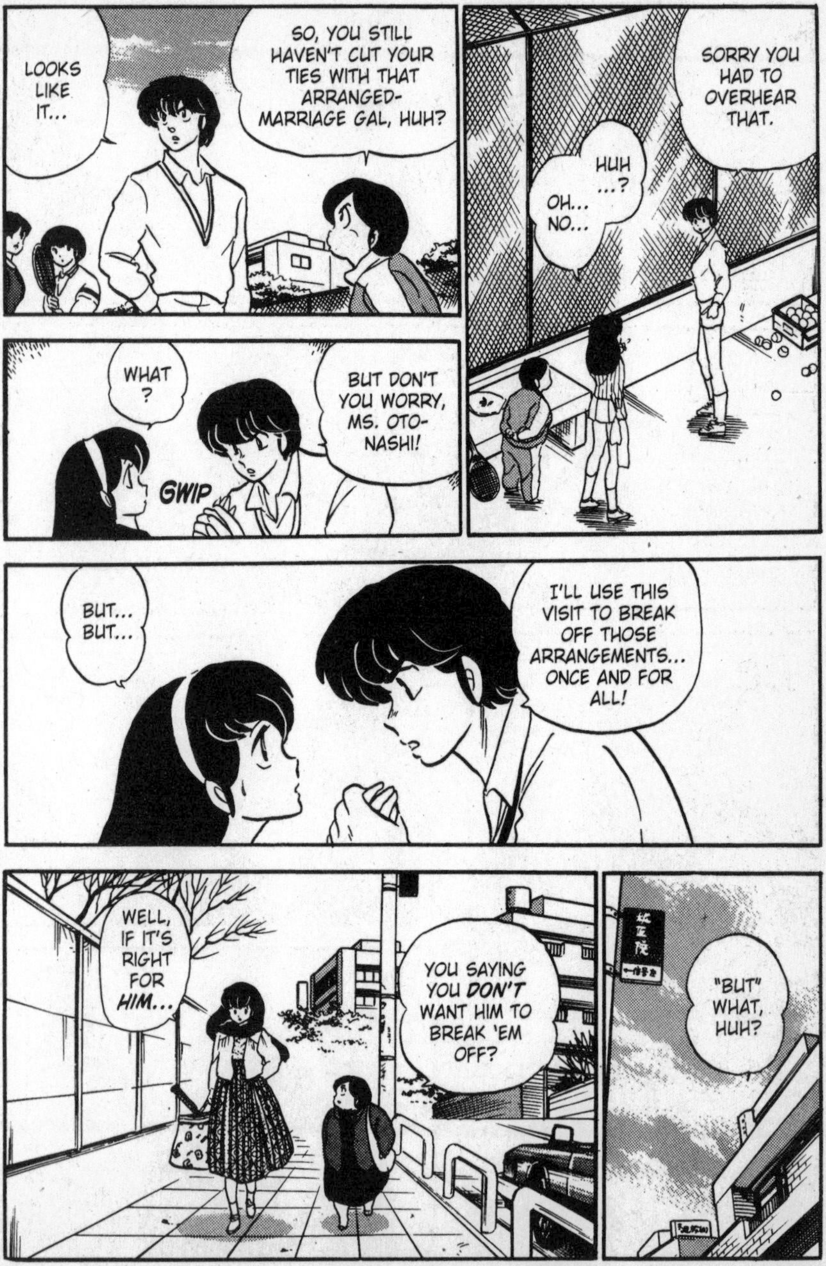
SORRY YOU HAD TO OVERHEAR THAT.
HUH ...?
OH... NO...
SO, YOU STILL HAVEN'T CUT YOUR TIES WITH THAT ARRANGED-MARRIAGE GAL, HUH?
LOOKS LIKE IT...
BUT DON'T YOU WORRY, MS. OTO-NASHI!
WHAT ?
GWIP
I'LL USE THIS VISIT TO BREAK OFF THOSE ARRANGEMENTS... ONCE AND FOR ALL!
BUT... BUT...
"BUT" WHAT, HUH?
YOU SAYING YOU ***DON'T*** WANT HIM TO BREAK 'EM OFF?
WELL, IF IT'S RIGHT FOR ***HIM...***

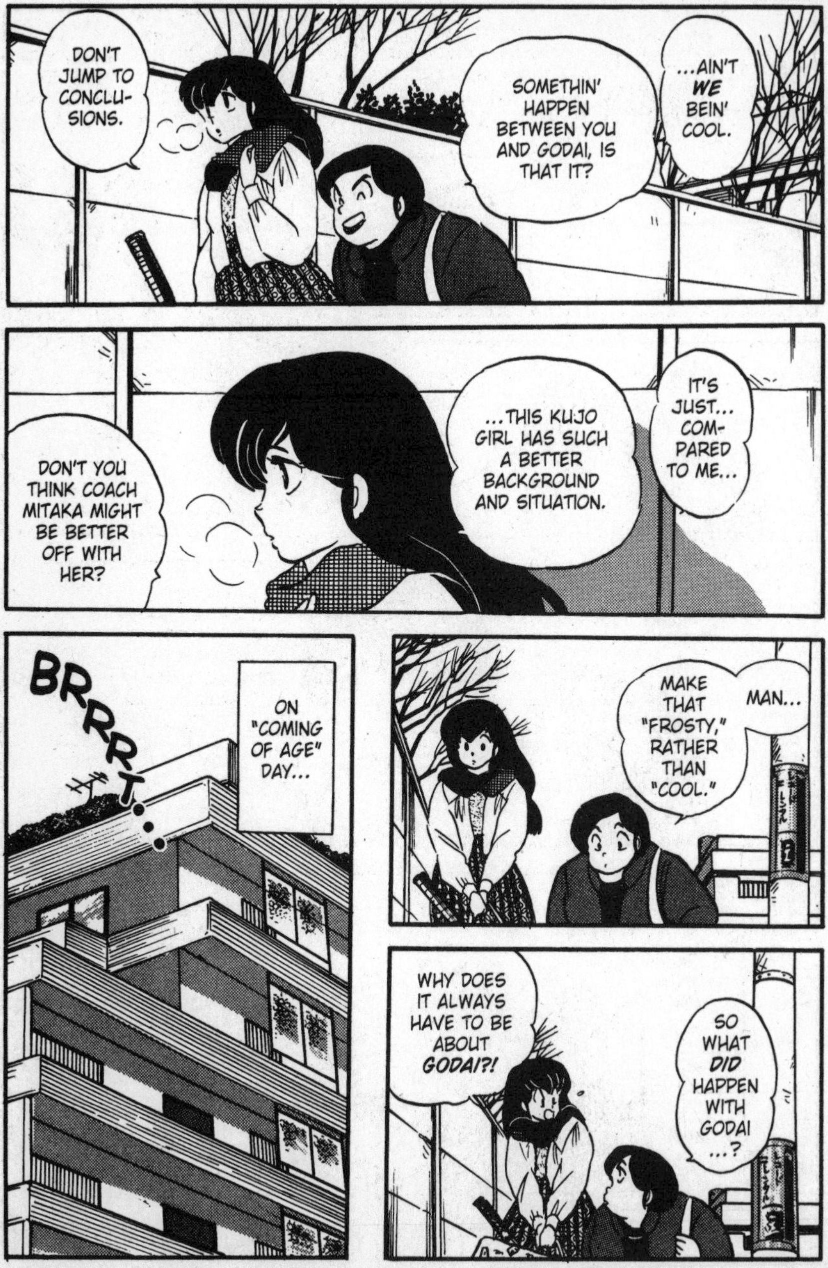
...AIN'T *WE* BEIN' COOL.
SOMETHIN' HAPPEN BETWEEN YOU AND GODAI, IS THAT IT?
DON'T JUMP TO CONCLU-SIONS.
IT'S JUST... COM-PARED TO ME...
...THIS KUJO GIRL HAS SUCH A BETTER BACKGROUND AND SITUATION.
DON'T YOU THINK COACH MITAKA MIGHT BE BETTER OFF WITH HER?
MAN...
MAKE THAT "FROSTY," RATHER THAN "COOL."
SO WHAT *DID* HAPPEN WITH GODAI ...?
WHY DOES IT ALWAYS HAVE TO BE ABOUT *GODAI?!*
ON "COMING OF AGE" DAY...
BRRRT...

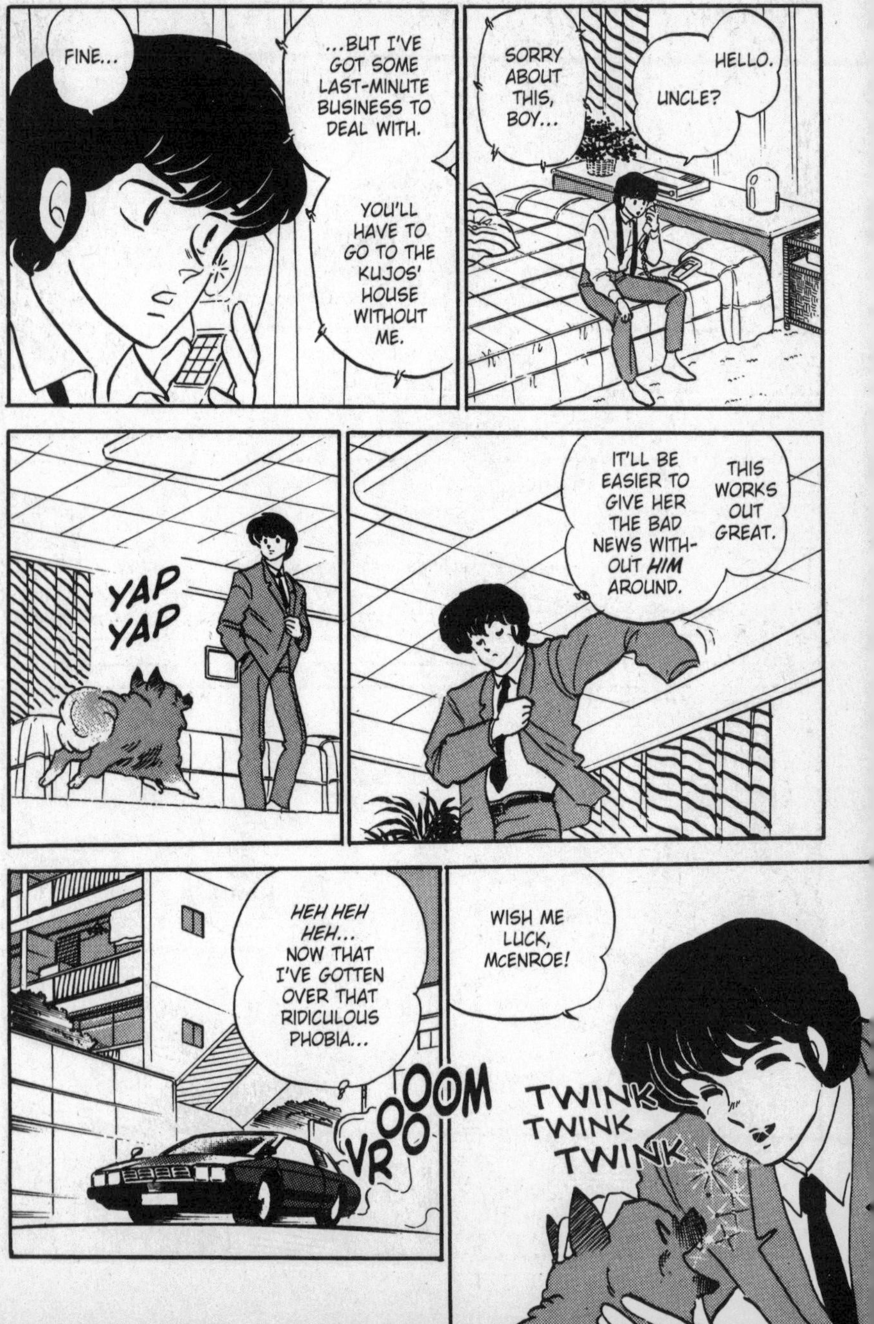
HELLO.
UNCLE?
SORRY ABOUT THIS, BOY...
FINE...
...BUT I'VE GOT SOME LAST-MINUTE BUSINESS TO DEAL WITH.
YOU'LL HAVE TO GO TO THE KUJOS' HOUSE WITHOUT ME.
THIS WORKS OUT GREAT.
IT'LL BE EASIER TO GIVE HER THE BAD NEWS WITH-OUT *HIM* AROUND.
YAP YAP
WISH ME LUCK, McENROE!
TWINK TWINK TWINK
HEH HEH HEH... NOW THAT I'VE GOTTEN OVER THAT RIDICULOUS PHOBIA...
VROOOOOM

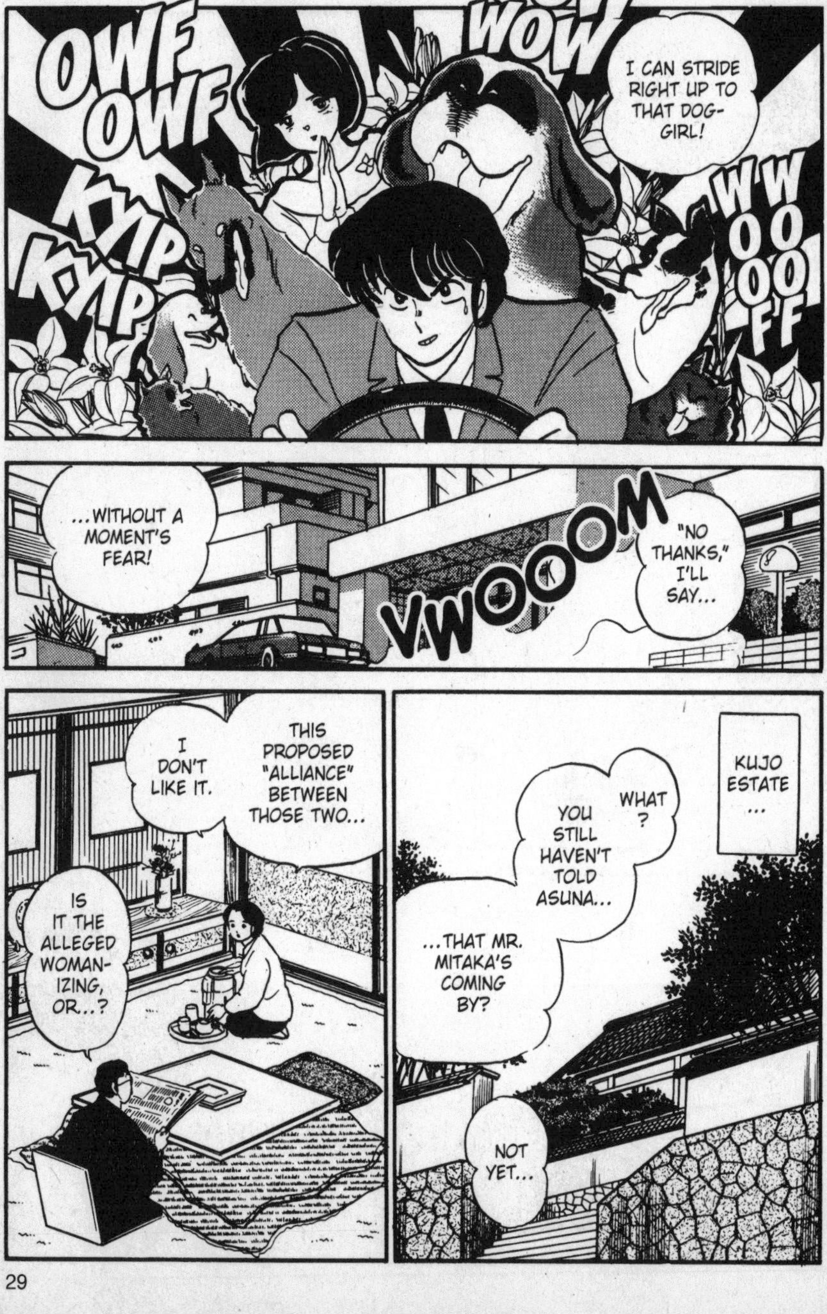
BOW WOW
I CAN STRIDE RIGHT UP TO THAT DOG-GIRL!
WWOOOOFF
OWF OWF
KYIP KYIP
"NO THANKS," I'LL SAY...
VWOOOM
...WITHOUT A MOMENT'S FEAR!
KUJO ESTATE ...
WHAT?
YOU STILL HAVEN'T TOLD ASUNA...
...THAT MR. MITAKA'S COMING BY?
NOT YET...
THIS PROPOSED "ALLIANCE" BETWEEN THOSE TWO...
I DON'T LIKE IT.
IS IT THE ALLEGED WOMAN-IZING, OR...?

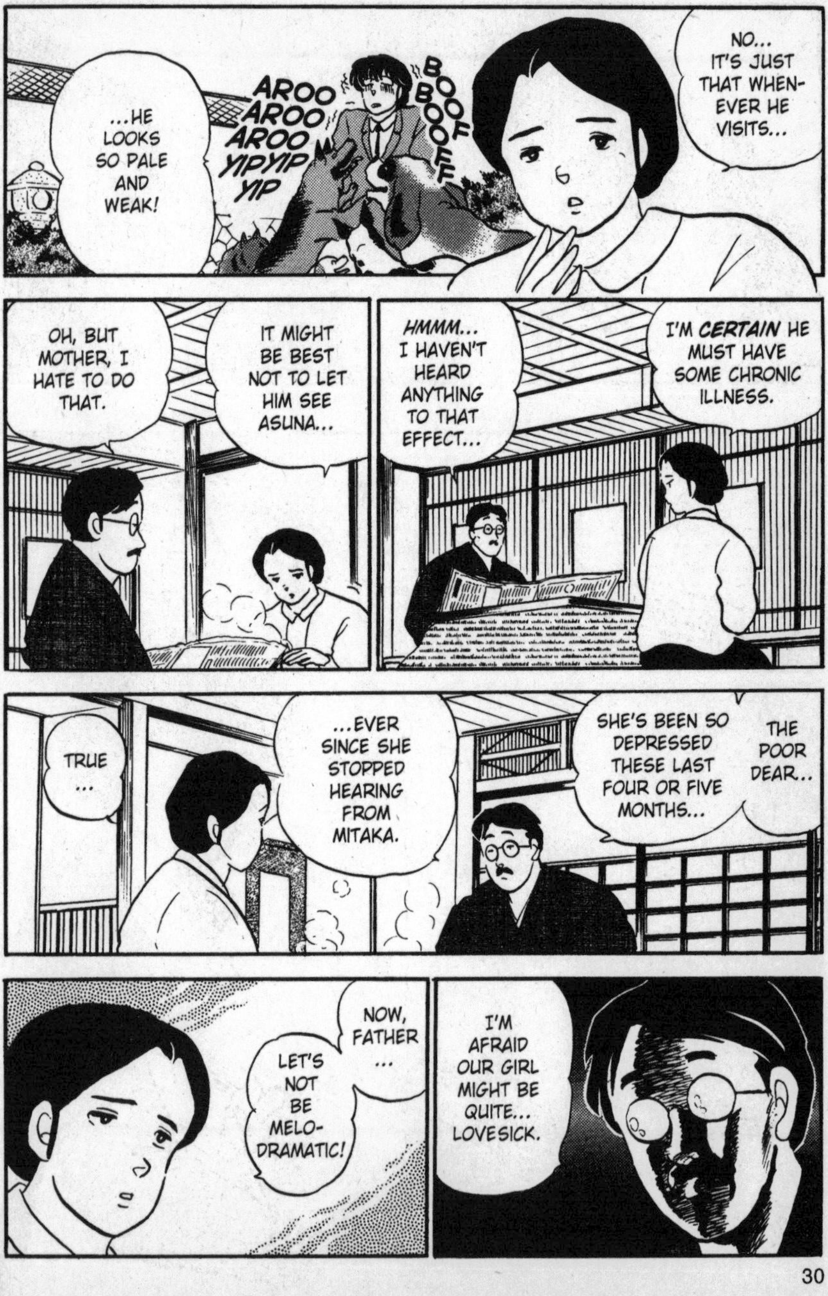
NO... IT'S JUST THAT WHEN-EVER HE VISITS...
BOOOF BOOOFF
AROO AROO AROO YIPYIP YIP
...HE LOOKS SO PALE AND WEAK!
I'M CERTAIN HE MUST HAVE SOME CHRONIC ILLNESS.
HMMM... I HAVEN'T HEARD ANYTHING TO THAT EFFECT...
IT MIGHT BE BEST NOT TO LET HIM SEE ASUNA...
OH, BUT MOTHER, I HATE TO DO THAT.
THE POOR DEAR...
SHE'S BEEN SO DEPRESSED THESE LAST FOUR OR FIVE MONTHS...
...EVER SINCE SHE STOPPED HEARING FROM MITAKA.
TRUE...
I'M AFRAID OUR GIRL MIGHT BE QUITE... LOVESICK.
NOW, FATHER...
LET'S NOT BE MELO-DRAMATIC!

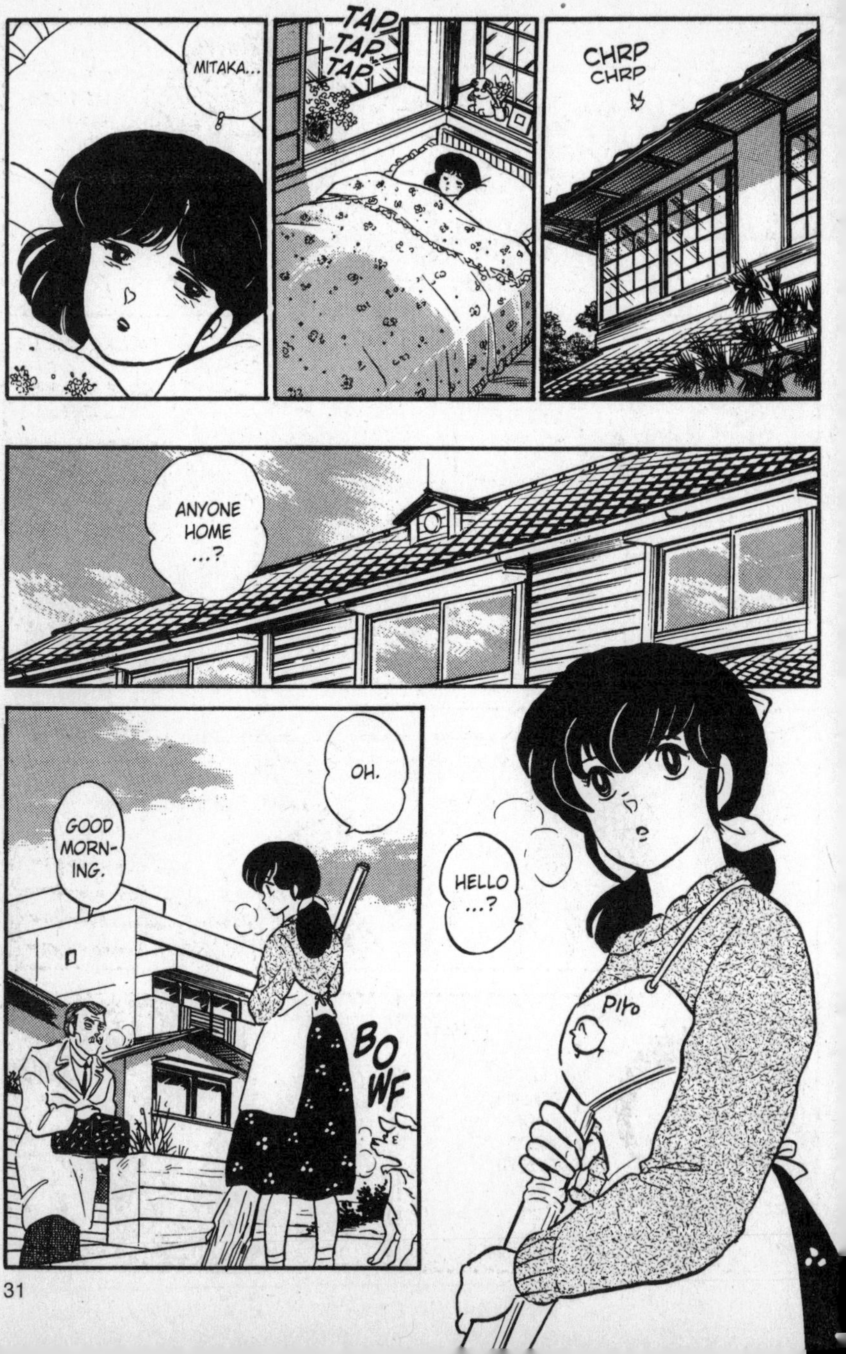
CHRP
CHRP
TAP
TAP
TAP
MITAKA...
ANYONE HOME ...?
HELLO ...?
PIYO
OH.
GOOD MORN-ING.
BOWF

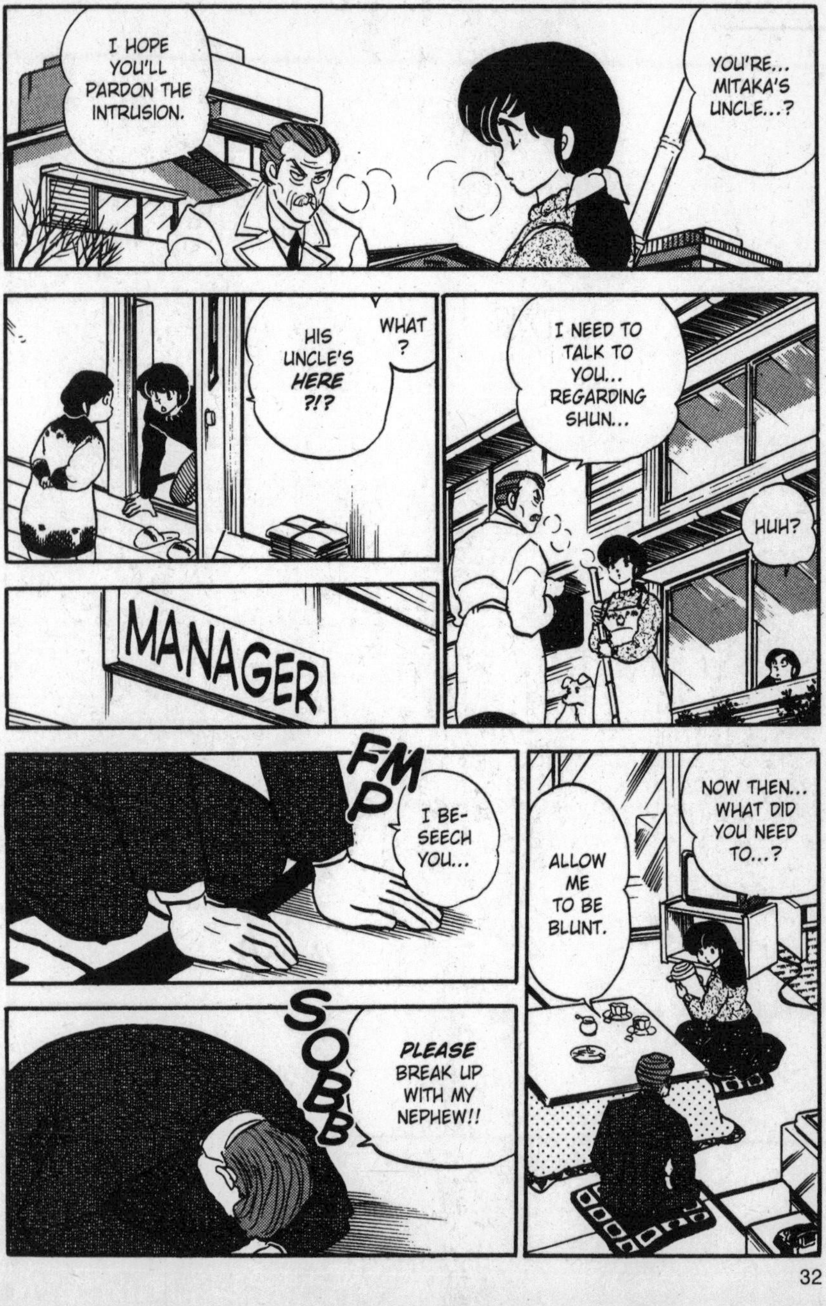
YOU'RE... MITAKA'S UNCLE...?
I HOPE YOU'LL PARDON THE INTRUSION.
I NEED TO TALK TO YOU... REGARDING SHUN...
HUH?
WHAT?
HIS UNCLE'S *HERE* ?!?
MANAGER
NOW THEN... WHAT DID YOU NEED TO...?
ALLOW ME TO BE BLUNT.
FMP
I BE-SEECH YOU...
SOBB
PLEASE BREAK UP WITH MY NEPHEW!!

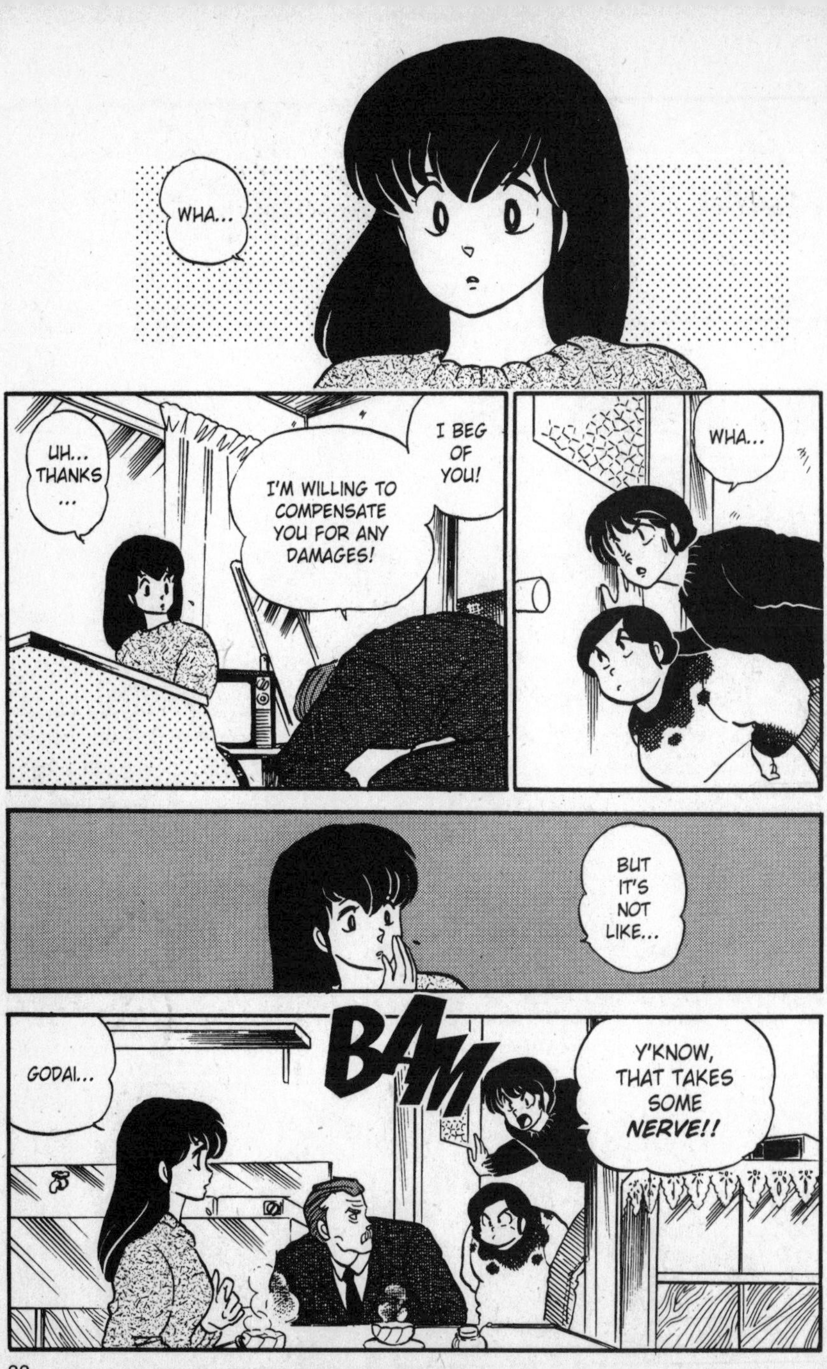
WHA...
WHA...
I BEG OF YOU!
I'M WILLING TO COMPENSATE YOU FOR ANY DAMAGES!
UH... THANKS ...
BUT IT'S NOT LIKE...
Y'KNOW, THAT TAKES SOME NERVE!!
BAM
GODAI...

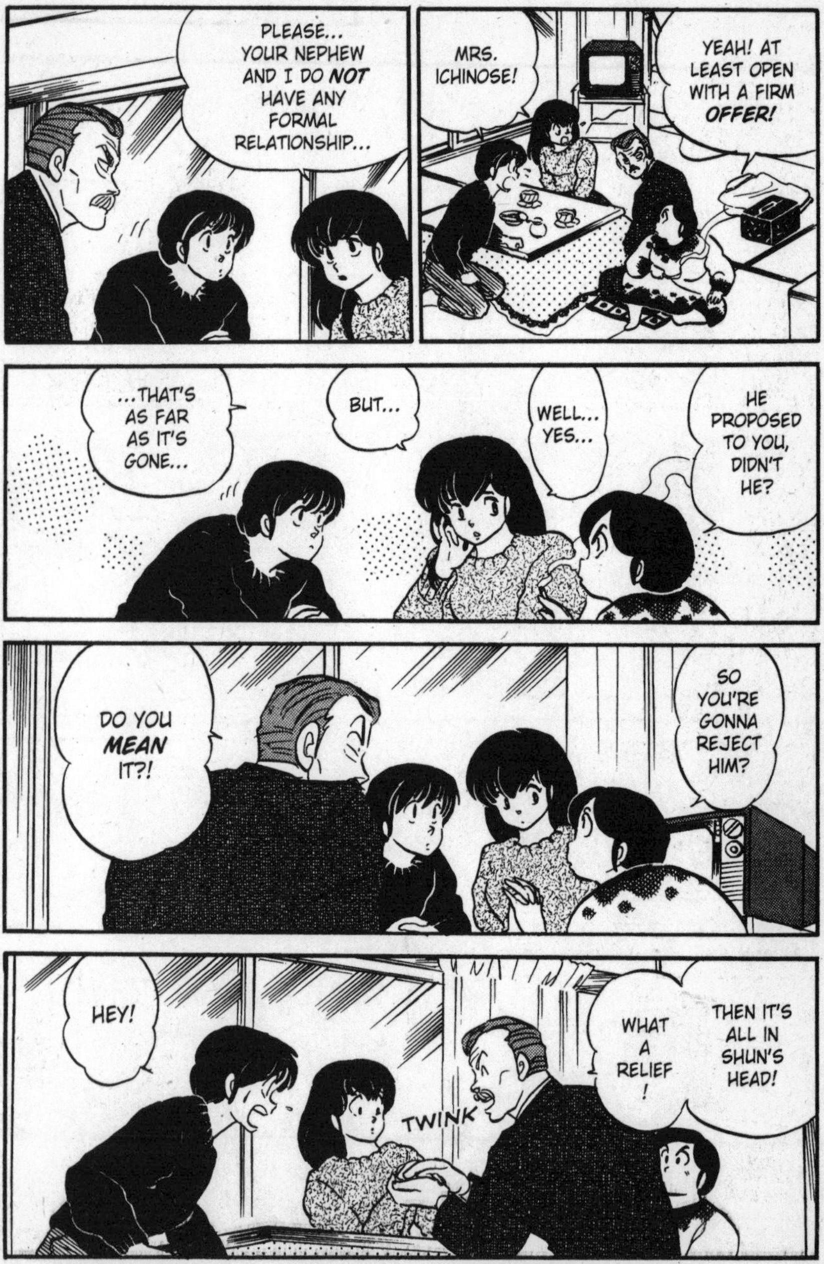
YEAH! AT LEAST OPEN WITH A FIRM OFFER!
MRS. ICHINOSE!
PLEASE... YOUR NEPHEW AND I DO NOT HAVE ANY FORMAL RELATIONSHIP...
HE PROPOSED TO YOU, DIDN'T HE?
WELL... YES...
BUT...
...THAT'S AS FAR AS IT'S GONE...
SO YOU'RE GONNA REJECT HIM?
DO YOU MEAN IT?!
THEN IT'S ALL IN SHUN'S HEAD!
WHAT A RELIEF!
TWINK
HEY!

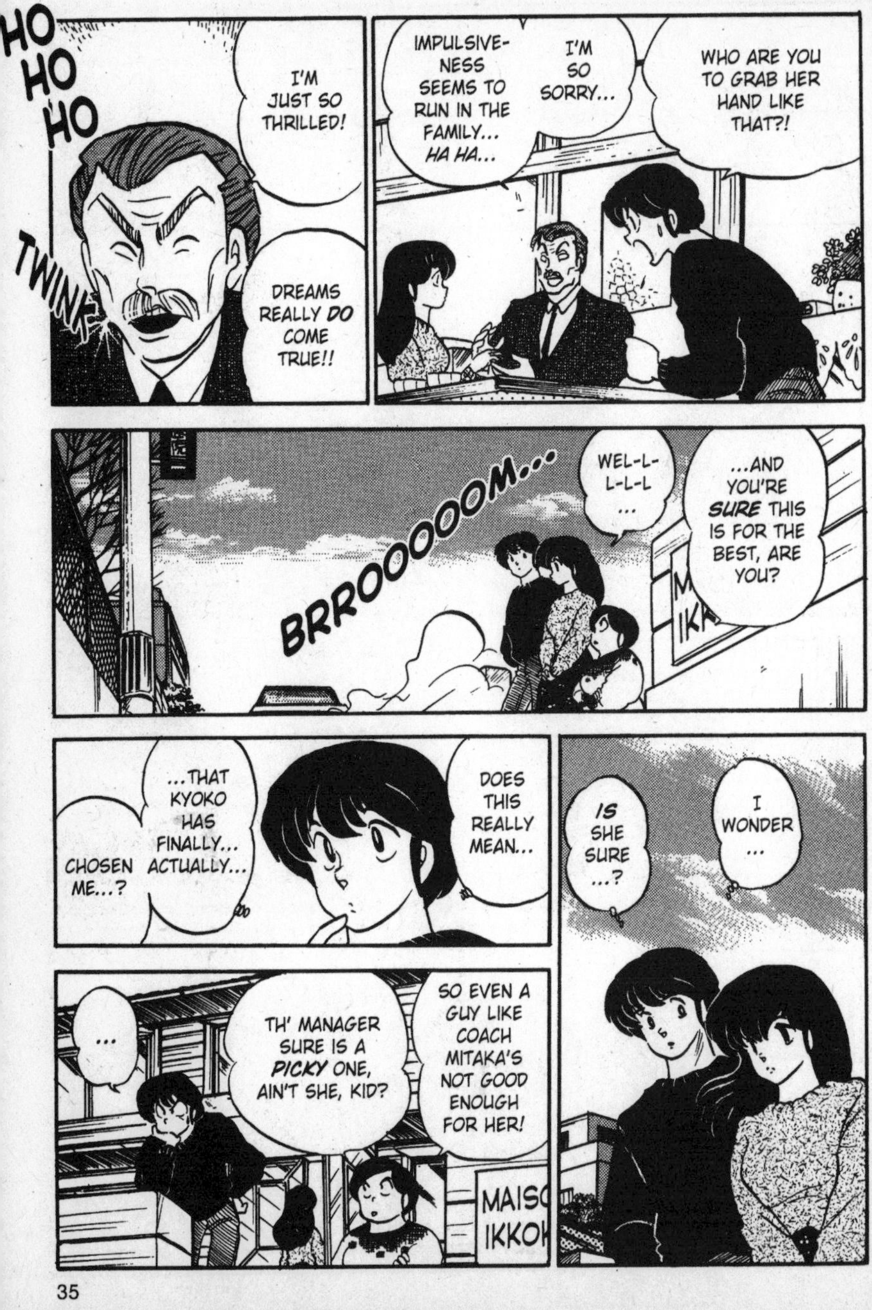
WHO ARE YOU TO GRAB HER HAND LIKE THAT?!
I'M SO SORRY...
IMPULSIVE-NESS SEEMS TO RUN IN THE FAMILY... *HA HA...*
HO HO HO
I'M JUST SO THRILLED!
TWINK
DREAMS REALLY *DO* COME TRUE!!
...AND YOU'RE *SURE* THIS IS FOR THE BEST, ARE YOU?
WEL-L-L-L-L ...
BRROOOOOM...
I WONDER ...
IS SHE SURE ...?
DOES THIS REALLY MEAN...
...THAT KYOKO HAS FINALLY... ACTUALLY...
CHOSEN ME...?
SO EVEN A GUY LIKE COACH MITAKA'S NOT GOOD ENOUGH FOR HER!
TH' MANAGER SURE IS A *PICKY* ONE, AIN'T SHE, KID?
...

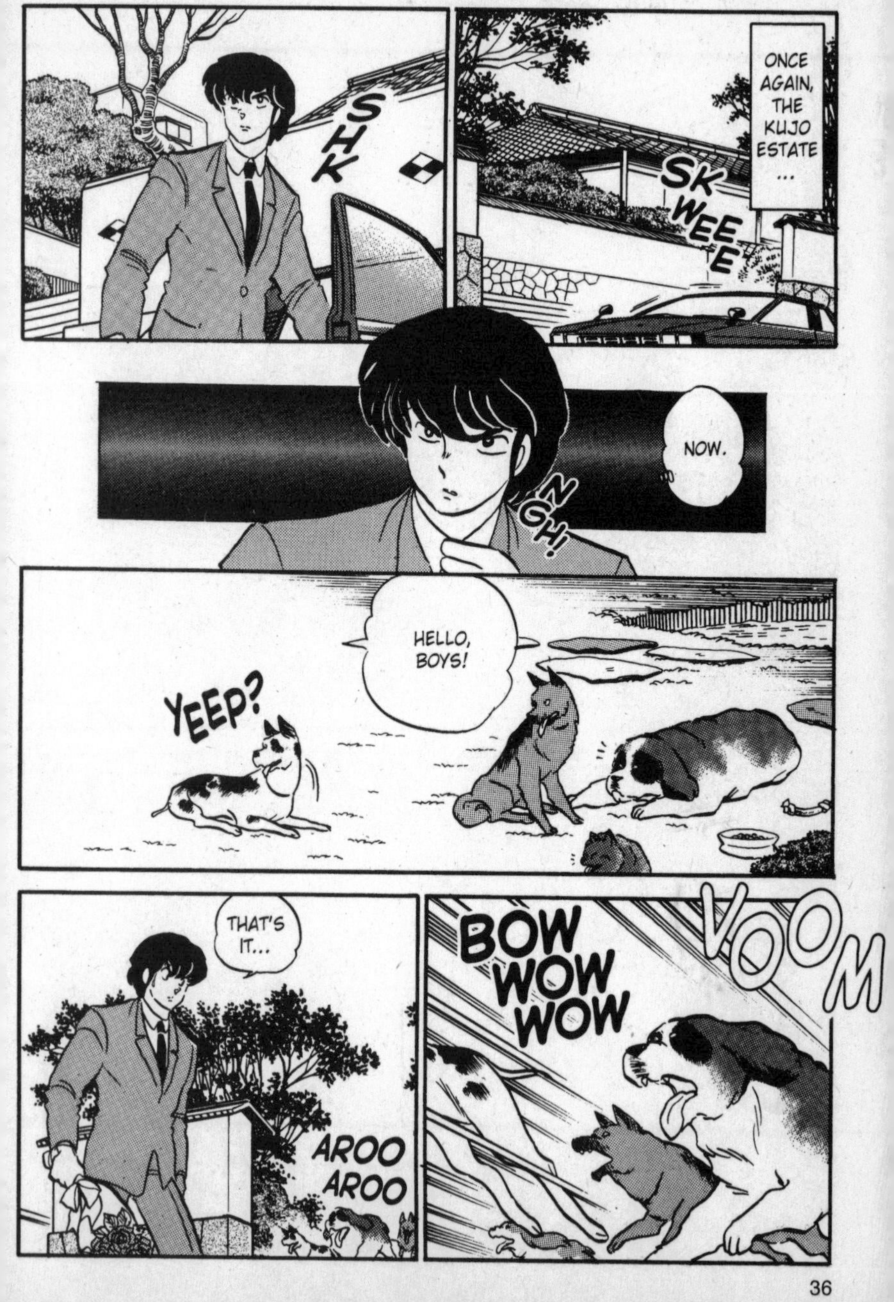
ONCE AGAIN, THE KUJO ESTATE ...
SKWEEEE
SHK
NOW.
NGH!
HELLO, BOYS!
YEEP?
VOOM
BOW WOW WOW
THAT'S IT...
AROO AROO

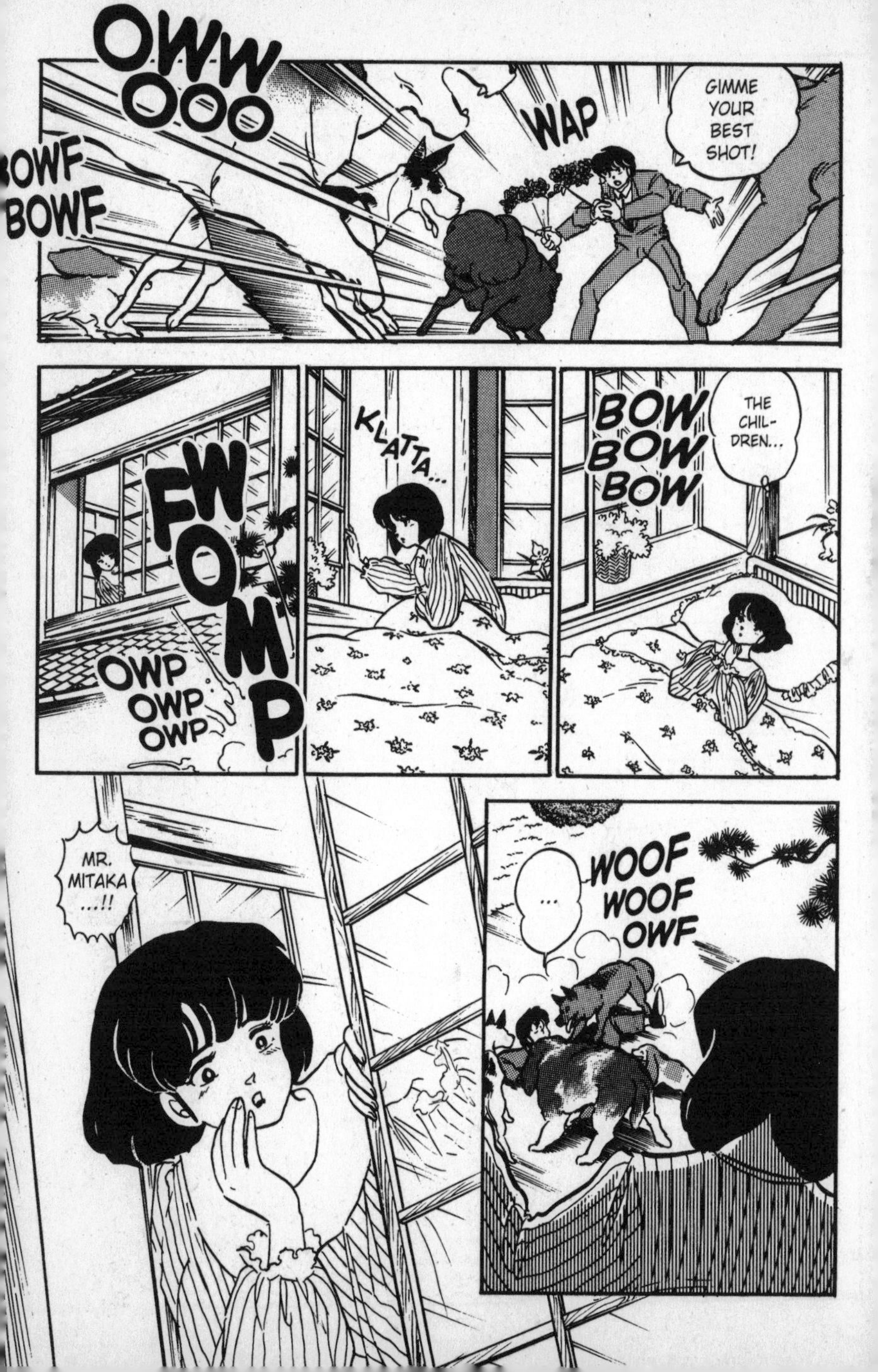
GIMME YOUR BEST SHOT!
OWW OOO
WAP
BOWF BOWF
THE CHIL-DREN...
BOW BOW BOW
KLATTA...
FWOMP
OWP OWP OWP
WOOF WOOF OWF
...
MR. MITAKA ...!!

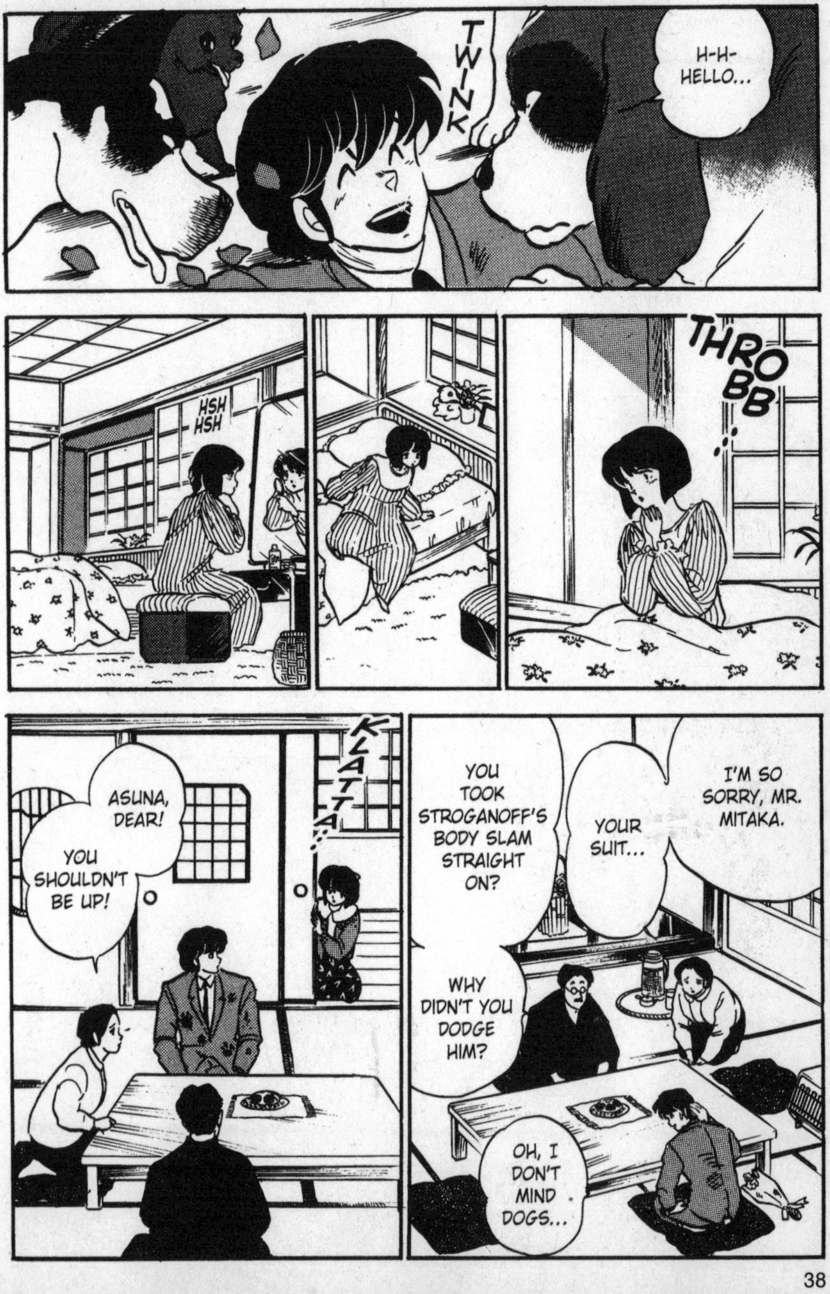
H-H-HELLO...
TWINK
THROBB
HSH HSH
I'M SO SORRY, MR. MITAKA.
YOUR SUIT...
YOU TOOK STROGANOFF'S BODY SLAM STRAIGHT ON?
WHY DIDN'T YOU DODGE HIM?
OH, I DON'T MIND DOGS...
KLATTA
ASUNA, DEAR!
YOU SHOULDN'T BE UP!

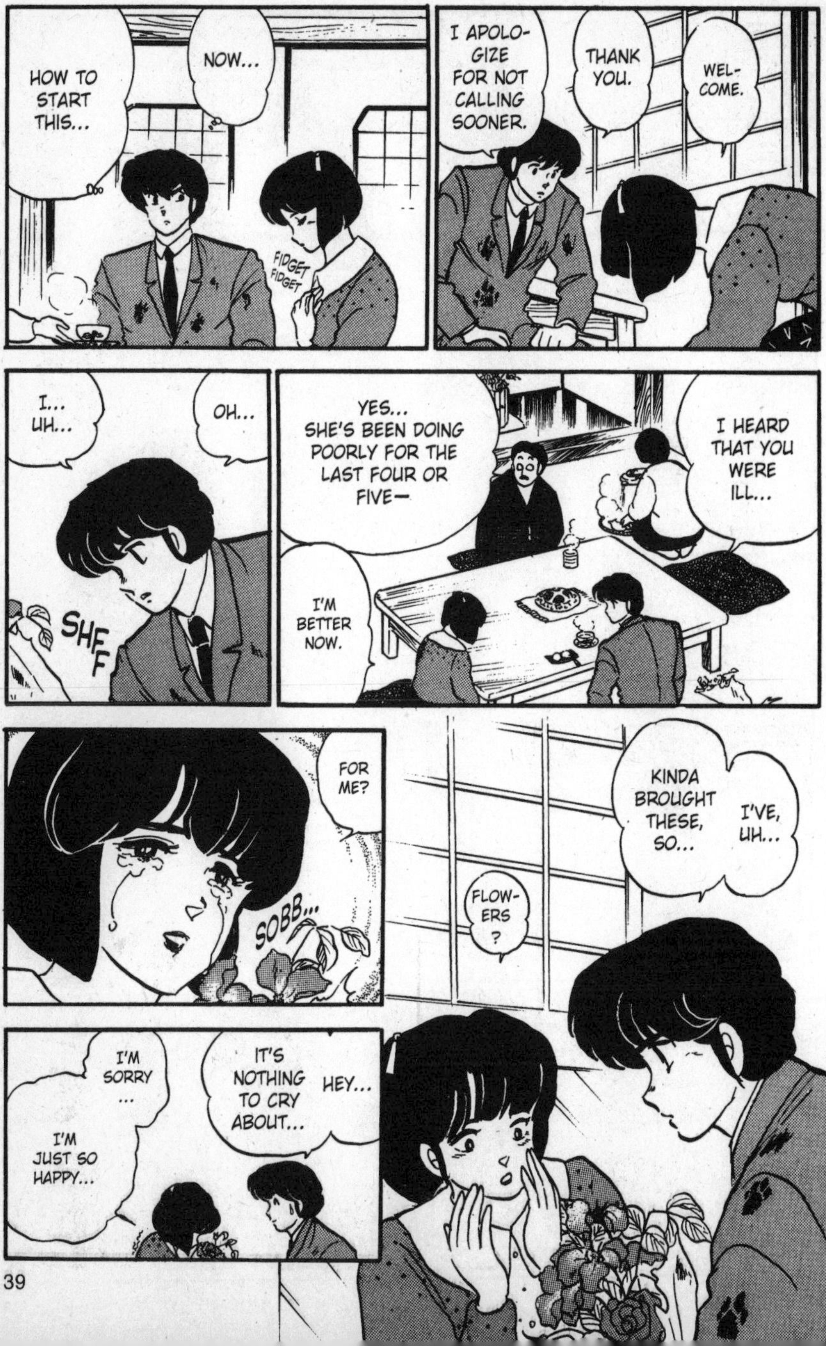

WEL-COME.
THANK YOU.
I APOLO-GIZE FOR NOT CALLING SOONER.
NOW...
HOW TO START THIS...
FIDGET FIDGET
I HEARD THAT YOU WERE ILL...
YES... SHE'S BEEN DOING POORLY FOR THE LAST FOUR OR FIVE—
I'M BETTER NOW.
OH...
I... UH...
SHFF
I'VE, UH...
KINDA BROUGHT THESE, SO...
FLOW-ERS?
FOR ME?
SOBB...
HEY...
IT'S NOTHING TO CRY ABOUT...
I'M SORRY...
I'M JUST SO HAPPY...

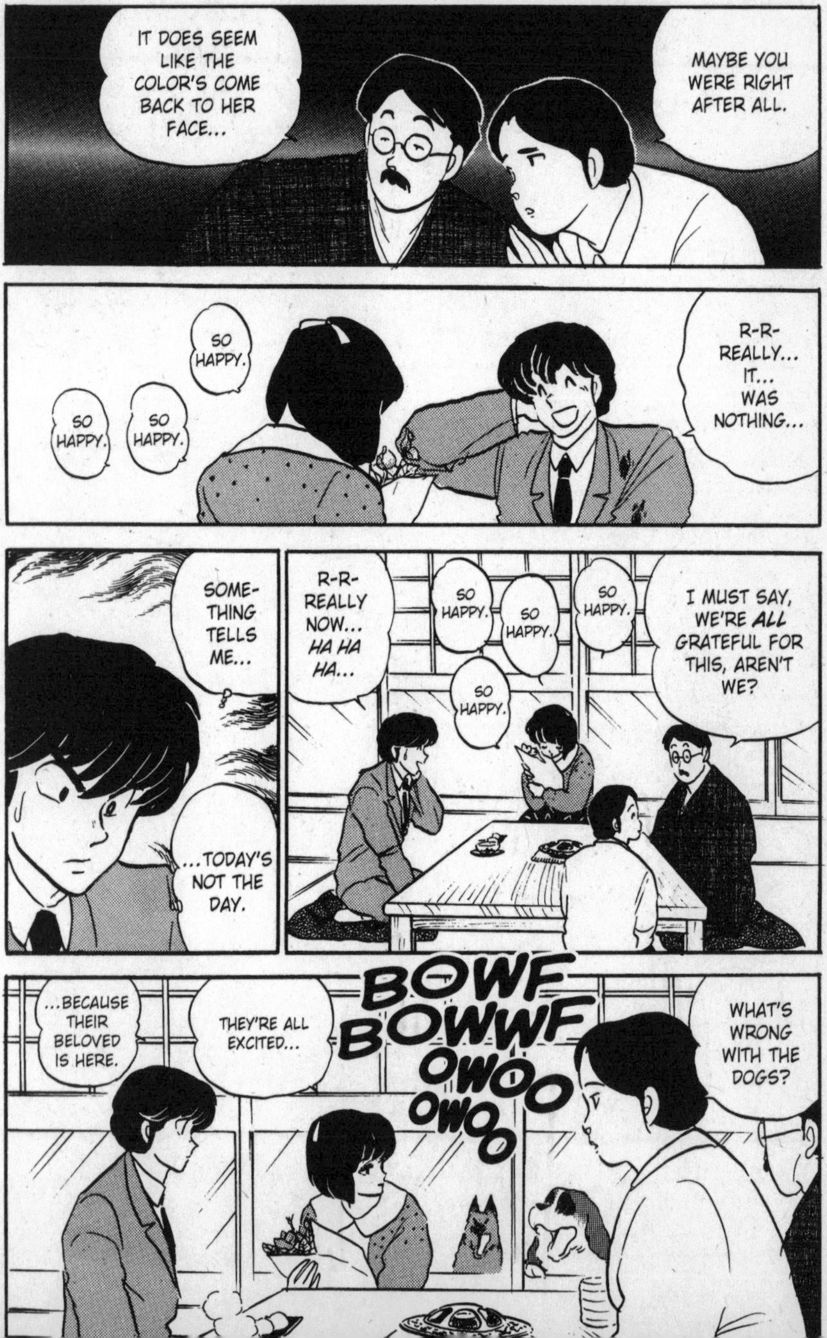
MAYBE YOU WERE RIGHT AFTER ALL.
IT DOES SEEM LIKE THE COLOR'S COME BACK TO HER FACE...
R-R-REALLY... IT... WAS NOTHING...
SO HAPPY.
SO HAPPY.
SO HAPPY.
I MUST SAY, WE'RE ALL GRATEFUL FOR THIS, AREN'T WE?
SO HAPPY.
SO HAPPY.
SO HAPPY.
SO HAPPY.
R-R-REALLY NOW... HA HA HA...
SOME-THING TELLS ME...
...TODAY'S NOT THE DAY.
WHAT'S WRONG WITH THE DOGS?
BOWF BOWWF
OWOO OWOO
THEY'RE ALL EXCITED...
...BECAUSE THEIR BELOVED IS HERE.

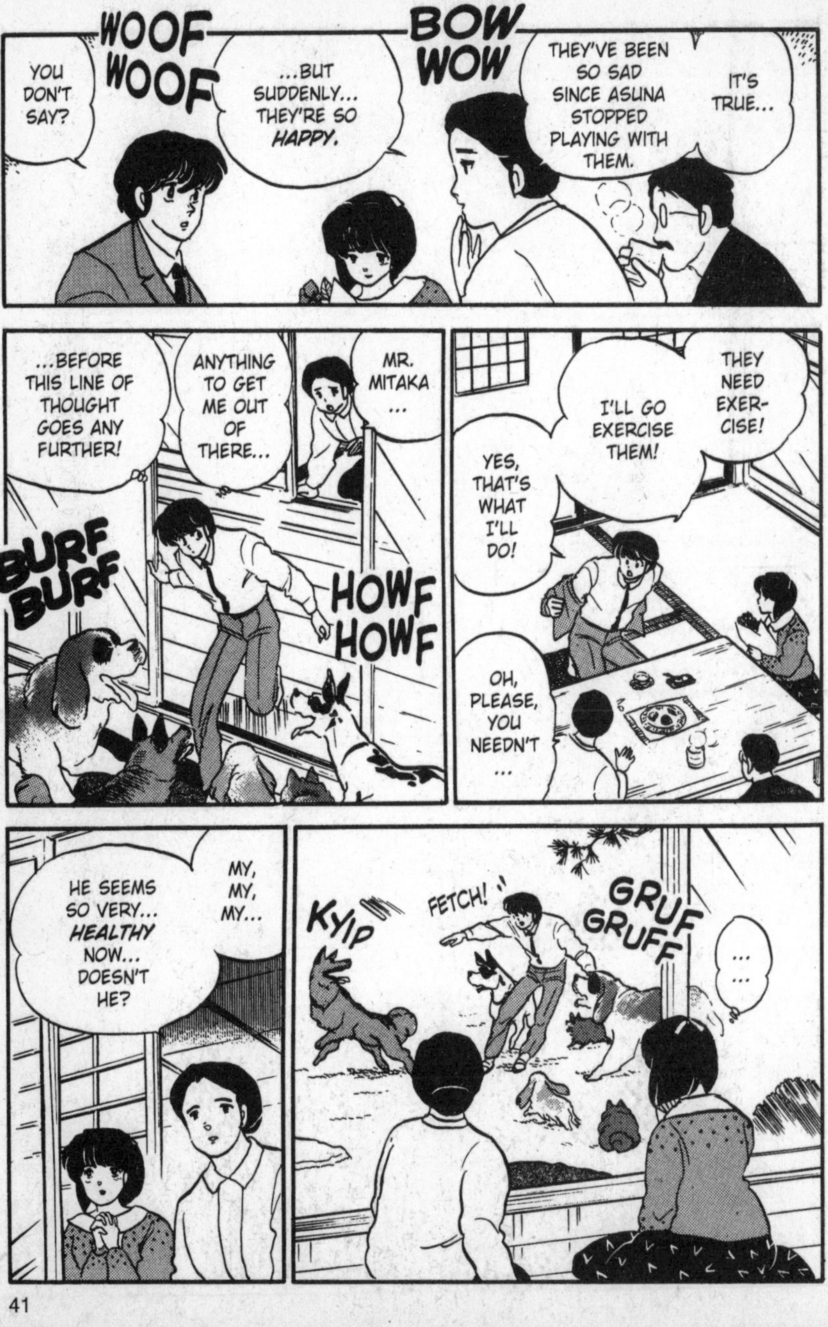
IT'S TRUE...
THEY'VE BEEN SO SAD SINCE ASUNA STOPPED PLAYING WITH THEM.
BOW WOW
...BUT SUDDENLY... THEY'RE SO *HAPPY*.
WOOF WOOF
YOU DON'T SAY?
THEY NEED EXER-CISE!
I'LL GO EXERCISE THEM!
YES, THAT'S WHAT I'LL DO!
OH, PLEASE, YOU NEEDN'T ...
MR. MITAKA ...
ANYTHING TO GET ME OUT OF THERE...
...BEFORE THIS LINE OF THOUGHT GOES ANY FURTHER!
HOWF HOWF
BURF BURF
GRUF GRUFF
... ...
FETCH!
KYIP
MY, MY, MY...
HE SEEMS SO VERY... *HEALTHY* NOW... DOESN'T HE?

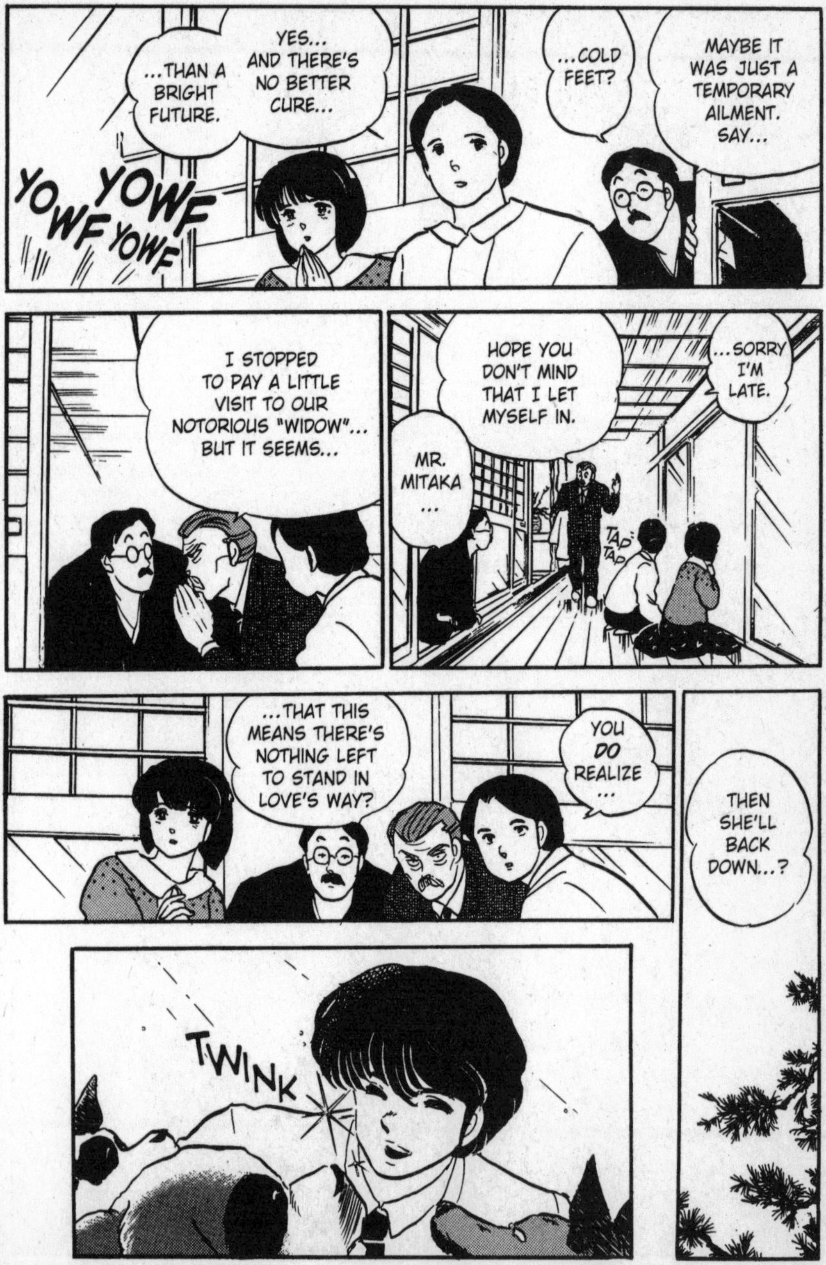
MAYBE IT WAS JUST A TEMPORARY AILMENT. SAY...
...COLD FEET?
YES... AND THERE'S NO BETTER CURE...
...THAN A BRIGHT FUTURE.
YOWF YOWF YOWF YOWF
...SORRY I'M LATE.
HOPE YOU DON'T MIND THAT I LET MYSELF IN.
MR. MITAKA ...
TAP TAP
I STOPPED TO PAY A LITTLE VISIT TO OUR NOTORIOUS "WIDOW"... BUT IT SEEMS...
THEN SHE'LL BACK DOWN...?
YOU *DO* REALIZE ...
...THAT THIS MEANS THERE'S NOTHING LEFT TO STAND IN LOVE'S WAY?
TWINK

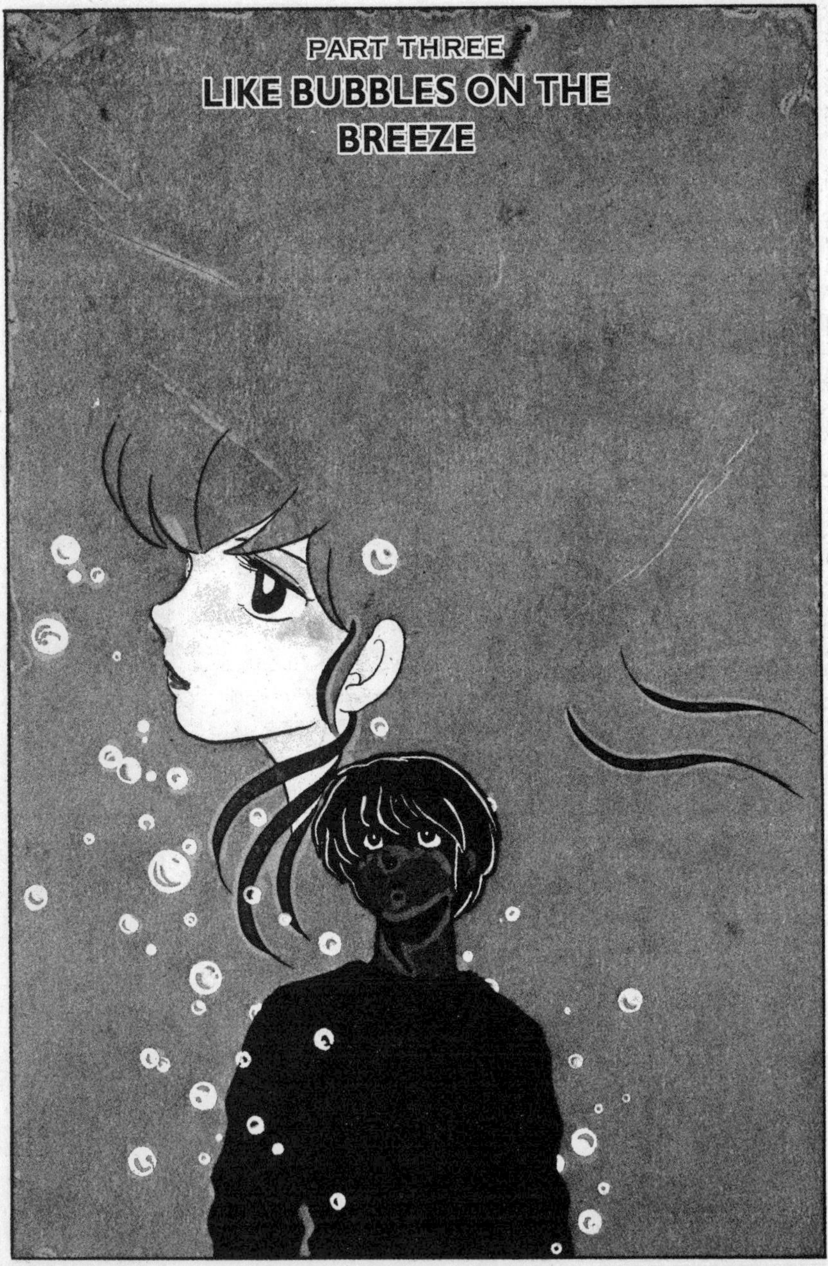
PART THREE
LIKE BUBBLES ON THE BREEZE

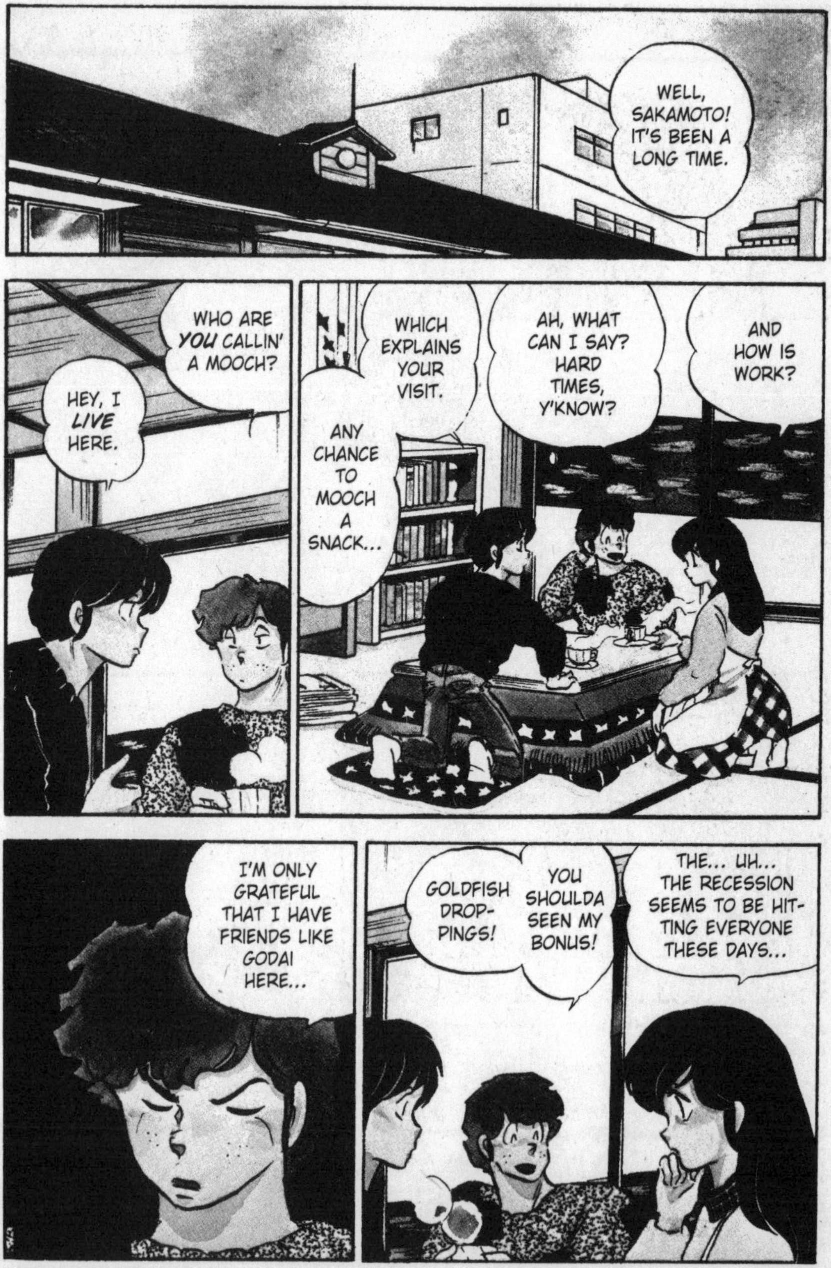
WELL, SAKAMOTO! IT'S BEEN A LONG TIME.
AND HOW IS WORK?
AH, WHAT CAN I SAY? HARD TIMES, Y'KNOW?
WHICH EXPLAINS YOUR VISIT.
ANY CHANCE TO MOOCH A SNACK...
WHO ARE *YOU* CALLIN' A MOOCH?
HEY, I *LIVE* HERE.
THE... UH... THE RECESSION SEEMS TO BE HITTING EVERYONE THESE DAYS...
YOU SHOULDA SEEN MY BONUS!
GOLDFISH DROPPINGS!
I'M ONLY GRATEFUL THAT I HAVE FRIENDS LIKE GODAI HERE...

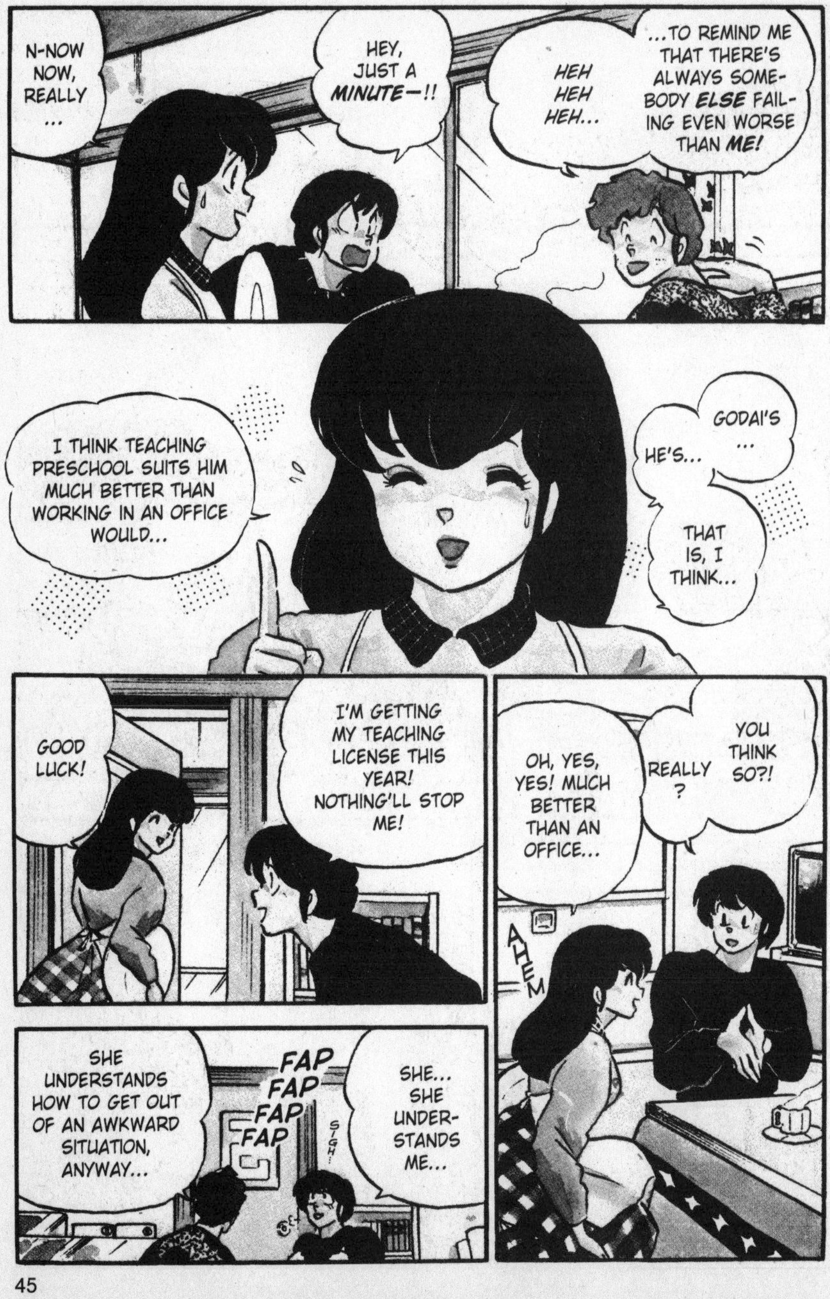
...TO REMIND ME THAT THERE'S ALWAYS SOMEBODY *ELSE* FAILING EVEN WORSE THAN *ME!*
HEH HEH HEH...
HEY, JUST A *MINUTE*—!!
N-NOW NOW, REALLY ...
GODAI'S ...
HE'S...
THAT IS, I THINK...
I THINK TEACHING PRESCHOOL SUITS HIM MUCH BETTER THAN WORKING IN AN OFFICE WOULD...
YOU THINK SO?!
REALLY ?
OH, YES, YES! MUCH BETTER THAN AN OFFICE...
AHEM
I'M GETTING MY TEACHING LICENSE THIS YEAR! NOTHING'LL STOP ME!
GOOD LUCK!
SHE... SHE UNDERSTANDS ME...
SIGH...
FAP FAP FAP FAP
SHE UNDERSTANDS HOW TO GET OUT OF AN AWKWARD SITUATION, ANYWAY...

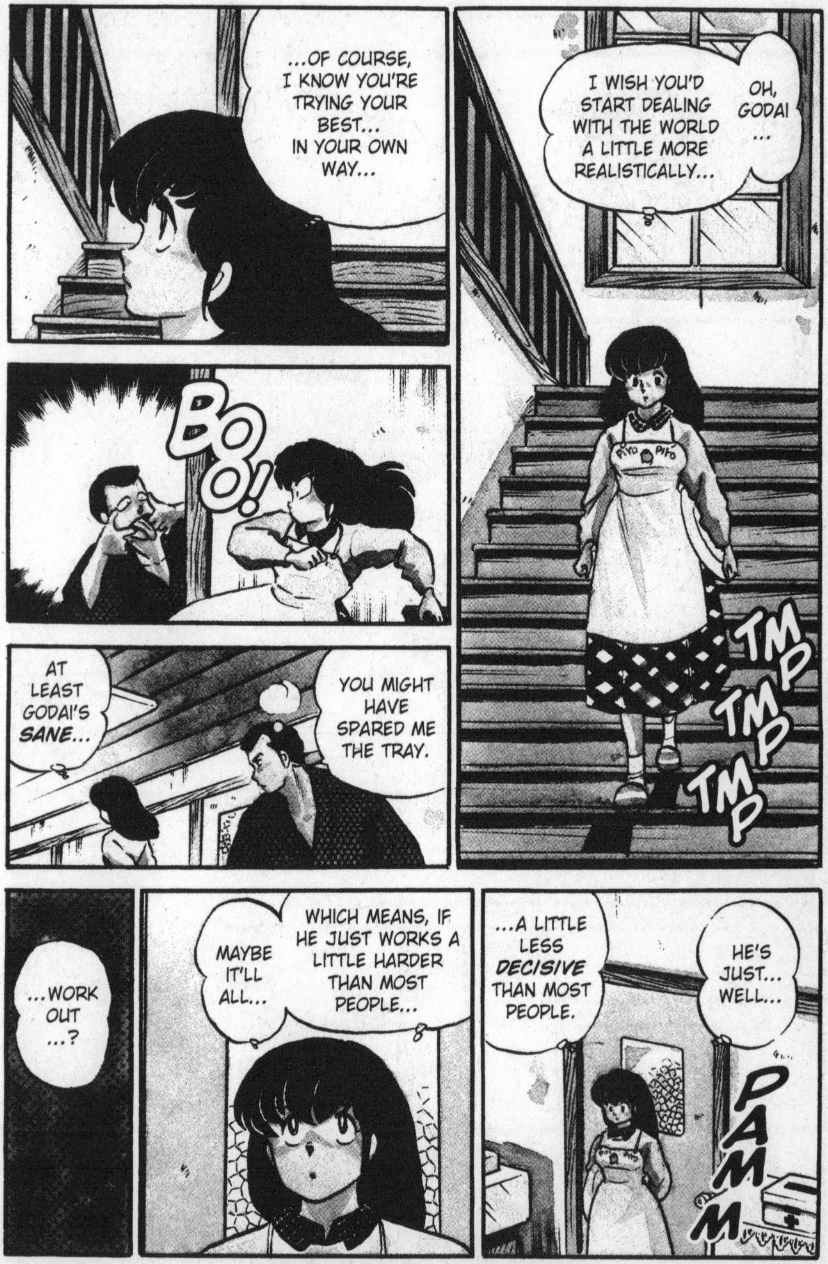
OH, GODAI ...
I WISH YOU'D START DEALING WITH THE WORLD A LITTLE MORE REALISTICALLY...
TMP TMP TMP
...OF COURSE, I KNOW YOU'RE TRYING YOUR BEST... IN YOUR OWN WAY...
BOO!
YOU MIGHT HAVE SPARED ME THE TRAY.
AT LEAST GODAI'S *SANE*...
HE'S JUST... WELL...
PAMM
...A LITTLE LESS *DECISIVE* THAN MOST PEOPLE.
WHICH MEANS, IF HE JUST WORKS A LITTLE HARDER THAN MOST PEOPLE...
MAYBE IT'LL ALL...
...WORK OUT ...?

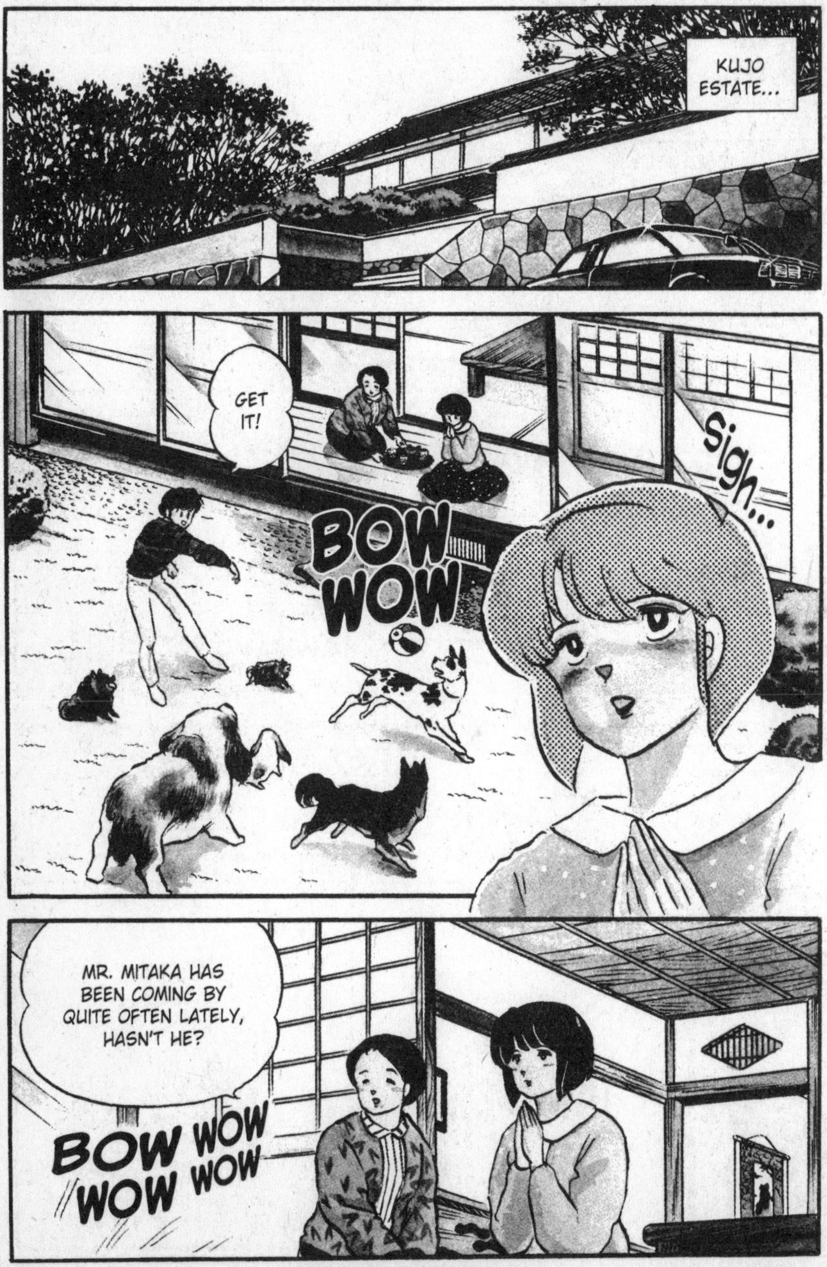
KUJO ESTATE...
Sigh...
GET IT!
BOW WOW
MR. MITAKA HAS BEEN COMING BY QUITE OFTEN LATELY, HASN'T HE?
BOW WOW WOW WOW

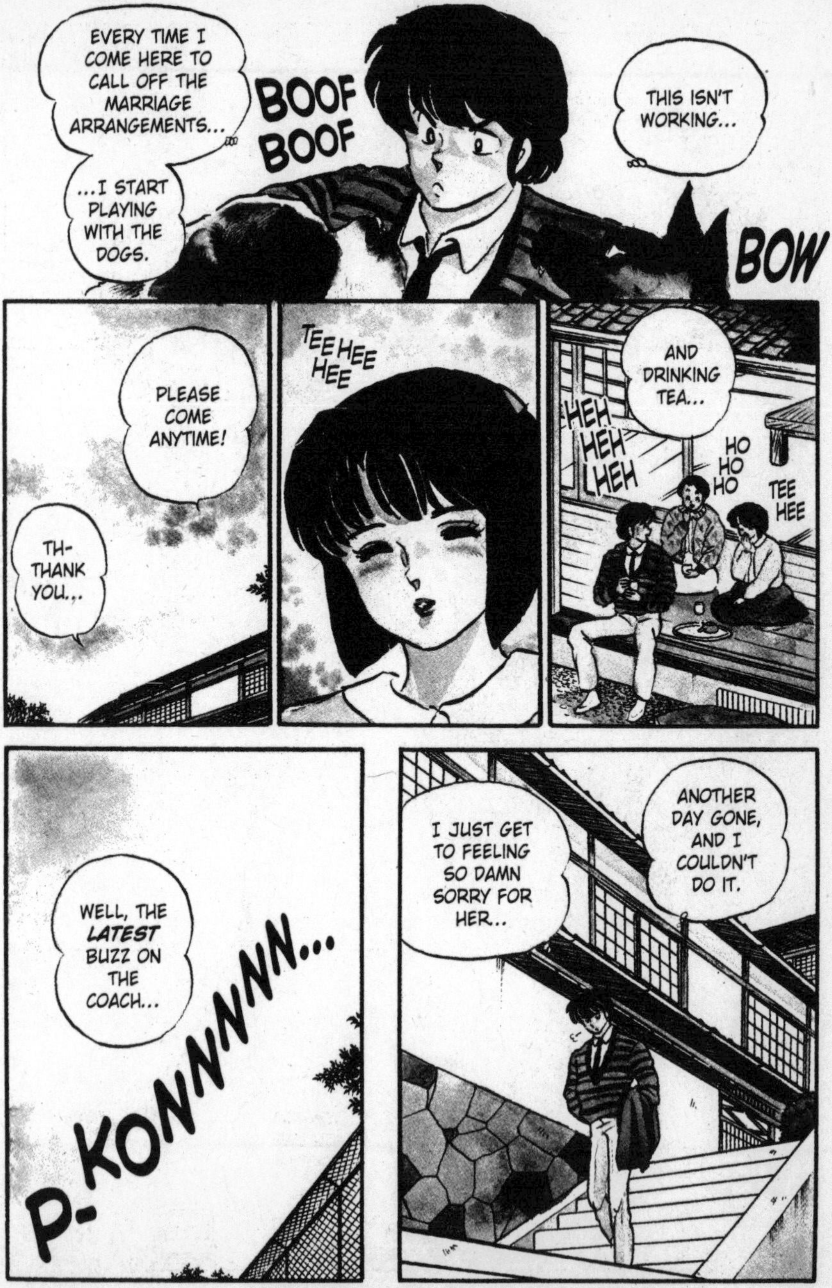
THIS ISN'T WORKING...
BOW
EVERY TIME I COME HERE TO CALL OFF THE MARRIAGE ARRANGEMENTS...
BOOF BOOF
...I START PLAYING WITH THE DOGS.
AND DRINKING TEA...
HO HO HO
TEE HEE
HEH HEH HEH
TEE HEE HEE
PLEASE COME ANYTIME!
TH-THANK YOU...
ANOTHER DAY GONE, AND I COULDN'T DO IT.
I JUST GET TO FEELING SO DAMN SORRY FOR HER...
WELL, THE *LATEST* BUZZ ON THE COACH...
P-KONNNNN...

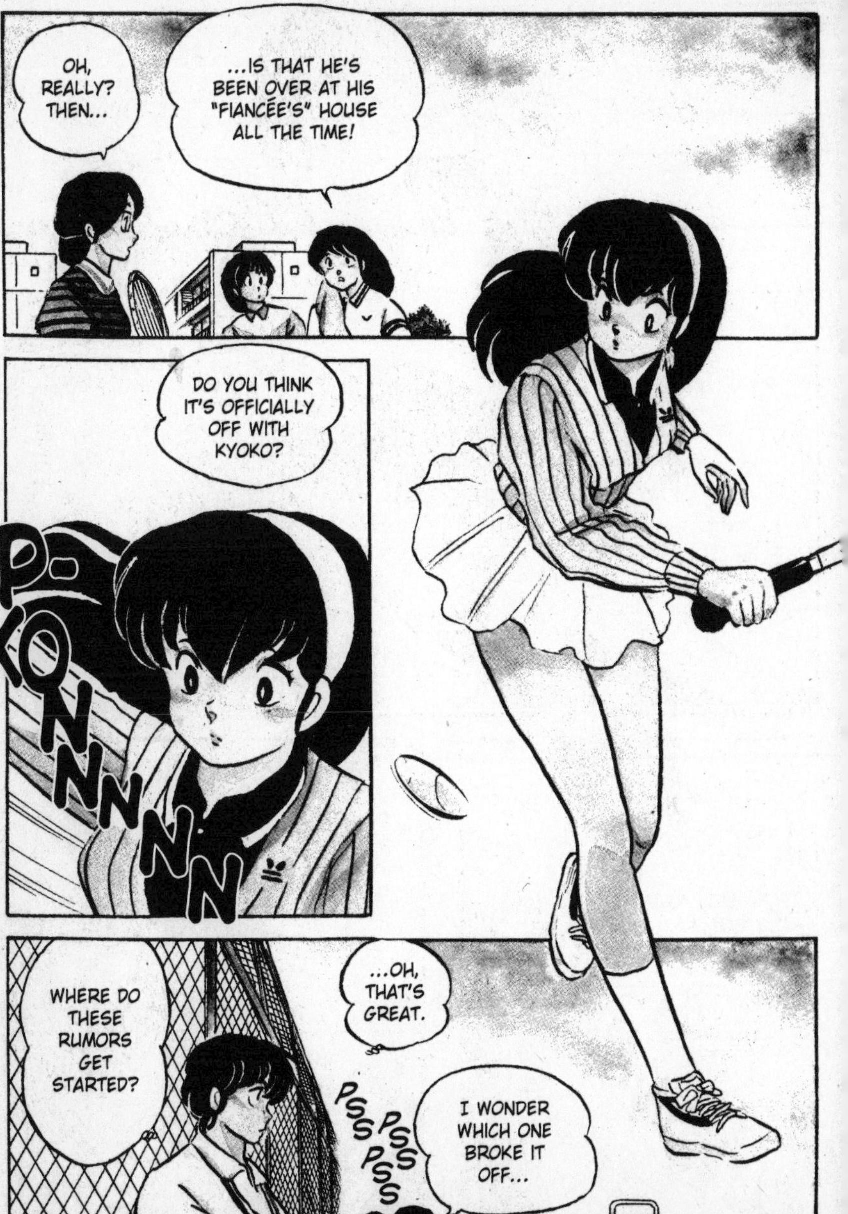
...IS THAT HE'S BEEN OVER AT HIS "FIANCÉE'S" HOUSE ALL THE TIME!
OH, REALLY? THEN...
DO YOU THINK IT'S OFFICIALLY OFF WITH KYOKO?
P-KONNNNNN
...OH, THAT'S GREAT.
I WONDER WHICH ONE BROKE IT OFF...
PSS PSS PSS PSS PSS
WHERE DO THESE RUMORS GET STARTED?

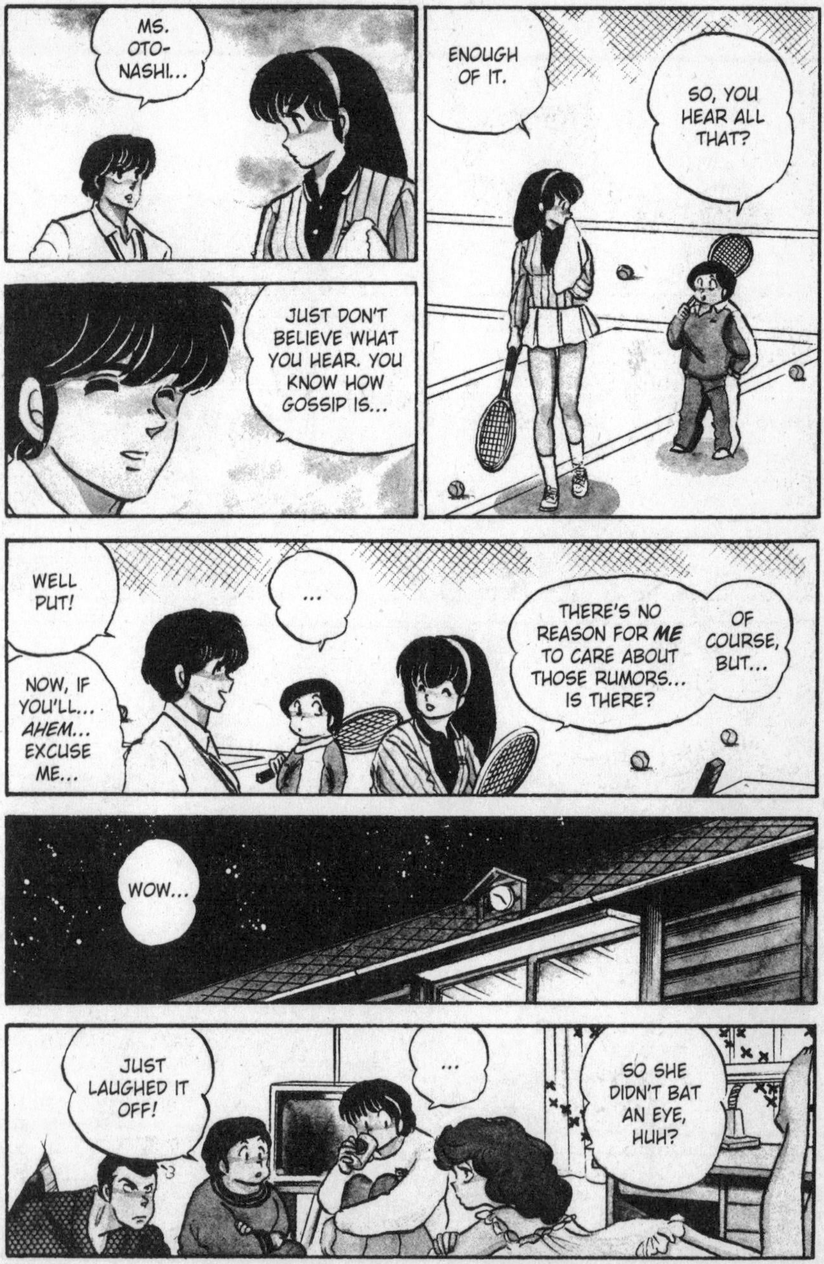
SO, YOU HEAR ALL THAT?
ENOUGH OF IT.
MS. OTO-NASHI...
JUST DON'T BELIEVE WHAT YOU HEAR. YOU KNOW HOW GOSSIP IS...
OF COURSE, BUT...
THERE'S NO REASON FOR *ME* TO CARE ABOUT THOSE RUMORS... IS THERE?
...
WELL PUT!
NOW, IF YOU'LL... *AHEM*... EXCUSE ME...
WOW...
SO SHE DIDN'T BAT AN EYE, HUH?
...
JUST LAUGHED IT OFF!

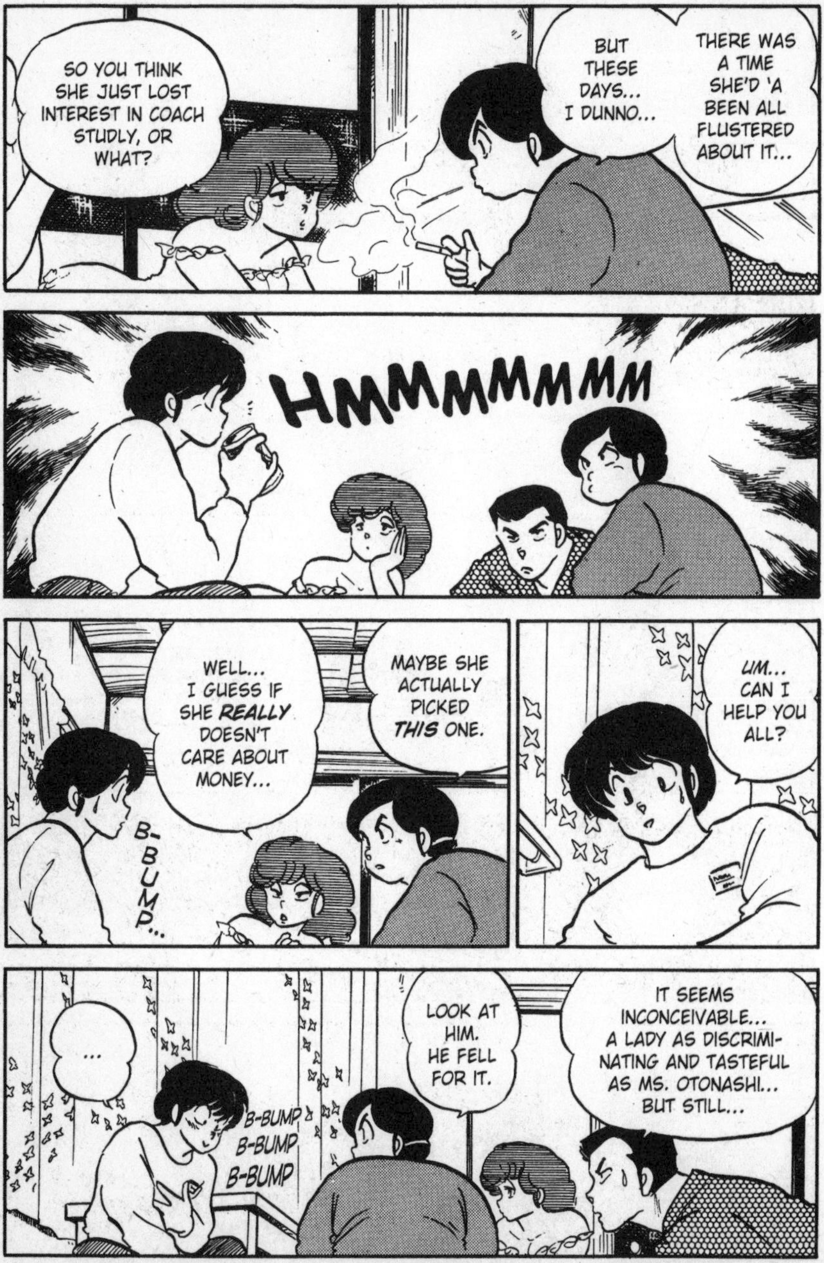
THERE WAS A TIME SHE'D 'A BEEN ALL FLUSTERED ABOUT IT...
BUT THESE DAYS... I DUNNO...
SO YOU THINK SHE JUST LOST INTEREST IN COACH STUDLY, OR WHAT?
HMMMMMMM
UM... CAN I HELP YOU ALL?
MAYBE SHE ACTUALLY PICKED THIS ONE.
WELL... I GUESS IF SHE REALLY DOESN'T CARE ABOUT MONEY...
B-BUMP...
IT SEEMS INCONCEIVABLE... A LADY AS DISCRIMI-NATING AND TASTEFUL AS MS. OTONASHI... BUT STILL...
LOOK AT HIM. HE FELL FOR IT.
B-BUMP
B-BUMP
B-BUMP
...

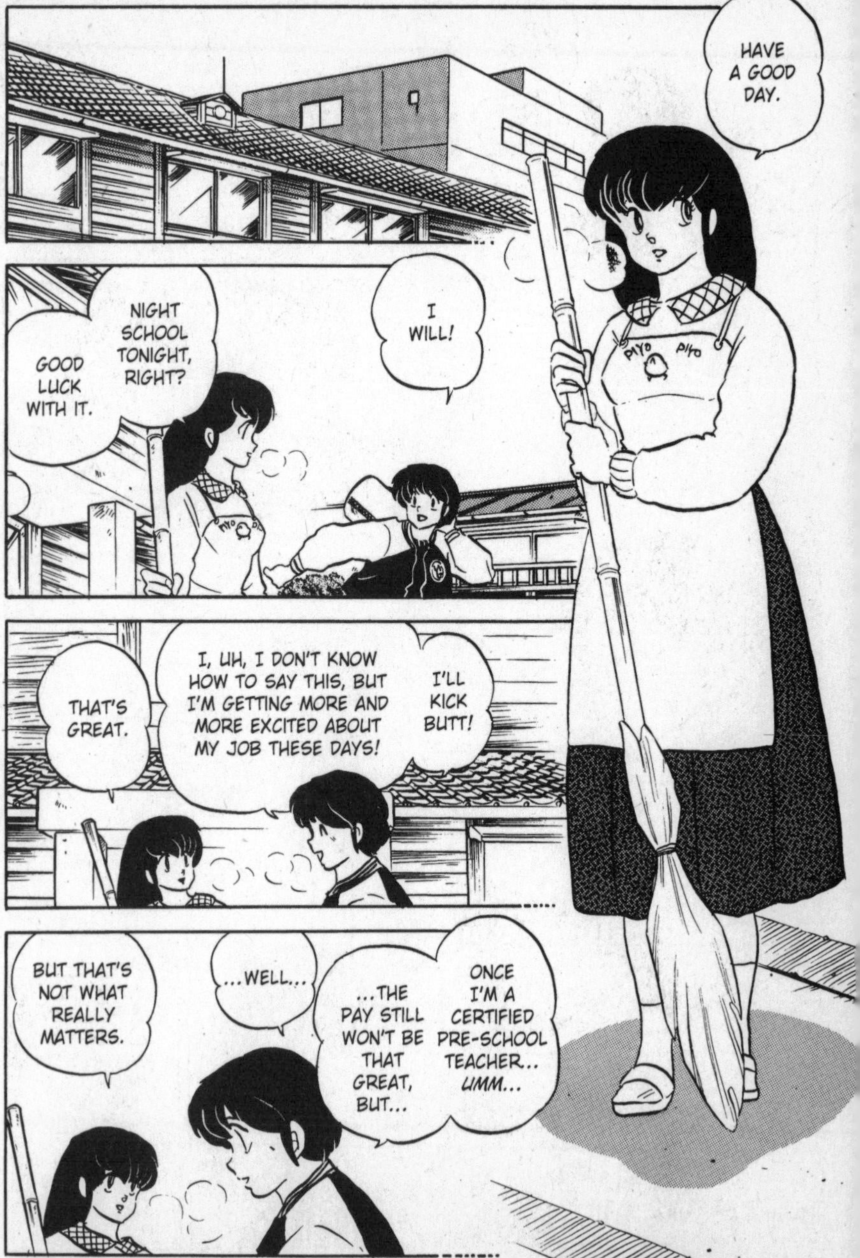
HAVE A GOOD DAY.
PIYO PIYO
I WILL!
NIGHT SCHOOL TONIGHT, RIGHT?
GOOD LUCK WITH IT.
I'LL KICK BUTT!
I, UH, I DON'T KNOW HOW TO SAY THIS, BUT I'M GETTING MORE AND MORE EXCITED ABOUT MY JOB THESE DAYS!
THAT'S GREAT.
ONCE I'M A CERTIFIED PRE-SCHOOL TEACHER.. UMM...
...THE PAY STILL WON'T BE THAT GREAT, BUT...
...WELL...
BUT THAT'S NOT WHAT REALLY MATTERS.

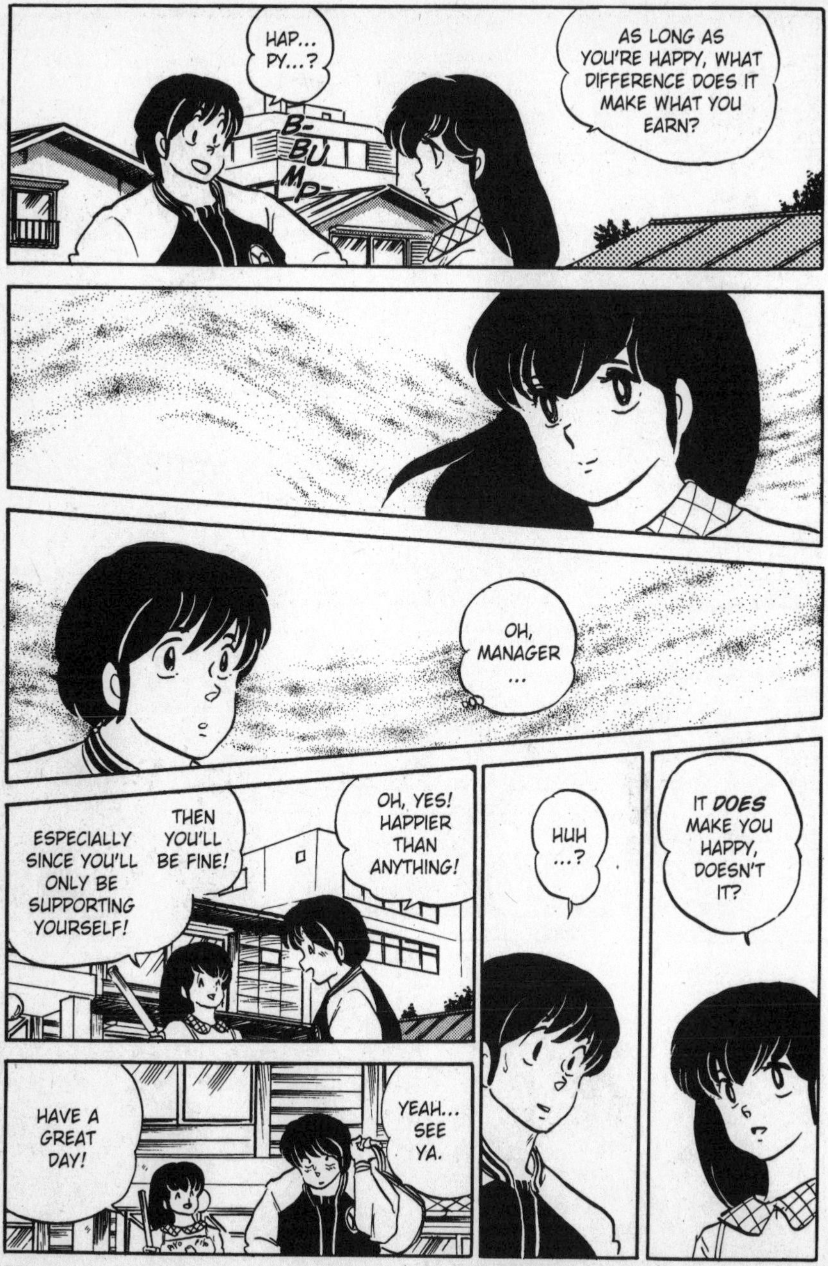
AS LONG AS YOU'RE HAPPY, WHAT DIFFERENCE DOES IT MAKE WHAT YOU EARN?
HAP... PY...?
B-BUMP-
OH, MANAGER ...
IT *DOES* MAKE YOU HAPPY, DOESN'T IT?
HUH ...?
OH, YES! HAPPIER THAN ANYTHING!
THEN YOU'LL BE FINE!
ESPECIALLY SINCE YOU'LL ONLY BE SUPPORTING YOURSELF!
YEAH... SEE YA.
HAVE A GREAT DAY!

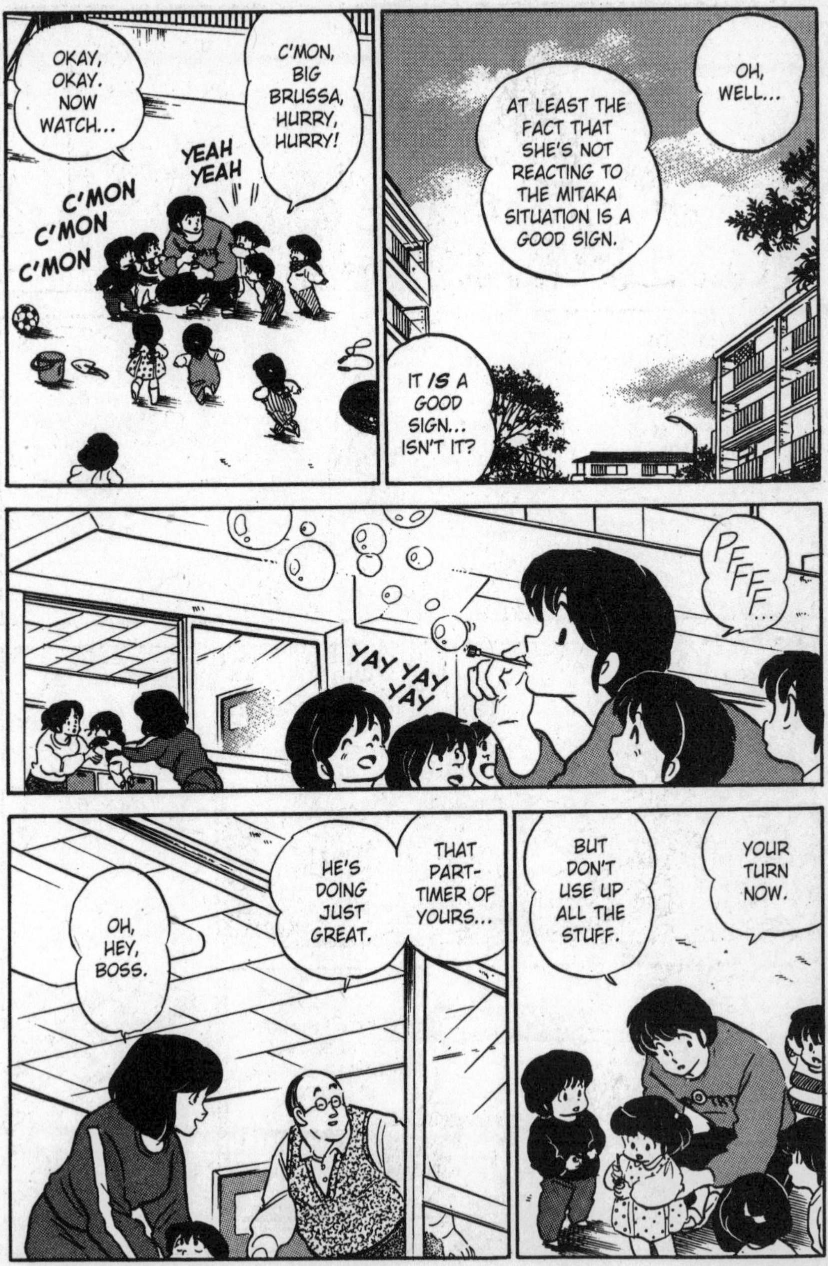
OH, WELL...
AT LEAST THE FACT THAT SHE'S NOT REACTING TO THE MITAKA SITUATION IS A GOOD SIGN.
IT IS A GOOD SIGN... ISN'T IT?
C'MON, BIG BRUSSA, HURRY, HURRY!
OKAY, OKAY. NOW WATCH...
YEAH YEAH
C'MON C'MON C'MON
PFFFF...
YAY YAY YAY
YOUR TURN NOW.
BUT DON'T USE UP ALL THE STUFF.
THAT PART-TIMER OF YOURS...
HE'S DOING JUST GREAT.
OH, HEY, BOSS.

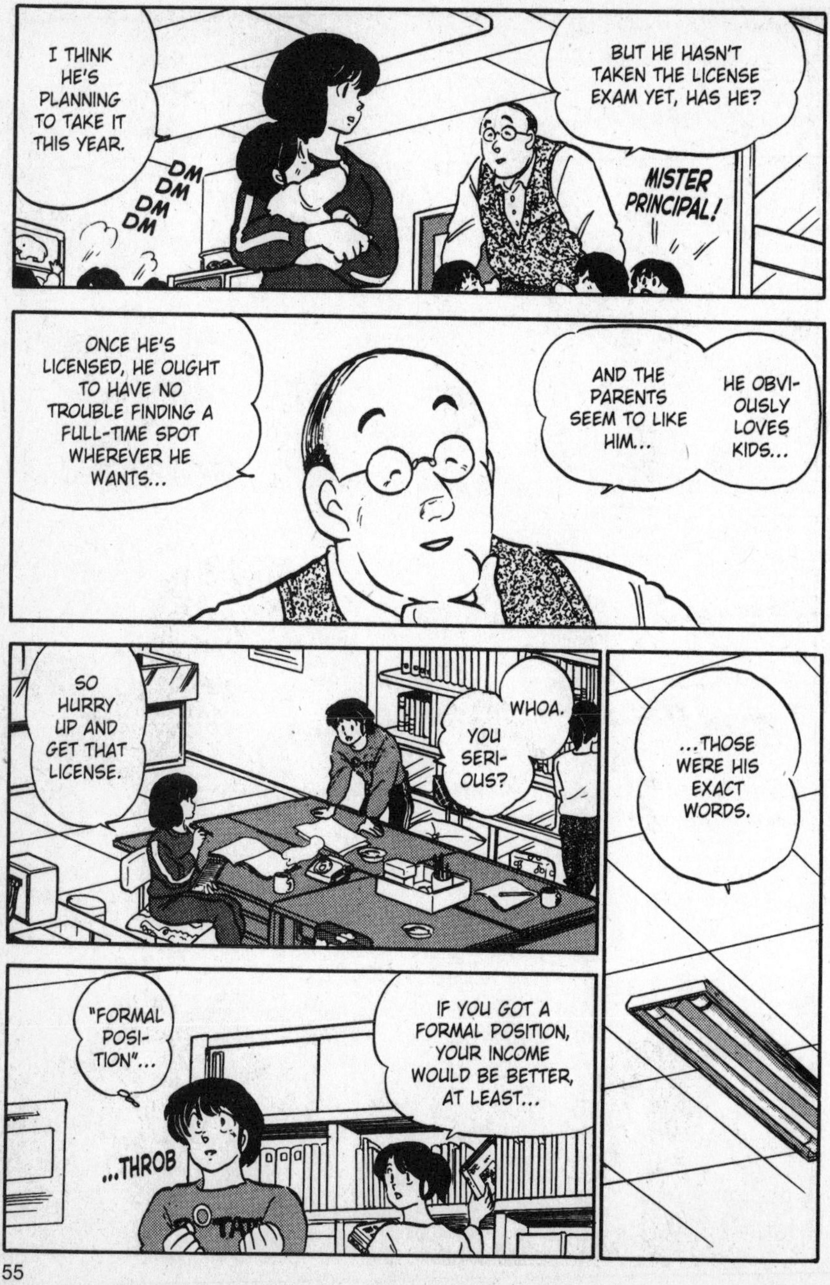
BUT HE HASN'T TAKEN THE LICENSE EXAM YET, HAS HE?
MISTER PRINCIPAL!
I THINK HE'S PLANNING TO TAKE IT THIS YEAR.
DM DM DM DM
HE OBVI-OUSLY LOVES KIDS...
AND THE PARENTS SEEM TO LIKE HIM...
ONCE HE'S LICENSED, HE OUGHT TO HAVE NO TROUBLE FINDING A FULL-TIME SPOT WHEREVER HE WANTS...
...THOSE WERE HIS EXACT WORDS.
WHOA.
YOU SERI-OUS?
SO HURRY UP AND GET THAT LICENSE.
IF YOU GOT A FORMAL POSITION, YOUR INCOME WOULD BE BETTER, AT LEAST...
...THROB
"FORMAL POSI-TION"...

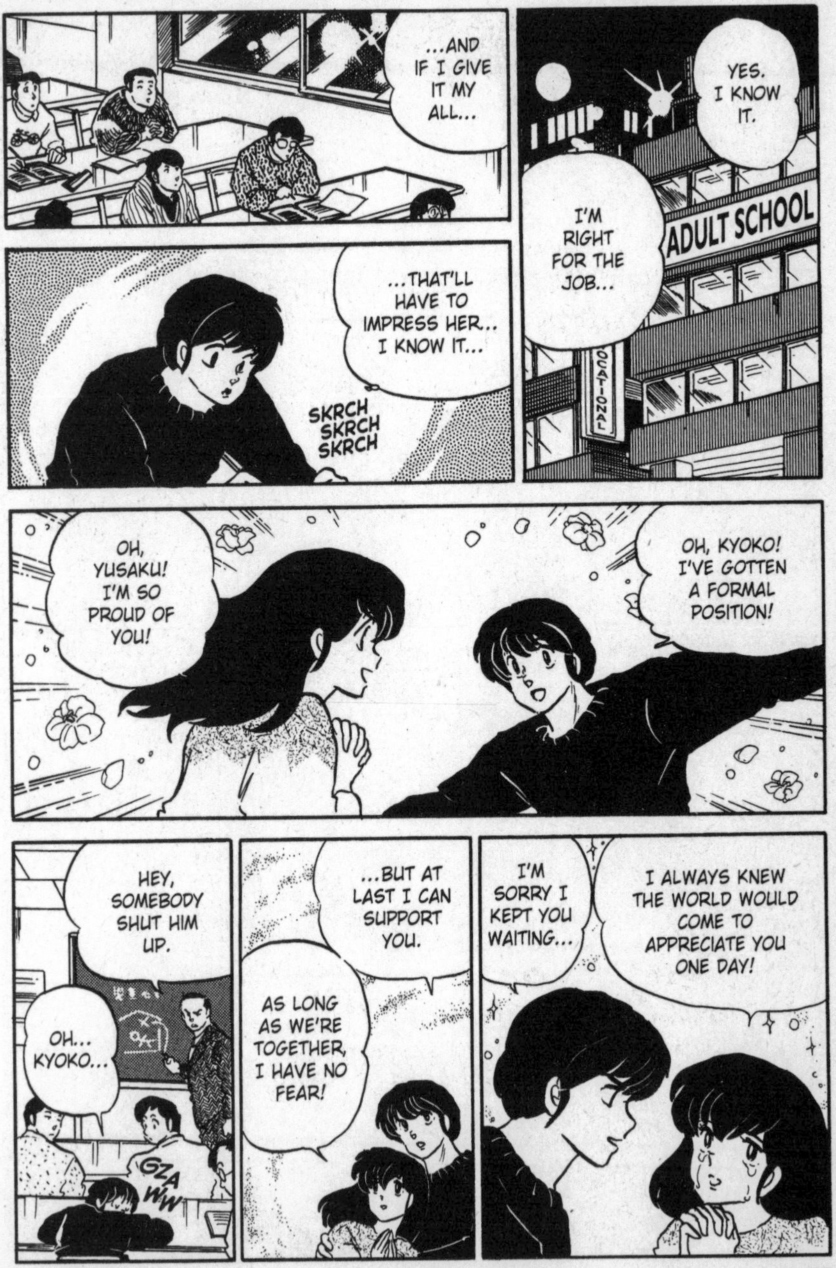
YES. I KNOW IT.
I'M RIGHT FOR THE JOB...
ADULT SCHOOL
OCATIONAL
...AND IF I GIVE IT MY ALL...
...THAT'LL HAVE TO IMPRESS HER... I KNOW IT...
SKRCH SKRCH SKRCH
OH, KYOKO! I'VE GOTTEN A FORMAL POSITION!
OH, YUSAKU! I'M SO PROUD OF YOU!
I ALWAYS KNEW THE WORLD WOULD COME TO APPRECIATE YOU ONE DAY!
I'M SORRY I KEPT YOU WAITING...
...BUT AT LAST I CAN SUPPORT YOU.
AS LONG AS WE'RE TOGETHER, I HAVE NO FEAR!
HEY, SOMEBODY SHUT HIM UP.
OH... KYOKO...
GZAWW

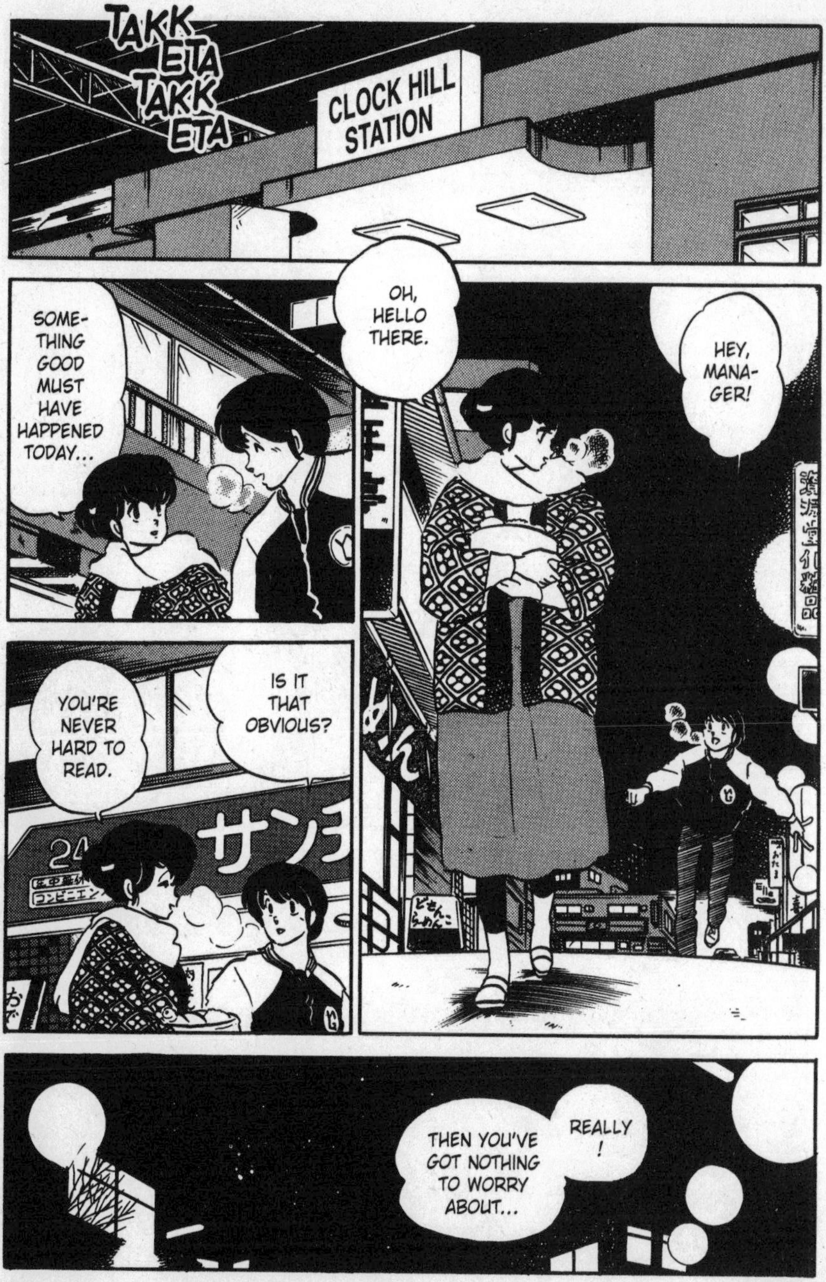
TAKK ETA TAKK ETA
CLOCK HILL STATION
HEY, MANAGER!
OH, HELLO THERE.
SOMETHING GOOD MUST HAVE HAPPENED TODAY...
IS IT THAT OBVIOUS?
YOU'RE NEVER HARD TO READ.
REALLY!
THEN YOU'VE GOT NOTHING TO WORRY ABOUT...

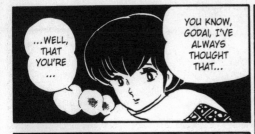

'COURSE, WE'RE TALK-ING ABOUT AFTER I'M CERTIFIED, BUT...
BY THE END OF THE YEAR, THOUGH, YOU'LL BE SET.
YOU KNOW, GODAI, I'VE ALWAYS THOUGHT THAT...
...WELL, THAT YOU'RE ...
YOU'RE ...
MORE SELF-EFFACING THAN MOST PEOPLE, SO YOU TEND TO GET SADDLED WITH MORE... AND STRANGER... TROUBLES...
BUT I ALWAYS KNEW THAT YOUR LUCK WOULD TURN...
THAT THE SUN WOULD SHINE ON YOU ONE OF THESE DAYS. AND...
...
WELL... GOOD LUCK.
THANKS.

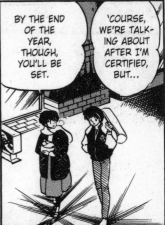

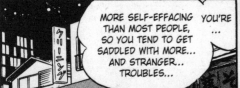

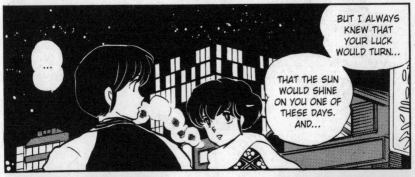

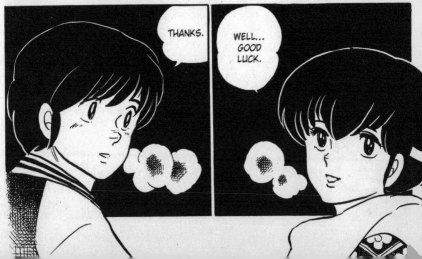

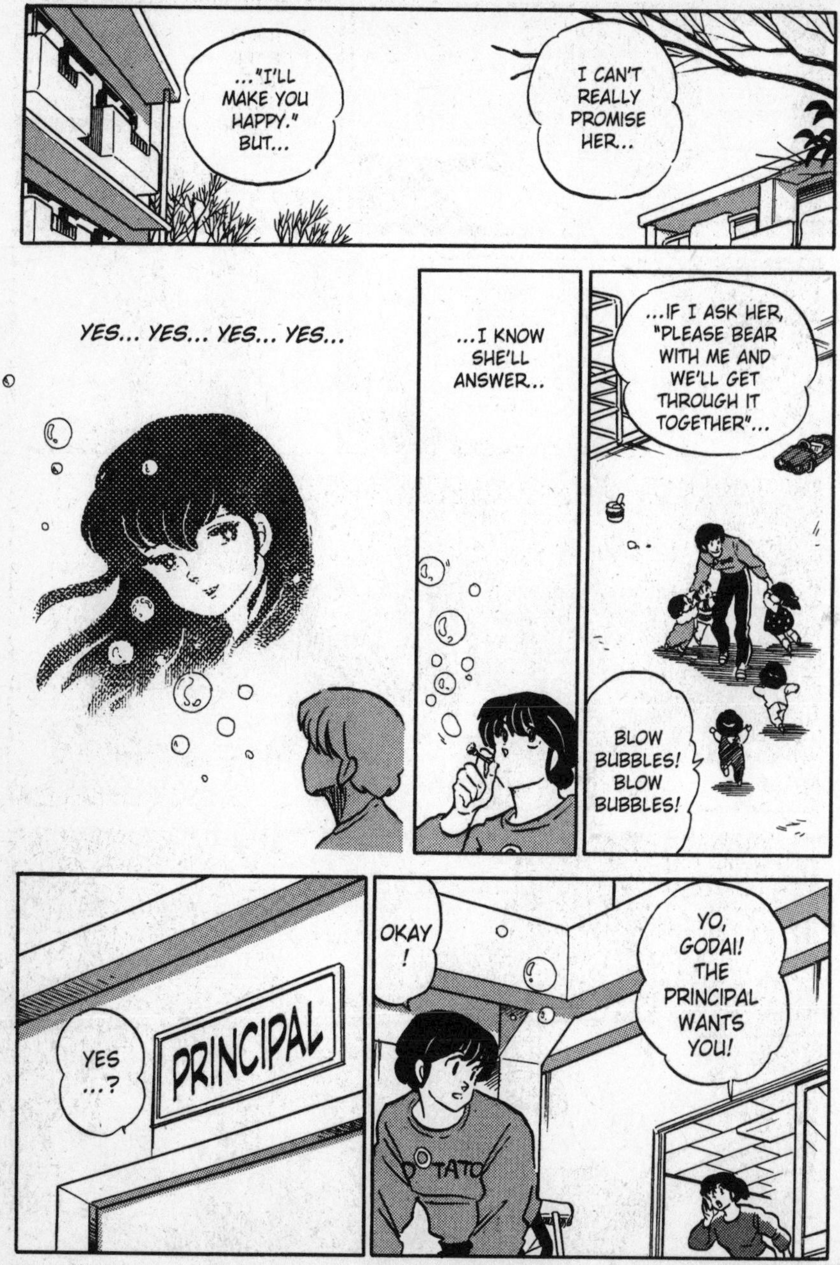
I CAN'T REALLY PROMISE HER...
..."I'LL MAKE YOU HAPPY." BUT...
...IF I ASK HER, "PLEASE BEAR WITH ME AND WE'LL GET THROUGH IT TOGETHER"...
BLOW BUBBLES! BLOW BUBBLES!
...I KNOW SHE'LL ANSWER...
YES... YES... YES... YES...
YO, GODAI! THE PRINCIPAL WANTS YOU!
OKAY!
PRINCIPAL
YES ...?

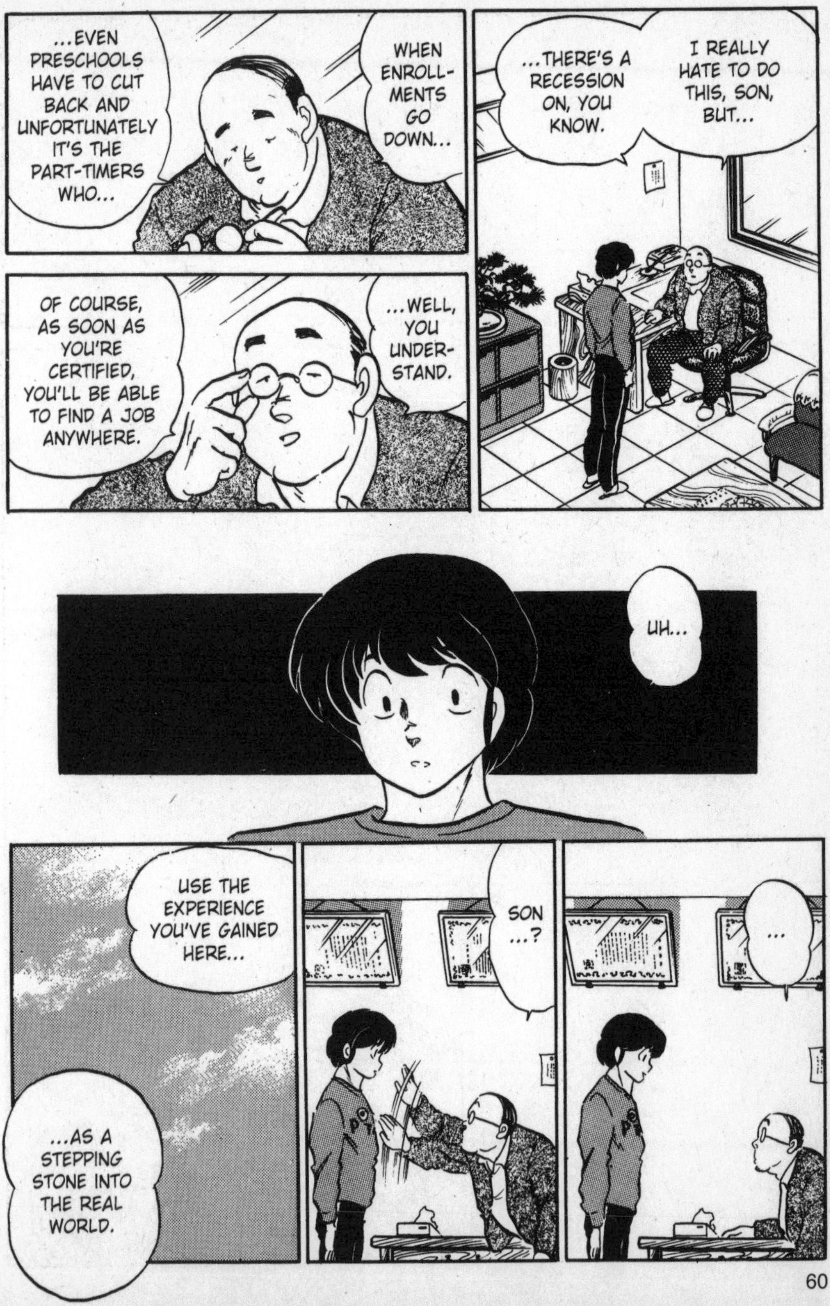
I REALLY HATE TO DO THIS, SON, BUT...
...THERE'S A RECESSION ON, YOU KNOW.
WHEN ENROLLMENTS GO DOWN...
...EVEN PRESCHOOLS HAVE TO CUT BACK AND UNFORTUNATELY IT'S THE PART-TIMERS WHO...
...WELL, YOU UNDERSTAND.
OF COURSE, AS SOON AS YOU'RE CERTIFIED, YOU'LL BE ABLE TO FIND A JOB ANYWHERE.
UH...
...
SON ...?
USE THE EXPERIENCE YOU'VE GAINED HERE...
...AS A STEPPING STONE INTO THE REAL WORLD.

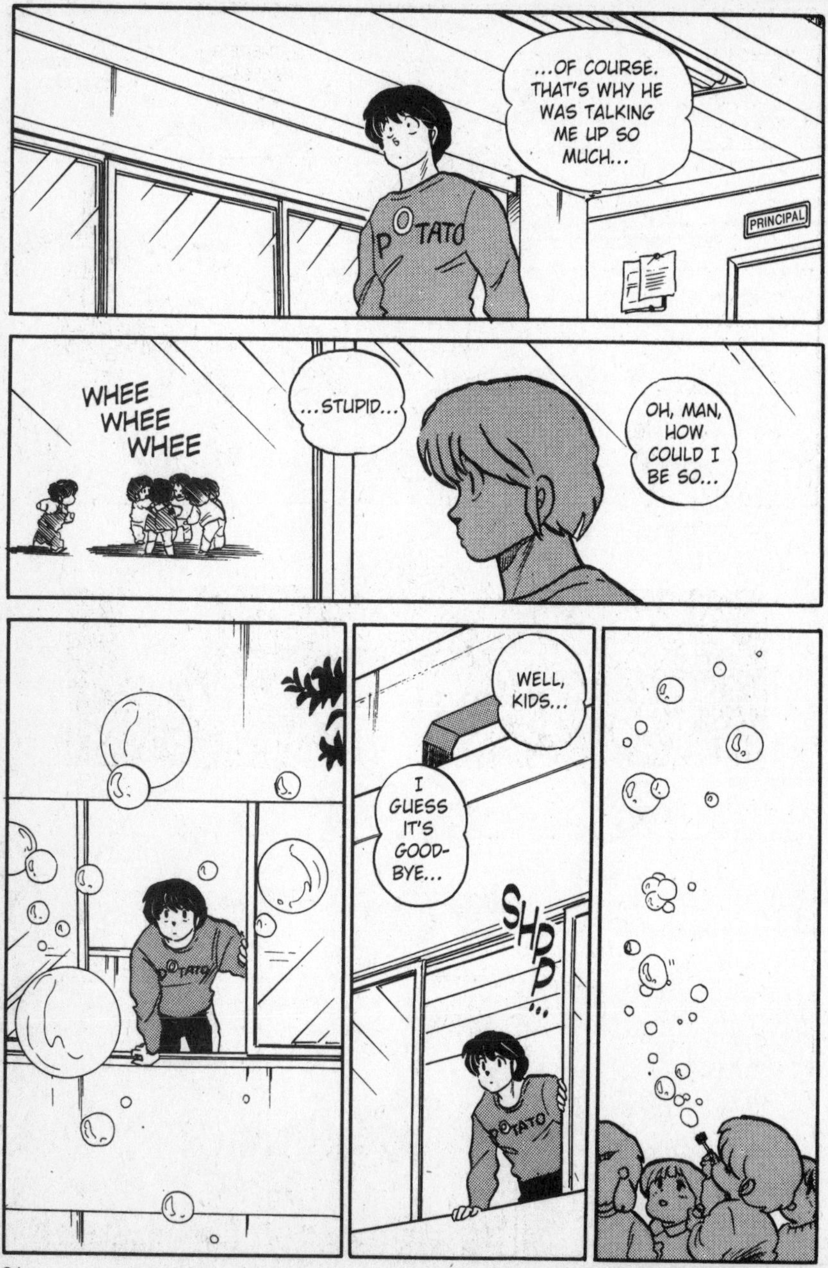
...OF COURSE. THAT'S WHY HE WAS TALKING ME UP SO MUCH...
PRINCIPAL
OH, MAN, HOW COULD I BE SO...
...STUPID...
WHEE WHEE WHEE
WELL, KIDS...
I GUESS IT'S GOOD-BYE...
SHPP...

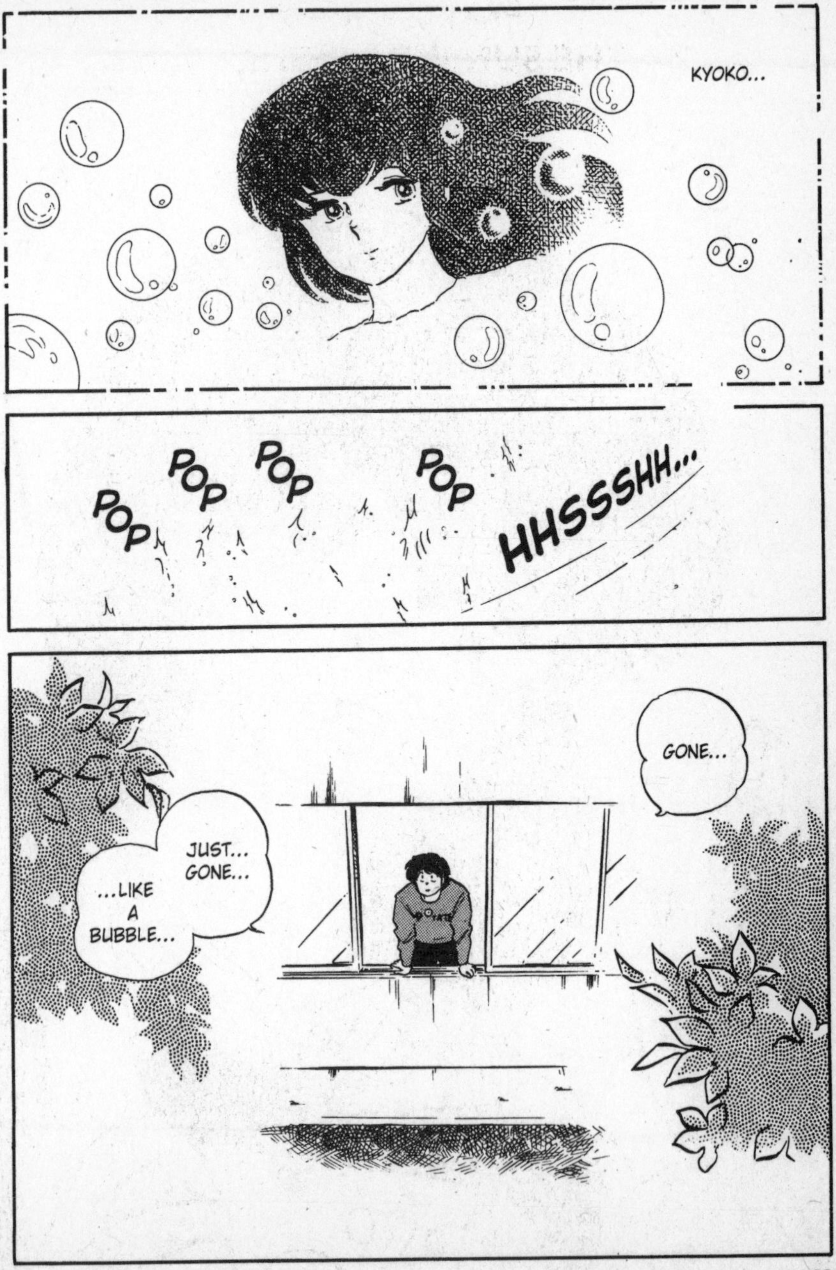
KYOKO...
HHSSSHH...
POP
POP
POP
POP
GONE...
JUST... GONE...
...LIKE A BUBBLE...

PART FOUR
THE SUN WILL SHINE

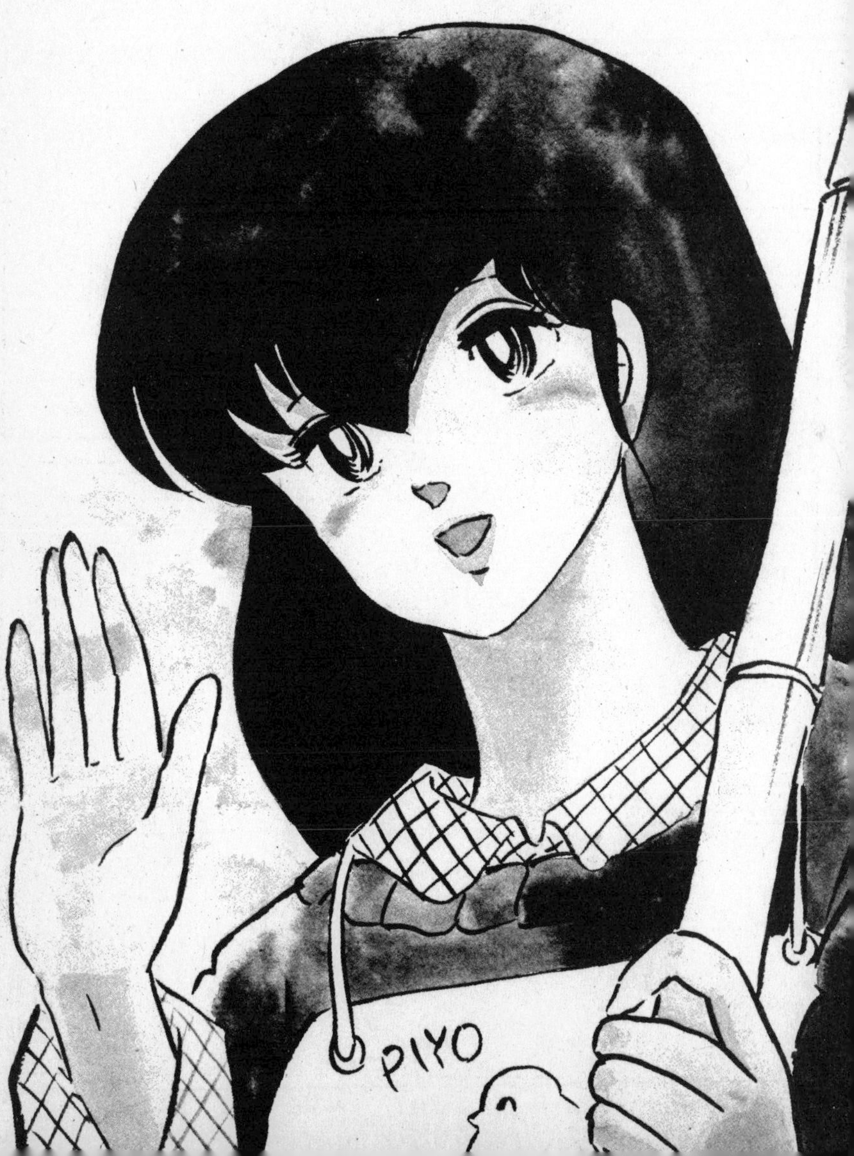
PIYO

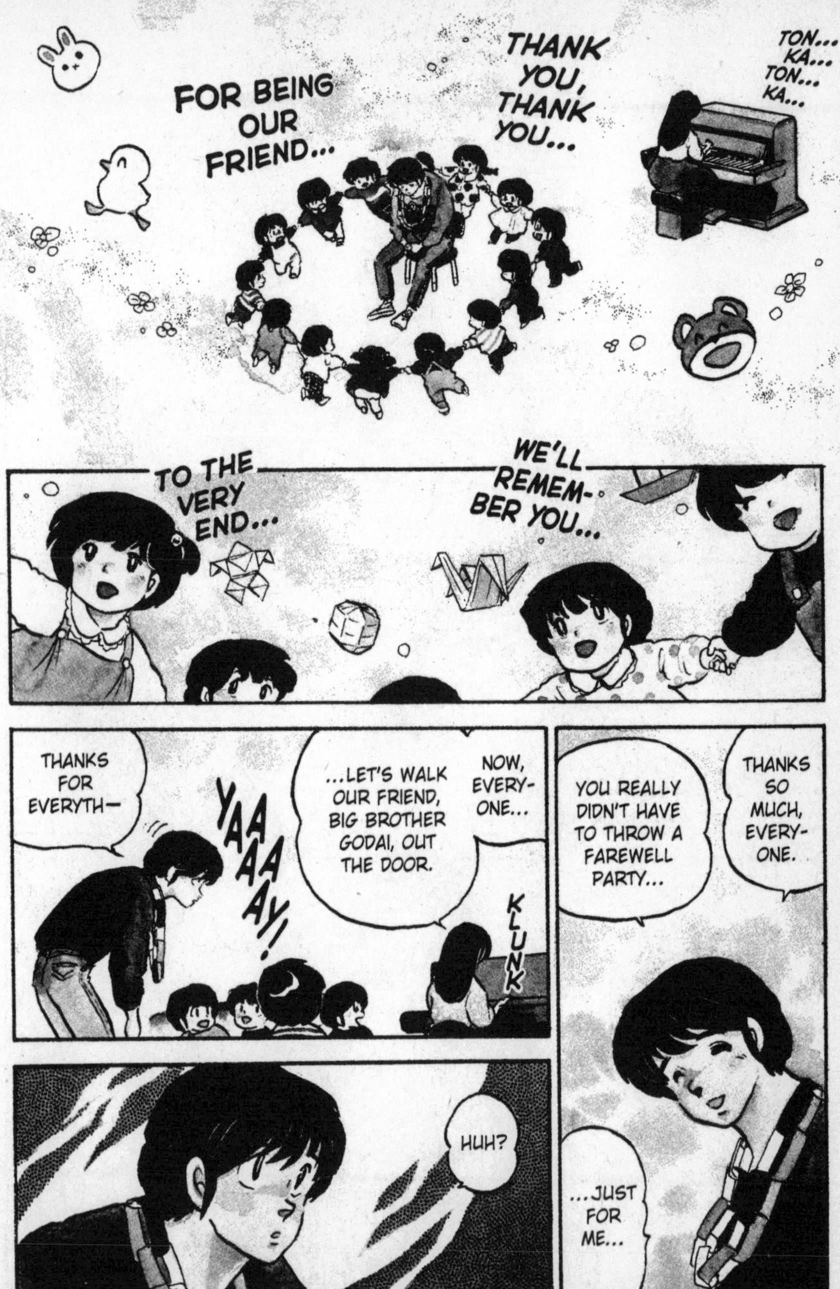
TON... KA... TON... KA...
THANK YOU, THANK YOU...
FOR BEING OUR FRIEND...
WE'LL REMEM-BER YOU...
TO THE VERY END...
THANKS SO MUCH, EVERY-ONE.
YOU REALLY DIDN'T HAVE TO THROW A FAREWELL PARTY...
...JUST FOR ME...
NOW, EVERY-ONE...
...LET'S WALK OUR FRIEND, BIG BROTHER GODAI, OUT THE DOOR.
KLUNK
YAAAAAY!
THANKS FOR EVERYTH—
HUH?

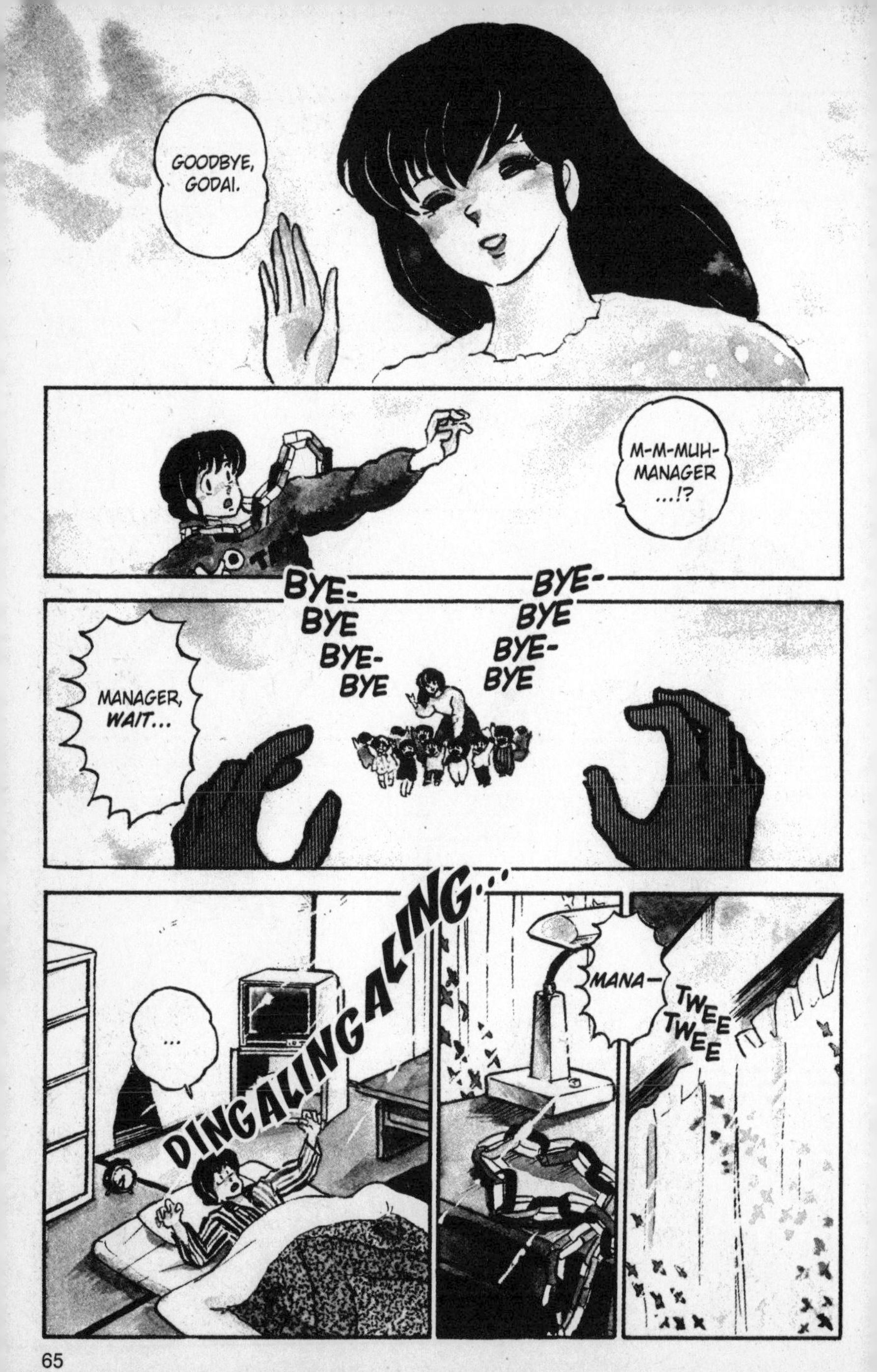

GOODBYE, GODAI.
M-M-MUH-MANAGER ...!?
BYE-BYE BYE-BYE
BYE-BYE BYE-BYE
MANAGER, WAIT...
TWEE TWEE
MANA—
DINGALINGALING...
...

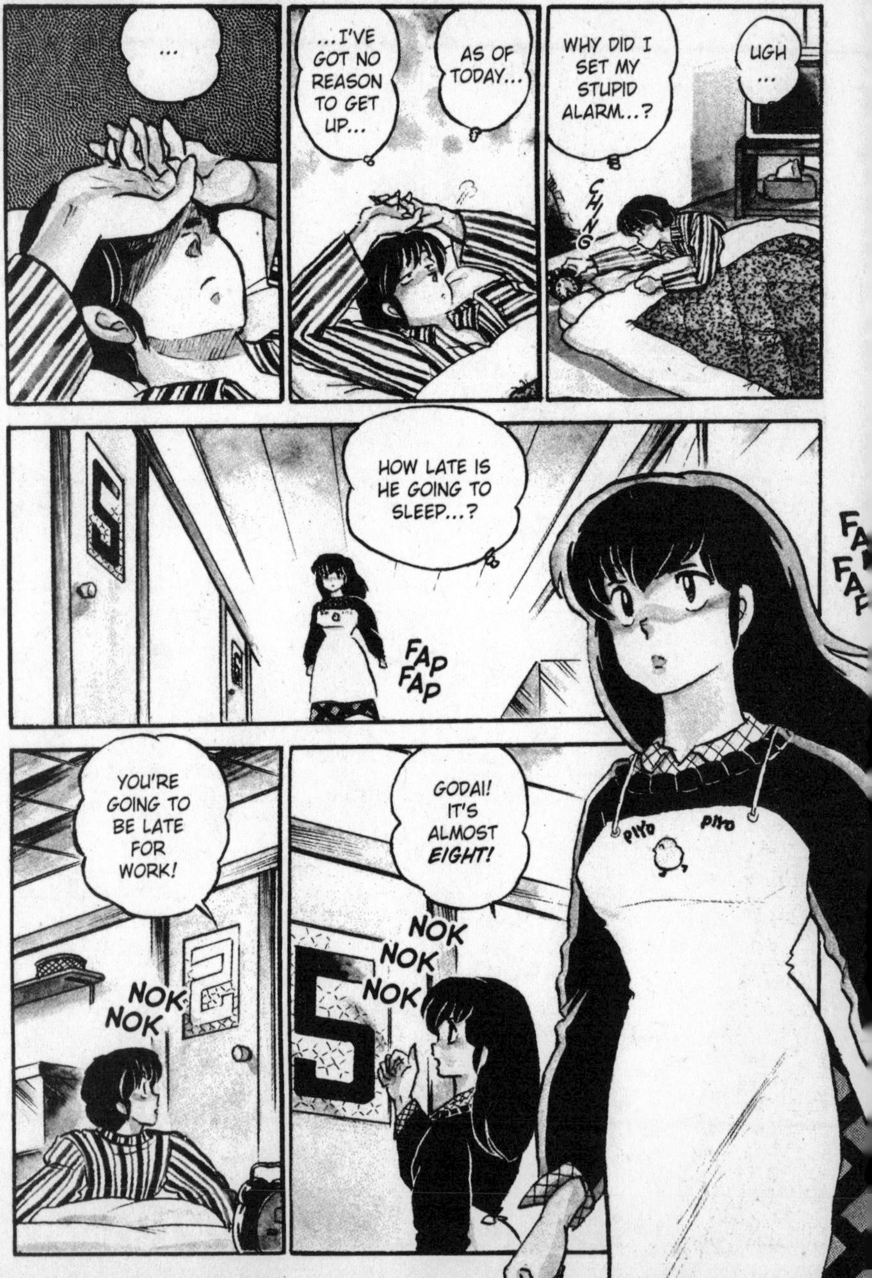
UGH ...
WHY DID I SET MY STUPID ALARM...?
CHING
AS OF TODAY...
...I'VE GOT NO REASON TO GET UP...
...
HOW LATE IS HE GOING TO SLEEP...?
FAP FAP
piyo piyo
NOK NOK NOK
GODAI! IT'S ALMOST EIGHT!
YOU'RE GOING TO BE LATE FOR WORK!
NOK NOK

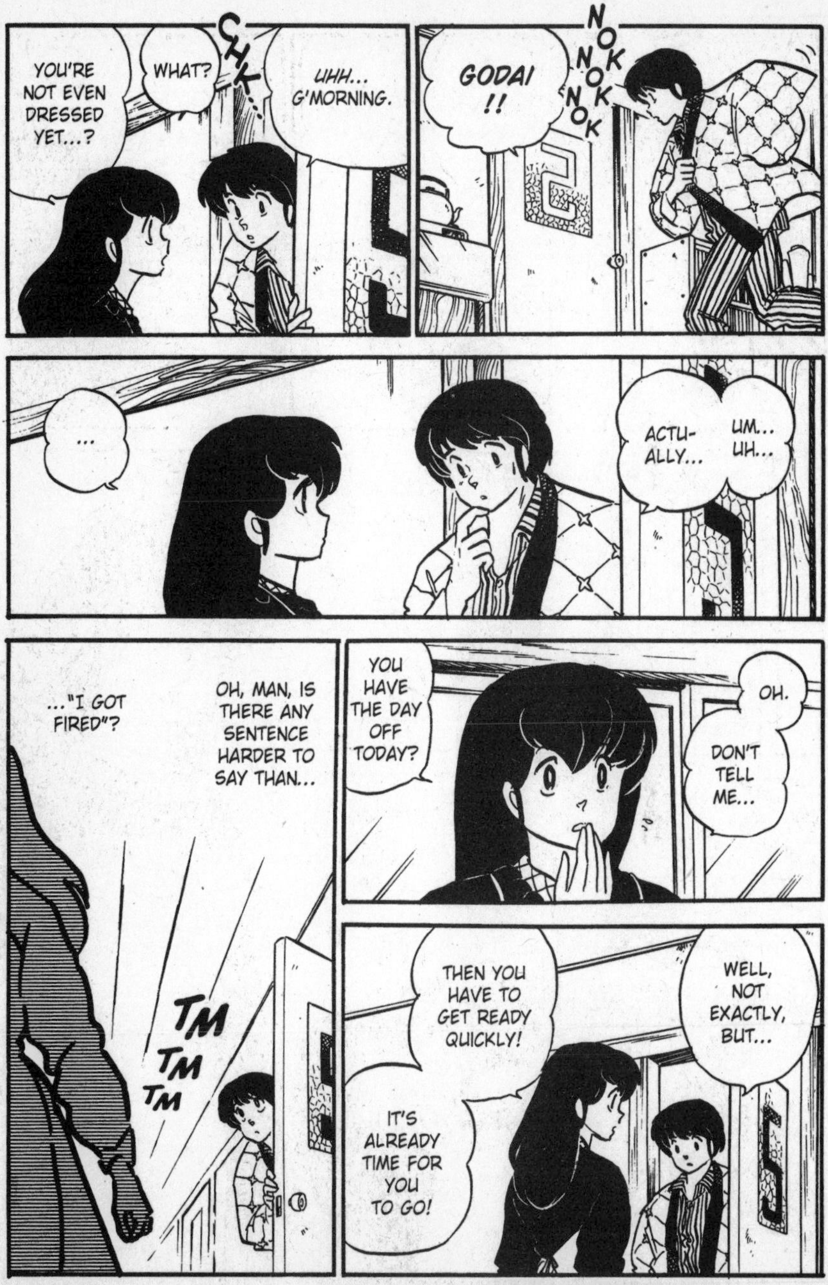
NOK NOK NOK NOK
GODAI !!
UHH... G'MORNING.
CHK...
WHAT?
YOU'RE NOT EVEN DRESSED YET...?
UM... UH...
ACTU- ALLY...
...
OH.
DON'T TELL ME...
YOU HAVE THE DAY OFF TODAY?
WELL, NOT EXACTLY, BUT...
THEN YOU HAVE TO GET READY QUICKLY!
IT'S ALREADY TIME FOR YOU TO GO!
OH, MAN, IS THERE ANY SENTENCE HARDER TO SAY THAN...
..."I GOT FIRED"?
TM TM TM

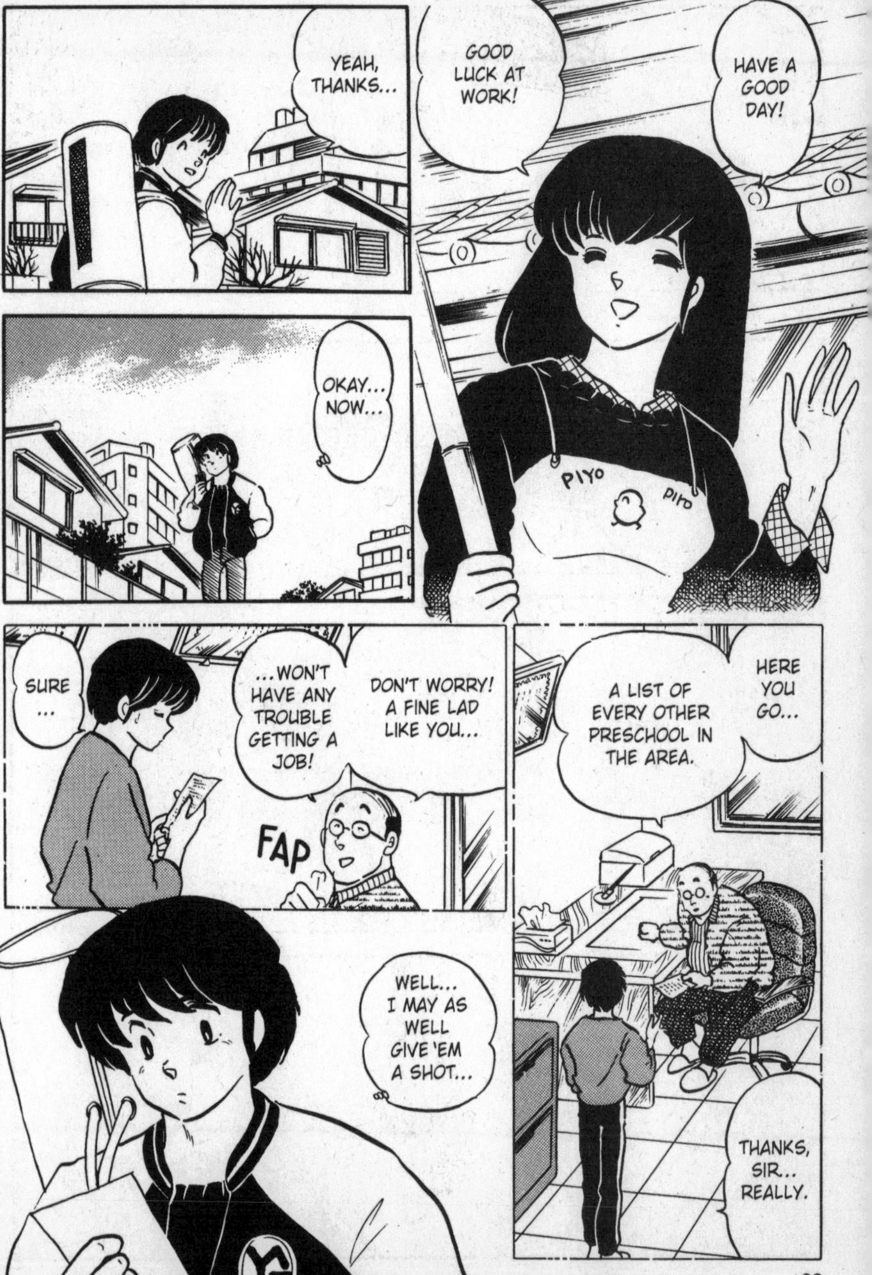
HAVE A GOOD DAY!
GOOD LUCK AT WORK!
YEAH, THANKS...
OKAY... NOW...
HERE YOU GO...
A LIST OF EVERY OTHER PRESCHOOL IN THE AREA.
THANKS, SIR... REALLY.
DON'T WORRY! A FINE LAD LIKE YOU...
...WON'T HAVE ANY TROUBLE GETTING A JOB!
FAP
SURE ...
WELL... I MAY AS WELL GIVE 'EM A SHOT...

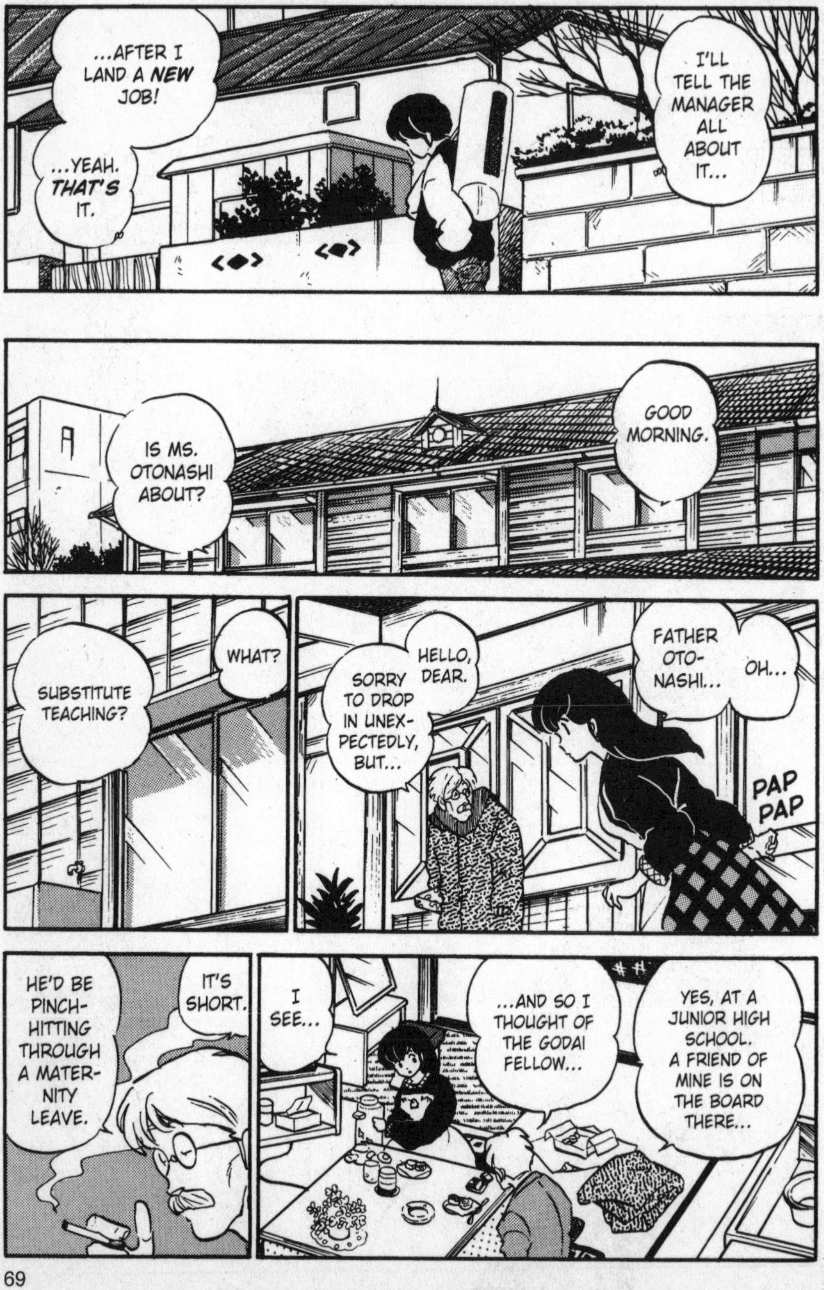

I'LL TELL THE MANAGER ALL ABOUT IT...
...AFTER I LAND A **NEW** JOB!
...YEAH. **THAT'S** IT.
GOOD MORNING.
IS MS. OTONASHI ABOUT?
OH...
FATHER OTO-NASHI...
PAP PAP
HELLO, DEAR.
SORRY TO DROP IN UNEX-PECTEDLY, BUT...
WHAT?
SUBSTITUTE TEACHING?
YES, AT A JUNIOR HIGH SCHOOL. A FRIEND OF MINE IS ON THE BOARD THERE...
...AND SO I THOUGHT OF THE GODAI FELLOW...
I SEE...
IT'S SHORT.
HE'D BE PINCH-HITTING THROUGH A MATER-NITY LEAVE.

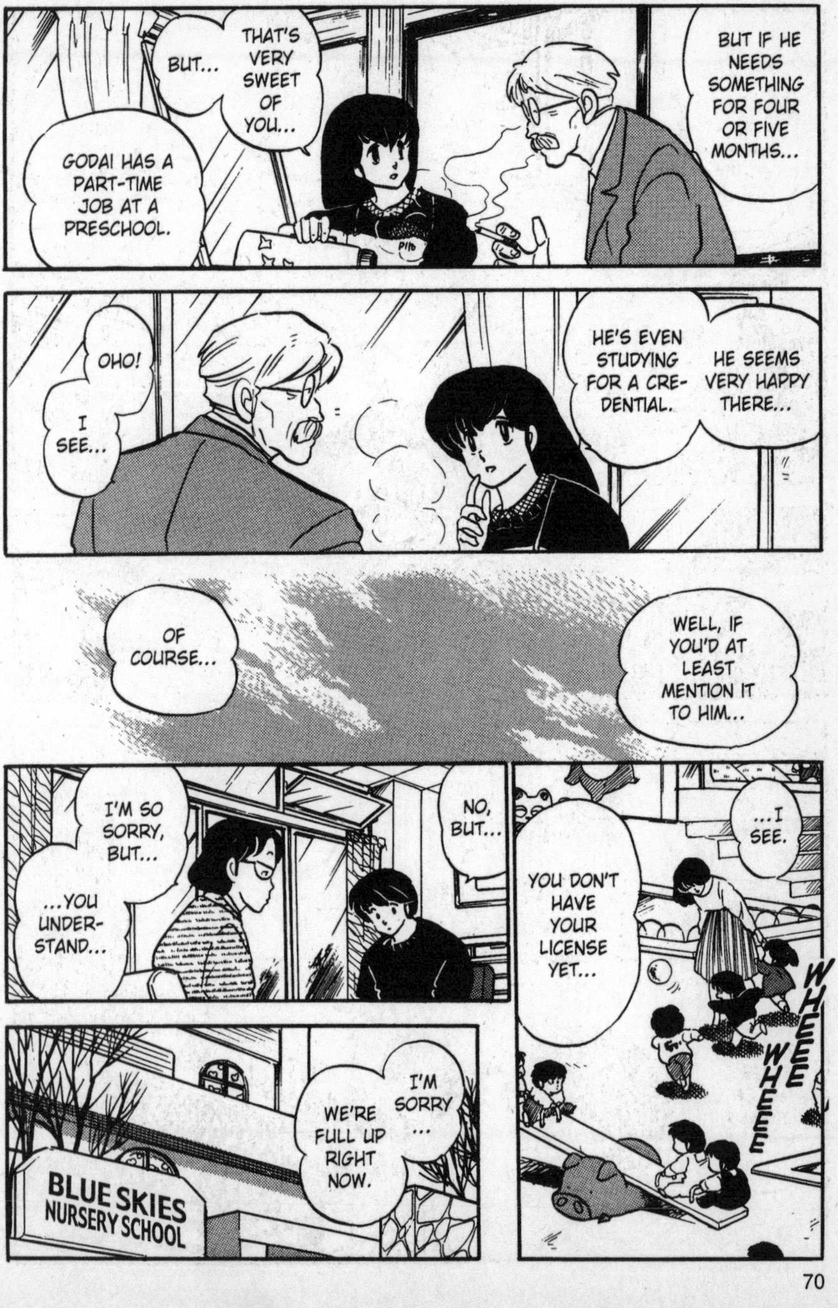

BUT IF HE NEEDS SOMETHING FOR FOUR OR FIVE MONTHS...
THAT'S VERY SWEET OF YOU...
BUT...
GODAI HAS A PART-TIME JOB AT A PRESCHOOL.
HE SEEMS VERY HAPPY THERE...
HE'S EVEN STUDYING FOR A CRE-DENTIAL.
OHO!
I SEE...
WELL, IF YOU'D AT LEAST MENTION IT TO HIM...
OF COURSE...
...I SEE.
YOU DON'T HAVE YOUR LICENSE YET...
WHEEE
WHEEE
WHEEE
NO, BUT...
I'M SO SORRY, BUT...
...YOU UNDER-STAND...
I'M SORRY...
WE'RE FULL UP RIGHT NOW.
BLUE SKIES NURSERY SCHOOL

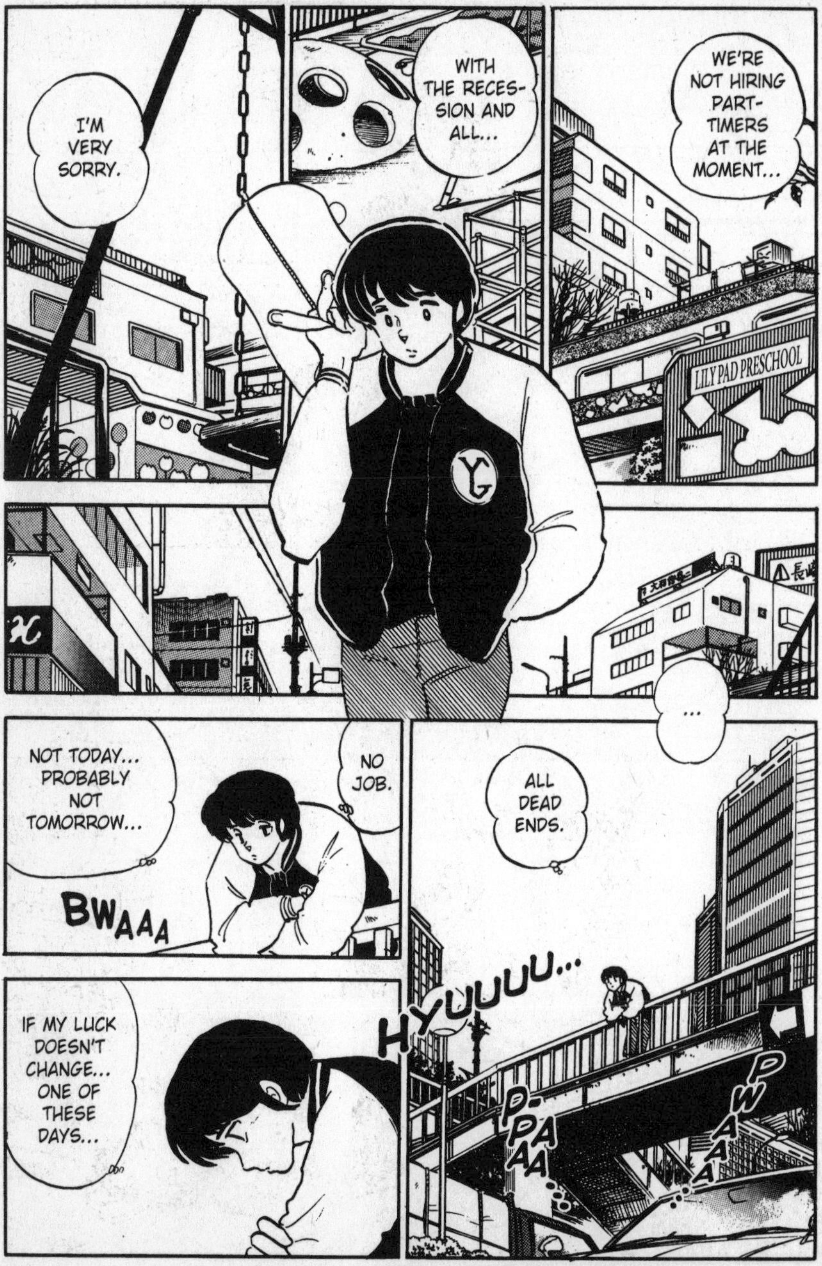
WE'RE NOT HIRING PART-TIMERS AT THE MOMENT...
LILY PAD PRESCHOOL
WITH THE RECES-SION AND ALL...
I'M VERY SORRY.
...
ALL DEAD ENDS.
HYUUUU...
PWAAAA...
P-PAAA...
NO JOB.
NOT TODAY... PROBABLY NOT TOMORROW...
BWAAA
IF MY LUCK DOESN'T CHANGE... ONE OF THESE DAYS...

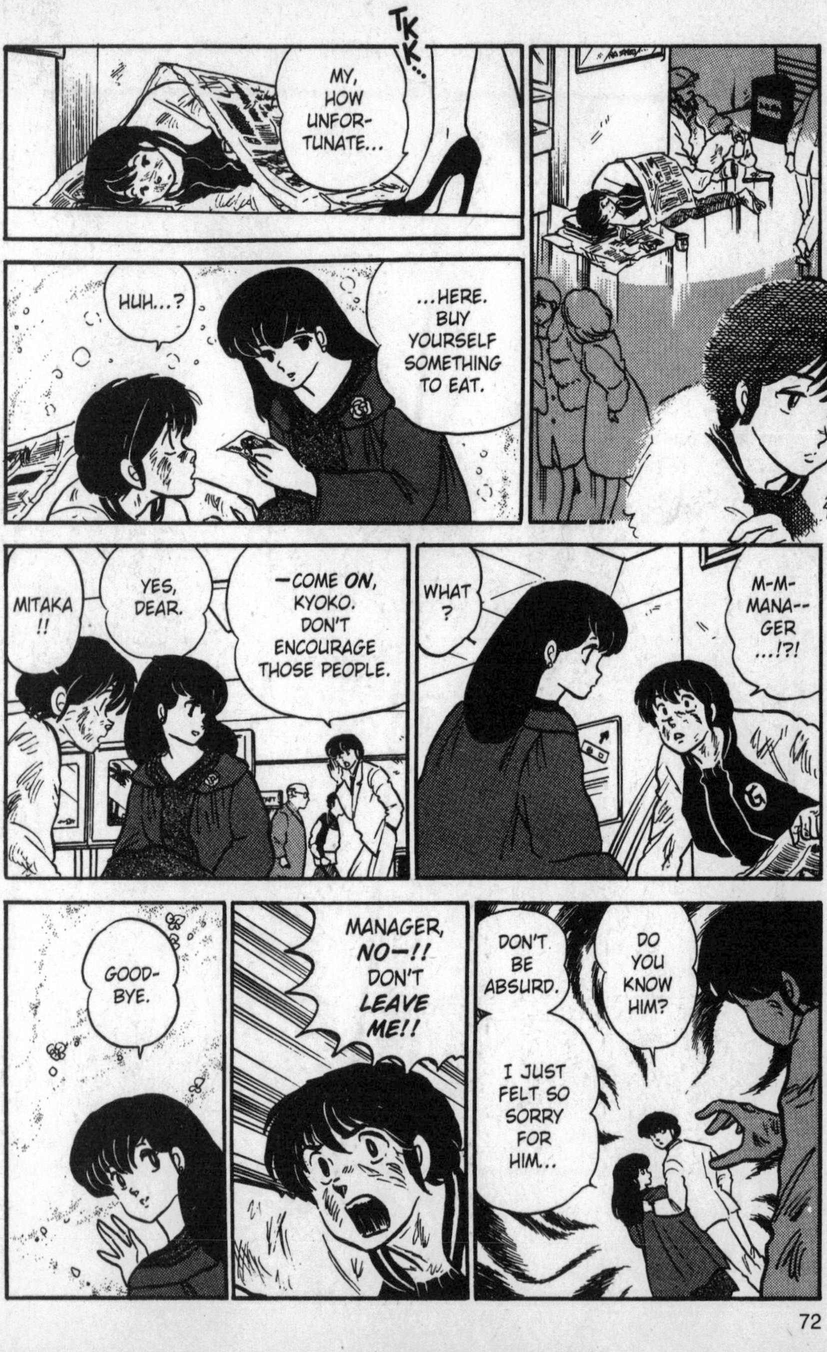
TKK...
MY, HOW UNFORTUNATE...
...HERE. BUY YOURSELF SOMETHING TO EAT.
HUH...?
M-M-MANA--GER ...!?!
WHAT ?
—COME ON, KYOKO. DON'T ENCOURAGE THOSE PEOPLE.
YES, DEAR.
MITAKA !!
DO YOU KNOW HIM?
DON'T BE ABSURD.
I JUST FELT SO SORRY FOR HIM...
MANAGER, NO—!! DON'T LEAVE ME!!
GOOD-BYE.

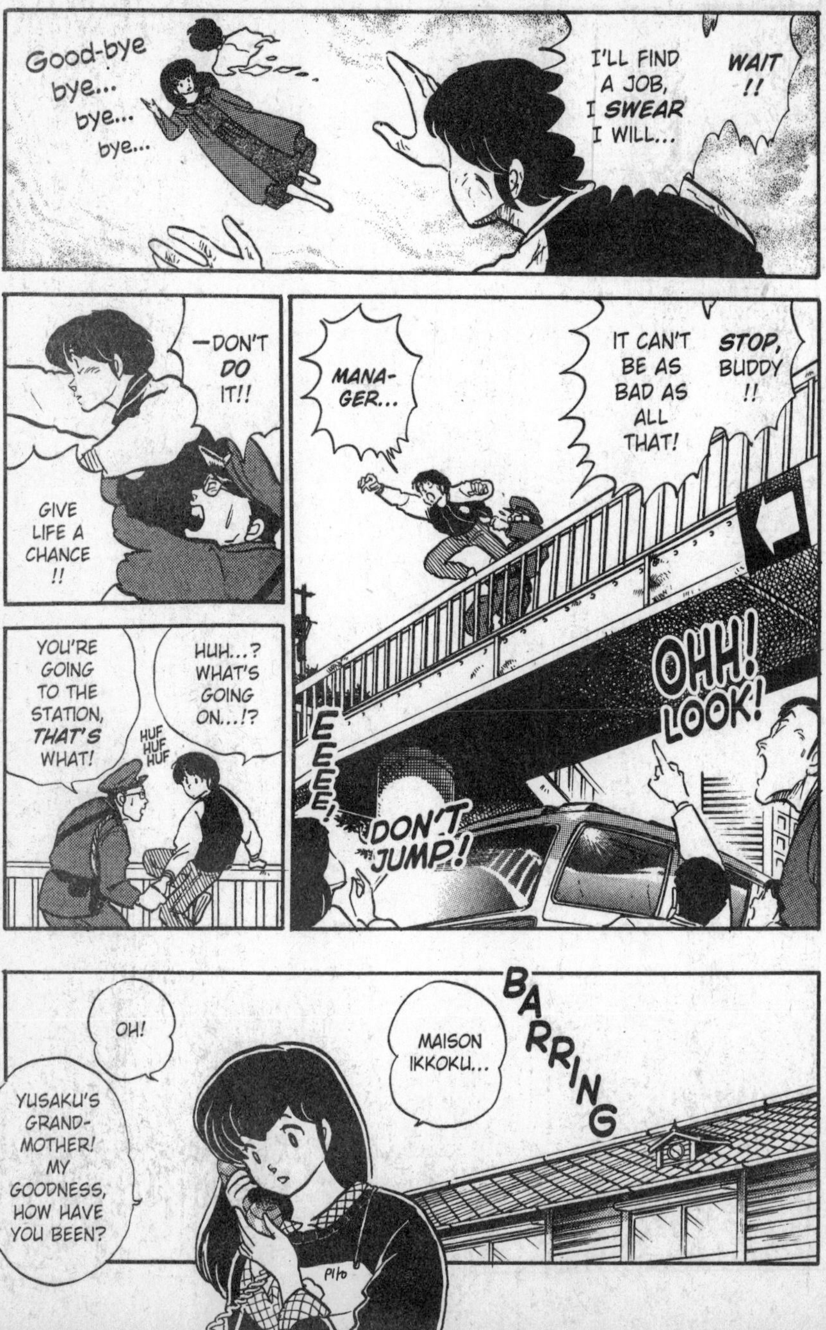
WAIT!!
I'LL FIND A JOB, I SWEAR I WILL...
Good-bye bye... bye... bye...
STOP, BUDDY!!
IT CAN'T BE AS BAD AS ALL THAT!
MANA-GER...
OHH! LOOK!
DON'T JUMP!
EEEEE!
—DON'T DO IT!!
GIVE LIFE A CHANCE!!
HUH...? WHAT'S GOING ON...!?
HUF HUF HUF
YOU'RE GOING TO THE STATION, THAT'S WHAT!
BARRING
MAISON IKKOKU...
OH!
YUSAKU'S GRAND-MOTHER! MY GOODNESS, HOW HAVE YOU BEEN?

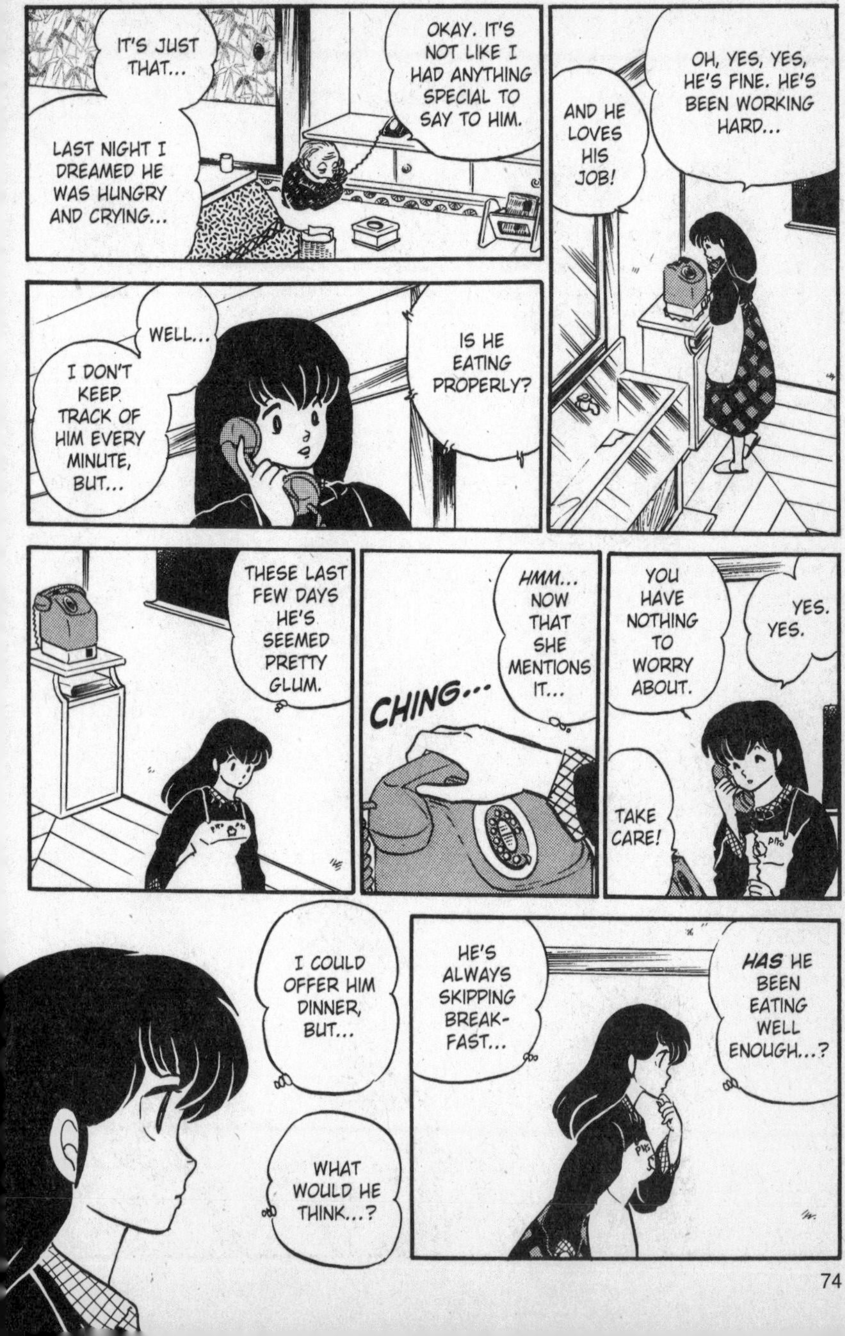
OH, YES, YES, HE'S FINE. HE'S BEEN WORKING HARD...
AND HE LOVES HIS JOB!
OKAY. IT'S NOT LIKE I HAD ANYTHING SPECIAL TO SAY TO HIM.
IT'S JUST THAT...
LAST NIGHT I DREAMED HE WAS HUNGRY AND CRYING...
IS HE EATING PROPERLY?
WELL...
I DON'T KEEP TRACK OF HIM EVERY MINUTE, BUT...
YES. YES.
YOU HAVE NOTHING TO WORRY ABOUT.
TAKE CARE!
HMM... NOW THAT SHE MENTIONS IT...
CHING...
THESE LAST FEW DAYS HE'S SEEMED PRETTY GLUM.
HAS HE BEEN EATING WELL ENOUGH...?
HE'S ALWAYS SKIPPING BREAK-FAST...
I COULD OFFER HIM DINNER, BUT...
WHAT WOULD HE THINK...?

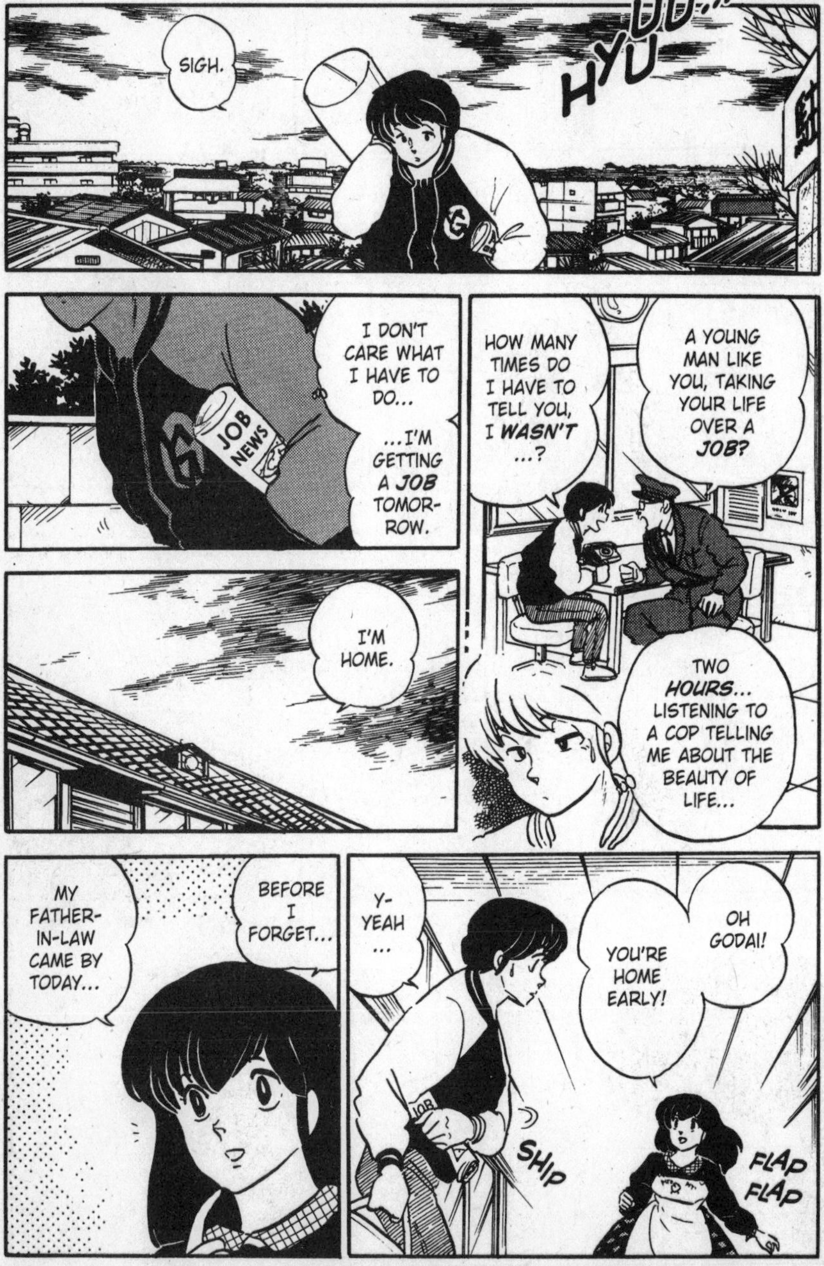

HYU UU...
SIGH.
A YOUNG MAN LIKE YOU, TAKING YOUR LIFE OVER A JOB?
HOW MANY TIMES DO I HAVE TO TELL YOU, I WASN'T ...?
TWO HOURS... LISTENING TO A COP TELLING ME ABOUT THE BEAUTY OF LIFE...
I DON'T CARE WHAT I HAVE TO DO...
...I'M GETTING A JOB TOMORROW.
JOB NEWS
I'M HOME.
OH GODAI!
YOU'RE HOME EARLY!
Y-YEAH ...
SHIP
FLAP FLAP
BEFORE I FORGET...
MY FATHER-IN-LAW CAME BY TODAY...

BUT I TOLD HIM YOU HAD THE PRE-SCHOOL JOB...

SO...

THAT'S RIGHT.

HE WANTED ME TO MENTION IT TO YOU...

A TEACHING JOB ...?!?

WHAT!?

IT'S GODAI!!

MR. OTO-NASHI!!

BMG

FWAP

!

YOU'D THINK HE COULD ...

SIGH. SUCH A SLOB...

JOB NEWS

I MEAN... I... I HEAR YOU WERE...

...

NO...

THEY'VE HIRED SOMEONE ELSE ALREADY.

I'M SORRY, SON...

THAT'S RIGHT, A SUB-STITUTE POSITION. BUT...

OH, YES, YES, THE JOB.

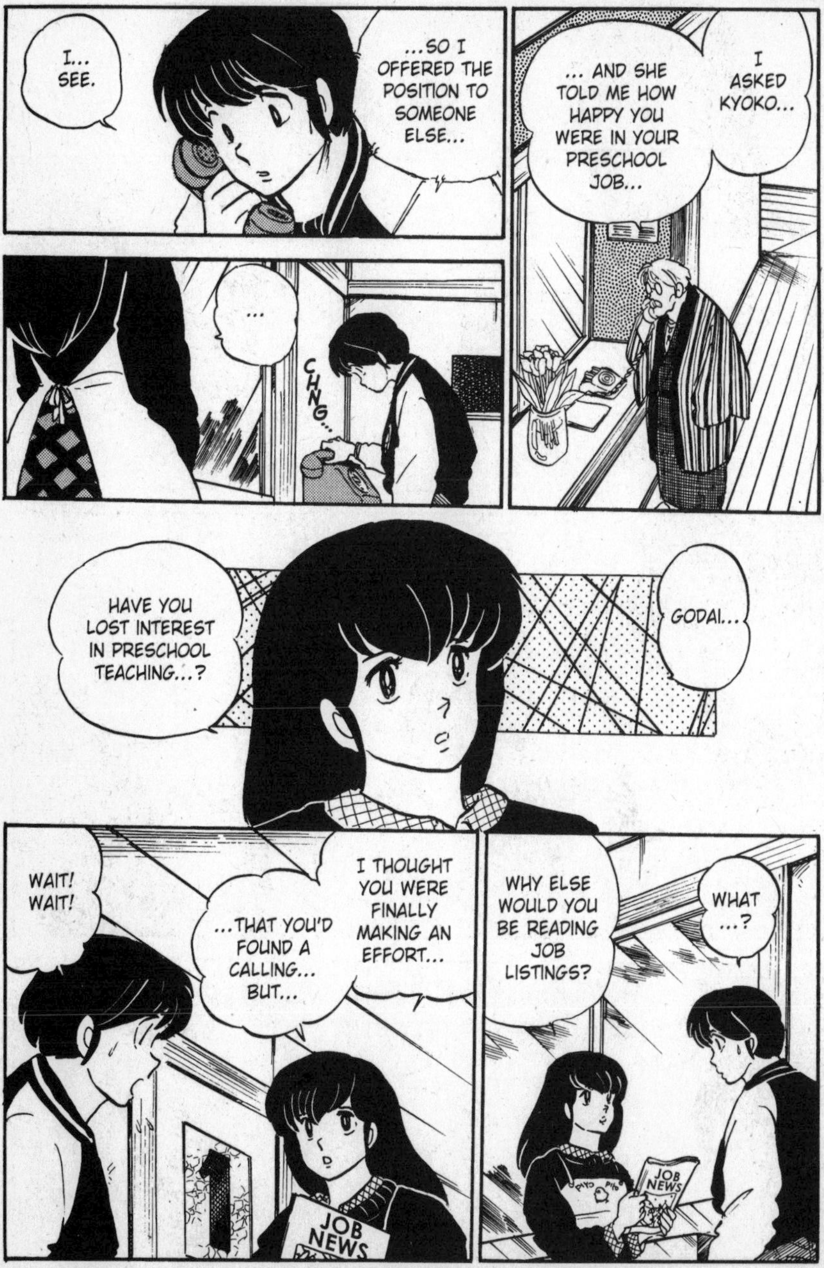
I ASKED KYOKO...
... AND SHE TOLD ME HOW HAPPY YOU WERE IN YOUR PRESCHOOL JOB...
...SO I OFFERED THE POSITION TO SOMEONE ELSE...
I... SEE.
...
CHNG...
GODAI...
HAVE YOU LOST INTEREST IN PRESCHOOL TEACHING...?
WHAT ...?
WHY ELSE WOULD YOU BE READING JOB LISTINGS?
JOB NEWS
I THOUGHT YOU WERE FINALLY MAKING AN EFFORT...
...THAT YOU'D FOUND A CALLING... BUT...
WAIT! WAIT!
JOB NEWS

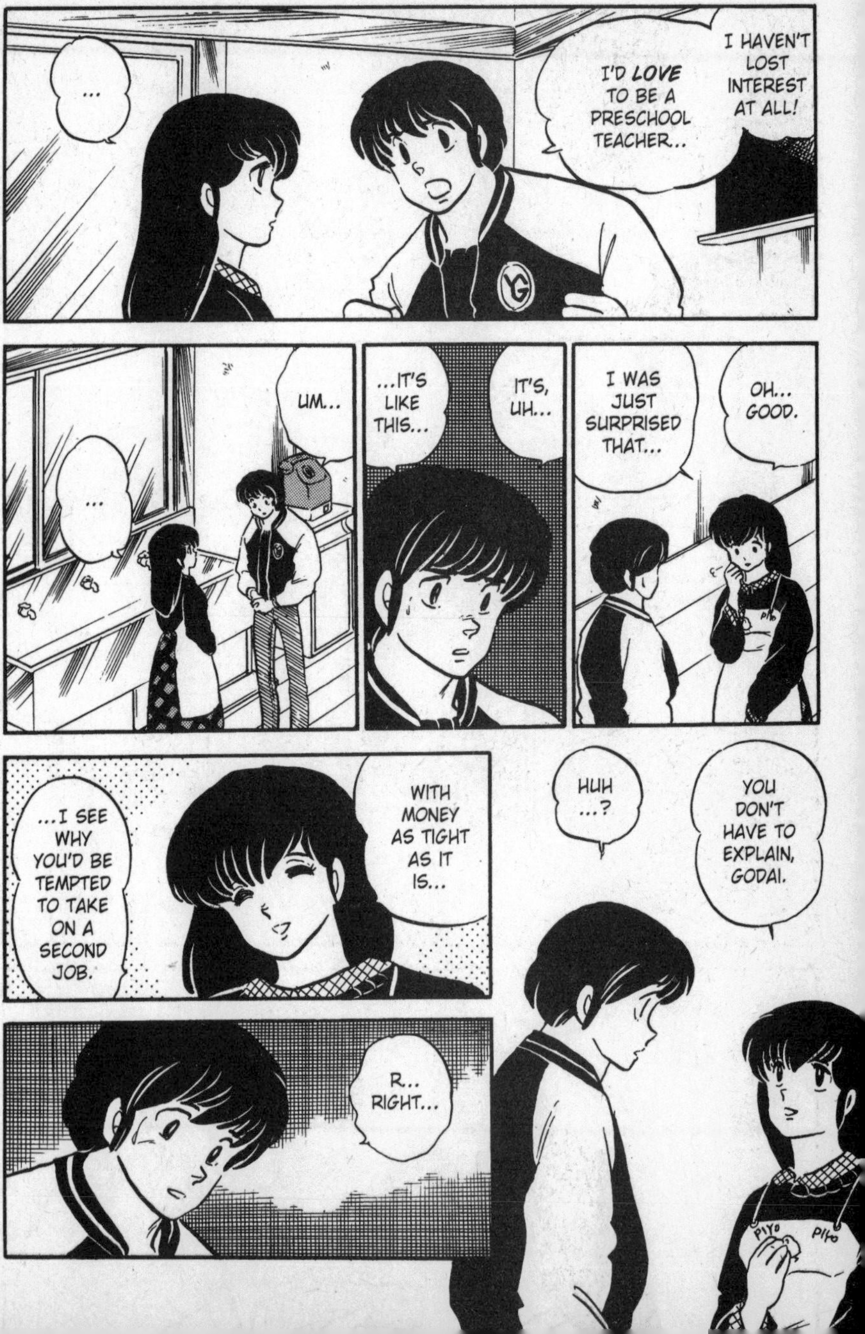
I HAVEN'T LOST INTEREST AT ALL!
I'D **LOVE** TO BE A PRESCHOOL TEACHER...
...
OH... GOOD.
I WAS JUST SURPRISED THAT...
IT'S, UH...
...IT'S LIKE THIS...
UM...
...
YOU DON'T HAVE TO EXPLAIN, GODAI.
HUH ...?
WITH MONEY AS TIGHT AS IT IS...
...I SEE WHY YOU'D BE TEMPTED TO TAKE ON A SECOND JOB.
R... RIGHT...

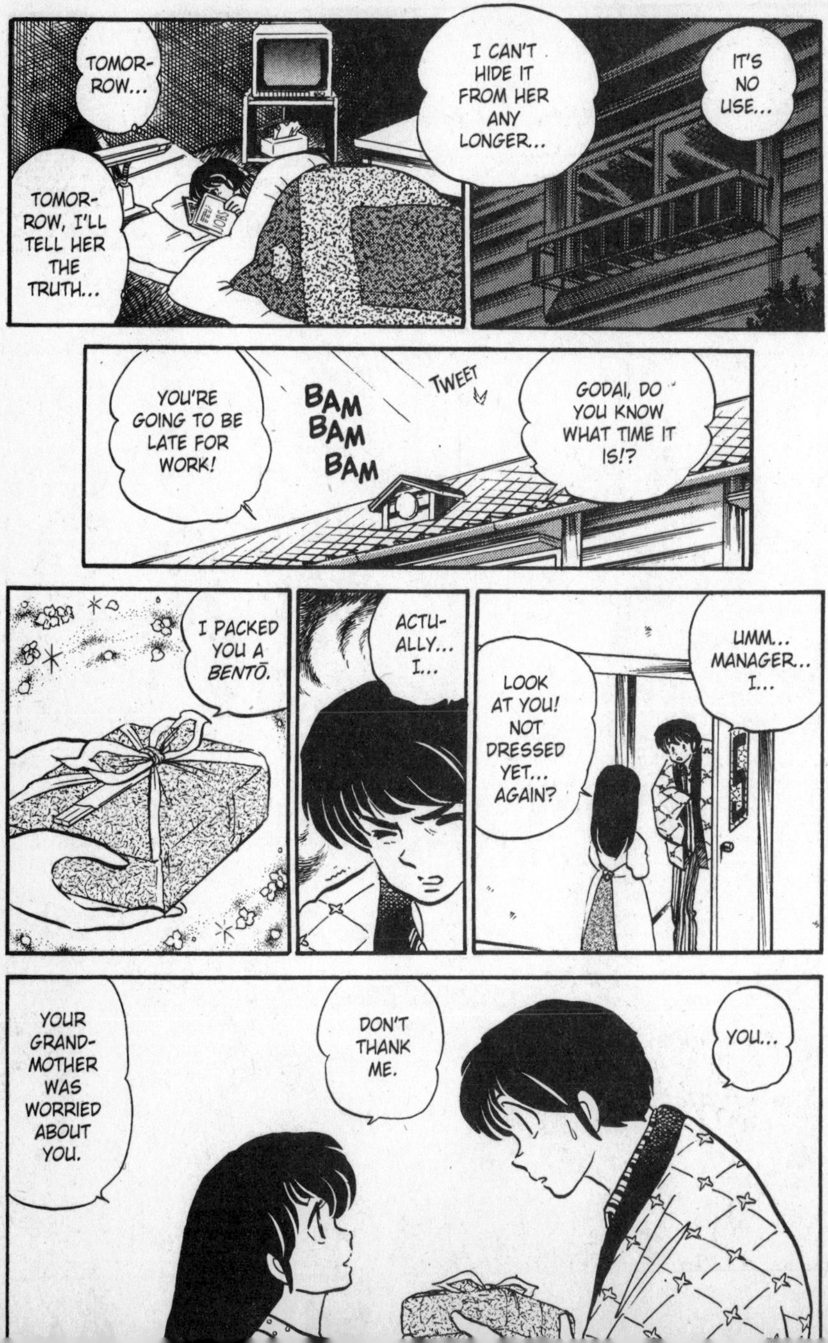
IT'S NO USE...
I CAN'T HIDE IT FROM HER ANY LONGER...
TOMORROW...
TOMORROW, I'LL TELL HER THE TRUTH...
GODAI, DO YOU KNOW WHAT TIME IT IS!?
TWEET
BAM BAM BAM
YOU'RE GOING TO BE LATE FOR WORK!
UMM... MANAGER... I...
LOOK AT YOU! NOT DRESSED YET... AGAIN?
ACTUALLY... I...
I PACKED YOU A BENTŌ.
YOU...
DON'T THANK ME.
YOUR GRANDMOTHER WAS WORRIED ABOUT YOU.

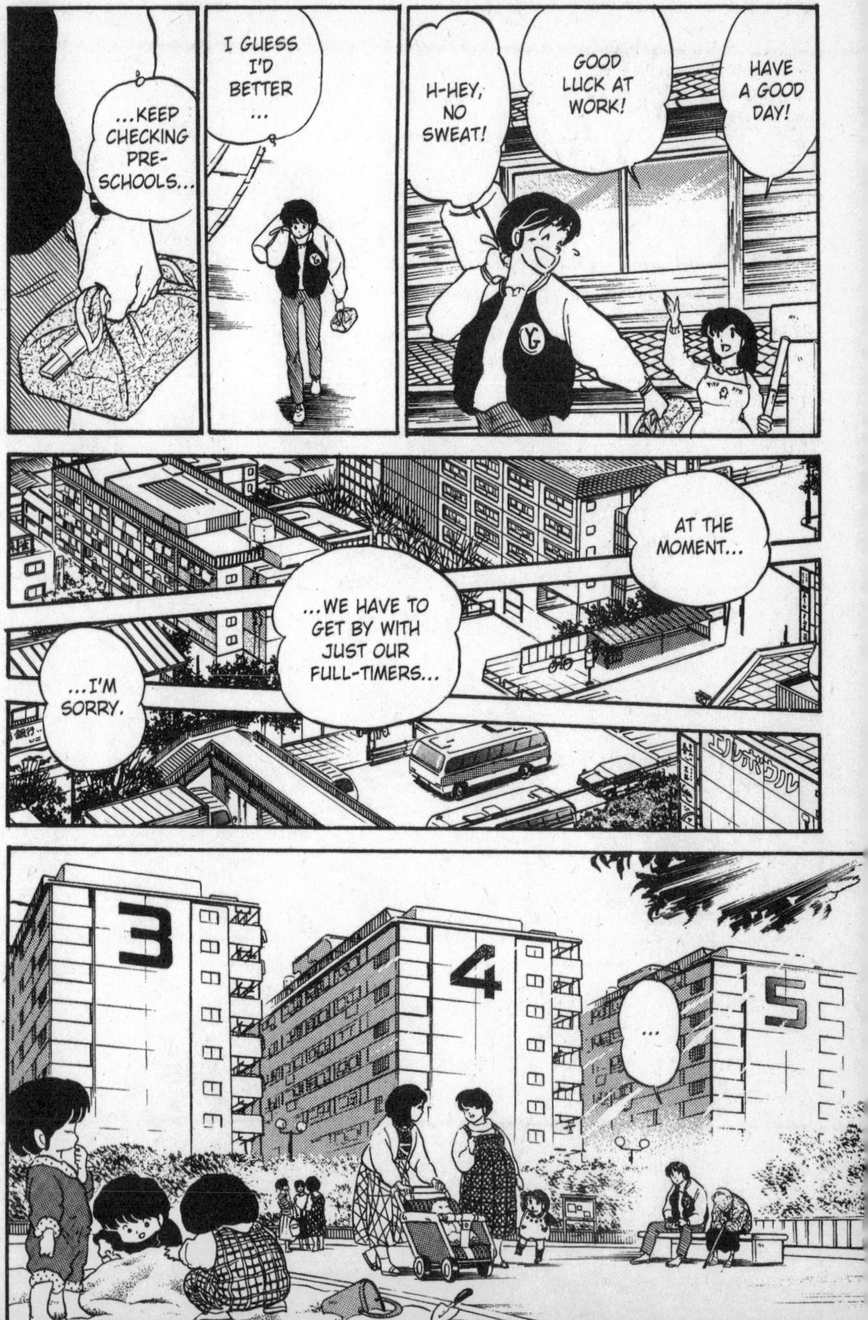
HAVE A GOOD DAY!
GOOD LUCK AT WORK!
H-HEY, NO SWEAT!
I GUESS I'D BETTER ...
...KEEP CHECKING PRE-SCHOOLS...
AT THE MOMENT...
...WE HAVE TO GET BY WITH JUST OUR FULL-TIMERS...
...I'M SORRY.
...

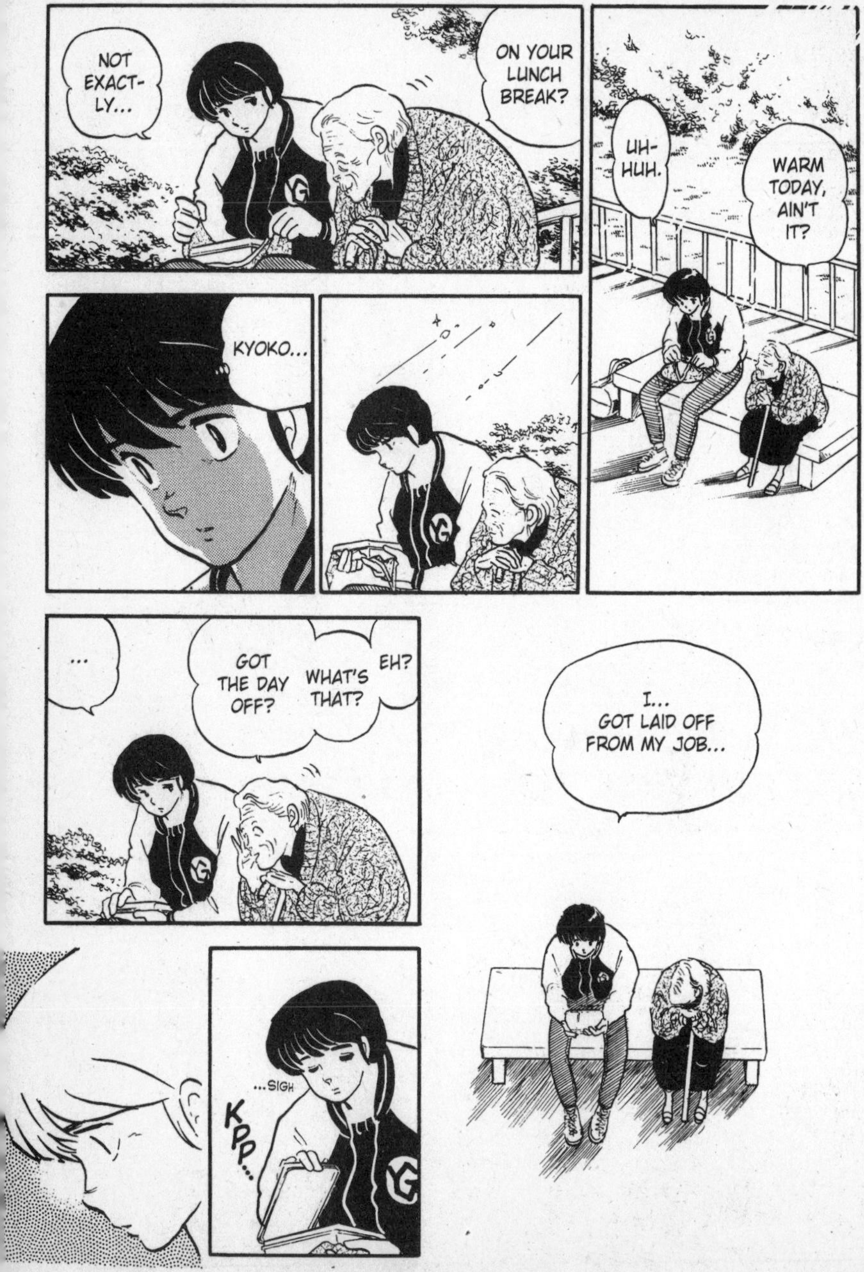
WARM TODAY, AIN'T IT?
UH-HUH.
ON YOUR LUNCH BREAK?
NOT EXACTLY...
KYOKO...
I... GOT LAID OFF FROM MY JOB...
EH?
WHAT'S THAT?
GOT THE DAY OFF?
...
...SIGH
KPP...

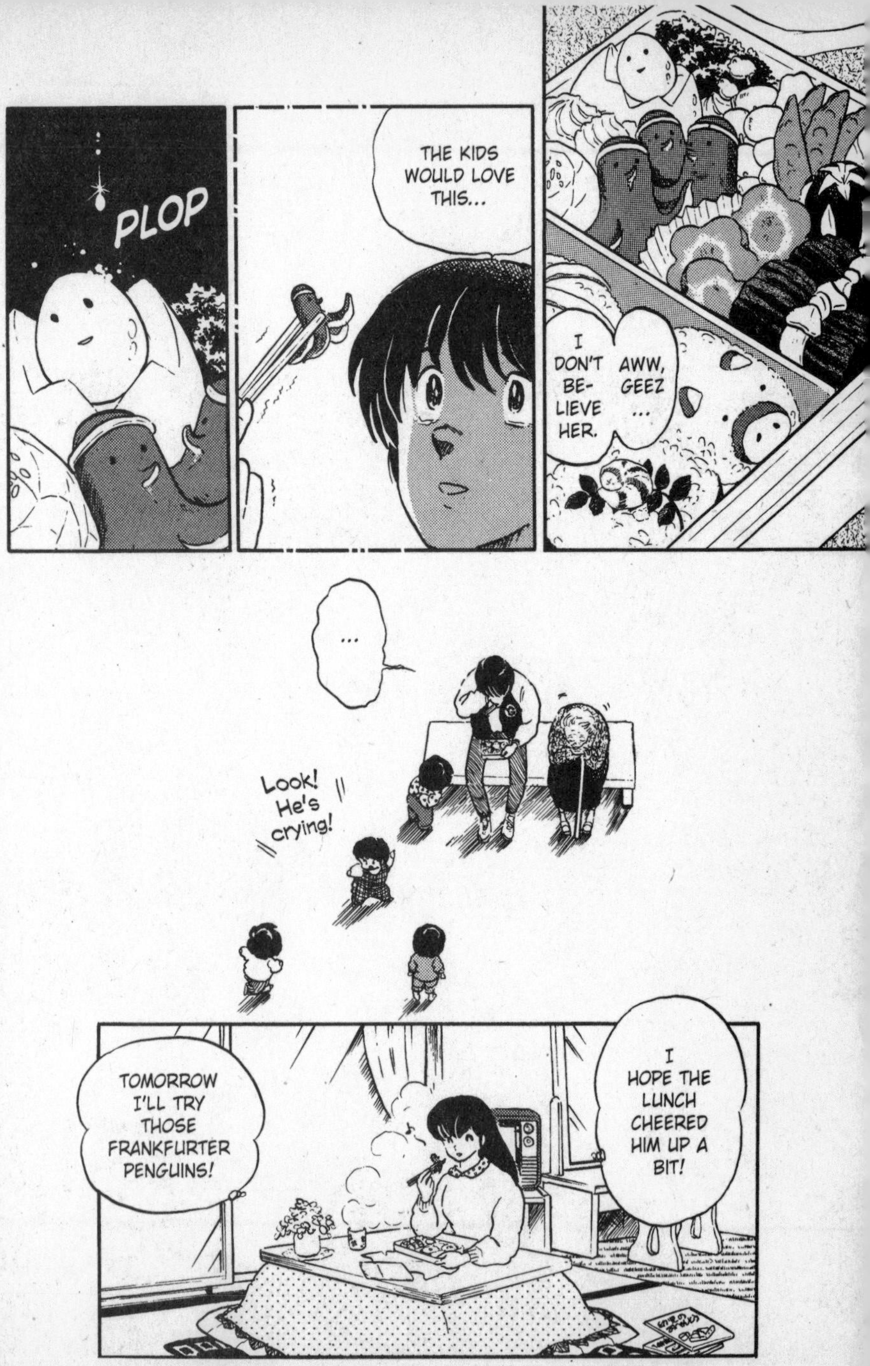
PLOP
THE KIDS WOULD LOVE THIS...
I DON'T BE-LIEVE HER.
AWW, GEEZ...
...
Look! He's crying!
TOMORROW I'LL TRY THOSE FRANKFURTER PENGUINS!
I HOPE THE LUNCH CHEERED HIM UP A BIT!

PART FIVE

SILENCE IS GOLDEN (OR AT LEAST VERY EXPENSIVE)

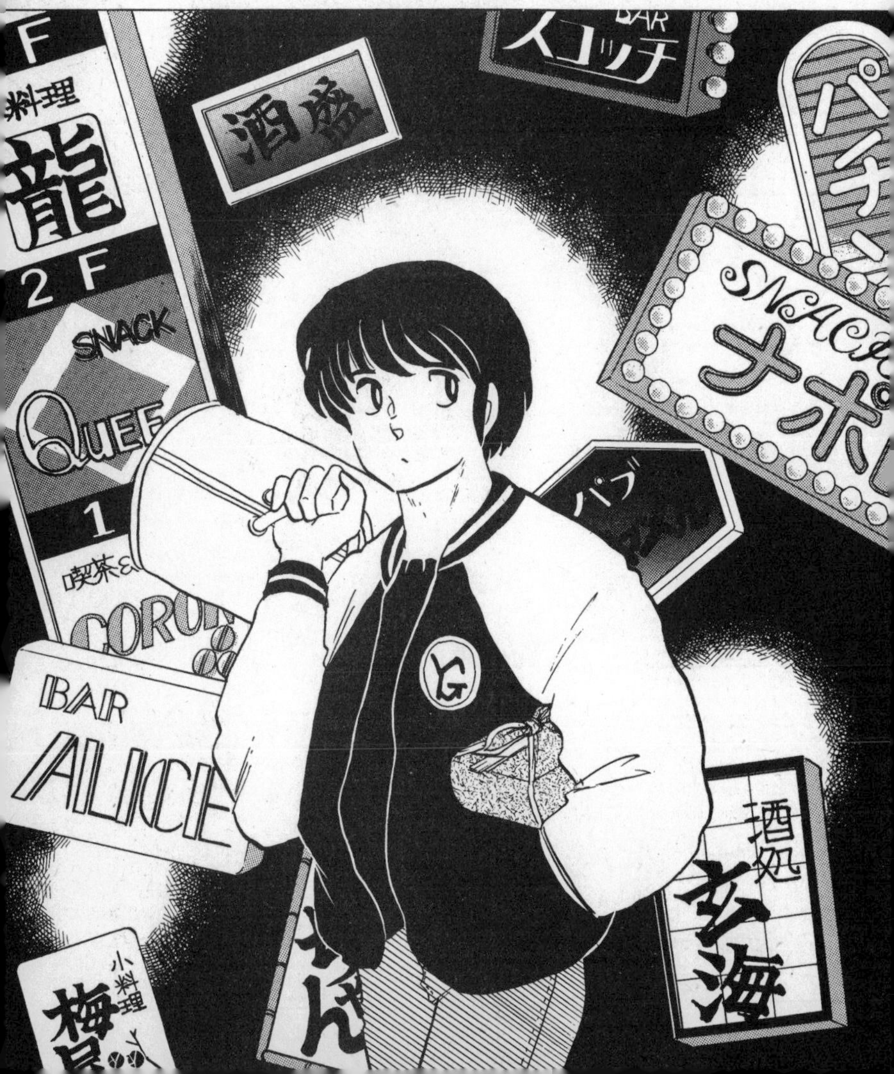

BAR
スコッチ
料理
龍
2 F
SNACK
1
BAR
ALICE
SNACK
パブ
酒処
玄海
小料理

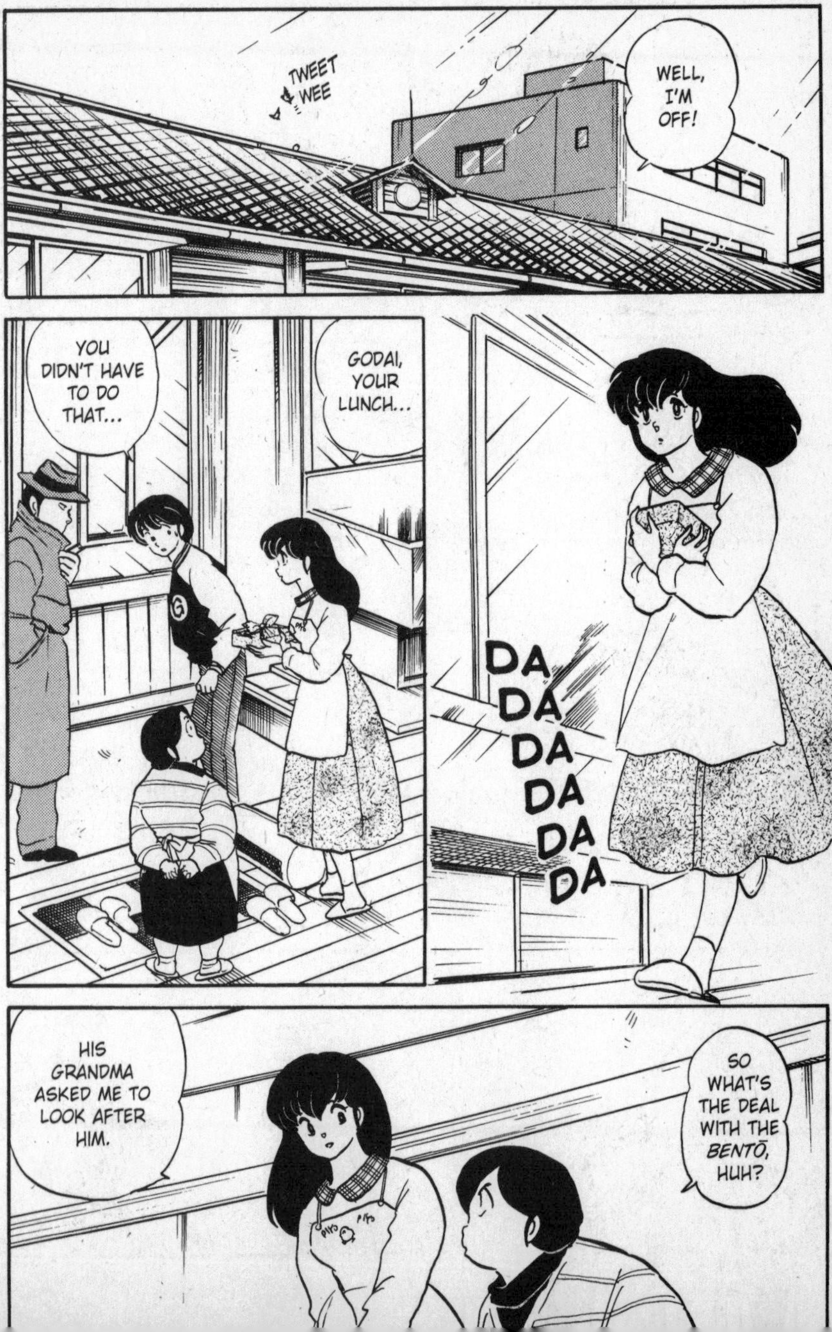
TWEET WEE
WELL, I'M OFF!
DA DA DA DA DA DA
GODAI, YOUR LUNCH...
YOU DIDN'T HAVE TO DO THAT...
SO WHAT'S THE DEAL WITH THE *BENTŌ*, HUH?
HIS GRANDMA ASKED ME TO LOOK AFTER HIM.

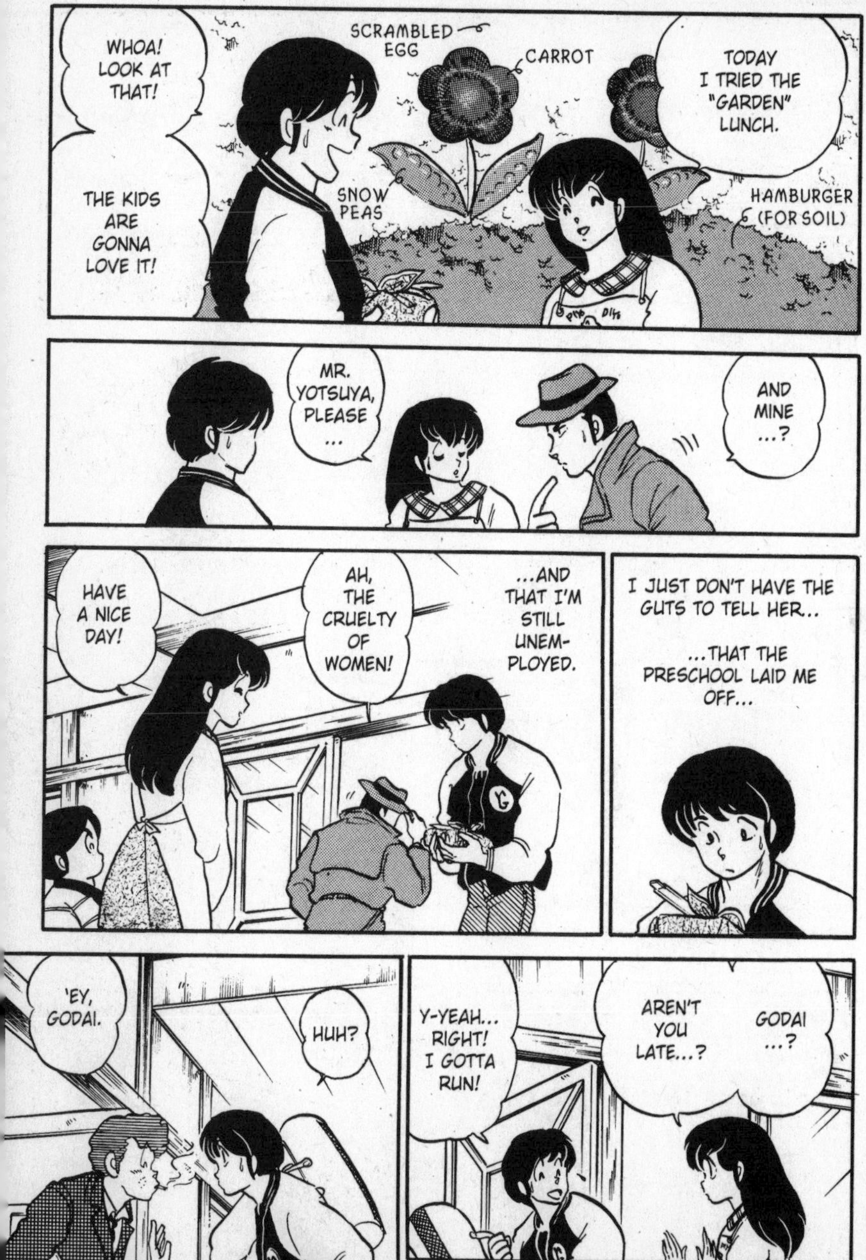
TODAY I TRIED THE "GARDEN" LUNCH.
CARROT
SCRAMBLED EGG
HAMBURGER (FOR SOIL)
SNOW PEAS
WHOA! LOOK AT THAT!
THE KIDS ARE GONNA LOVE IT!
AND MINE ...?
MR. YOTSUYA, PLEASE ...
I JUST DON'T HAVE THE GUTS TO TELL HER..
...THAT THE PRESCHOOL LAID ME OFF...
...AND THAT I'M STILL UNEMPLOYED.
AH, THE CRUELTY OF WOMEN!
HAVE A NICE DAY!
GODAI ...?
AREN'T YOU LATE...?
Y-YEAH... RIGHT! I GOTTA RUN!
'EY, GODAI.
HUH?

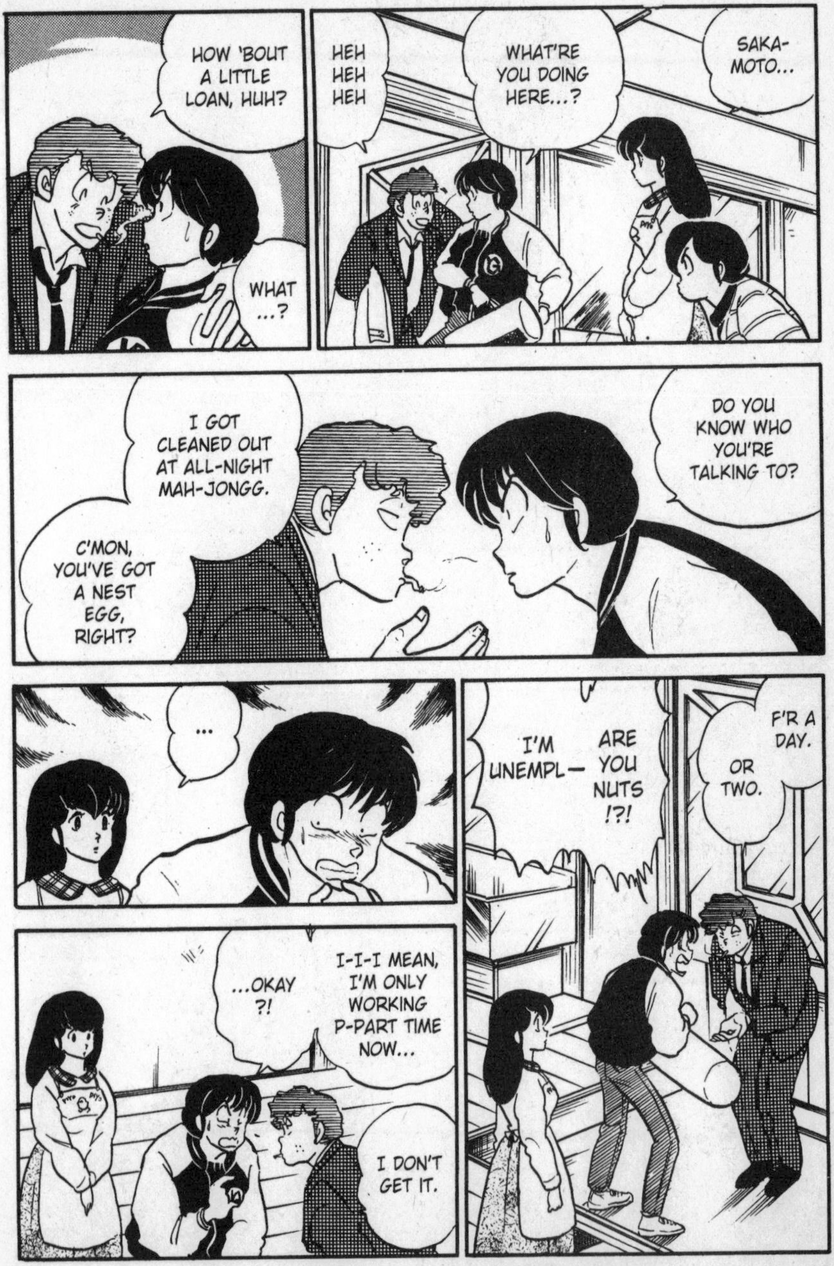
SAKA-MOTO...
WHAT'RE YOU DOING HERE...?
HEH HEH HEH
HOW 'BOUT A LITTLE LOAN, HUH?
WHAT ...?
DO YOU KNOW WHO YOU'RE TALKING TO?
I GOT CLEANED OUT AT ALL-NIGHT MAH-JONGG.
C'MON, YOU'VE GOT A NEST EGG, RIGHT?
F'R A DAY.
OR TWO.
ARE YOU NUTS !?!
I'M UNEMPL—
...
I-I-I MEAN, I'M ONLY WORKING P-PART TIME NOW...
...OKAY ?!
I DON'T GET IT.

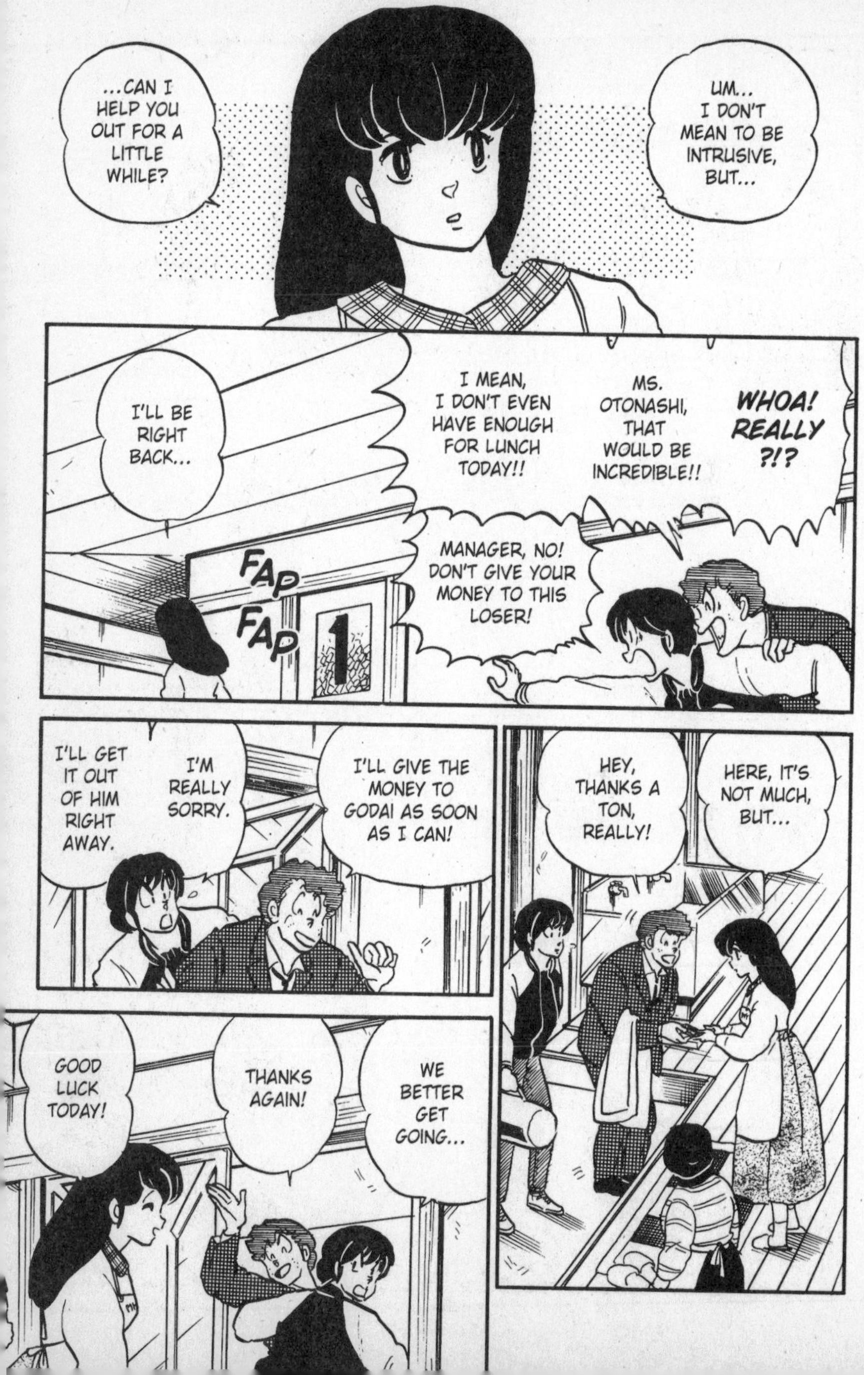
UM... I DON'T MEAN TO BE INTRUSIVE, BUT...
...CAN I HELP YOU OUT FOR A LITTLE WHILE?
WHOA! REALLY ?!?
MS. OTONASHI, THAT WOULD BE INCREDIBLE!!
I MEAN, I DON'T EVEN HAVE ENOUGH FOR LUNCH TODAY!!
MANAGER, NO! DON'T GIVE YOUR MONEY TO THIS LOSER!
FAP
FAP
1
I'LL BE RIGHT BACK...
HERE, IT'S NOT MUCH, BUT...
HEY, THANKS A TON, REALLY!
I'LL GIVE THE MONEY TO GODAI AS SOON AS I CAN!
I'M REALLY SORRY.
I'LL GET IT OUT OF HIM RIGHT AWAY.
WE BETTER GET GOING...
THANKS AGAIN!
GOOD LUCK TODAY!

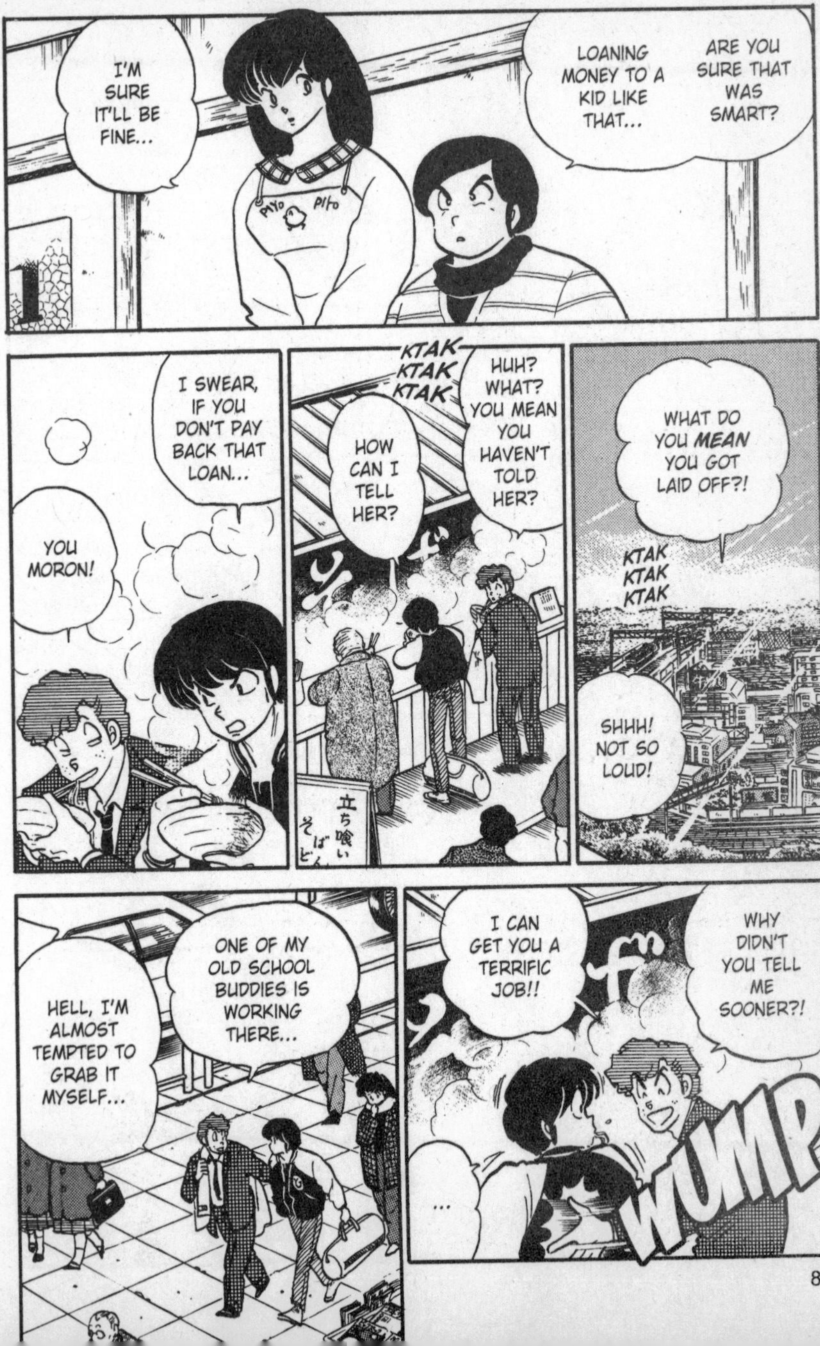
LOANING MONEY TO A KID LIKE THAT... ARE YOU SURE THAT WAS SMART?
I'M SURE IT'LL BE FINE...
WHAT DO YOU *MEAN* YOU GOT LAID OFF?!
KTAK KTAK KTAK
SHHH! NOT SO LOUD!
KTAK KTAK KTAK
HUH? WHAT? YOU MEAN YOU HAVEN'T TOLD HER?
HOW CAN I TELL HER?
立ち喰い
そば
I SWEAR, IF YOU DON'T PAY BACK THAT LOAN...
YOU MORON!
WHY DIDN'T YOU TELL ME SOONER?!
I CAN GET YOU A TERRIFIC JOB!!
WUMP
...
ONE OF MY OLD SCHOOL BUDDIES IS WORKING THERE...
HELL, I'M ALMOST TEMPTED TO GRAB IT MYSELF...

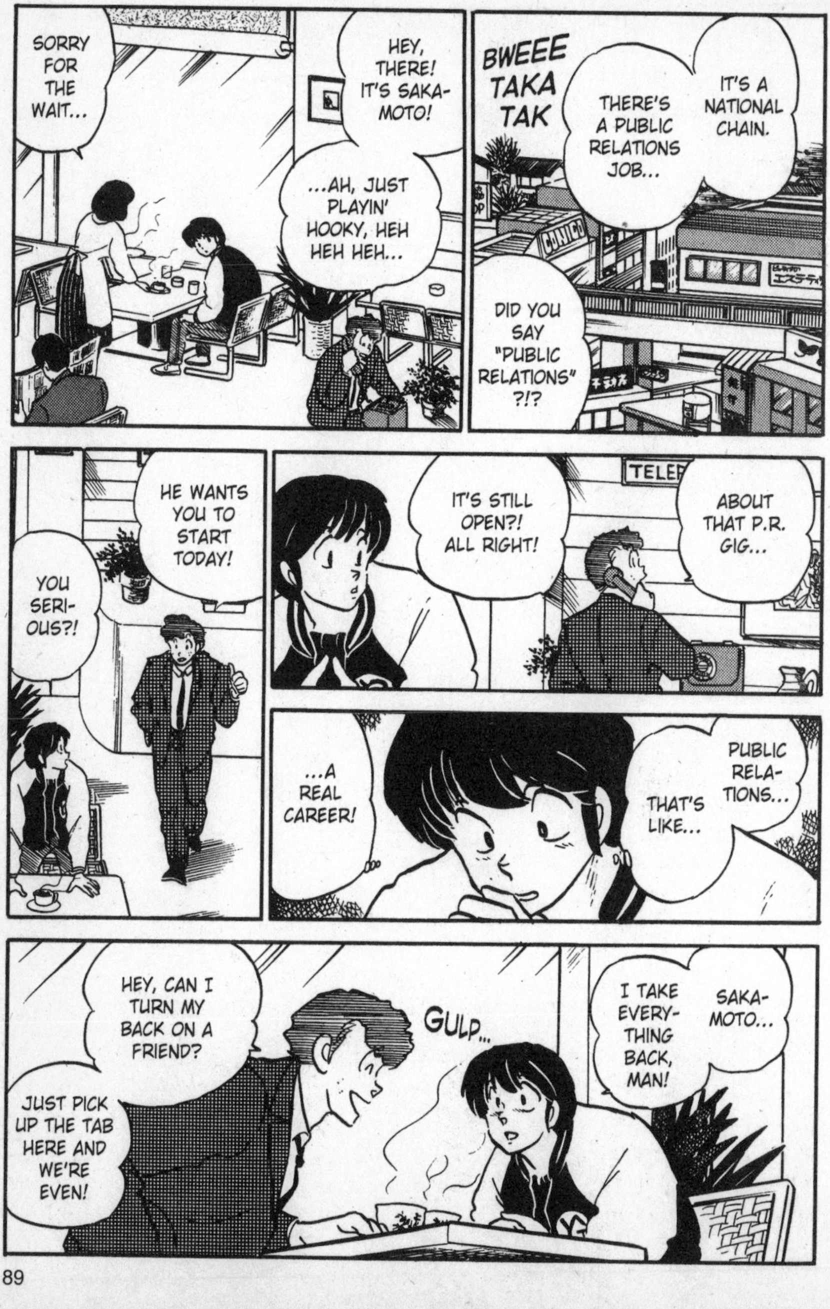
BWEEE TAKA TAK
IT'S A NATIONAL CHAIN.
THERE'S A PUBLIC RELATIONS JOB...
DID YOU SAY "PUBLIC RELATIONS" ?!?
HEY, THERE! IT'S SAKA-MOTO!
SORRY FOR THE WAIT...
...AH, JUST PLAYIN' HOOKY, HEH HEH HEH...
ABOUT THAT P.R. GIG...
IT'S STILL OPEN?! ALL RIGHT!
PUBLIC RELA-TIONS...
THAT'S LIKE...
...A REAL CAREER!
HE WANTS YOU TO START TODAY!
YOU SERI-OUS?!
SAKA-MOTO...
I TAKE EVERY-THING BACK, MAN!
GULP...
HEY, CAN I TURN MY BACK ON A FRIEND?
JUST PICK UP THE TAB HERE AND WE'RE EVEN!

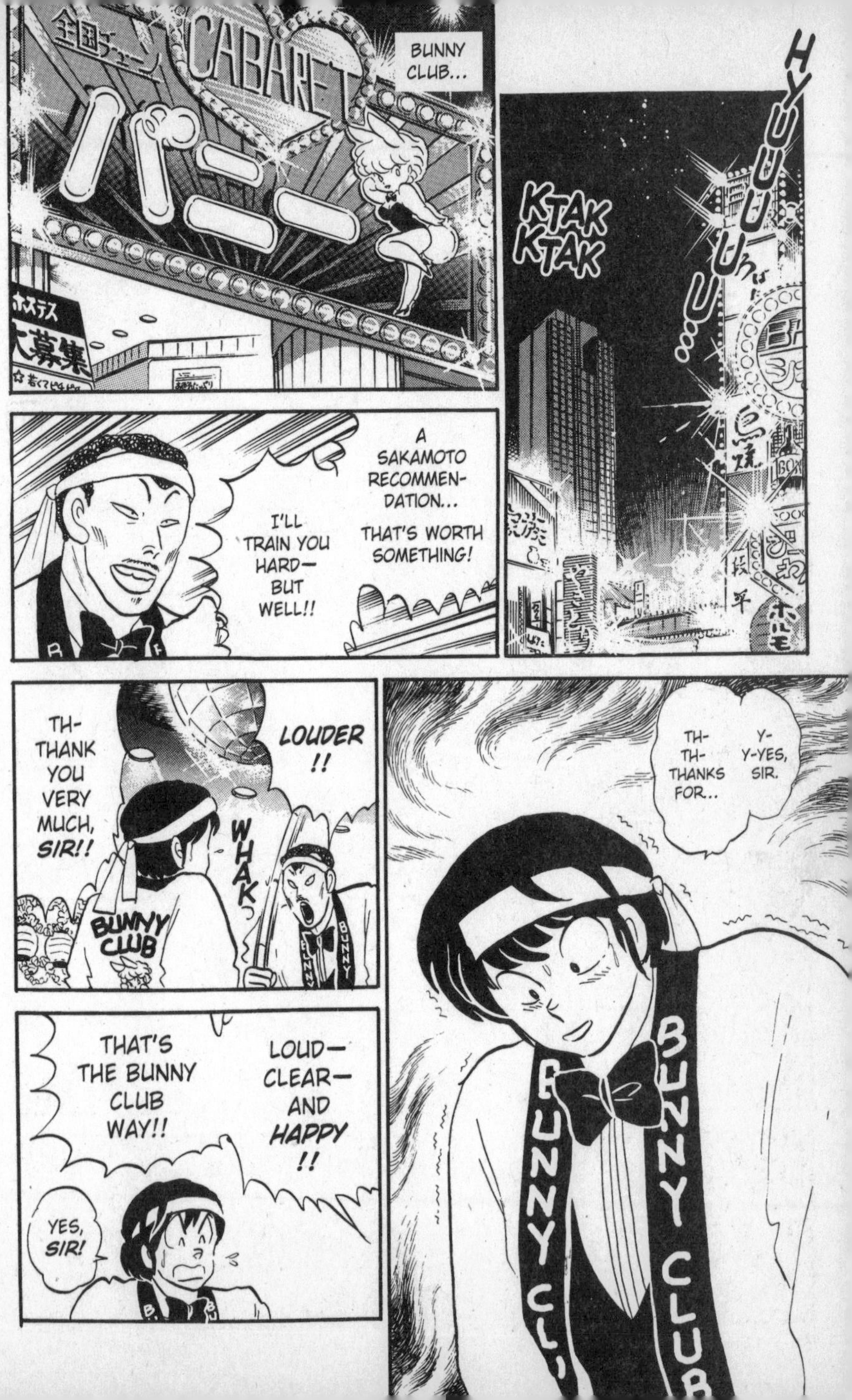

HYUUUUUU...
KTAK KTAK
全国チェーン
CABARET
バニー
BUNNY CLUB...
ホステス
大募集
A SAKAMOTO RECOMMENDATION...
THAT'S WORTH SOMETHING!
I'LL TRAIN YOU HARD—BUT WELL!!
Y-Y-YES, SIR.
TH-TH-THANKS FOR..
BUNNY CLUB
BUNNY CLUB
LOUDER!!
WHAK
TH-THANK YOU VERY MUCH, SIR!!
BUNNY CLUB
LOUD—CLEAR—AND HAPPY!!
THAT'S THE BUNNY CLUB WAY!!
YES, SIR!

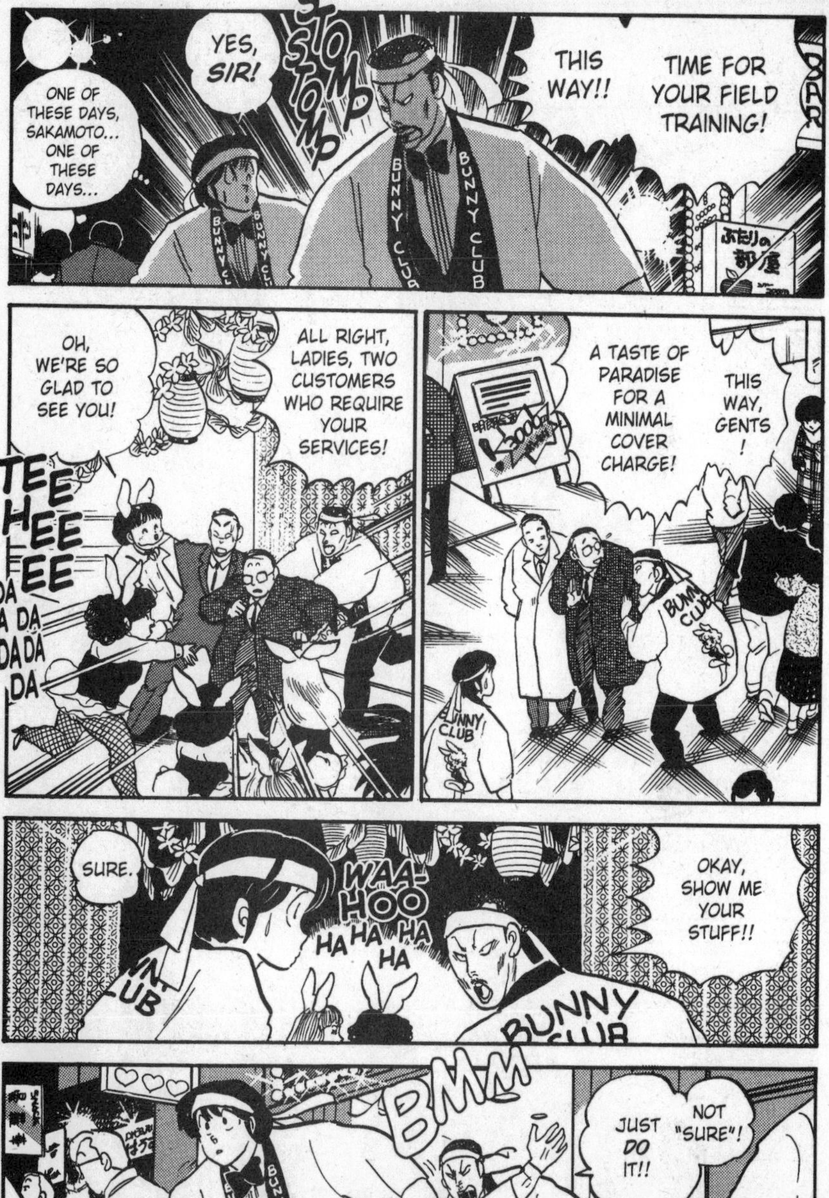
TIME FOR YOUR FIELD TRAINING!
THIS WAY!!
STOMP STOMP
YES, SIR!
ONE OF THESE DAYS, SAKAMOTO... ONE OF THESE DAYS...
BUNNY CLUB
ふたりの部屋
THIS WAY, GENTS!
A TASTE OF PARADISE FOR A MINIMAL COVER CHARGE!
ALL RIGHT, LADIES, TWO CUSTOMERS WHO REQUIRE YOUR SERVICES!
OH, WE'RE SO GLAD TO SEE YOU!
TEE HEE EE EE
DA DA DA DA DA DA
OKAY, SHOW ME YOUR STUFF!!
WAA-HOO
HA HA HA HA
SURE.
NOT "SURE"!
JUST DO IT!!
BMM

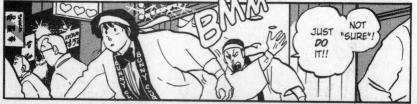

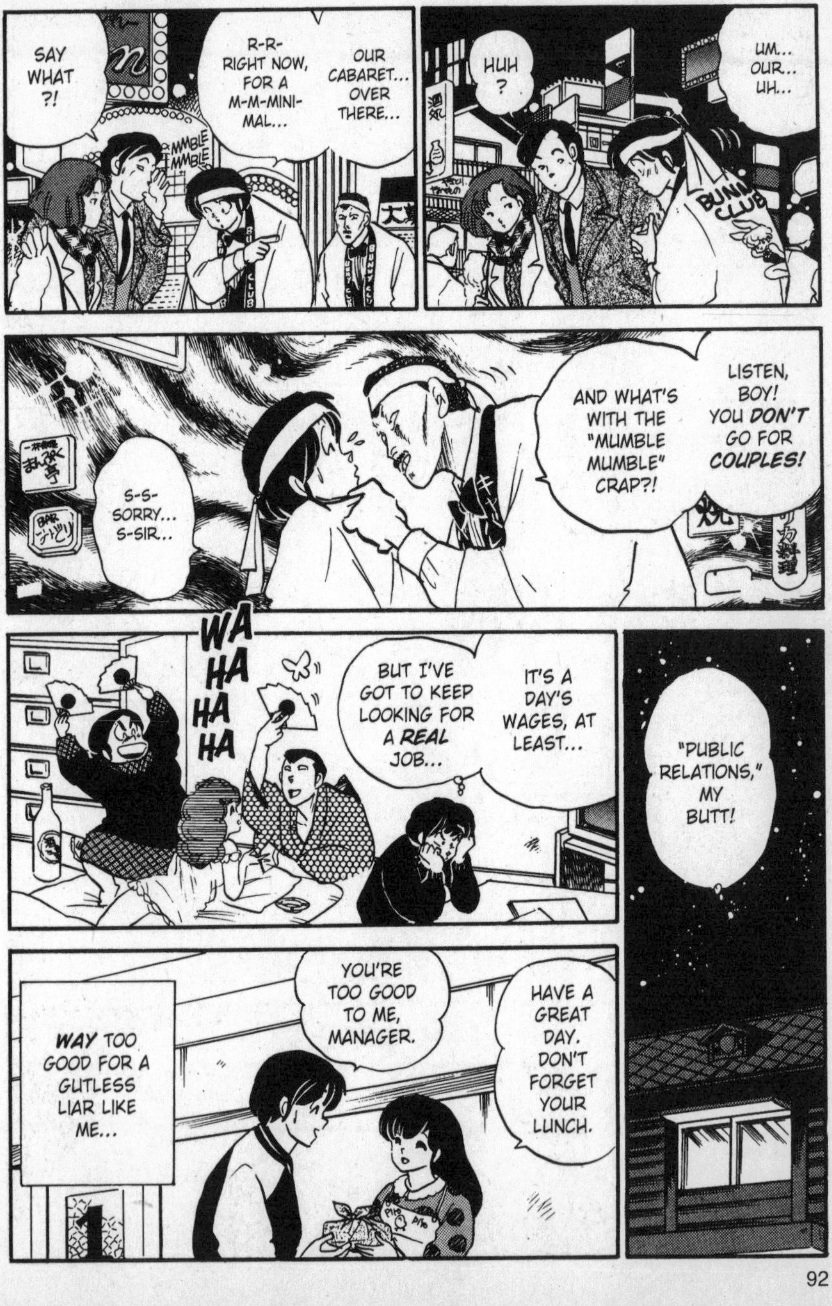
UM... OUR... UH...
HUH?
OUR CABARET... OVER THERE...
R-R-RIGHT NOW, FOR A M-M-MINI-MAL...
MMBLE MMBLE
SAY WHAT?!
LISTEN, BOY! YOU *DON'T* GO FOR *COUPLES!*
AND WHAT'S WITH THE "MUMBLE MUMBLE" CRAP?!
S-S-SORRY... S-SIR...
"PUBLIC RELATIONS," MY BUTT!
IT'S A DAY'S WAGES, AT LEAST...
BUT I'VE GOT TO KEEP LOOKING FOR A *REAL* JOB...
WA HA HA HA HA
HAVE A GREAT DAY. DON'T FORGET YOUR LUNCH.
YOU'RE TOO GOOD TO ME, MANAGER.
WAY TOO GOOD FOR A GUTLESS LIAR LIKE ME...

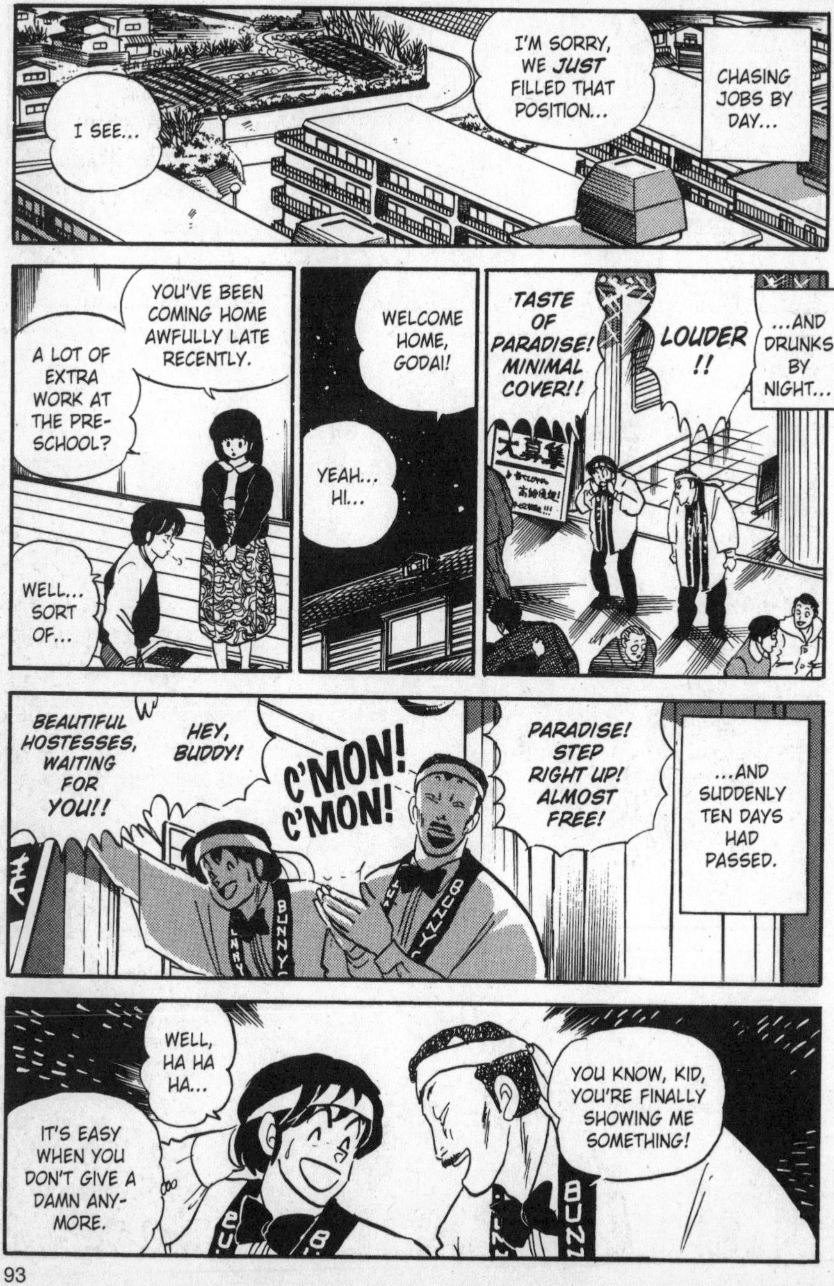
CHASING JOBS BY DAY...
I'M SORRY, WE JUST FILLED THAT POSITION...
I SEE...
...AND DRUNKS BY NIGHT...
LOUDER!!
TASTE OF PARADISE! MINIMAL COVER!!
WELCOME HOME, GODAI!
YEAH... HI...
YOU'VE BEEN COMING HOME AWFULLY LATE RECENTLY.
A LOT OF EXTRA WORK AT THE PRE-SCHOOL?
WELL... SORT OF...
...AND SUDDENLY TEN DAYS HAD PASSED.
PARADISE! STEP RIGHT UP! ALMOST FREE!
C'MON! C'MON!
HEY, BUDDY!
BEAUTIFUL HOSTESSES, WAITING FOR YOU!!
YOU KNOW, KID, YOU'RE FINALLY SHOWING ME SOMETHING!
WELL, HA HA HA...
IT'S EASY WHEN YOU DON'T GIVE A DAMN ANYMORE.

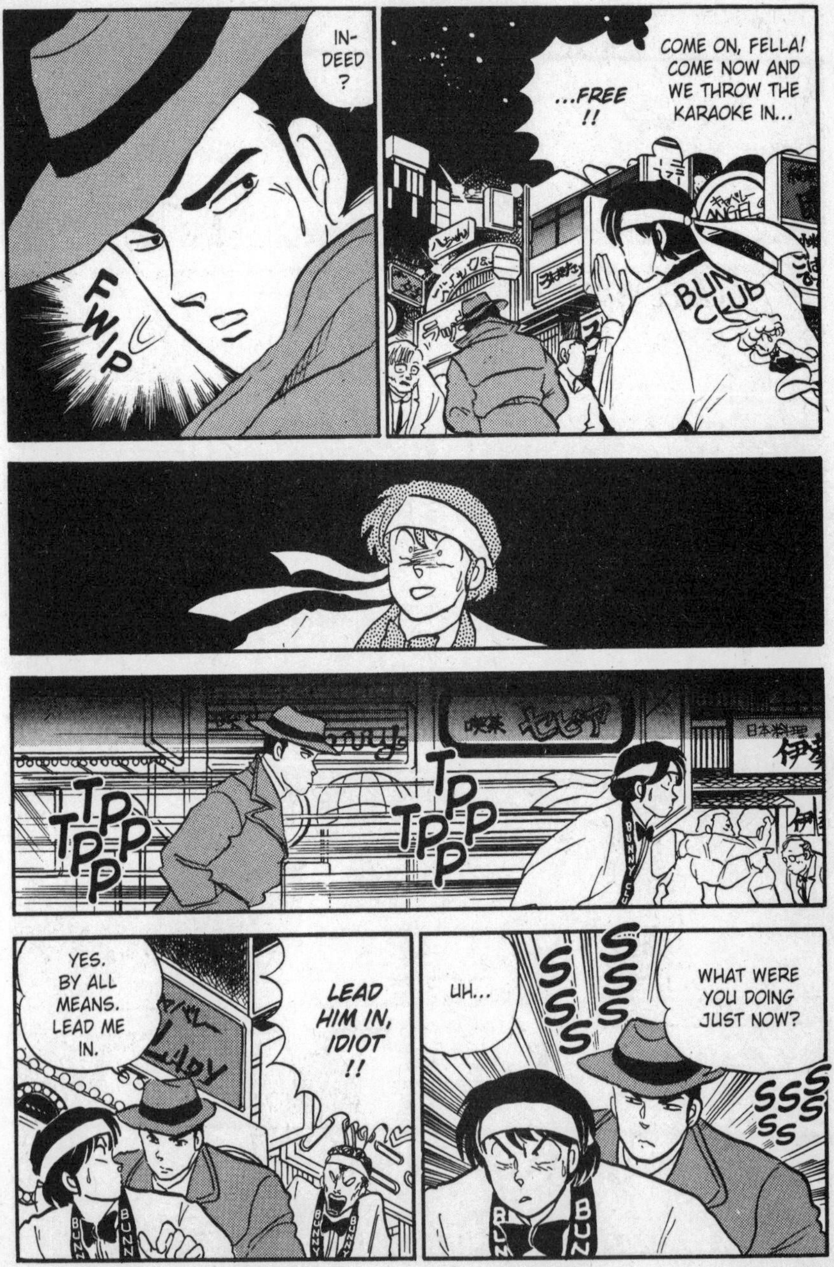
COME ON, FELLA! COME NOW AND WE THROW THE KARAOKE IN...
...FREE !!
IN-DEED ?
FWIP
TPPPP
TPPPP
WHAT WERE YOU DOING JUST NOW?
SSSSS
UH...
SSSSS
LEAD HIM IN, IDIOT !!
YES. BY ALL MEANS. LEAD ME IN.

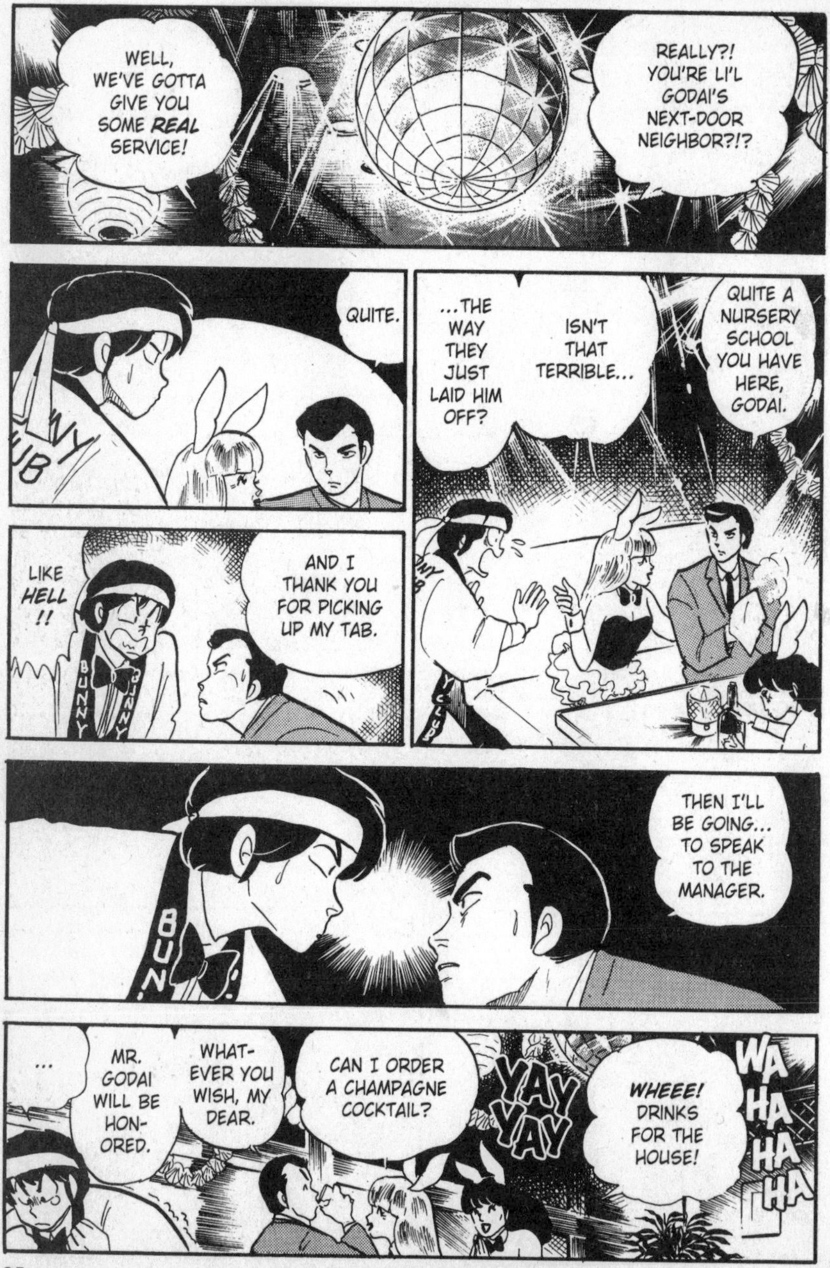
REALLY?! YOU'RE LI'L GODAI'S NEXT-DOOR NEIGHBOR?!?
WELL, WE'VE GOTTA GIVE YOU SOME *REAL* SERVICE!
QUITE A NURSERY SCHOOL YOU HAVE HERE, GODAI.
ISN'T THAT TERRIBLE...
...THE WAY THEY JUST LAID HIM OFF?
QUITE.
AND I THANK YOU FOR PICKING UP MY TAB.
LIKE *HELL* !!
THEN I'LL BE GOING... TO SPEAK TO THE MANAGER.
WA HA HA HA HA
WHEEE! DRINKS FOR THE HOUSE!
YAY YAY
CAN I ORDER A CHAMPAGNE COCKTAIL?
WHAT-EVER YOU WISH, MY DEAR.
MR. GODAI WILL BE HON-ORED.
...

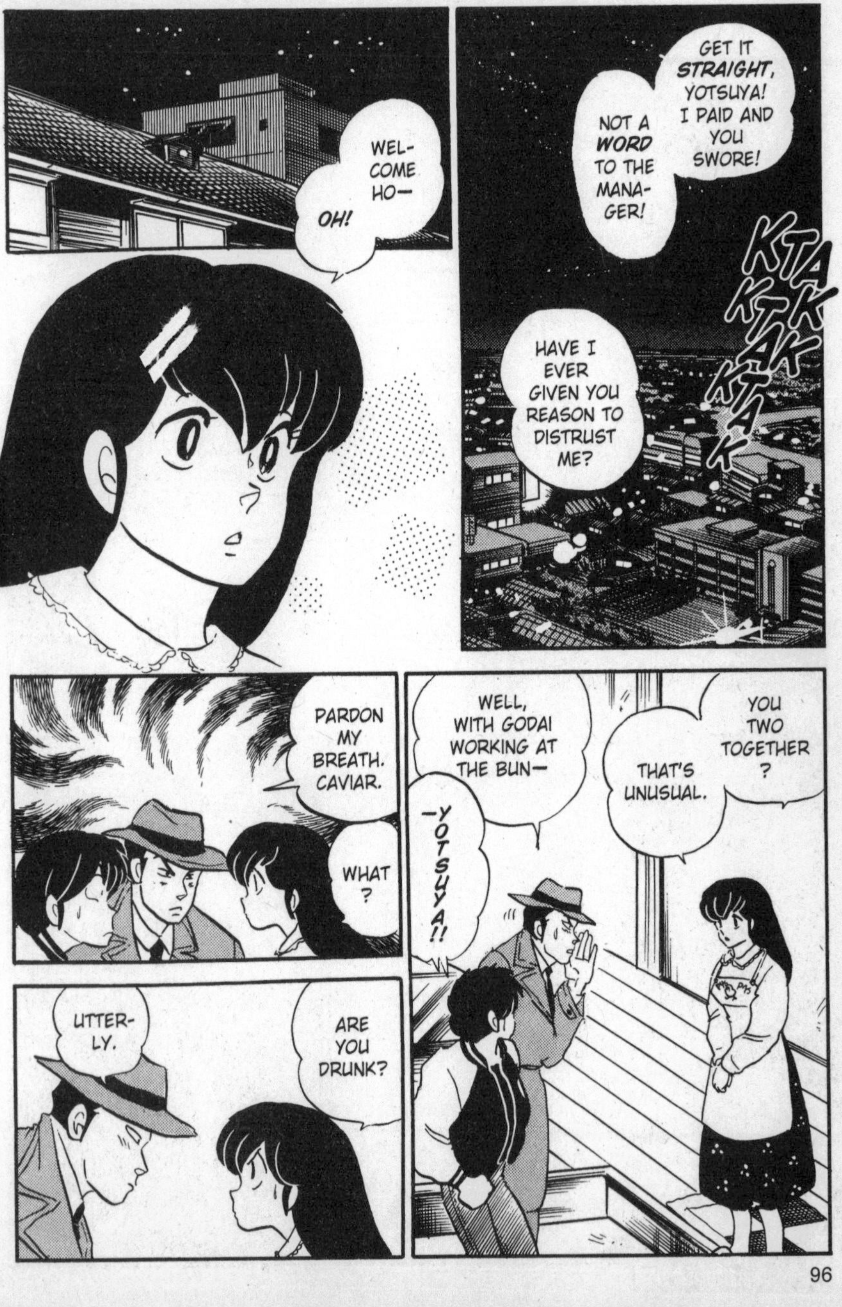
GET IT STRAIGHT, YOTSUYA! I PAID AND YOU SWORE!
NOT A WORD TO THE MANAGER!
KTAK KTAK KTAK KTAK
HAVE I EVER GIVEN YOU REASON TO DISTRUST ME?
WEL-COME HO— OH!
YOU TWO TOGETHER?
THAT'S UNUSUAL.
WELL, WITH GODAI WORKING AT THE BUN—
—YOTSUYA!!
PARDON MY BREATH. CAVIAR.
WHAT?
ARE YOU DRUNK?
UTTER-LY.

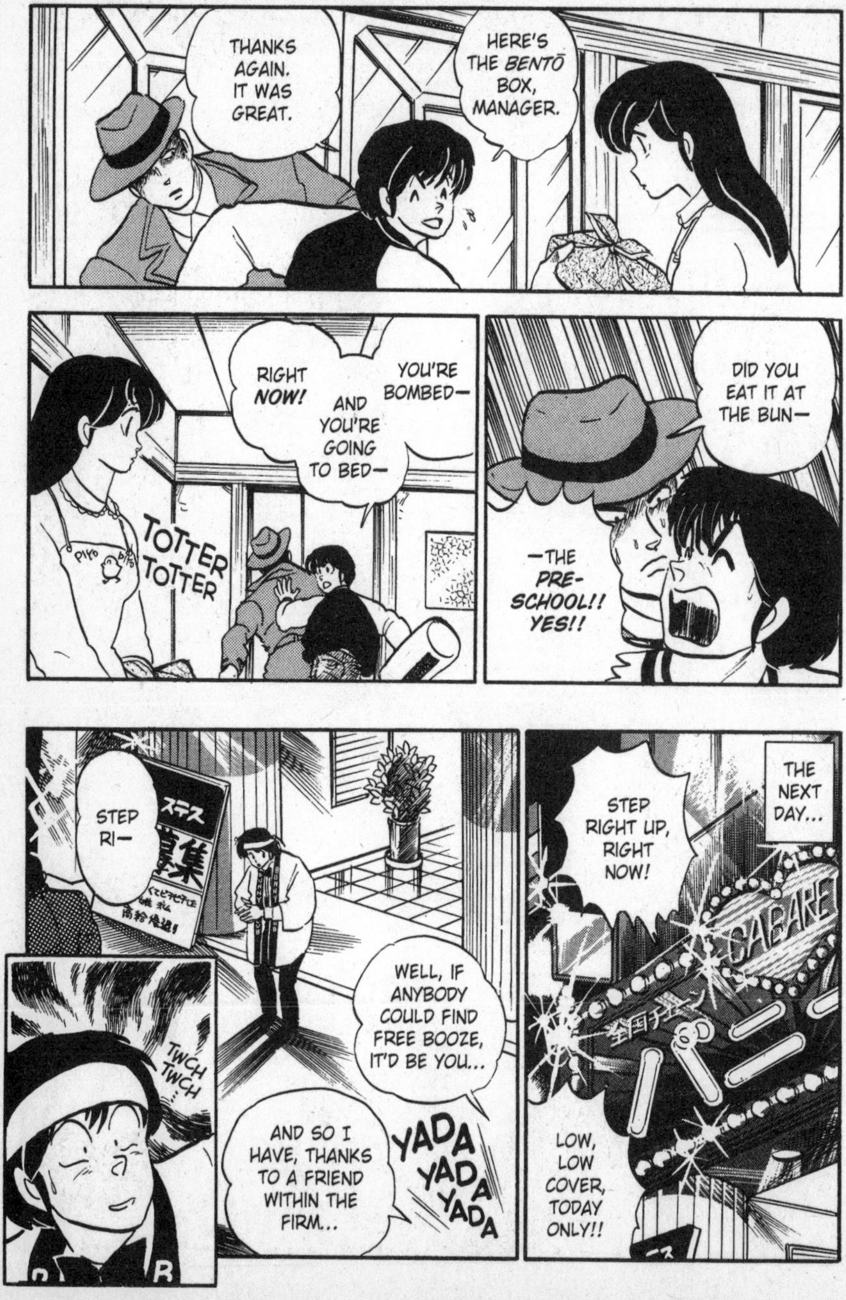
HERE'S THE *BENTŌ* BOX, MANAGER.
THANKS AGAIN. IT WAS GREAT.
DID YOU EAT IT AT THE BUN—
—THE *PRE-SCHOOL!! YES!!*
YOU'RE BOMBED—
RIGHT *NOW!*
AND YOU'RE GOING TO BED—
TOTTER TOTTER
THE NEXT DAY...
STEP RIGHT UP, RIGHT NOW!
CABARET
LOW, LOW COVER, TODAY ONLY!!
STEP RI—
WELL, IF ANYBODY COULD FIND FREE BOOZE, IT'D BE YOU...
AND SO I HAVE, THANKS TO A FRIEND WITHIN THE FIRM...
YADA YADA YADA YADA
TWCH TWCH

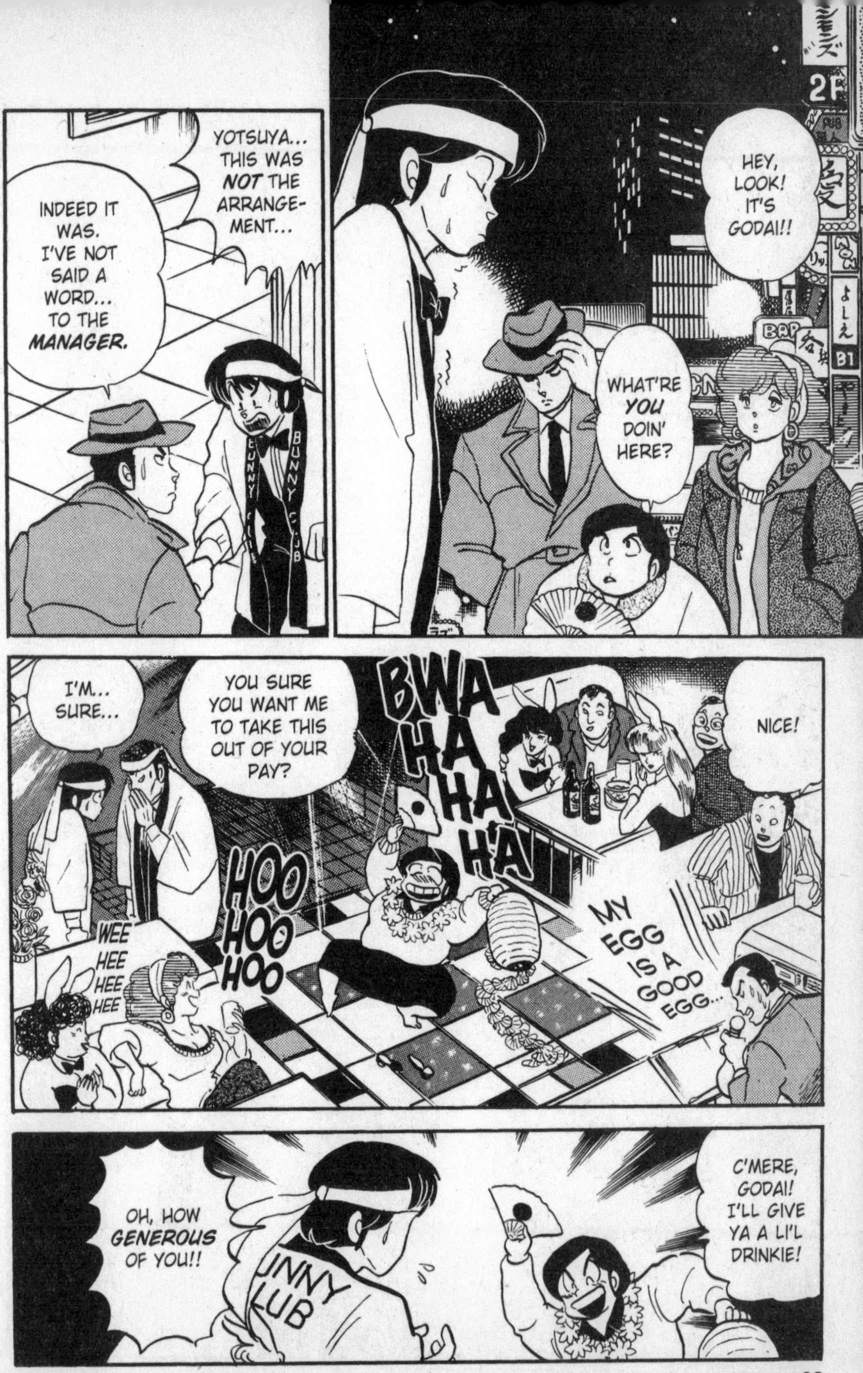

HEY, LOOK! IT'S GODAI!!
WHAT'RE YOU DOIN' HERE?
YOTSUYA... THIS WAS NOT THE ARRANGE-MENT...
INDEED IT WAS. I'VE NOT SAID A WORD... TO THE MANAGER.
BUNNY CLUB
NICE!
BWA HA HA HA HA
YOU SURE YOU WANT ME TO TAKE THIS OUT OF YOUR PAY?
I'M... SURE...
MY EGG IS A GOOD EGG...
HOO HOO HOO
WEE HEE HEE HEE
C'MERE, GODAI! I'LL GIVE YA A LI'L DRINKIE!
UNNY LUB
OH, HOW GENEROUS OF YOU!!

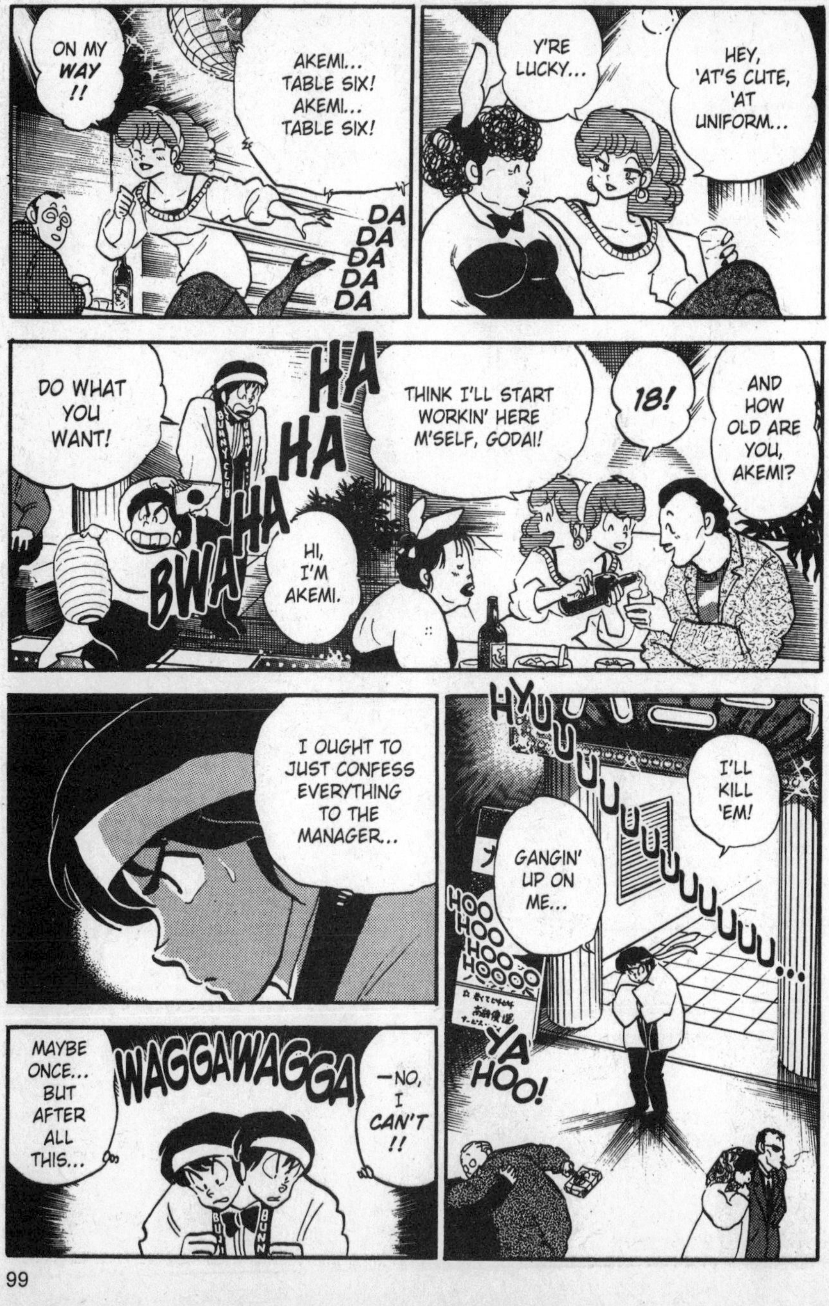
HEY, 'AT'S CUTE, 'AT UNIFORM...
Y'RE LUCKY...
AKEMI... TABLE SIX! AKEMI... TABLE SIX!
ON MY WAY !!
DA DA DA DA DA DA
AND HOW OLD ARE YOU, AKEMI?
18!
THINK I'LL START WORKIN' HERE M'SELF, GODAI!
HA HA HA HA
HI, I'M AKEMI.
BWA
DO WHAT YOU WANT!
HYUUUUUUUUUUUUUU...
I'LL KILL 'EM!
GANGIN' UP ON ME...
HOO HOO HOOO HOOOO
YAHOO!
I OUGHT TO JUST CONFESS EVERYTHING TO THE MANAGER...
—NO, I CAN'T !!
WAGGAWAGGA
MAYBE ONCE... BUT AFTER ALL THIS...

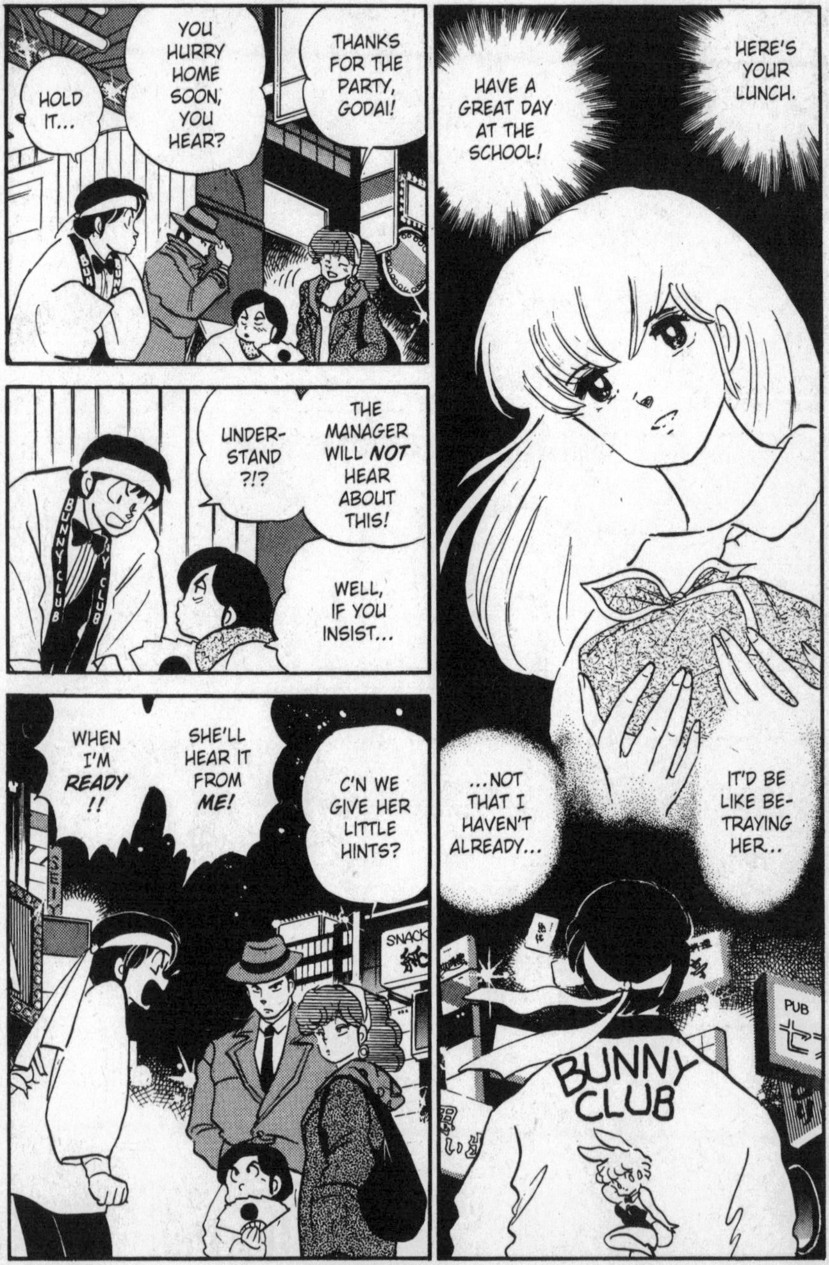
HERE'S YOUR LUNCH.
HAVE A GREAT DAY AT THE SCHOOL!
IT'D BE LIKE BE-TRAYING HER...
...NOT THAT I HAVEN'T ALREADY...
PUB
BUNNY CLUB
THANKS FOR THE PARTY, GODAI!
YOU HURRY HOME SOON, YOU HEAR?
HOLD IT...
THE MANAGER WILL ***NOT*** HEAR ABOUT THIS!
UNDER-STAND?!?
WELL, IF YOU INSIST...
C'N WE GIVE HER LITTLE HINTS?
SHE'LL HEAR IT FROM ***ME!***
WHEN I'M ***READY*** !!
SNACK

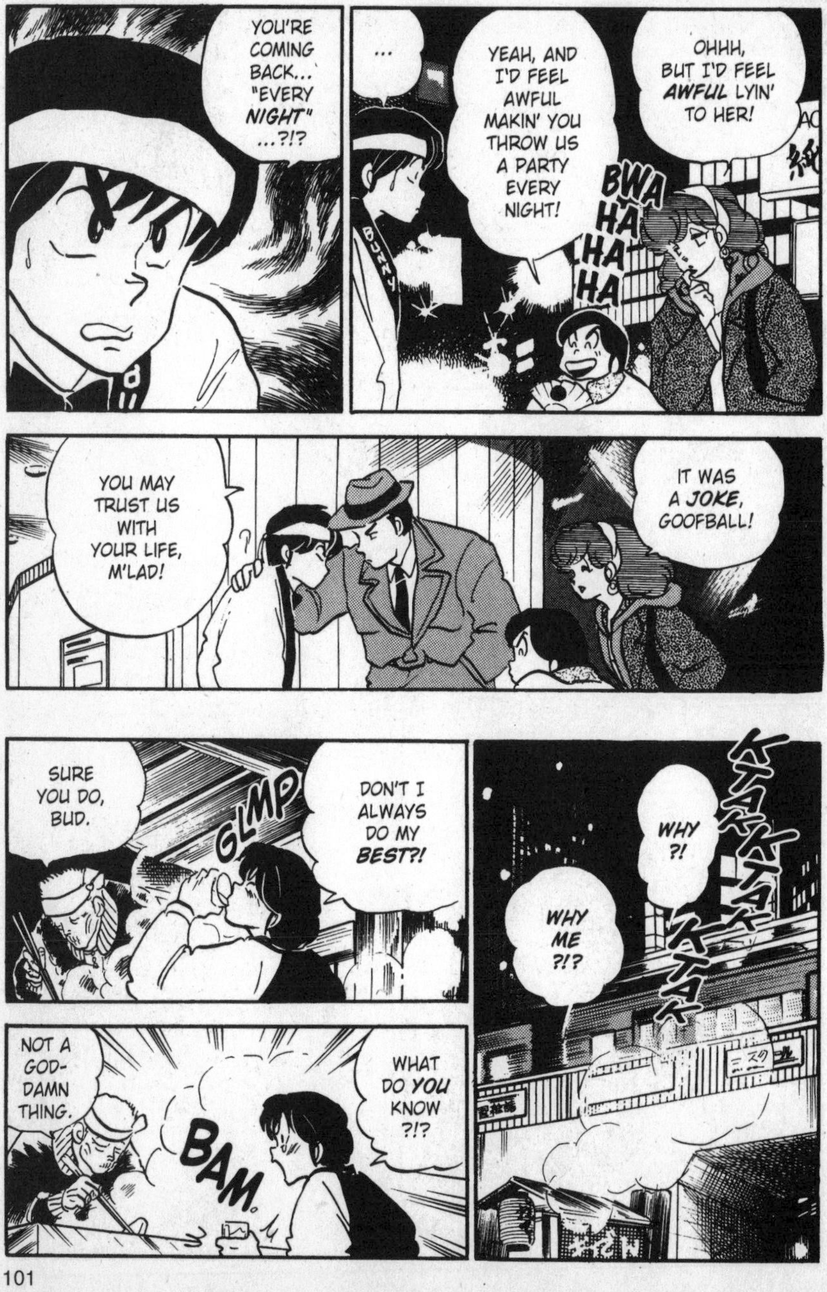
OHHH, BUT I'D FEEL AWFUL LYIN' TO HER!
YEAH, AND I'D FEEL AWFUL MAKIN' YOU THROW US A PARTY EVERY NIGHT!
BWA HA HA HA
...
YOU'RE COMING BACK... "EVERY NIGHT" ...?!?
IT WAS A JOKE, GOOFBALL!
YOU MAY TRUST US WITH YOUR LIFE, M'LAD!
KTAK KTAK KTAK
WHY ?!
WHY ME ?!?
DON'T I ALWAYS DO MY BEST?!
GLMP
SURE YOU DO, BUD.
WHAT DO YOU KNOW ?!?
BAM
NOT A GOD-DAMN THING.

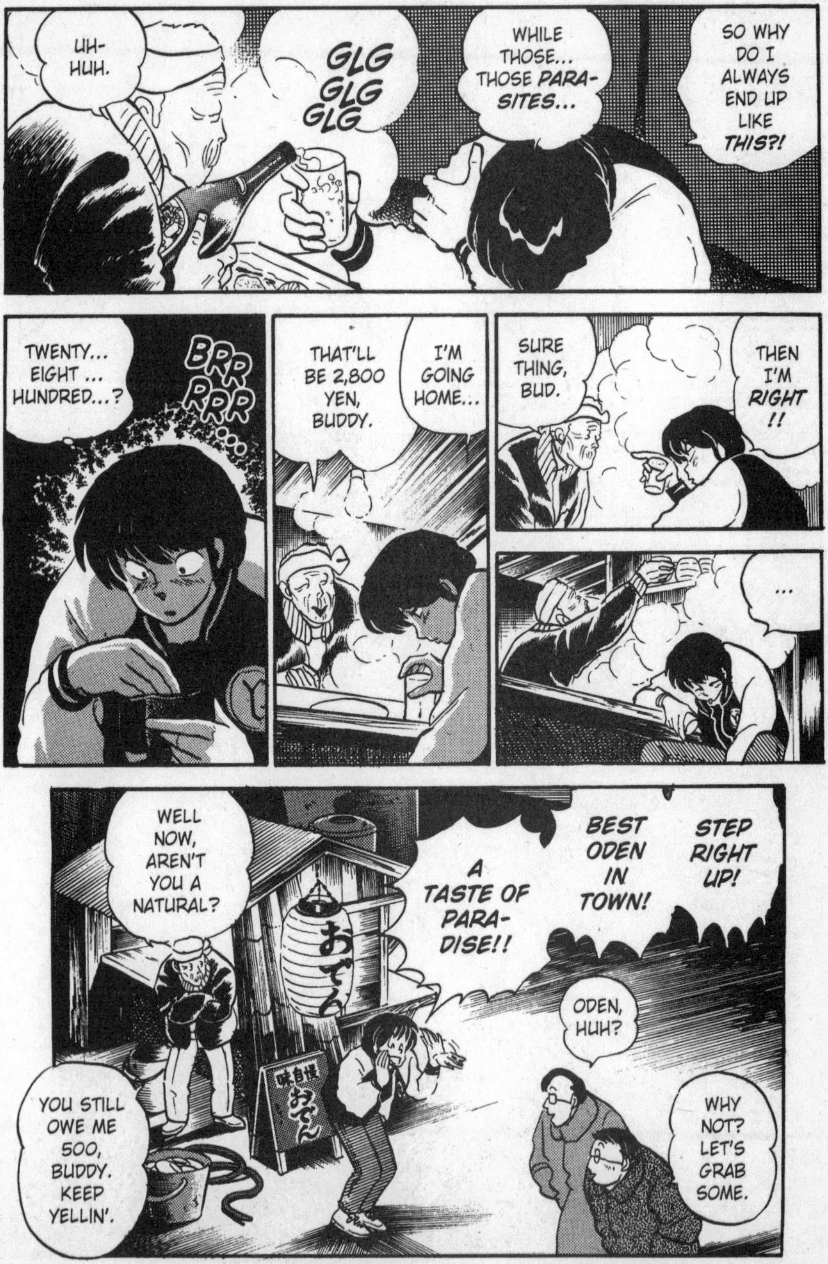
SO WHY DO I ALWAYS END UP LIKE *THIS?!*
WHILE THOSE... THOSE *PARA-SITES...*
GLG GLG GLG
UH-HUH.
THEN I'M *RIGHT* !!
SURE THING, BUD.
...
I'M GOING HOME...
THAT'LL BE 2,800 YEN, BUDDY.
BRRRRR...
TWENTY... EIGHT ... HUNDRED...?
STEP RIGHT UP!
BEST ODEN IN TOWN!
A TASTE OF PARA-DISE!!
WELL NOW, AREN'T YOU A NATURAL?
おでん
ODEN, HUH?
WHY NOT? LET'S GRAB SOME.
味自慢 おでん
YOU STILL OWE ME 500, BUDDY. KEEP YELLIN'.

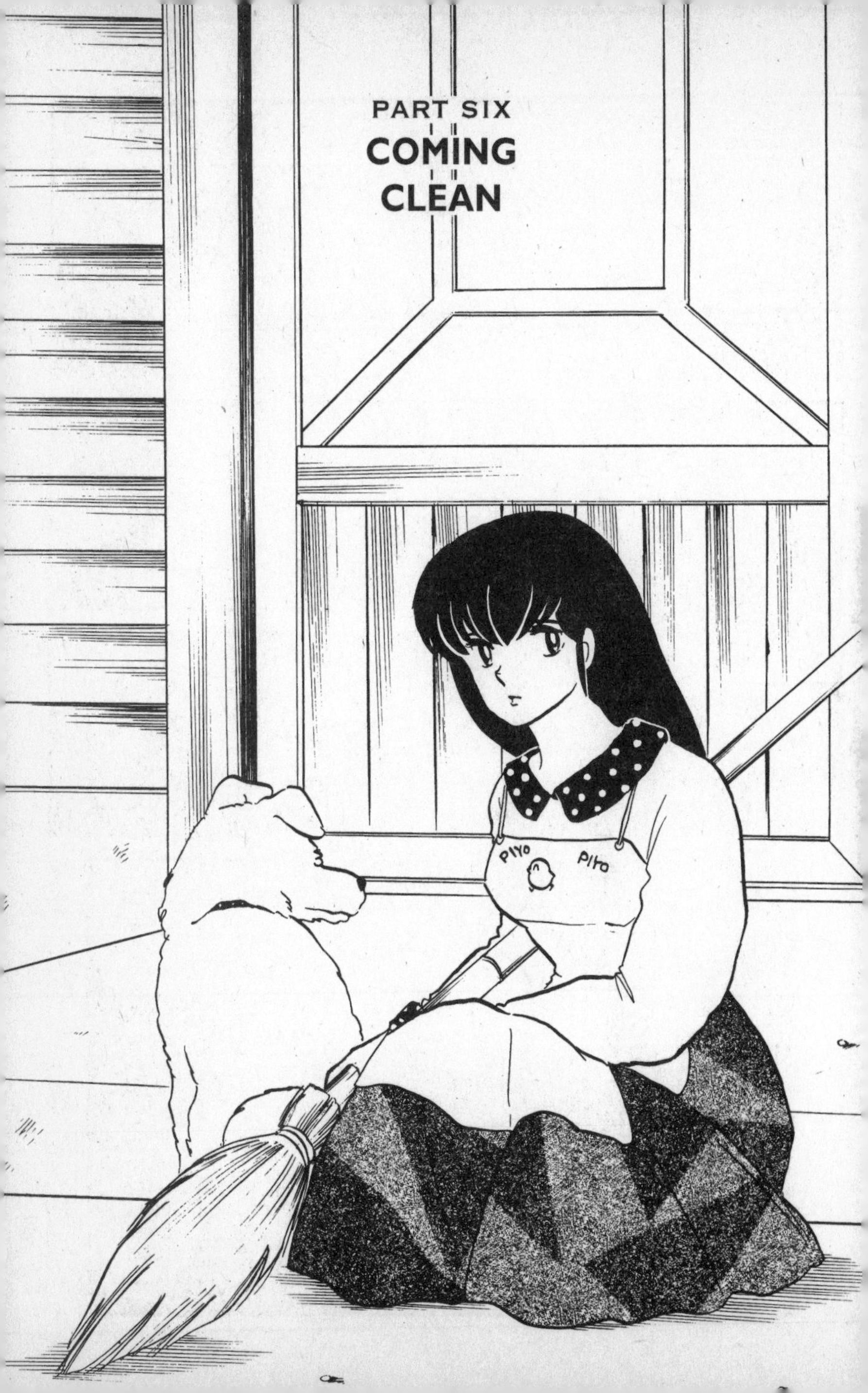
PART SIX
COMING CLEAN
Piyo
Piyo

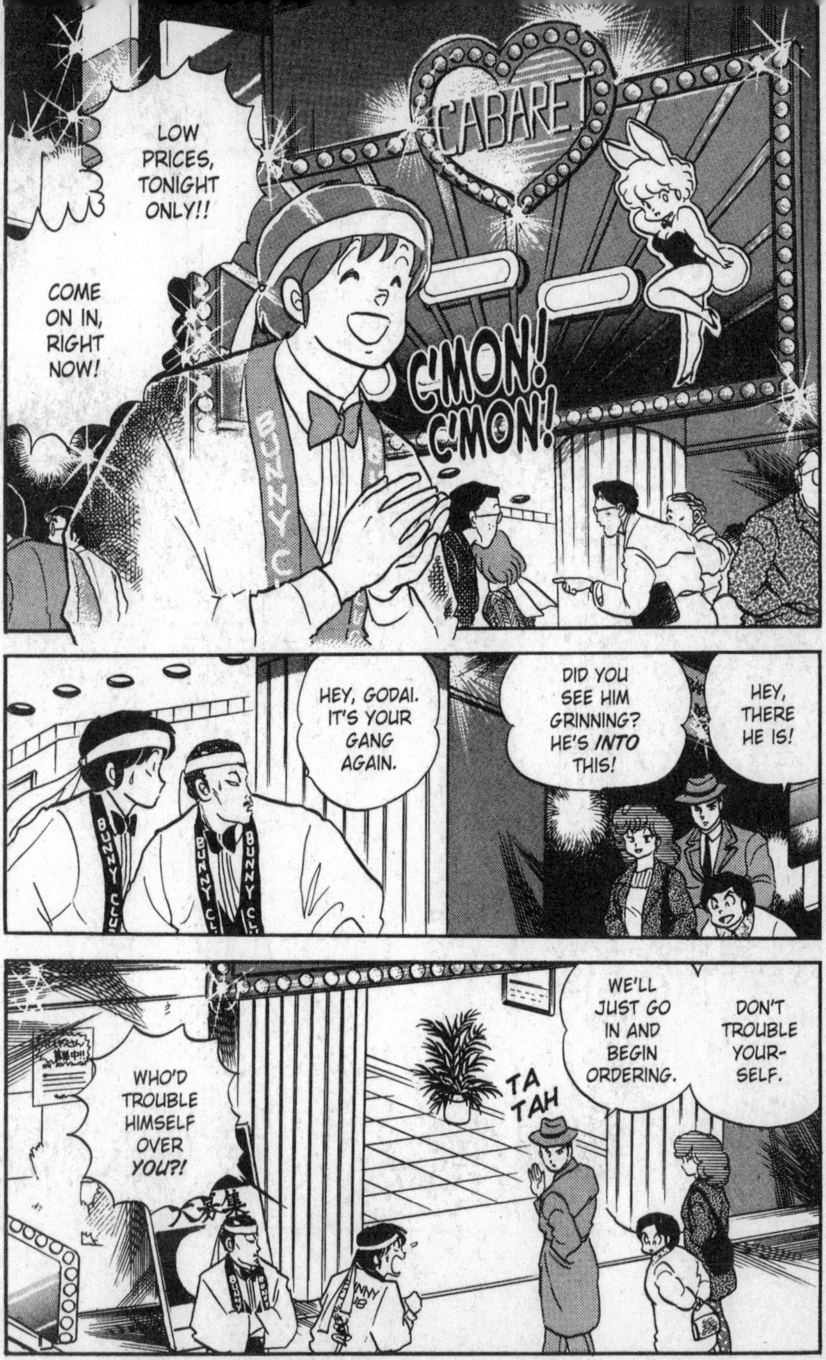
LOW PRICES, TONIGHT ONLY!!
COME ON IN, RIGHT NOW!
C'MON! C'MON!
CABARET
BUNNY CL
HEY, THERE HE IS!
DID YOU SEE HIM GRINNING? HE'S *INTO* THIS!
HEY, GODAI. IT'S YOUR GANG AGAIN.
BUNNY CL
DON'T TROUBLE YOUR-SELF.
WE'LL JUST GO IN AND BEGIN ORDERING.
TA TAH
WHO'D TROUBLE HIMSELF OVER *YOU*?!
大募集

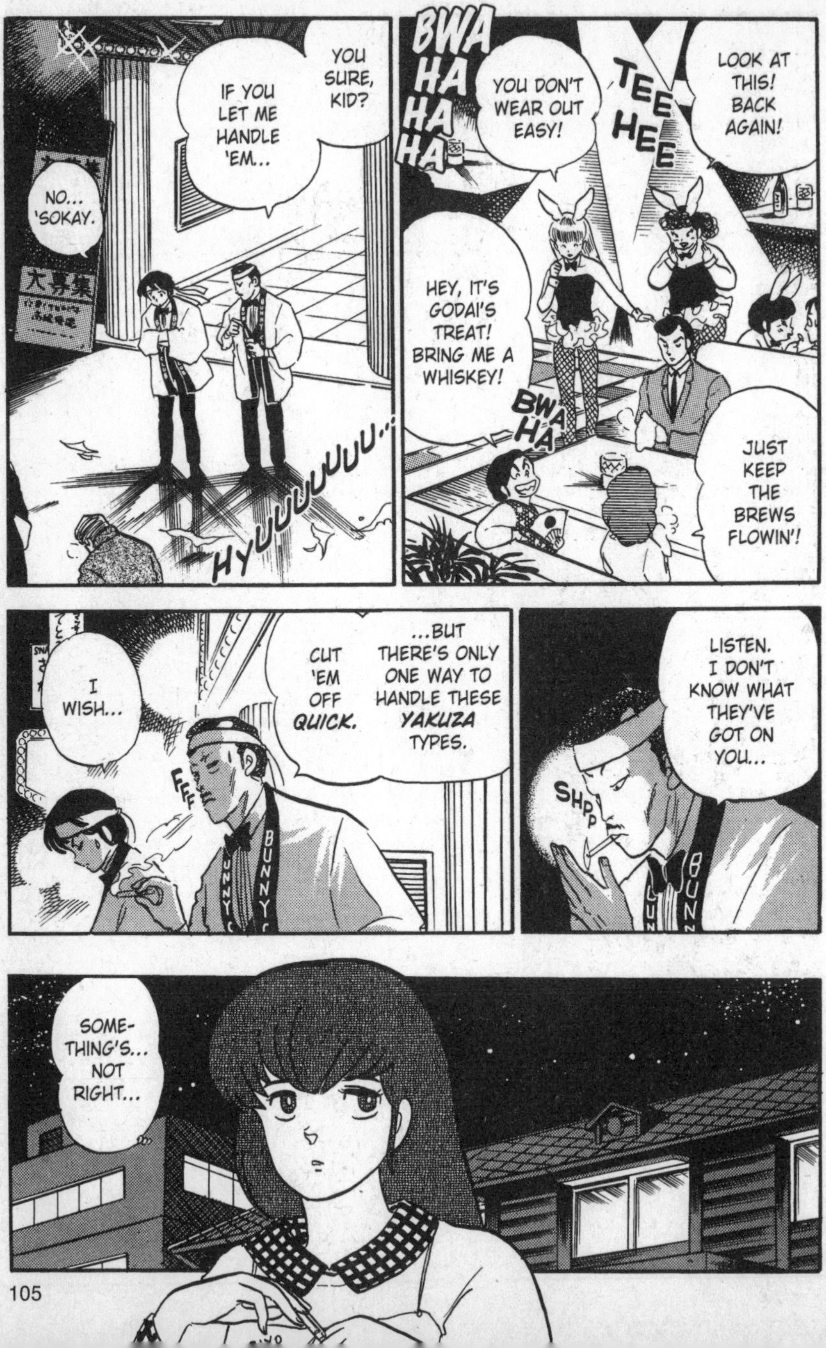
LOOK AT THIS! BACK AGAIN!
TEE HEE
YOU DON'T WEAR OUT EASY!
BWA HA HA HA HA
HEY, IT'S GODAI'S TREAT! BRING ME A WHISKEY!
JUST KEEP THE BREWS FLOWIN'!
BWA HA
YOU SURE, KID?
IF YOU LET ME HANDLE 'EM...
NO... 'SOKAY.
HYUUUUUUU...
LISTEN. I DON'T KNOW WHAT THEY'VE GOT ON YOU...
SHPP
...BUT THERE'S ONLY ONE WAY TO HANDLE THESE YAKUZA TYPES.
CUT 'EM OFF QUICK.
I WISH...
FFF
SOME-THING'S... NOT RIGHT...

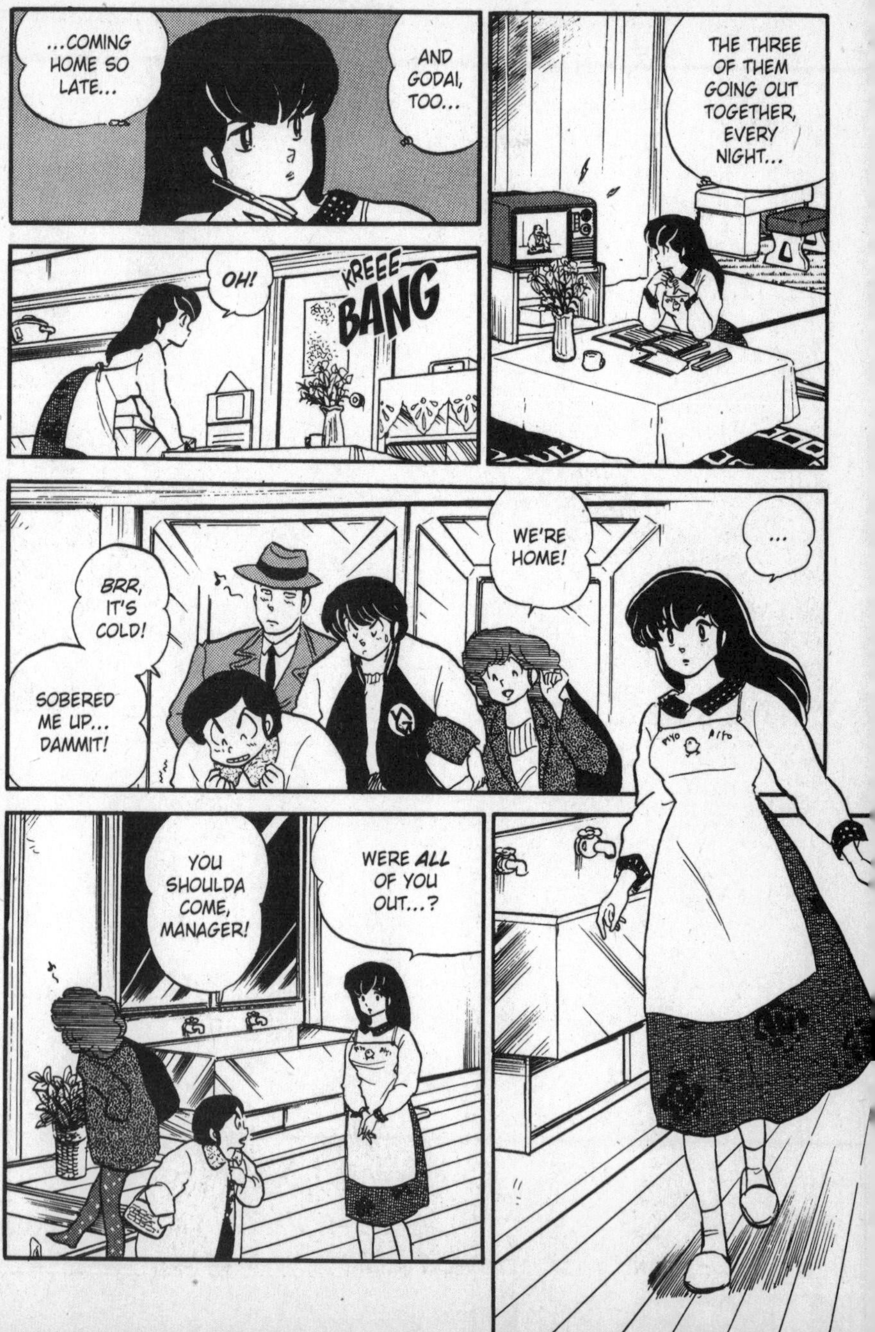
THE THREE OF THEM GOING OUT TOGETHER, EVERY NIGHT...
AND GODAI, TOO...
...COMING HOME SO LATE...
OH!
KREEE
BANG
...
WE'RE HOME!
BRR, IT'S COLD!
SOBERED ME UP... DAMMIT!
WERE *ALL* OF YOU OUT...?
YOU SHOULDA COME, MANAGER!

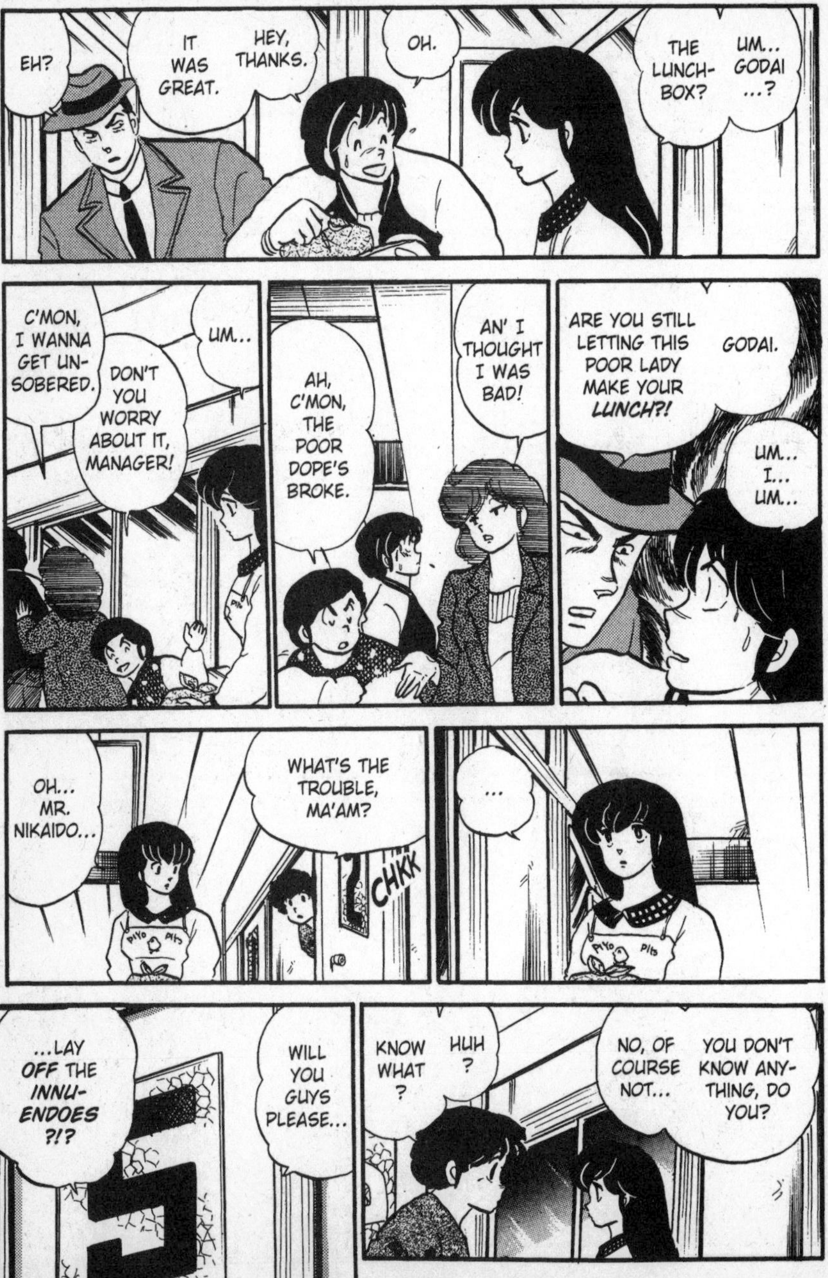
UM... GODAI ...?
THE LUNCH-BOX?
OH.
HEY, THANKS.
IT WAS GREAT.
EH?
GODAI.
ARE YOU STILL LETTING THIS POOR LADY MAKE YOUR *LUNCH?!*
UM... I... UM...
AN' I THOUGHT I WAS BAD!
AH, C'MON, THE POOR DOPE'S BROKE.
UM...
C'MON, I WANNA GET UN-SOBERED.
DON'T YOU WORRY ABOUT IT, MANAGER!
...
WHAT'S THE TROUBLE, MA'AM?
CHKK
OH... MR. NIKAIDO...
YOU DON'T KNOW ANY-THING, DO YOU?
NO, OF COURSE NOT...
HUH?
KNOW WHAT?
WILL YOU GUYS PLEASE...
...LAY *OFF* THE *INNU-ENDOES* ?!?

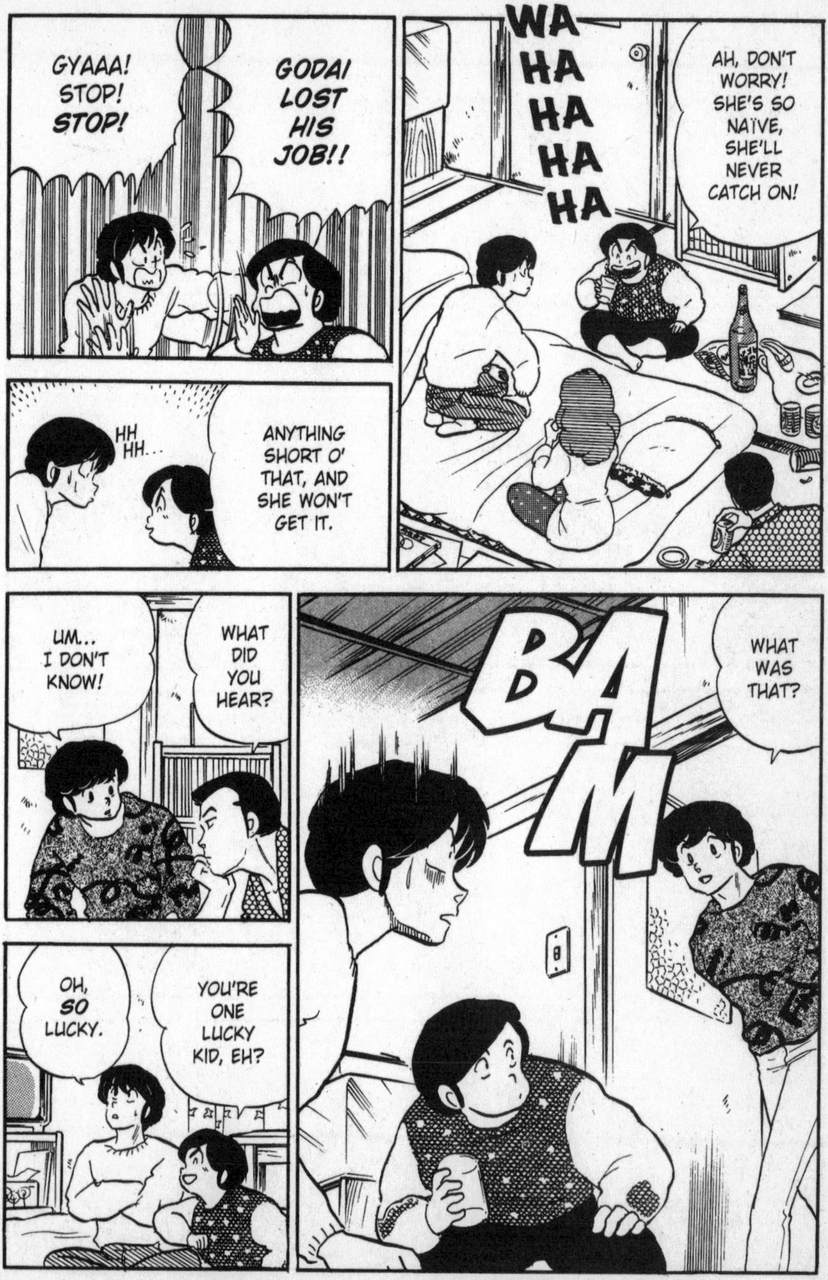
WA HA HA HA HA HA
AH, DON'T WORRY! SHE'S SO NAÏVE, SHE'LL NEVER CATCH ON!
GODAI LOST HIS JOB!!
GYAAA! STOP! STOP!
ANYTHING SHORT O' THAT, AND SHE WON'T GET IT.
HH HH...
WHAT WAS THAT?
BAM
WHAT DID YOU HEAR?
UM... I DON'T KNOW!
YOU'RE ONE LUCKY KID, EH?
OH, SO LUCKY.

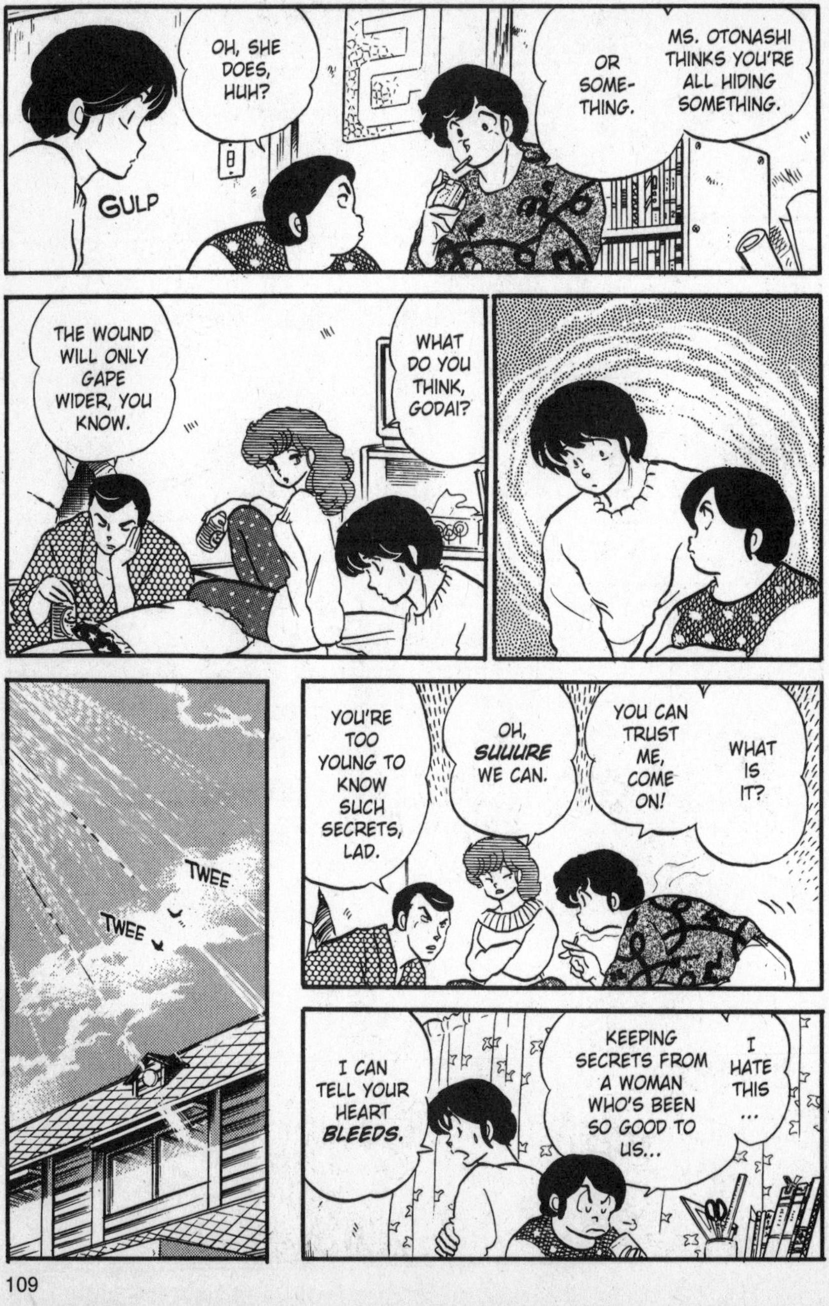
MS. OTONASHI THINKS YOU'RE ALL HIDING SOMETHING.
OR SOME-THING.
OH, SHE DOES, HUH?
GULP
WHAT DO YOU THINK, GODAI?
THE WOUND WILL ONLY GAPE WIDER, YOU KNOW.
WHAT IS IT?
YOU CAN TRUST ME, COME ON!
OH, ***SUUURE*** WE CAN.
YOU'RE TOO YOUNG TO KNOW SUCH SECRETS, LAD.
I HATE THIS...
KEEPING SECRETS FROM A WOMAN WHO'S BEEN SO GOOD TO US...
I CAN TELL YOUR HEART ***BLEEDS.***
TWEE
TWEE

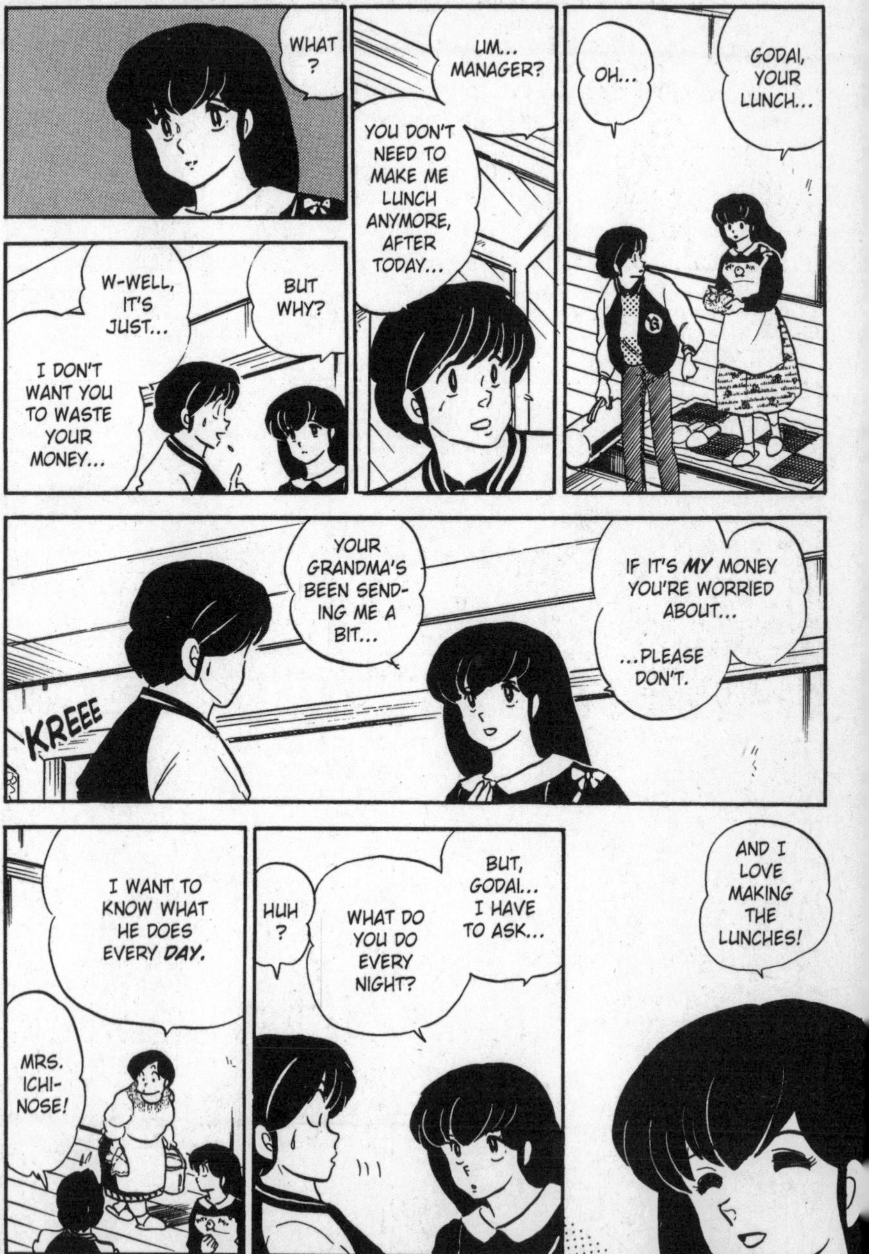
GODAI, YOUR LUNCH...
OH...
UM... MANAGER?
YOU DON'T NEED TO MAKE ME LUNCH ANYMORE, AFTER TODAY...
WHAT?
BUT WHY?
W-WELL, IT'S JUST...
I DON'T WANT YOU TO WASTE YOUR MONEY...
IF IT'S *MY* MONEY YOU'RE WORRIED ABOUT...
...PLEASE DON'T.
YOUR GRANDMA'S BEEN SENDING ME A BIT...
KREEE
AND I LOVE MAKING THE LUNCHES!
BUT, GODAI... I HAVE TO ASK...
WHAT DO YOU DO EVERY NIGHT?
HUH?
I WANT TO KNOW WHAT HE DOES EVERY *DAY*.
MRS. ICHINOSE!

MEAN BY WHAT?

WHAT DID YOU MEAN BY THAT?

OH...

I'D BETTER RUN!!

VROOOM

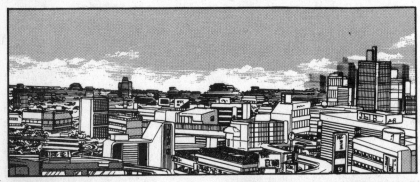

YEAH, SURE.

HEY, GODAI, WE'LL BE HANDING OUT FLYERS AT THE TRAIN STATION THIS AFTERNOON, OKAY?

CHK

BUNNY CLUB

CHIRIRIN

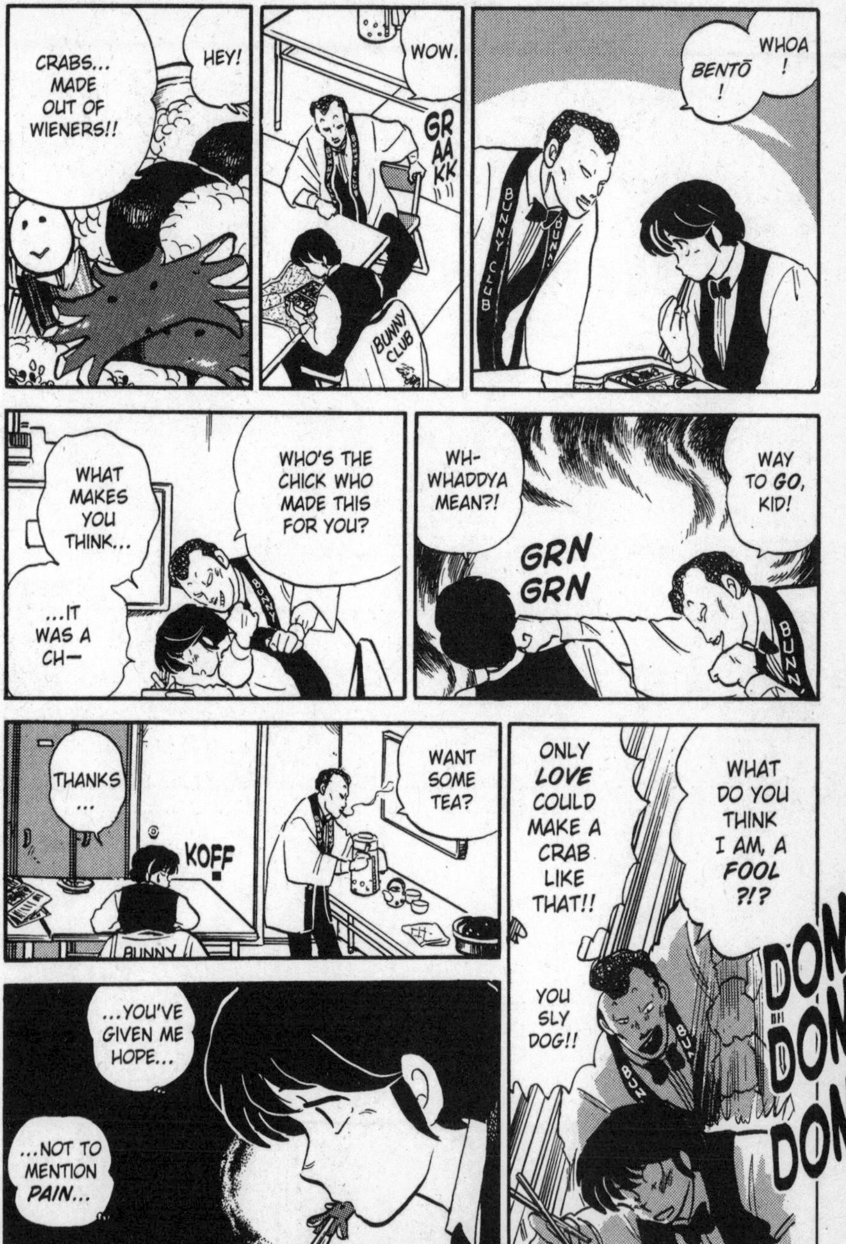
WHOA! BENTŌ!
WOW.
GRAAKK
HEY!
CRABS... MADE OUT OF WIENERS!!
WAY TO GO, KID!
WH-WHADDYA MEAN?!
GRN GRN
WHO'S THE CHICK WHO MADE THIS FOR YOU?
WHAT MAKES YOU THINK...
...IT WAS A CH—
WHAT DO YOU THINK I AM, A FOOL?!?
ONLY LOVE COULD MAKE A CRAB LIKE THAT!!
DOM DOM DOM
YOU SLY DOG!!
WANT SOME TEA?
THANKS...
KOFF
...YOU'VE GIVEN ME HOPE...
...NOT TO MENTION PAIN...

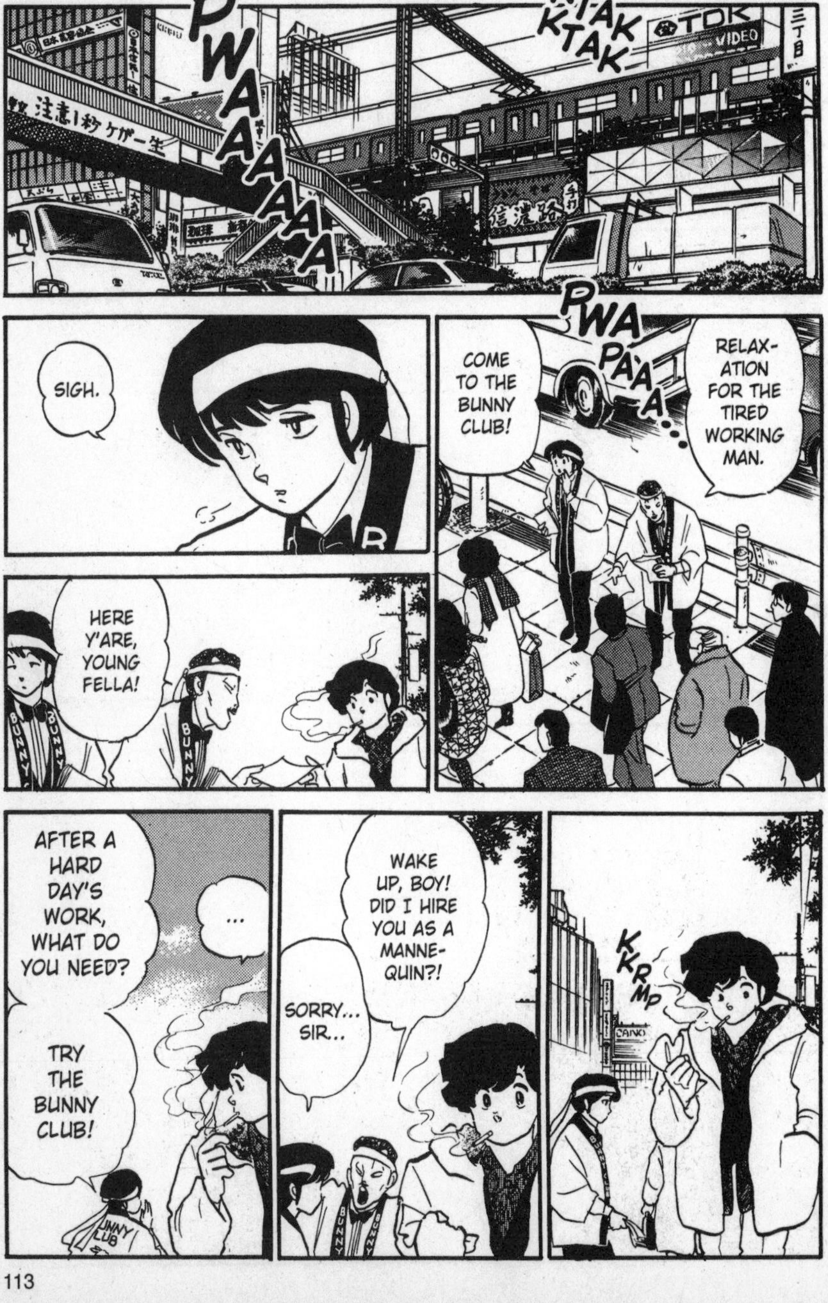

PWAAAAAAA
KTAK KTAK
TDK
VIDEO
三丁目
注意1秒ケガ一生
信濃路
PWA PAAAA...
RELAXATION FOR THE TIRED WORKING MAN.
COME TO THE BUNNY CLUB!
SIGH.
HERE Y'ARE, YOUNG FELLA!
KKRMP
WAKE UP, BOY! DID I HIRE YOU AS A MANNEQUIN?!
SORRY... SIR...
AFTER A HARD DAY'S WORK, WHAT DO YOU NEED?
...
TRY THE BUNNY CLUB!

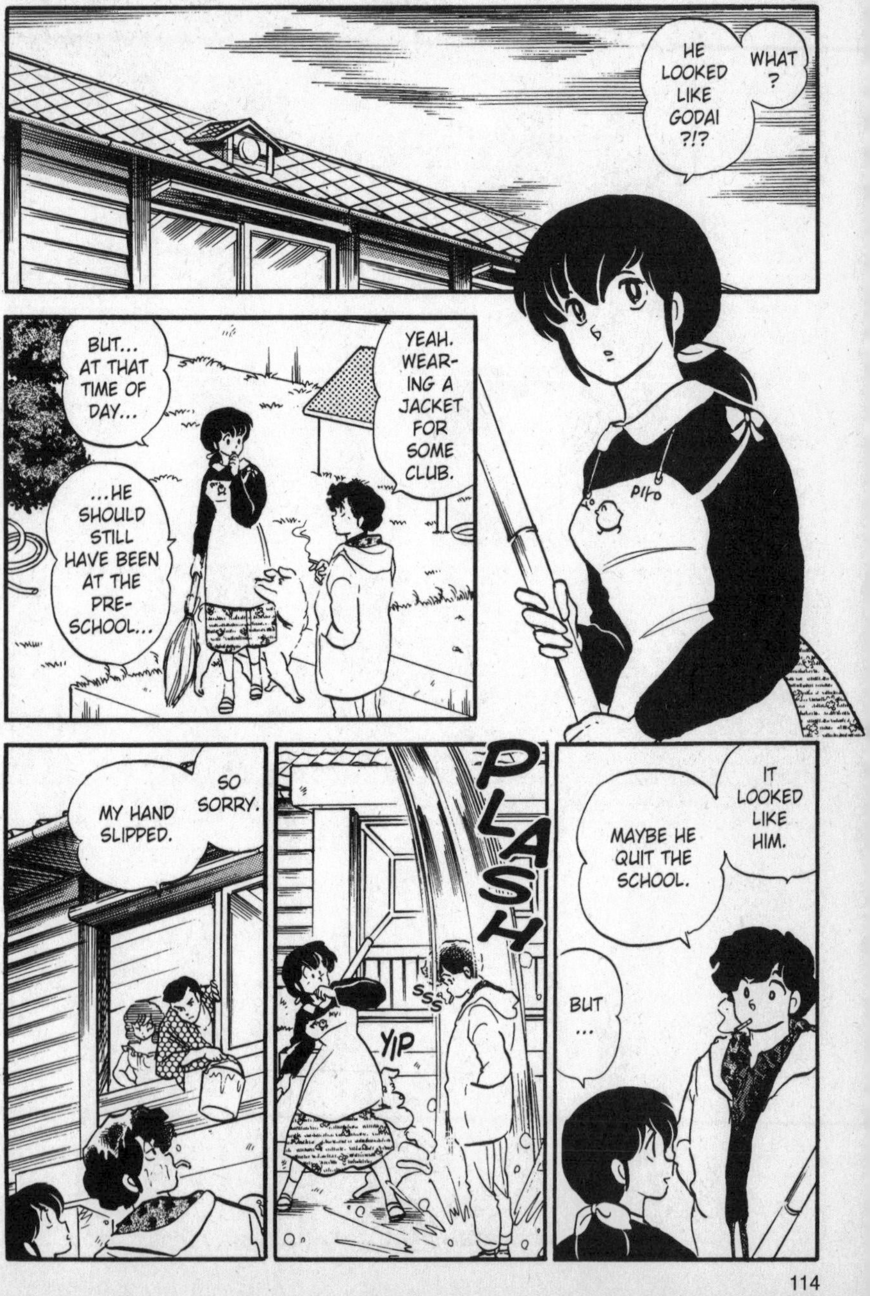
WHAT?
HE LOOKED LIKE GODAI ?!?
YEAH. WEAR-ING A JACKET FOR SOME CLUB.
BUT... AT THAT TIME OF DAY...
...HE SHOULD STILL HAVE BEEN AT THE PRE-SCHOOL...
PIYO
IT LOOKED LIKE HIM.
MAYBE HE QUIT THE SCHOOL.
BUT ...
PLASH
SSS
YIP
SO SORRY.
MY HAND SLIPPED.

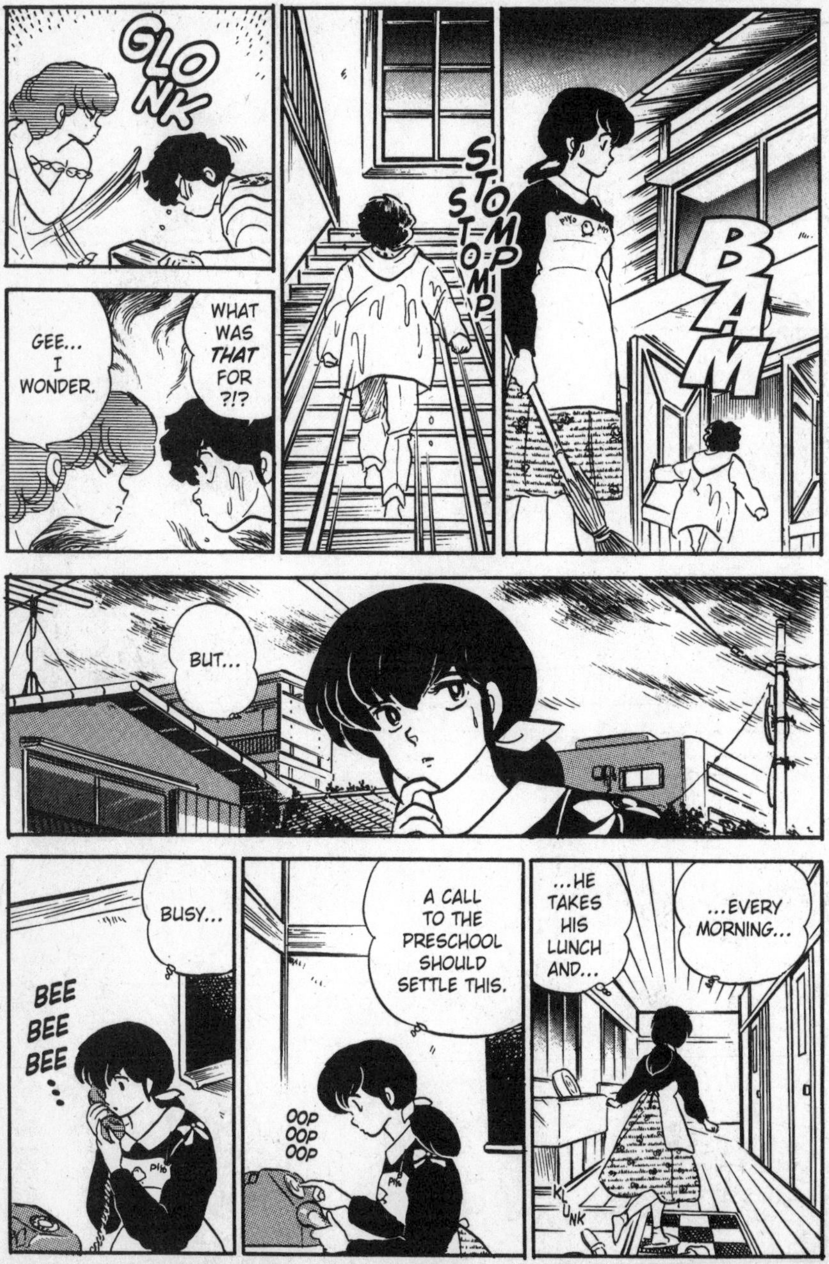
BAM
STOMP STOMP
GLONK
WHAT WAS *THAT* FOR ?!?
GEE... I WONDER.
BUT...
...EVERY MORNING...
...HE TAKES HIS LUNCH AND...
KLUNK
A CALL TO THE PRESCHOOL SHOULD SETTLE THIS.
OOP OOP OOP
BUSY...
BEE BEE BEE...

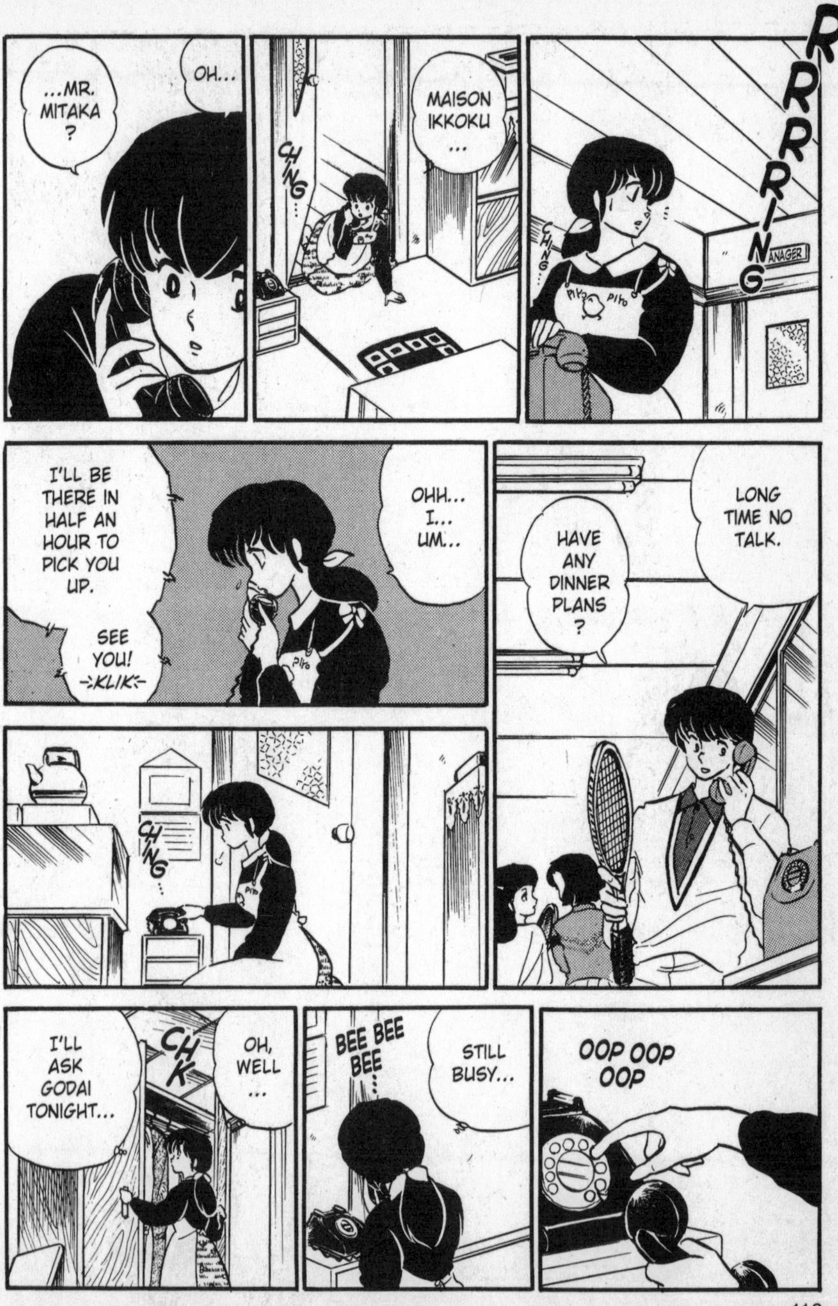
RRRRRING
ANAGER
CHING...
MAISON IKKOKU...
CHING...
OH...
...MR. MITAKA?
LONG TIME NO TALK.
HAVE ANY DINNER PLANS?
OHH... I... UM...
I'LL BE THERE IN HALF AN HOUR TO PICK YOU UP.
SEE YOU! -KLIK-
CHING...
OOP OOP OOP
STILL BUSY...
BEE BEE BEE...
OH, WELL...
CHK
I'LL ASK GODAI TONIGHT...

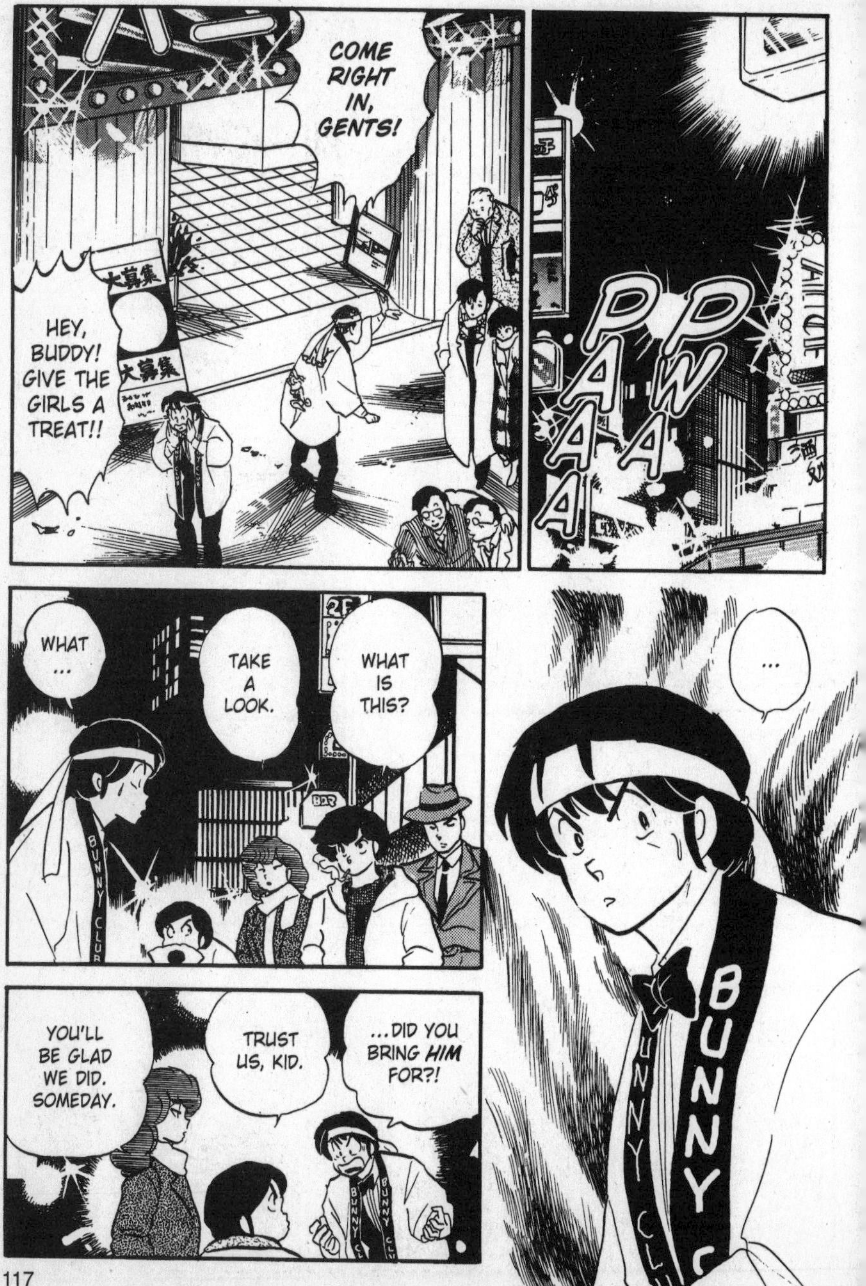
PAAAA
PWAA
COME RIGHT IN, GENTS!
HEY, BUDDY! GIVE THE GIRLS A TREAT!!
...
BUNNY C
WHAT IS THIS?
TAKE A LOOK.
WHAT ...
...DID YOU BRING *HIM* FOR?!
TRUST US, KID.
YOU'LL BE GLAD WE DID. SOMEDAY.

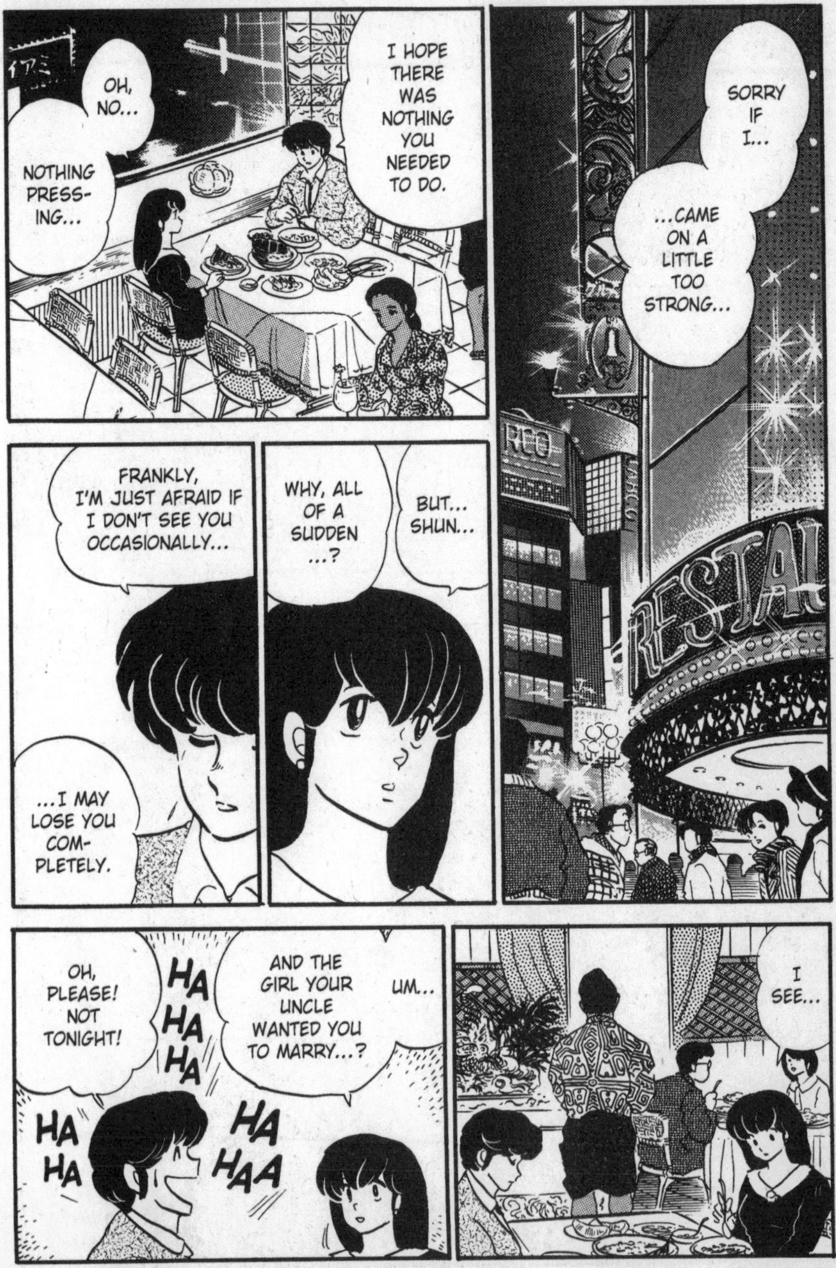
SORRY IF I...
...CAME ON A LITTLE TOO STRONG...
I HOPE THERE WAS NOTHING YOU NEEDED TO DO.
OH, NO...
NOTHING PRESSING...
BUT... SHUN...
WHY, ALL OF A SUDDEN...?
FRANKLY, I'M JUST AFRAID IF I DON'T SEE YOU OCCASIONALLY...
...I MAY LOSE YOU COMPLETELY.
I SEE...
UM...
AND THE GIRL YOUR UNCLE WANTED YOU TO MARRY...?
HA HA HA
OH, PLEASE! NOT TONIGHT!
HA HAA
HA HA

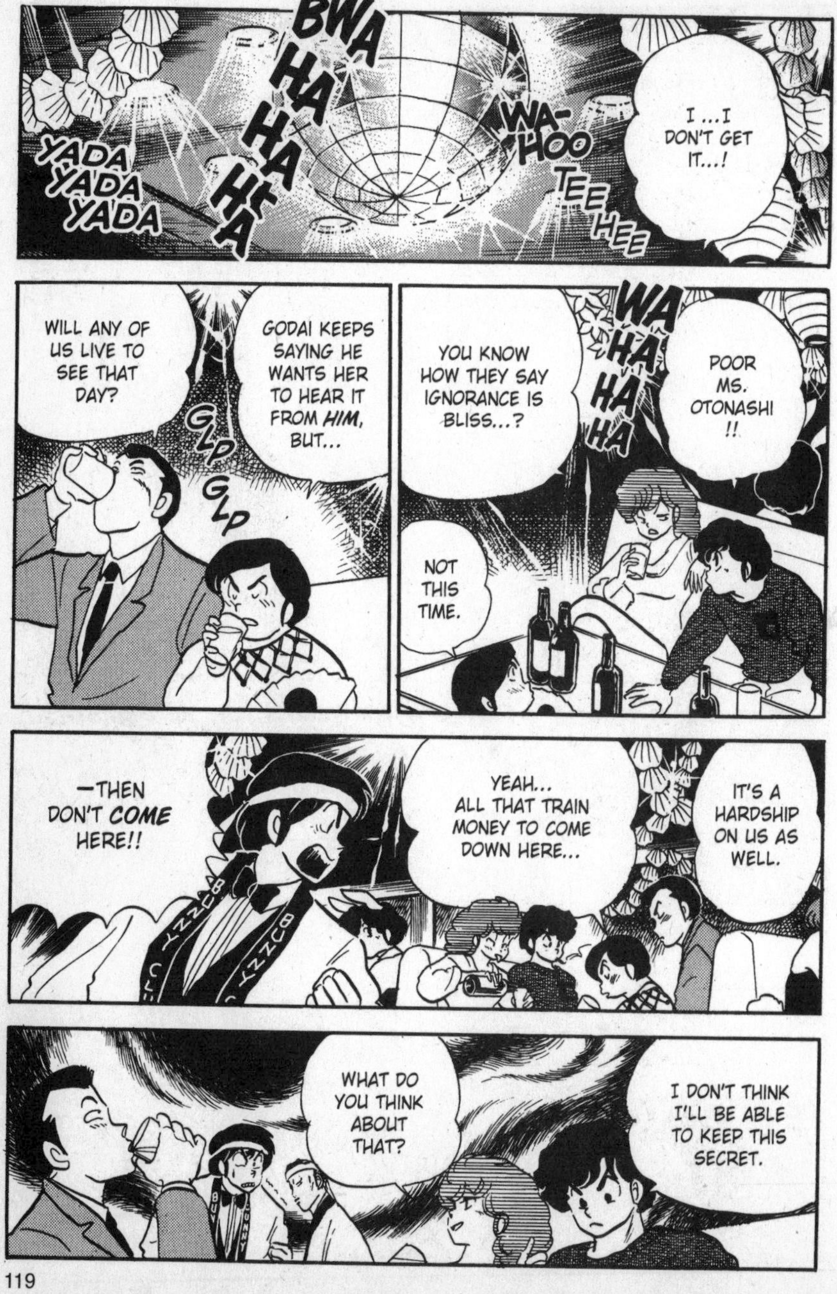

I ...I DON'T GET IT...!
WA-HOO
TEE HEE
BWA HA HA HA HA
YADA YADA YADA
POOR MS. OTONASHI !!
WA HA HA HA HA
YOU KNOW HOW THEY SAY IGNORANCE IS BLISS...?
NOT THIS TIME.
GODAI KEEPS SAYING HE WANTS HER TO HEAR IT FROM *HIM*, BUT...
WILL ANY OF US LIVE TO SEE THAT DAY?
GLP GLP
IT'S A HARDSHIP ON US AS WELL.
YEAH... ALL THAT TRAIN MONEY TO COME DOWN HERE...
—THEN DON'T *COME* HERE!!
I DON'T THINK I'LL BE ABLE TO KEEP THIS SECRET.
WHAT DO YOU THINK ABOUT THAT?

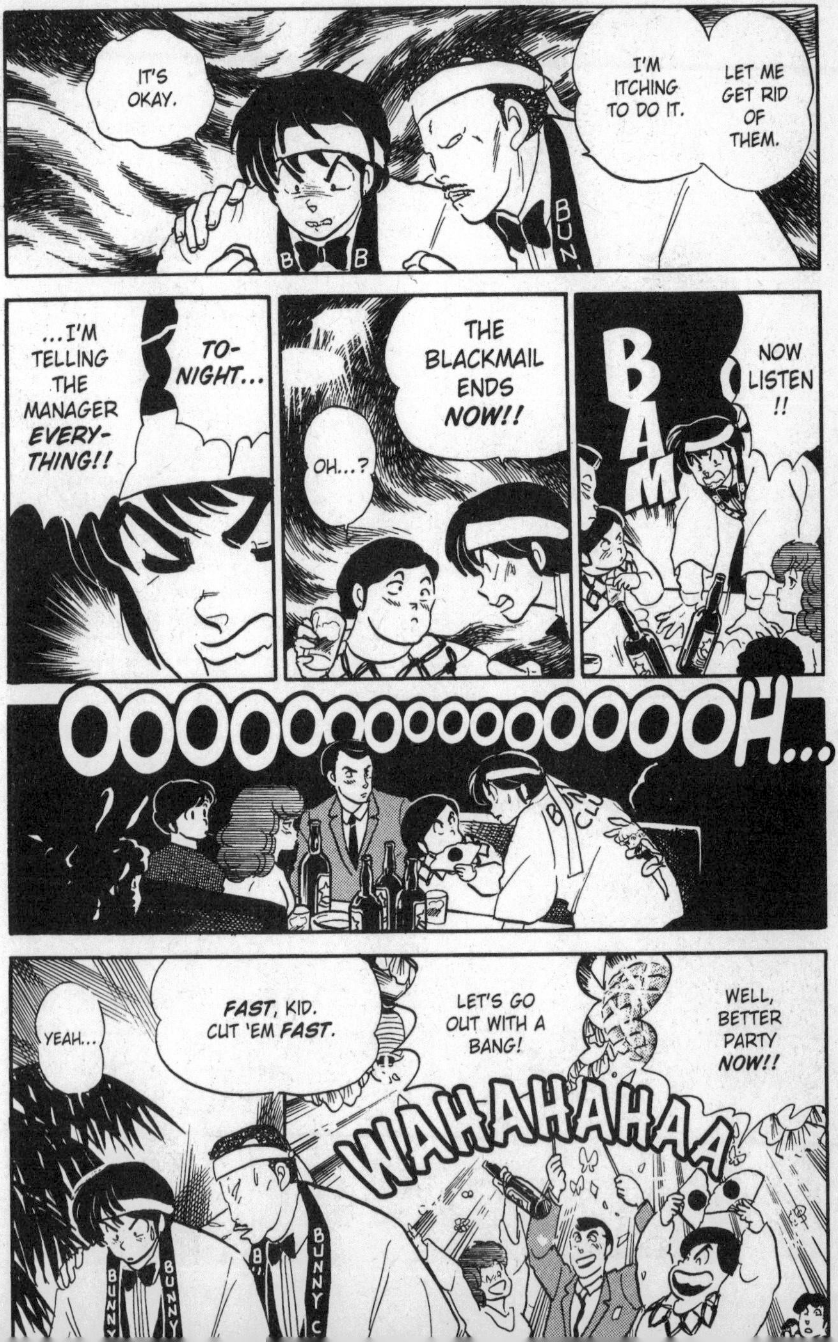
LET ME GET RID OF THEM.
I'M ITCHING TO DO IT.
IT'S OKAY.
NOW LISTEN !!
BAM
THE BLACKMAIL ENDS *NOW!!*
OH...?
TO-NIGHT...
...I'M TELLING THE MANAGER *EVERYTHING!!*
OOOOOOOOOOOOOOH...
WELL, BETTER PARTY *NOW!!*
LET'S GO OUT WITH A BANG!
WAHAHAHAHAA
FAST, KID. CUT 'EM *FAST*.
YEAH...

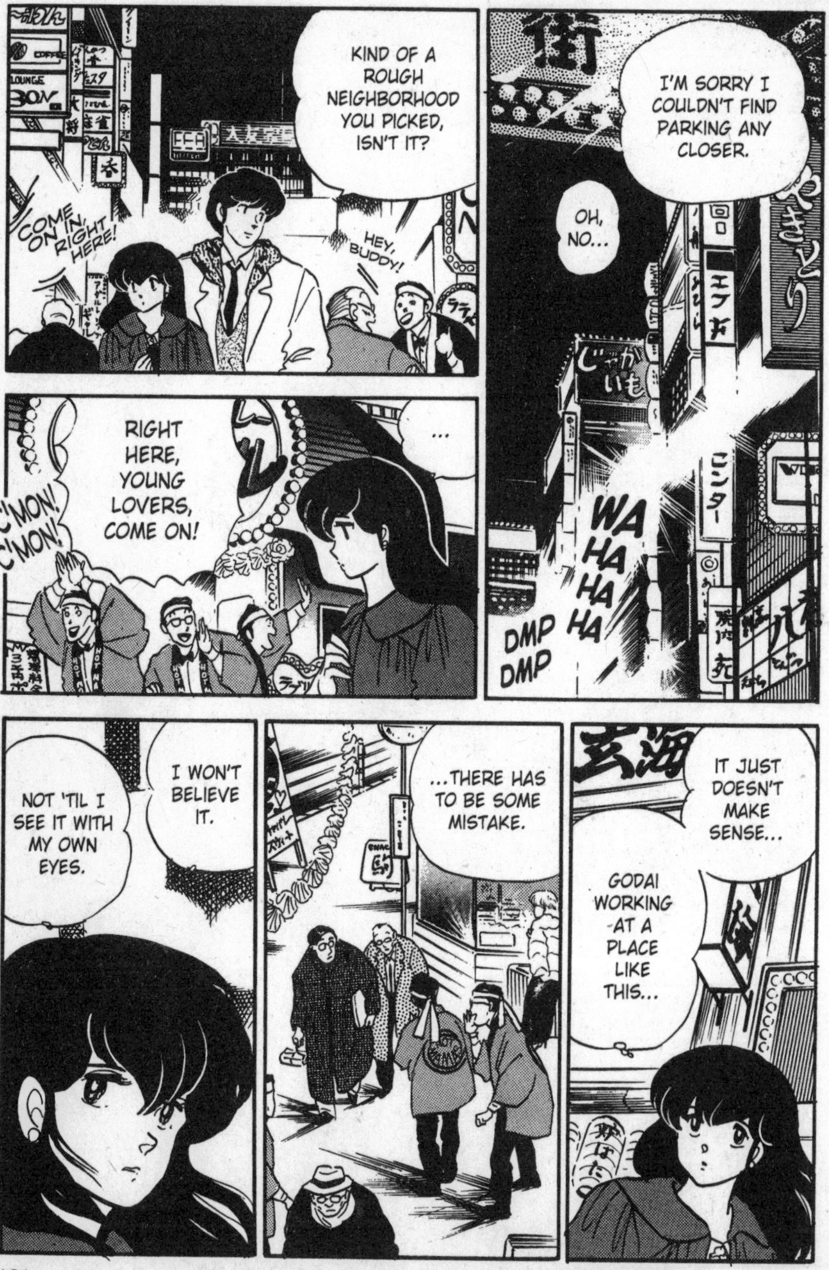
I'M SORRY I COULDN'T FIND PARKING ANY CLOSER.
OH, NO...
WA HA HA HA
DMP DMP
KIND OF A ROUGH NEIGHBORHOOD YOU PICKED, ISN'T IT?
HEY, BUDDY!
COME ON IN, RIGHT HERE!
...
RIGHT HERE, YOUNG LOVERS, COME ON!
C'MON! C'MON!
IT JUST DOESN'T MAKE SENSE...
GODAI WORKING AT A PLACE LIKE THIS...
...THERE HAS TO BE SOME MISTAKE.
I WON'T BELIEVE IT.
NOT 'TIL I SEE IT WITH MY OWN EYES.

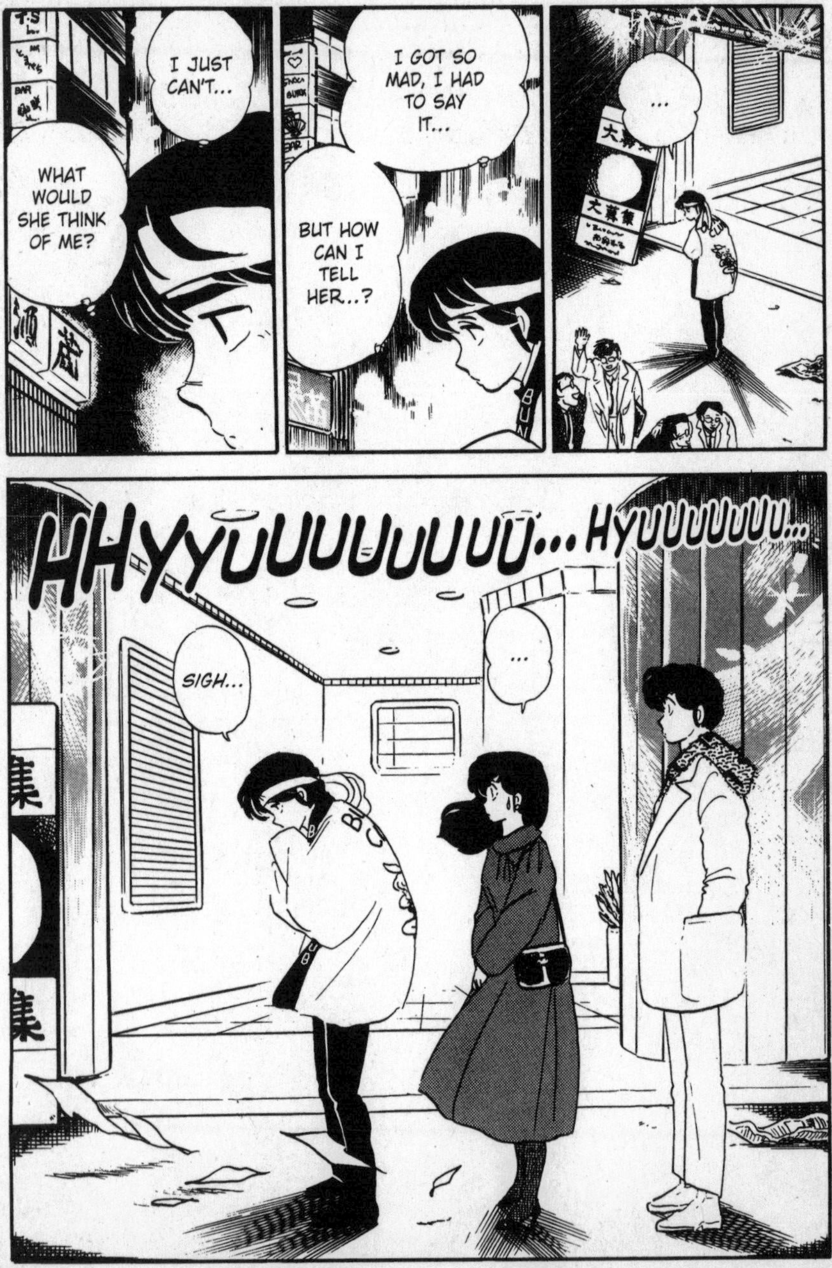
...
I GOT SO MAD, I HAD TO SAY IT...
BUT HOW CAN I TELL HER...?
I JUST CAN'T...
WHAT WOULD SHE THINK OF ME?
HHYYUUUUUUUUU... HYUUUUUUUU...
...
SIGH...

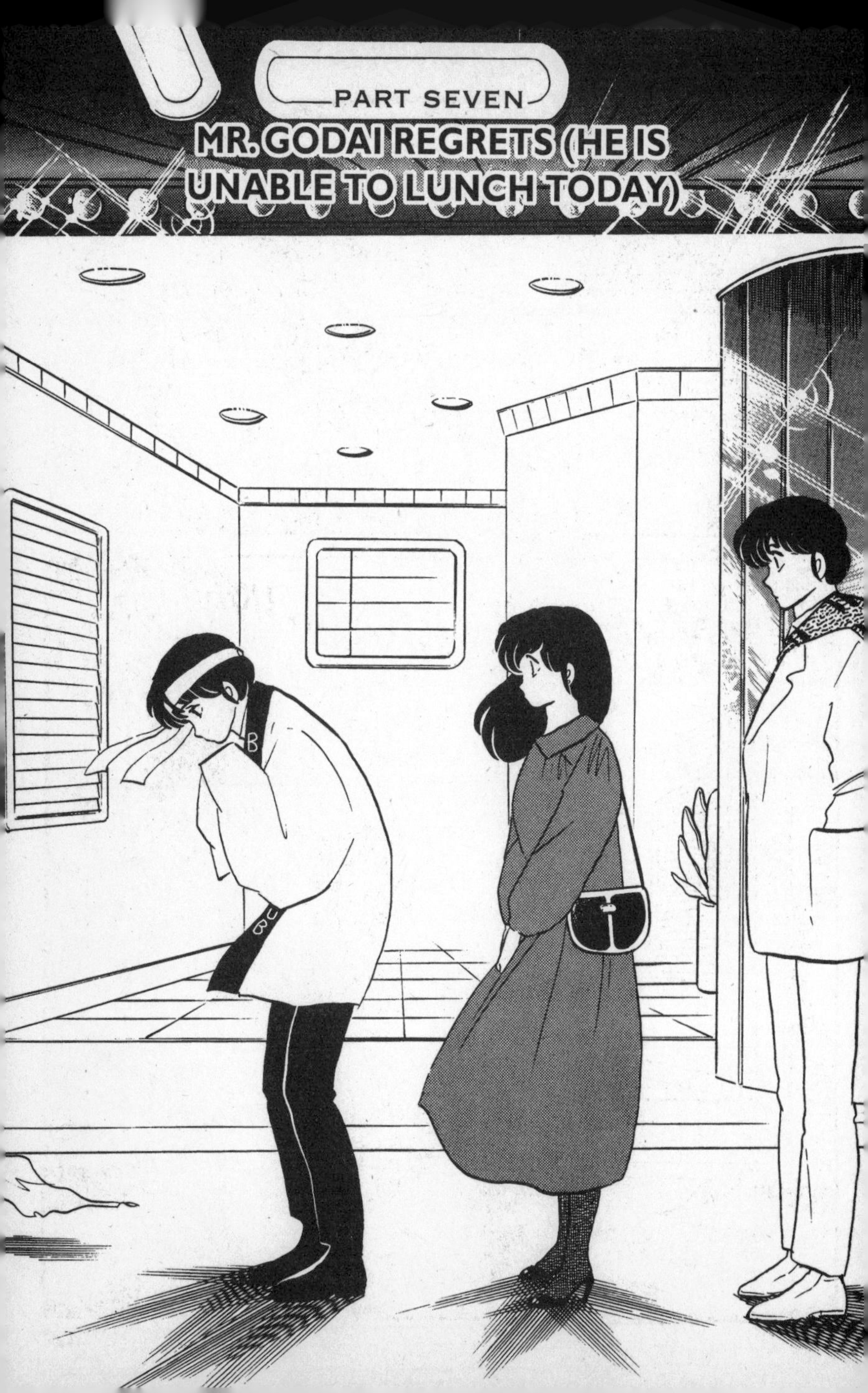
PART SEVEN
MR. GODAI REGRETS (HE IS
UNABLE TO LUNCH TODAY)

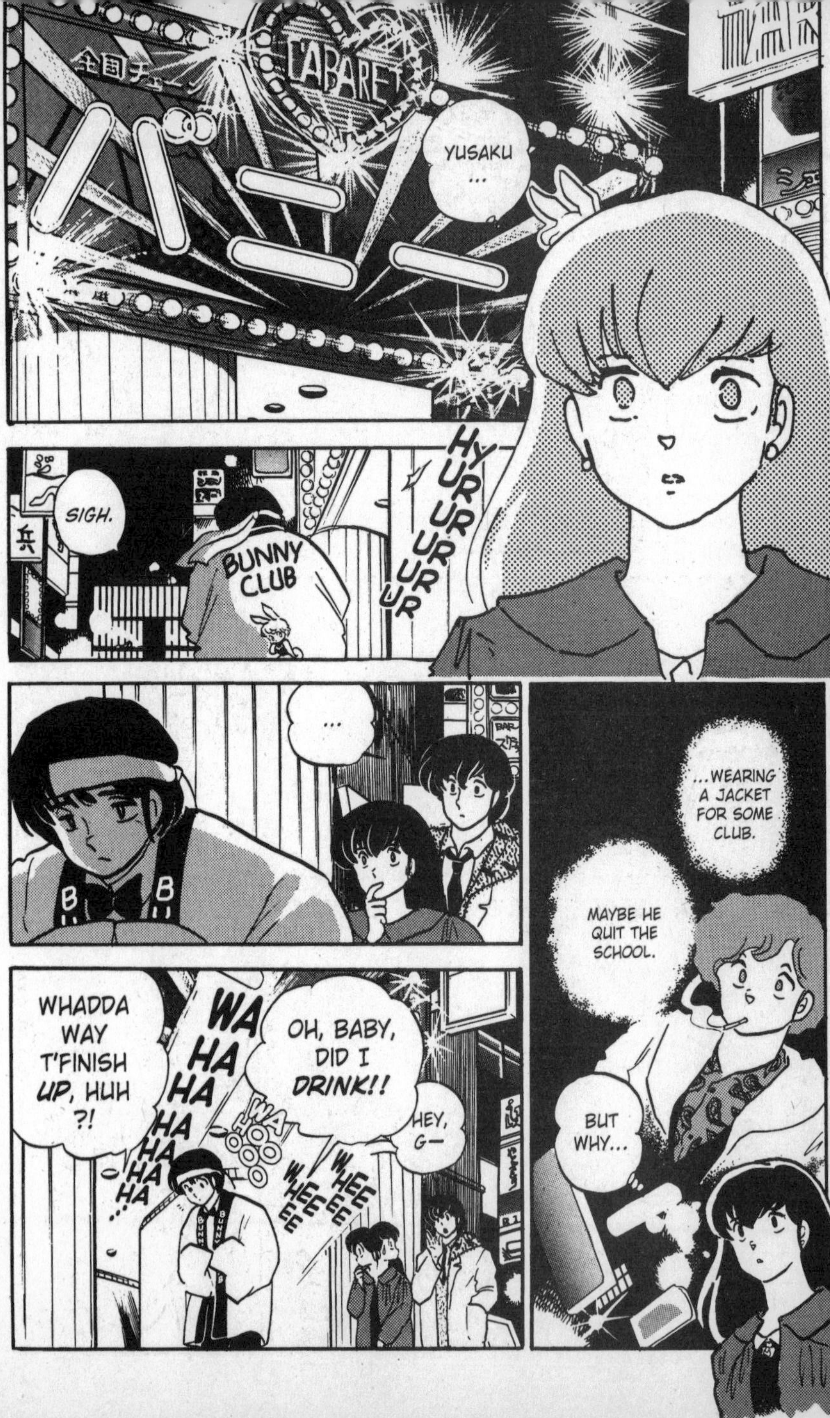
CABARET
YUSAKU ...
SIGH.
BUNNY CLUB
HYURURURURURUR
...WEARING A JACKET FOR SOME CLUB.
MAYBE HE QUIT THE SCHOOL.
BUT WHY...
...
OH, BABY, DID I DRINK!!
HEY, G—
WAHOOOOO
WHEEEE
WHEEEE
WAHAHAHAHAHAHAHA...
WHADDA WAY T'FINISH UP, HUH ?!
BAR

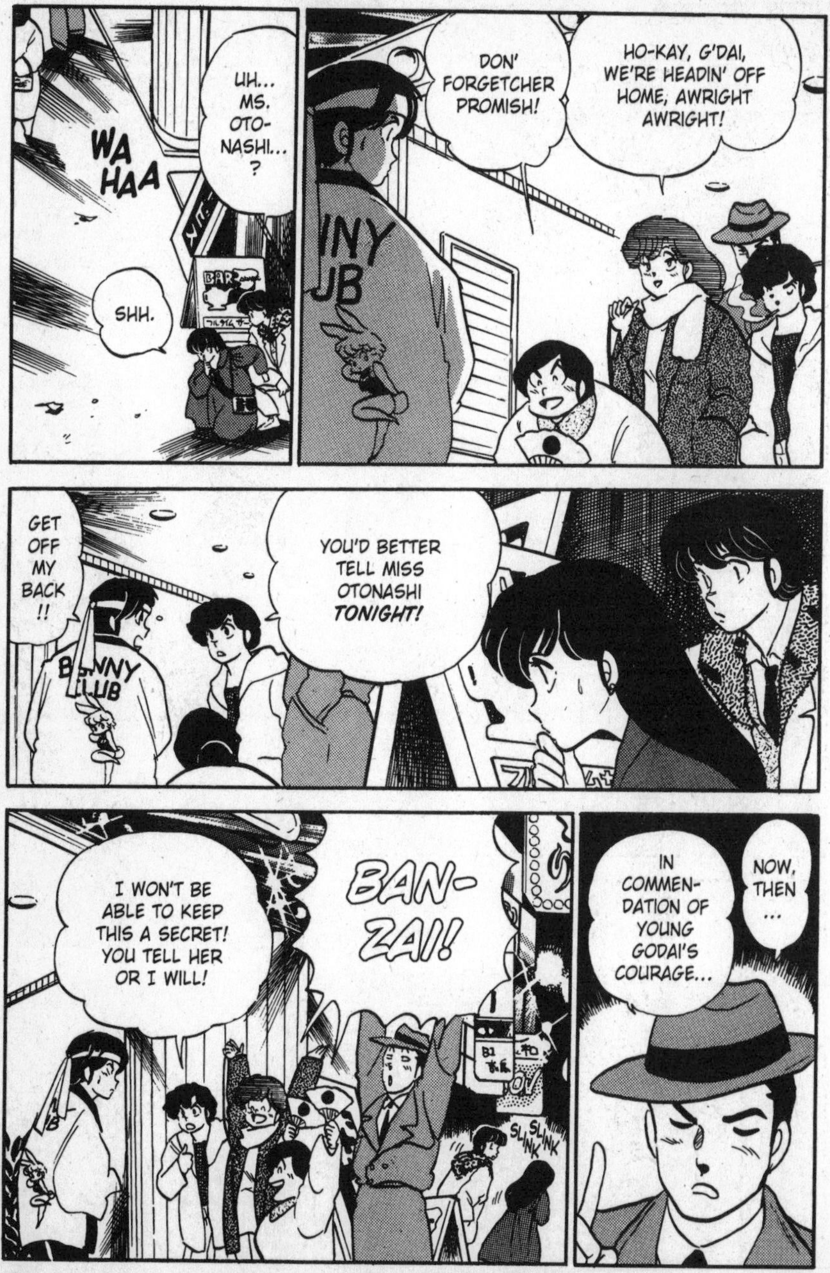
HO-KAY, G'DAI, WE'RE HEADIN' OFF HOME, AWRIGHT AWRIGHT!
DON' FORGETCHER PROMISH!
UH... MS. OTO-NASHI...?
WA HAA
SHH.
YOU'D BETTER TELL MISS OTONASHI *TONIGHT!*
!
GET OFF MY BACK!!
NOW, THEN...
IN COMMENDATION OF YOUNG GODAI'S COURAGE...
BAN-ZAI!
I WON'T BE ABLE TO KEEP THIS A SECRET! YOU TELL HER OR I WILL!
SLINK SLINK

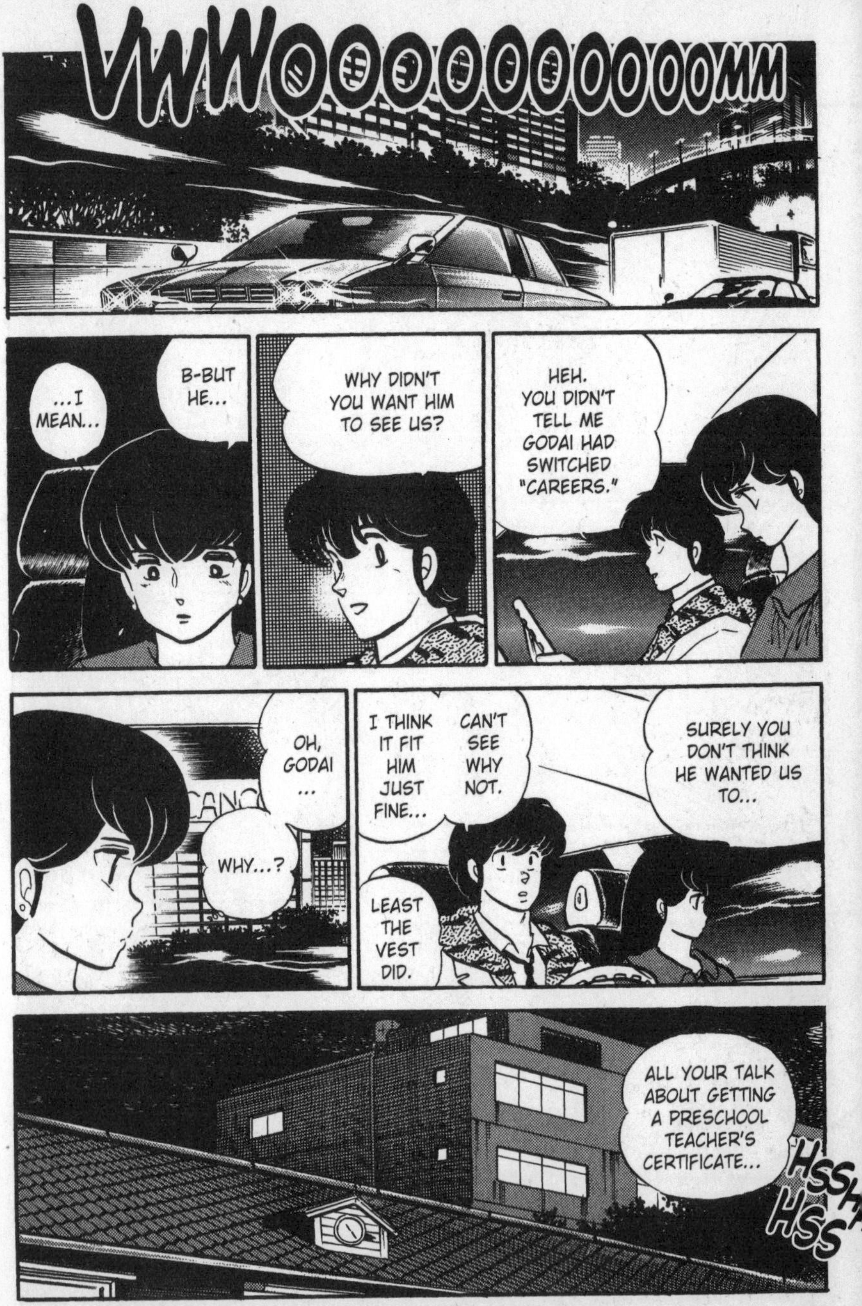

VWWOOOOOOOOOOOMM
HEH. YOU DIDN'T TELL ME GODAI HAD SWITCHED "CAREERS."
WHY DIDN'T YOU WANT HIM TO SEE US?
B-BUT HE...
...I MEAN...
SURELY YOU DON'T THINK HE WANTED US TO...
CAN'T SEE WHY NOT.
I THINK IT FIT HIM JUST FINE...
LEAST THE VEST DID.
OH, GODAI ...
WHY...?
ALL YOUR TALK ABOUT GETTING A PRESCHOOL TEACHER'S CERTIFICATE...
HSSH, HSS

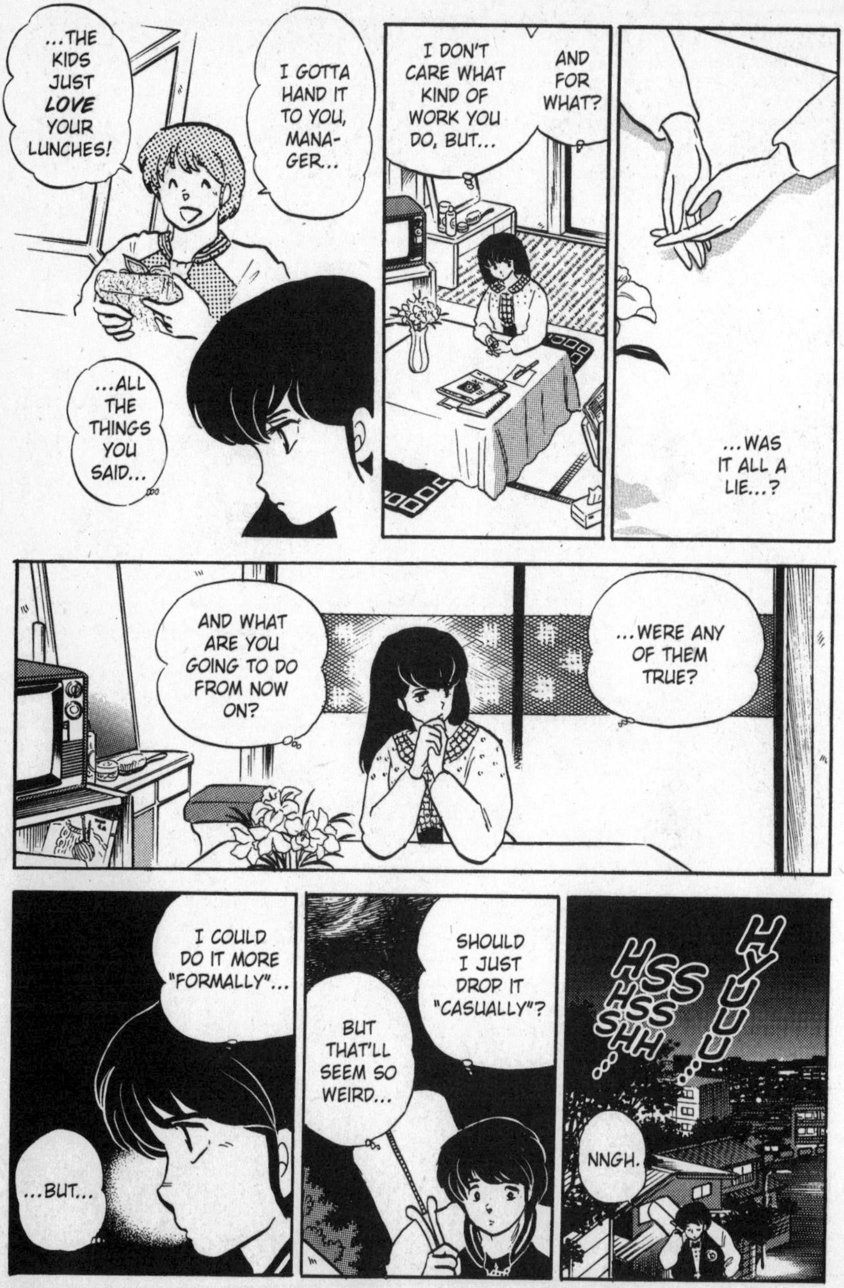
...WAS IT ALL A LIE...?
I DON'T CARE WHAT KIND OF WORK YOU DO, BUT...
AND FOR WHAT?
I GOTTA HAND IT TO YOU, MANAGER...
...THE KIDS JUST **LOVE** YOUR LUNCHES!
...ALL THE THINGS YOU SAID...
...WERE ANY OF THEM TRUE?
AND WHAT ARE YOU GOING TO DO FROM NOW ON?
HYUUU...
HSS HSS SHH...
NNGH.
SHOULD I JUST DROP IT "CASUALLY"?
BUT THAT'LL SEEM SO WEIRD...
I COULD DO IT MORE "FORMALLY"...
...BUT...

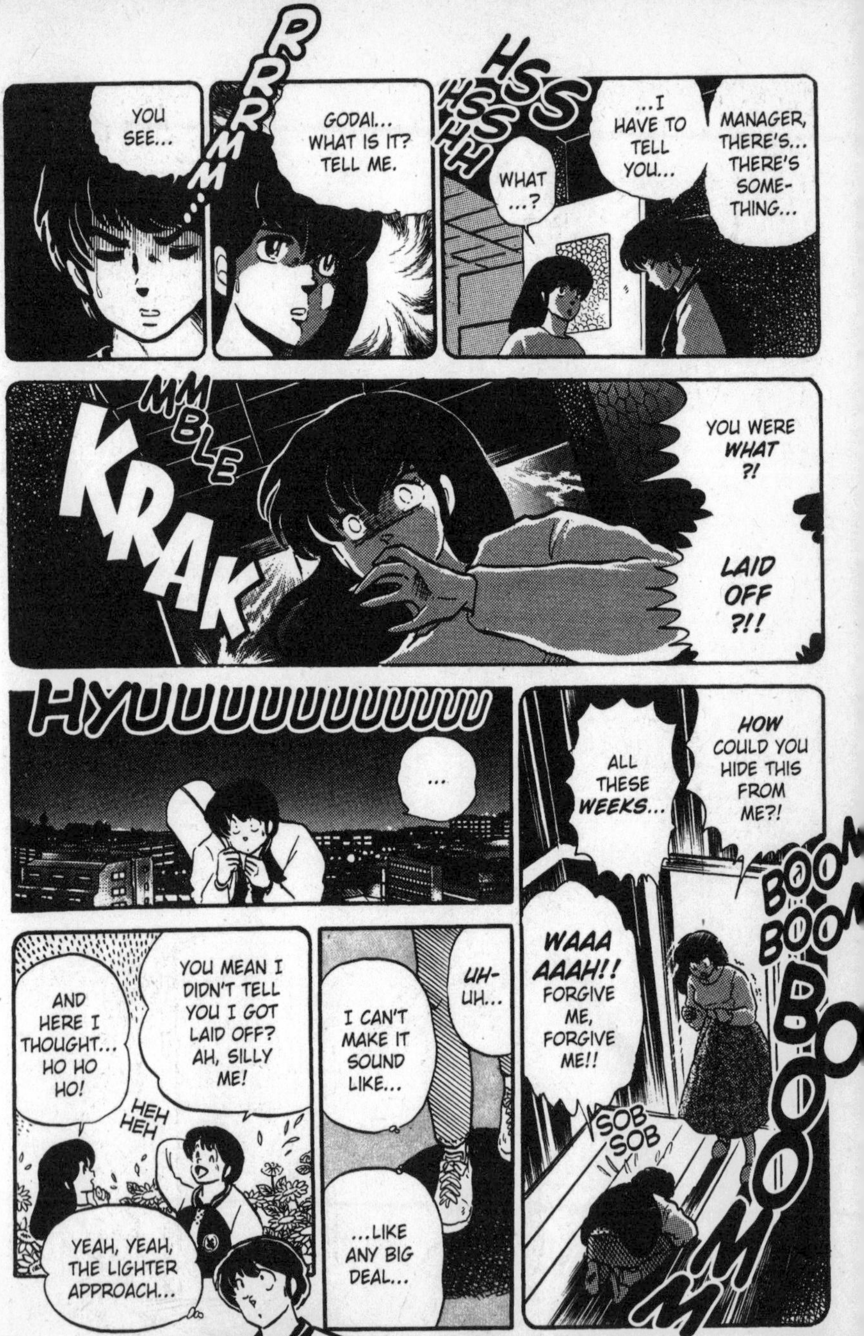
HSS
HSS
HH
MANAGER, THERE'S... THERE'S SOME-THING...
...I HAVE TO TELL YOU...
WHAT ...?
RRRMMM...
GODAI... WHAT IS IT? TELL ME.
YOU SEE...
YOU WERE *WHAT* ?!
LAID OFF ?!!
MMBLE
KRAK
HOW COULD YOU HIDE THIS FROM ME?!
ALL THESE *WEEKS*...
WAAA AAAH!! FORGIVE ME, FORGIVE ME!!
SOB SOB
BOOM
BOOM
HYUUUUUUUUUUUU
...
UH-UH...
I CAN'T MAKE IT SOUND LIKE...
...LIKE ANY BIG DEAL...
YOU MEAN I DIDN'T TELL YOU I GOT LAID OFF? AH, SILLY ME!
AND HERE I THOUGHT... HO HO HO!
HEH HEH
YEAH, YEAH, THE LIGHTER APPROACH...

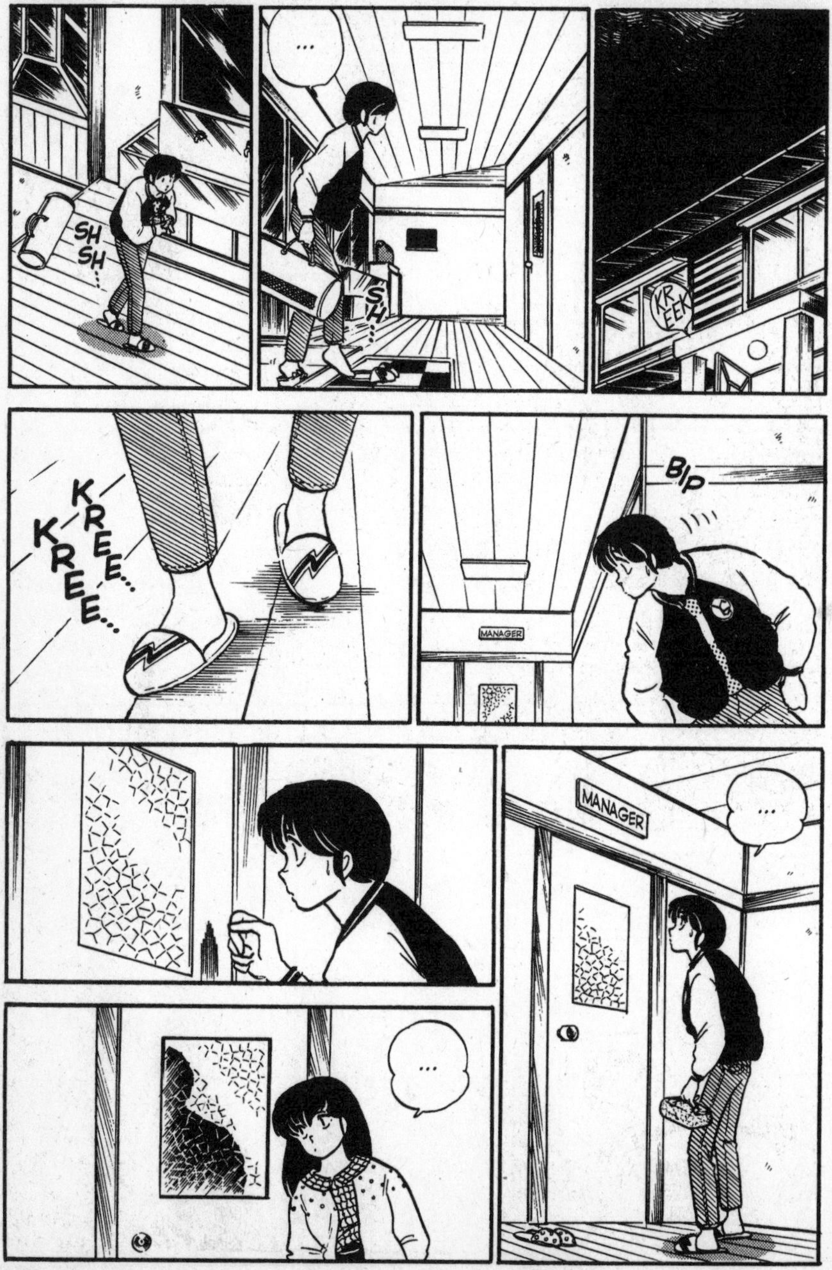
KREEK
...
SH...
SH SH...
BIP
MANAGER
KREE... KREE...
MANAGER
...
...

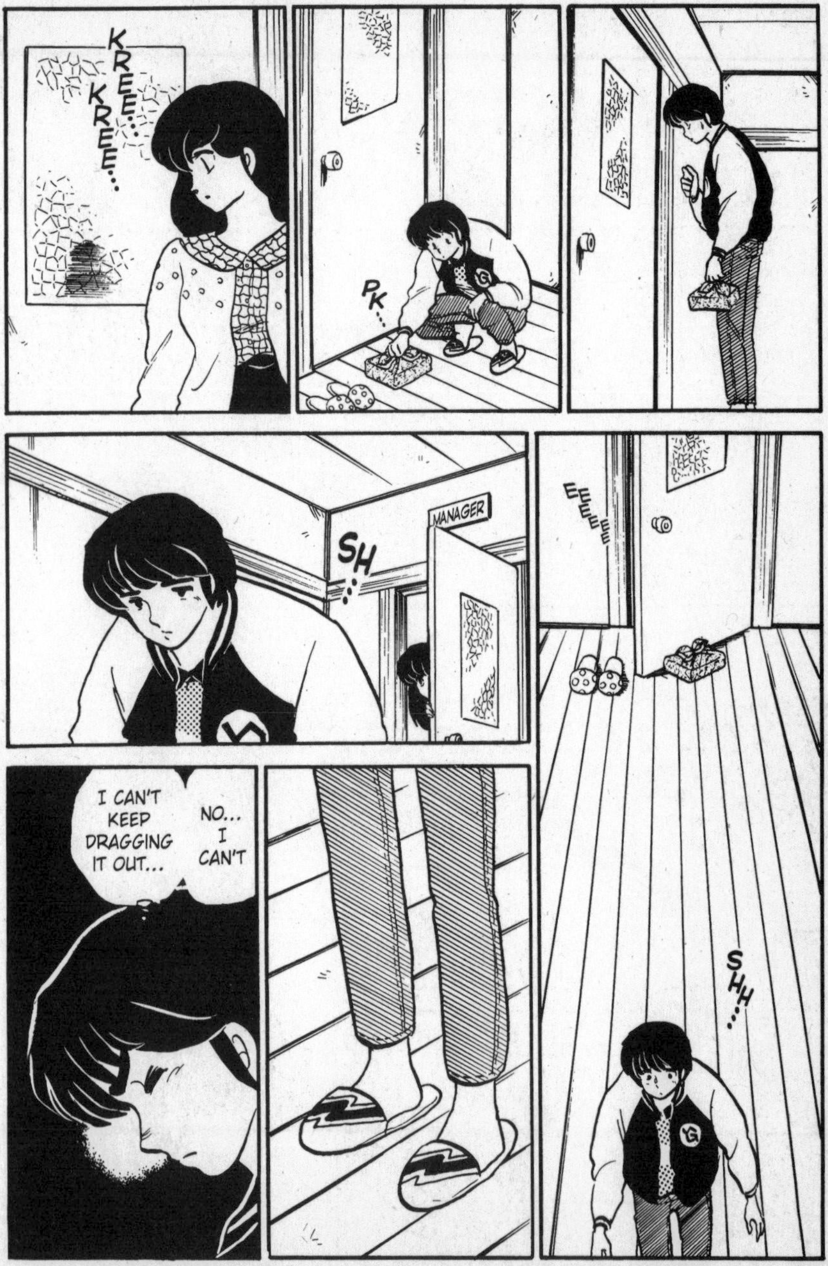
PK...
KREE... KREE...
EEEEE
SHH...
MANAGER
SH...
NO... I CAN'T
I CAN'T KEEP DRAGGING IT OUT...

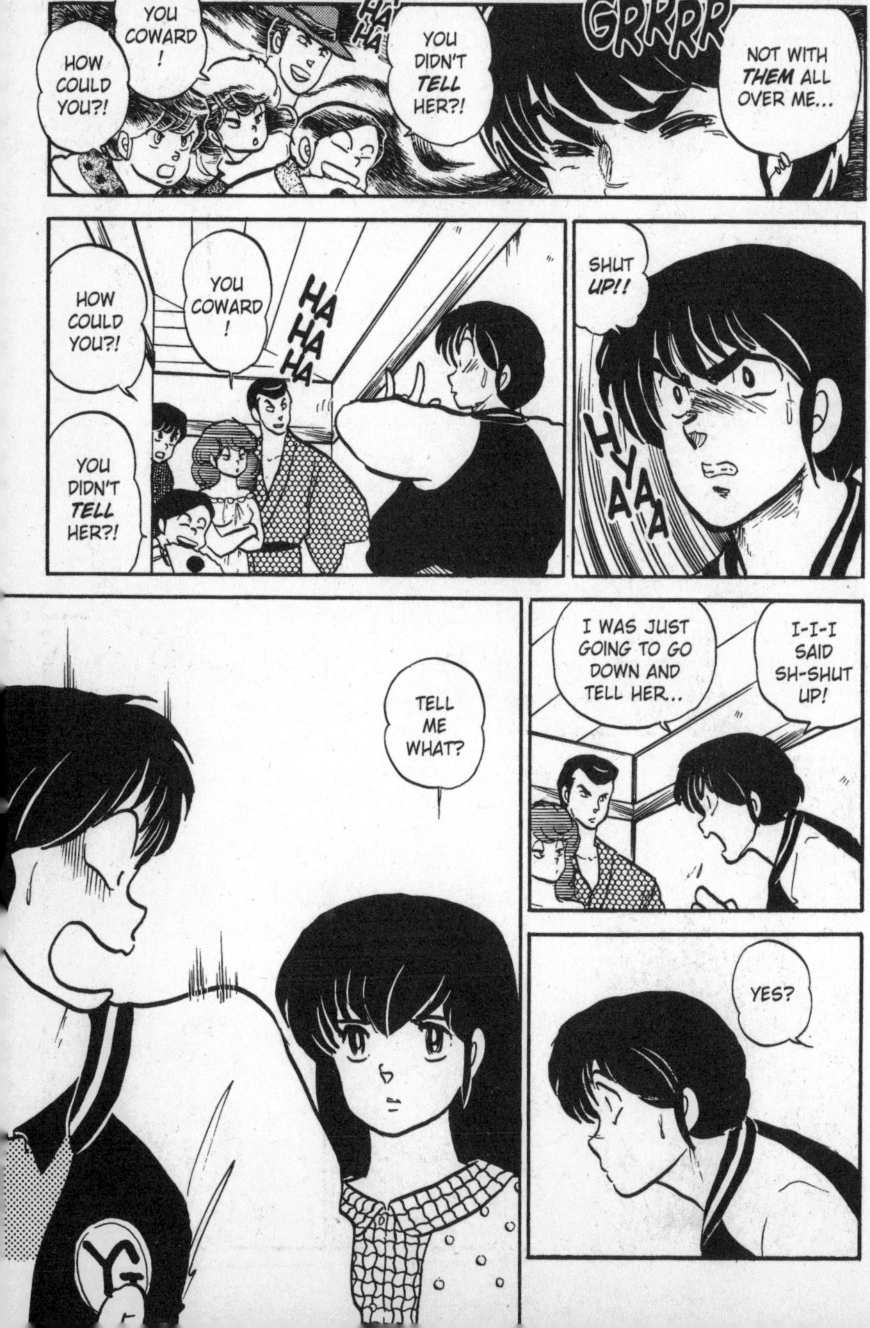
GRRRR
NOT WITH THEM ALL OVER ME...
YOU DIDN'T TELL HER?!
HA HA HA
YOU COWARD!
HOW COULD YOU?!
SHUT UP!!
HYAAA
HAHAHA
YOU COWARD!
HOW COULD YOU?!
YOU DIDN'T TELL HER?!
I-I-I SAID SH-SHUT UP!
I WAS JUST GOING TO GO DOWN AND TELL HER...
YES?
TELL ME WHAT?

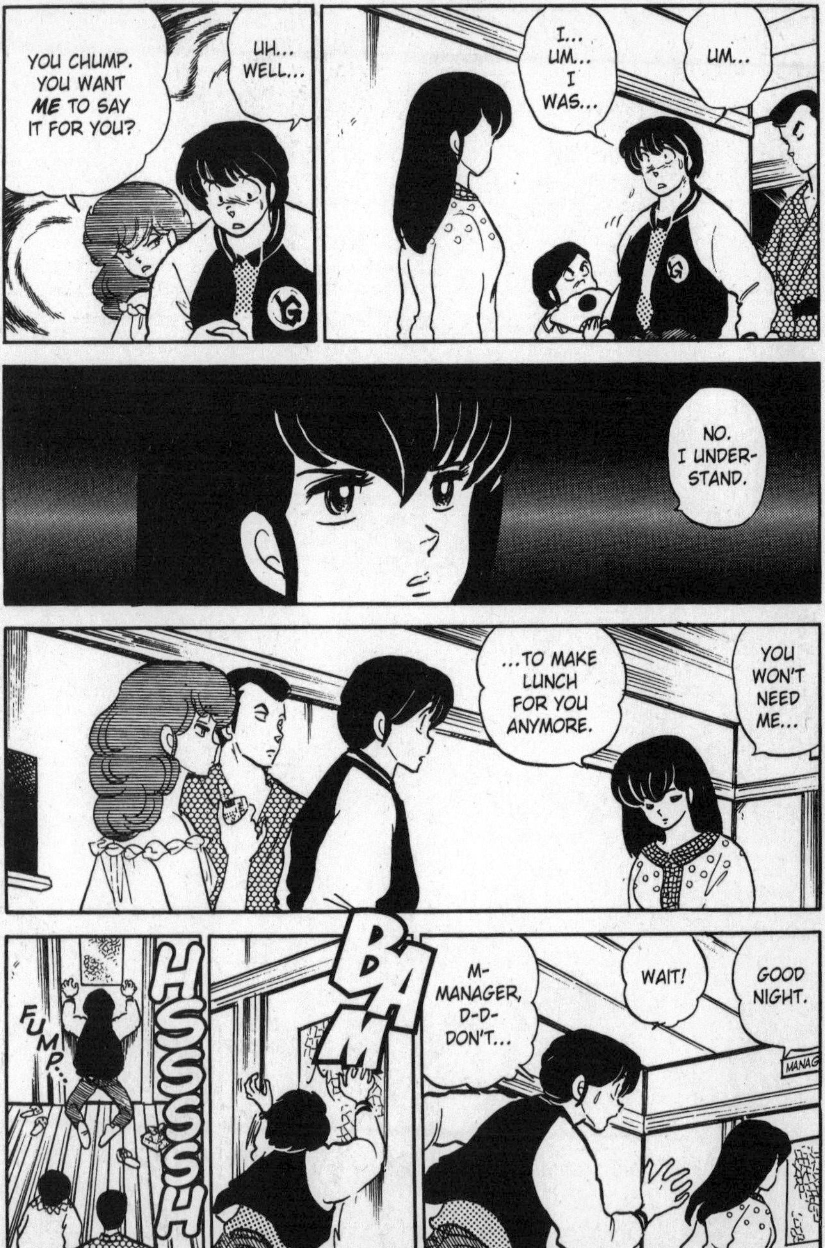
UM...
I... UM... I WAS...
UH... WELL...
YOU CHUMP. YOU WANT ME TO SAY IT FOR YOU?
NO. I UNDER-STAND.
YOU WON'T NEED ME...
...TO MAKE LUNCH FOR YOU ANYMORE.
GOOD NIGHT.
MANAG
WAIT!
M-MANAGER, D-D-DON'T...
BAM
HSSSSH
FUMP...

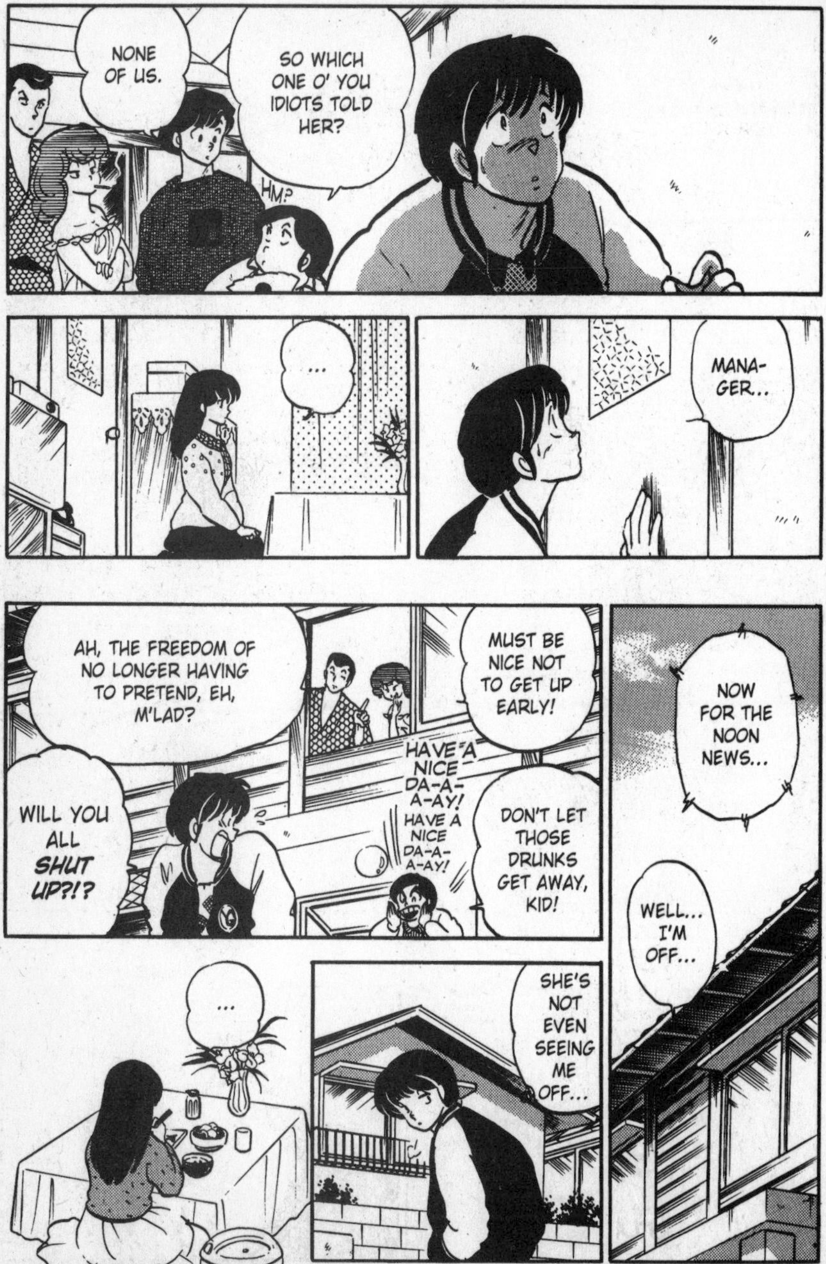
SO WHICH ONE O' YOU IDIOTS TOLD HER?
NONE OF US.
HM?
MANA-GER...
...
NOW FOR THE NOON NEWS...
WELL... I'M OFF...
MUST BE NICE NOT TO GET UP EARLY!
AH, THE FREEDOM OF NO LONGER HAVING TO PRETEND, EH, M'LAD?
DON'T LET THOSE DRUNKS GET AWAY, KID!
HAVE A NICE DA-A-A-AY!
HAVE A NICE DA-A-A-AY!
WILL YOU ALL SHUT UP?!?
SHE'S NOT EVEN SEEING ME OFF...
...

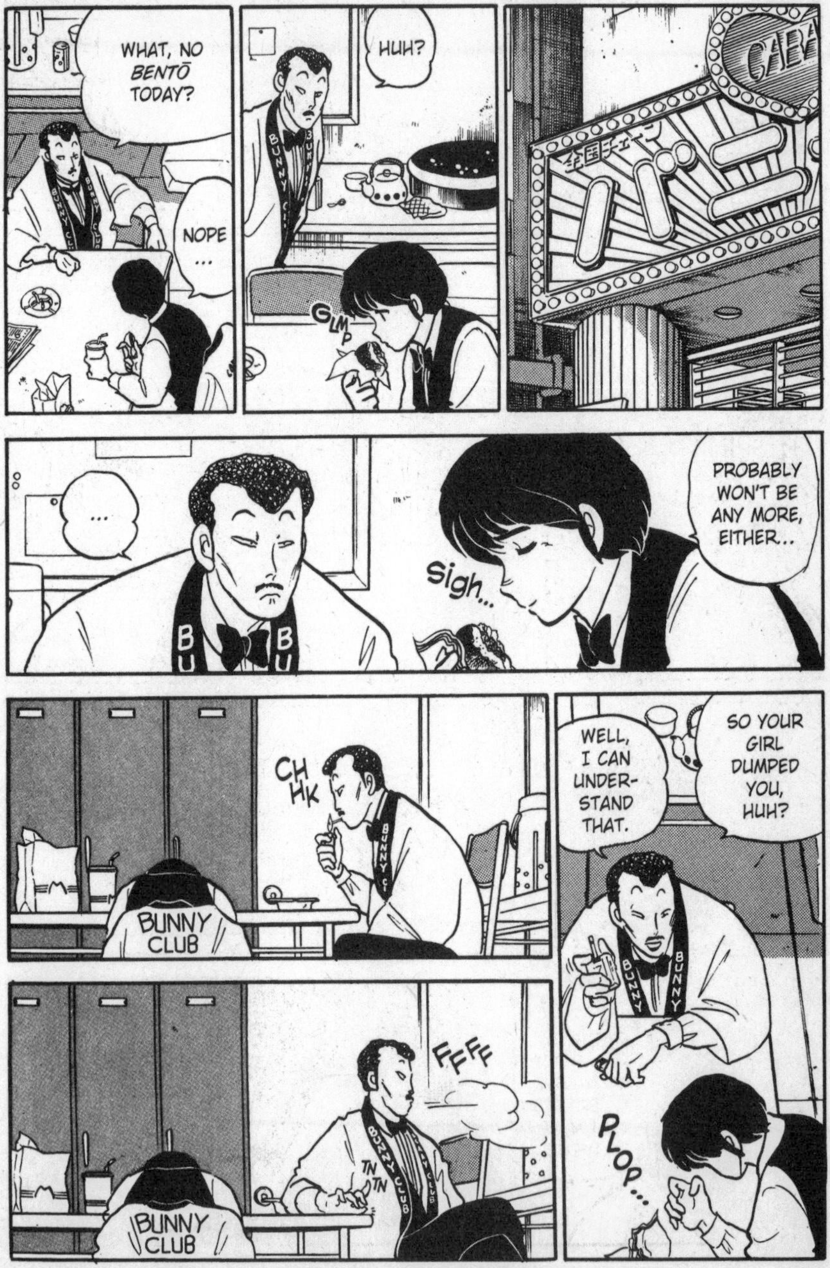
WHAT, NO BENTŌ TODAY?
NOPE ...
HUH?
GLMP
...
Sigh...
PROBABLY WON'T BE ANY MORE, EITHER...
CHHK
BUNNY CLUB
TN TN
FFFF
SO YOUR GIRL DUMPED YOU, HUH?
WELL, I CAN UNDER-STAND THAT.
PLOP...

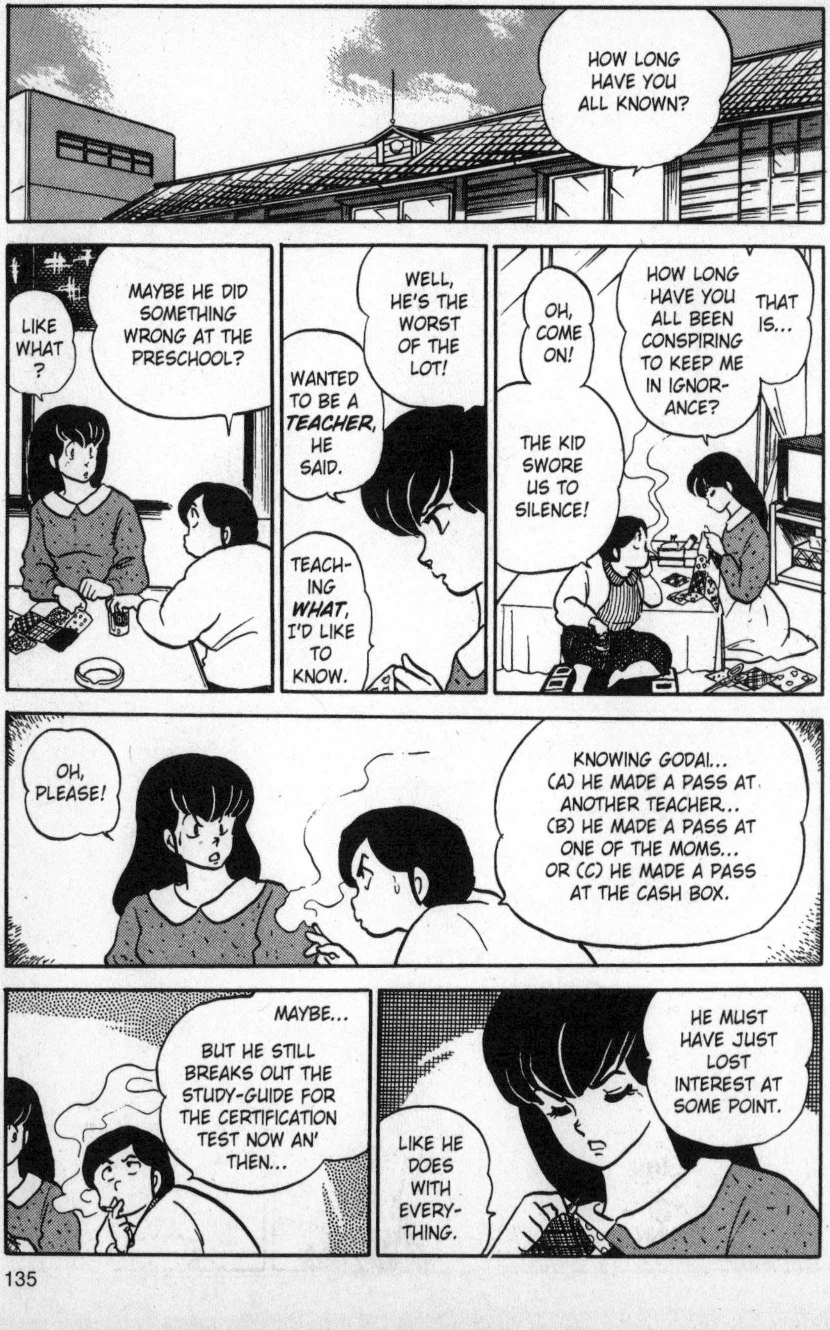
HOW LONG HAVE YOU ALL KNOWN?
THAT IS...
HOW LONG HAVE YOU ALL BEEN CONSPIRING TO KEEP ME IN IGNOR-ANCE?
OH, COME ON!
THE KID SWORE US TO SILENCE!
WELL, HE'S THE WORST OF THE LOT!
WANTED TO BE A *TEACHER*, HE SAID.
TEACH-ING *WHAT*, I'D LIKE TO KNOW.
MAYBE HE DID SOMETHING WRONG AT THE PRESCHOOL?
LIKE WHAT ?
KNOWING GODAI... (A) HE MADE A PASS AT ANOTHER TEACHER... (B) HE MADE A PASS AT ONE OF THE MOMS... OR (C) HE MADE A PASS AT THE CASH BOX.
OH, PLEASE!
HE MUST HAVE JUST LOST INTEREST AT SOME POINT.
LIKE HE DOES WITH EVERY-THING.
MAYBE...
BUT HE STILL BREAKS OUT THE STUDY-GUIDE FOR THE CERTIFICATION TEST NOW AN' THEN...

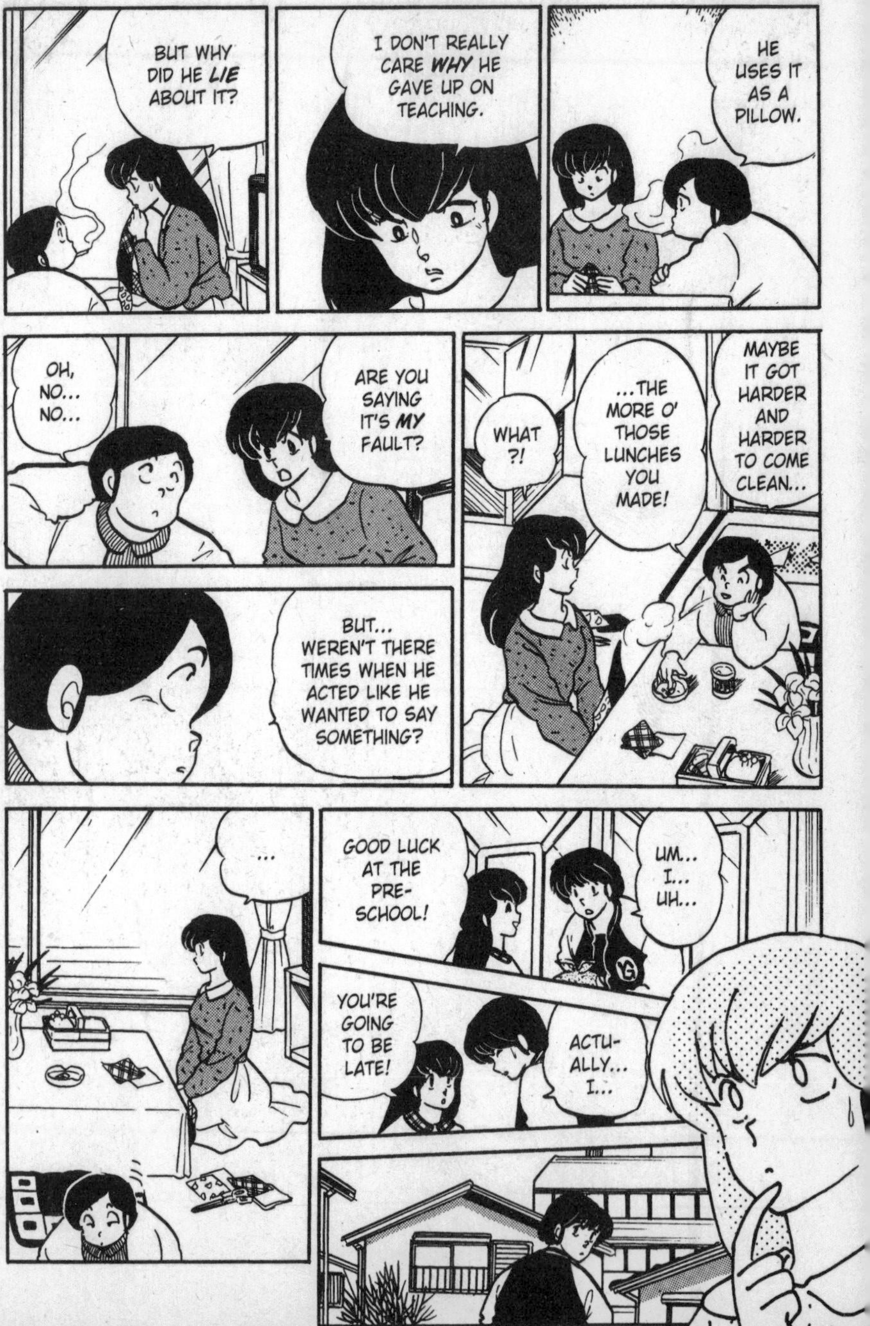
HE USES IT AS A PILLOW.
I DON'T REALLY CARE WHY HE GAVE UP ON TEACHING.
BUT WHY DID HE LIE ABOUT IT?
MAYBE IT GOT HARDER AND HARDER TO COME CLEAN...
...THE MORE O' THOSE LUNCHES YOU MADE!
WHAT?!
ARE YOU SAYING IT'S MY FAULT?
OH, NO... NO...
BUT... WEREN'T THERE TIMES WHEN HE ACTED LIKE HE WANTED TO SAY SOMETHING?
UM... I... UH...
GOOD LUCK AT THE PRE-SCHOOL!
ACTU-ALLY... I...
YOU'RE GOING TO BE LATE!
...

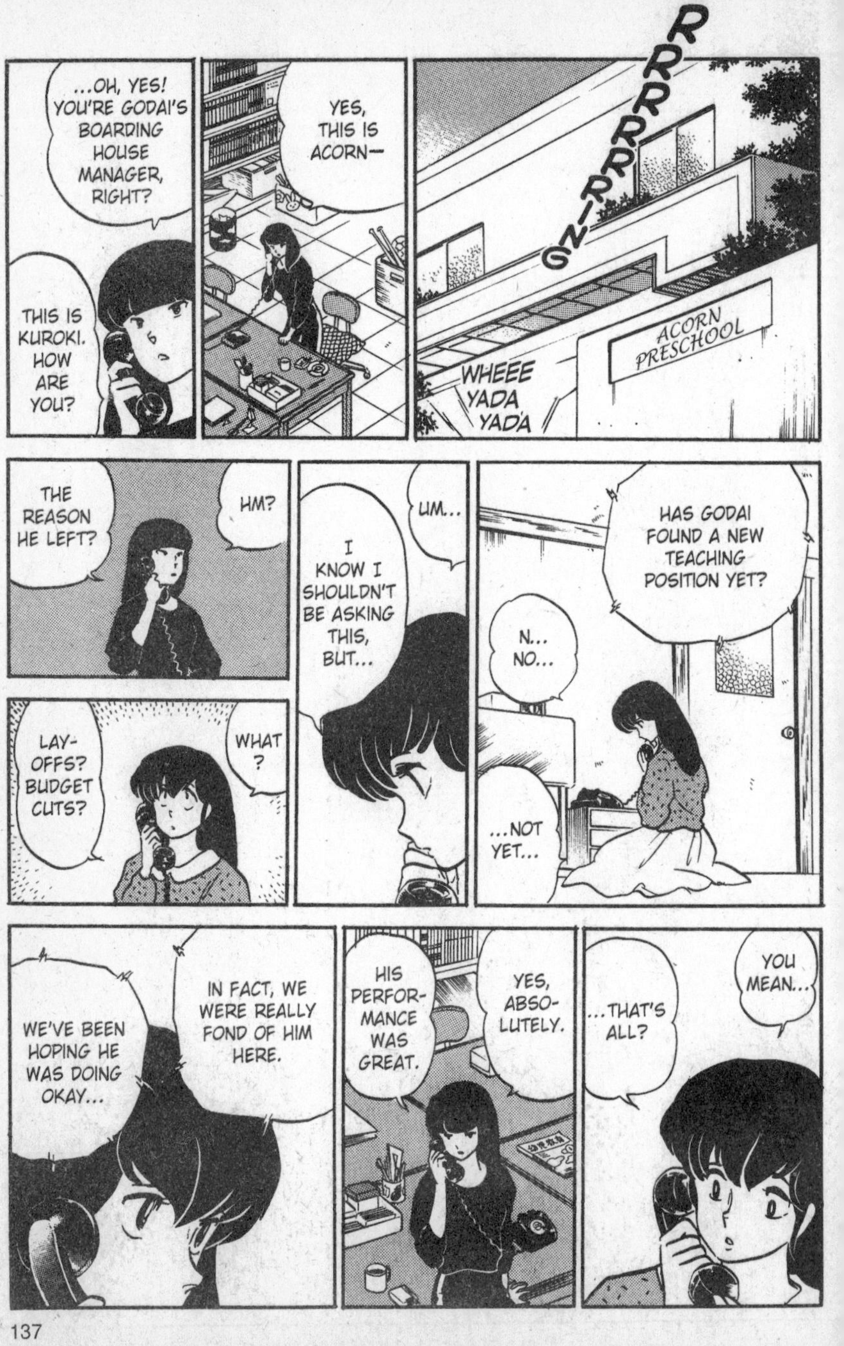
RRRRRRRING
ACORN PRESCHOOL
WHEEE YADA YADA
YES, THIS IS ACORN—
...OH, YES! YOU'RE GODAI'S BOARDING HOUSE MANAGER, RIGHT?
THIS IS KUROKI. HOW ARE YOU?
HAS GODAI FOUND A NEW TEACHING POSITION YET?
N... NO...
...NOT YET...
UM...
I KNOW I SHOULDN'T BE ASKING THIS, BUT...
HM?
THE REASON HE LEFT?
WHAT?
LAY-OFFS? BUDGET CUTS?
YOU MEAN...
...THAT'S ALL?
YES, ABSOLUTELY.
HIS PERFORMANCE WAS GREAT.
IN FACT, WE WERE REALLY FOND OF HIM HERE.
WE'VE BEEN HOPING HE WAS DOING OKAY...

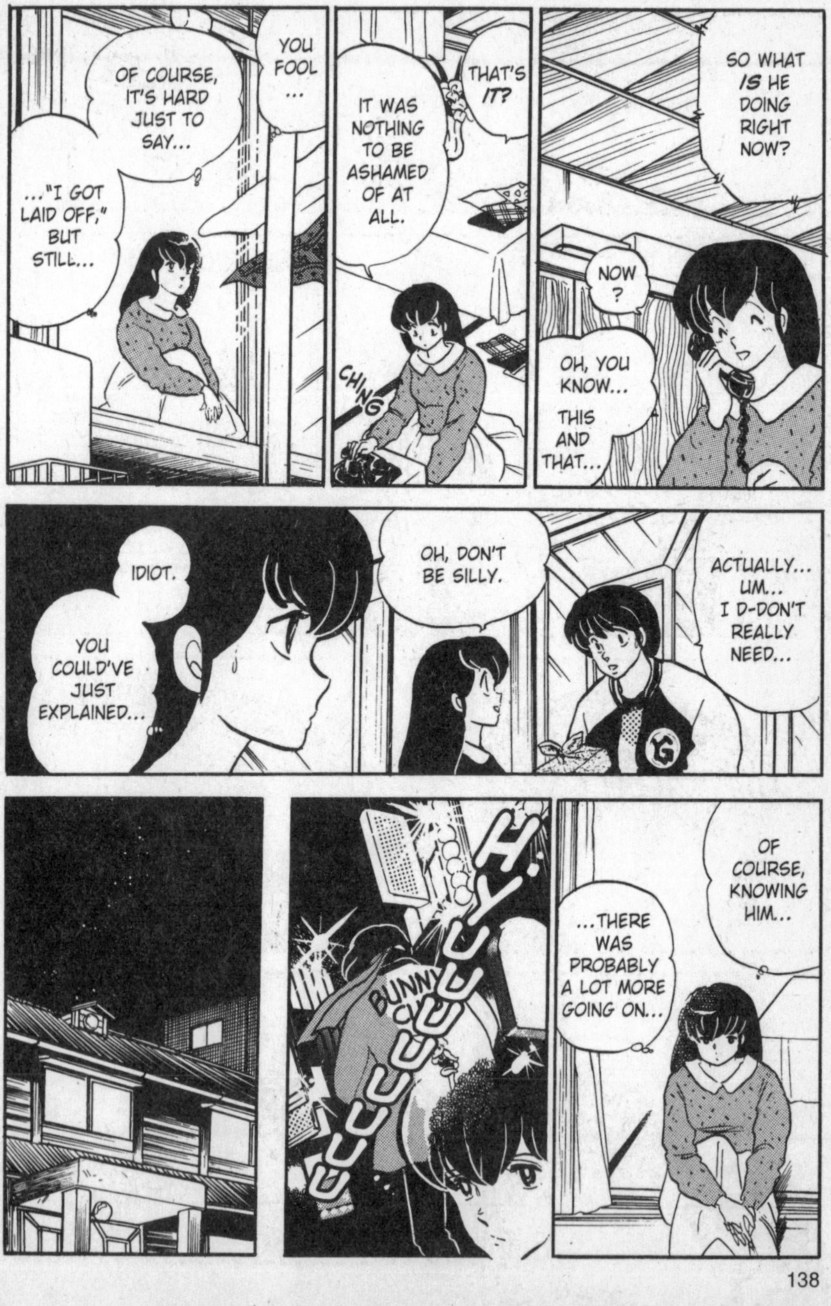
SO WHAT *IS* HE DOING RIGHT NOW?
NOW?
OH, YOU KNOW...
THIS AND THAT...
THAT'S *IT?*
IT WAS NOTHING TO BE ASHAMED OF AT ALL.
CHING
YOU FOOL ...
OF COURSE, IT'S HARD JUST TO SAY...
..."I GOT LAID OFF," BUT STILL...
ACTUALLY... UM... I D-DON'T REALLY NEED...
OH, DON'T BE SILLY.
IDIOT.
YOU COULD'VE JUST EXPLAINED...
OF COURSE, KNOWING HIM...
...THERE WAS PROBABLY A LOT MORE GOING ON...
HYUUUUUUUU
BUNNY

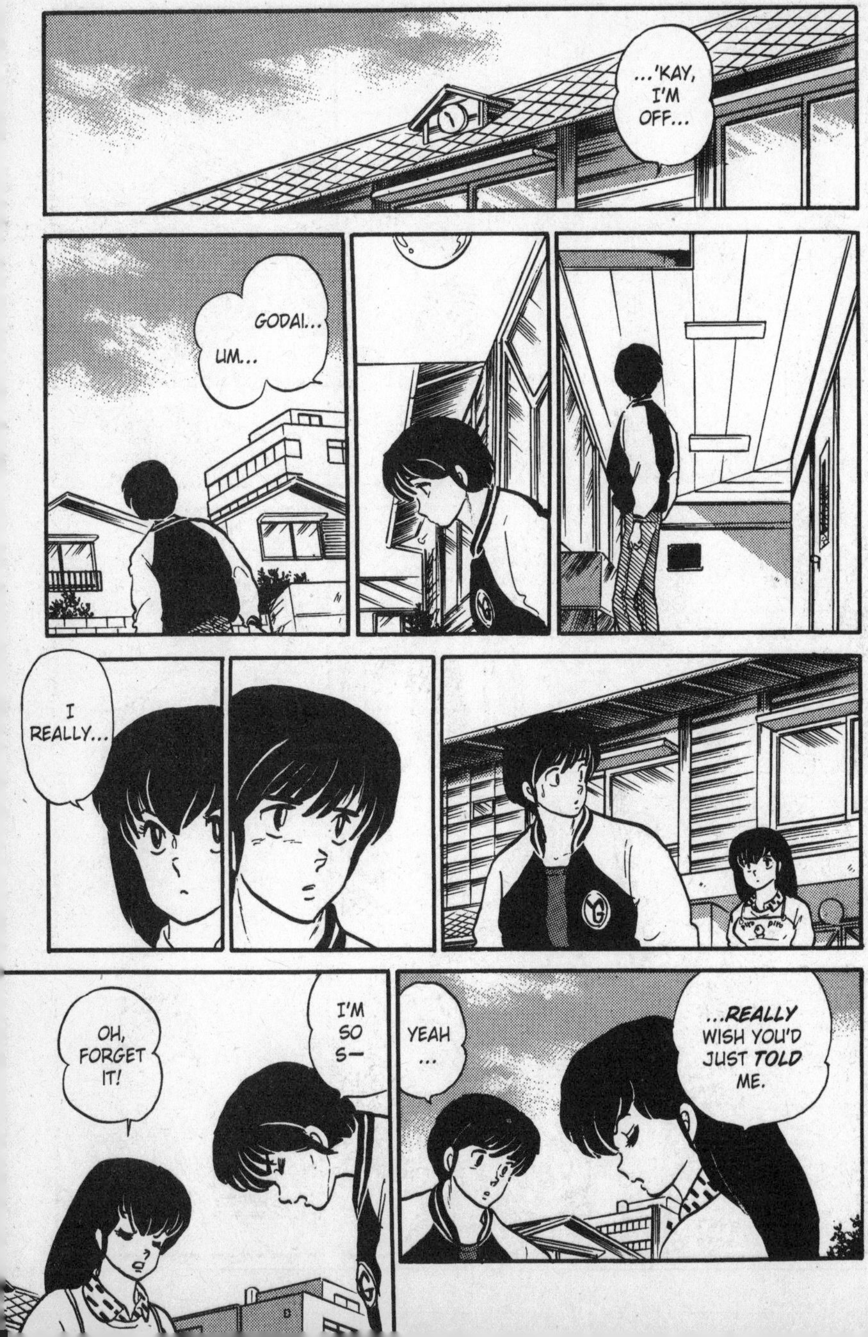
...'KAY, I'M OFF...
GODAI... UM...
I REALLY...
...**REALLY** WISH YOU'D JUST **TOLD** ME.
YEAH ...
I'M SO S—
OH, FORGET IT!

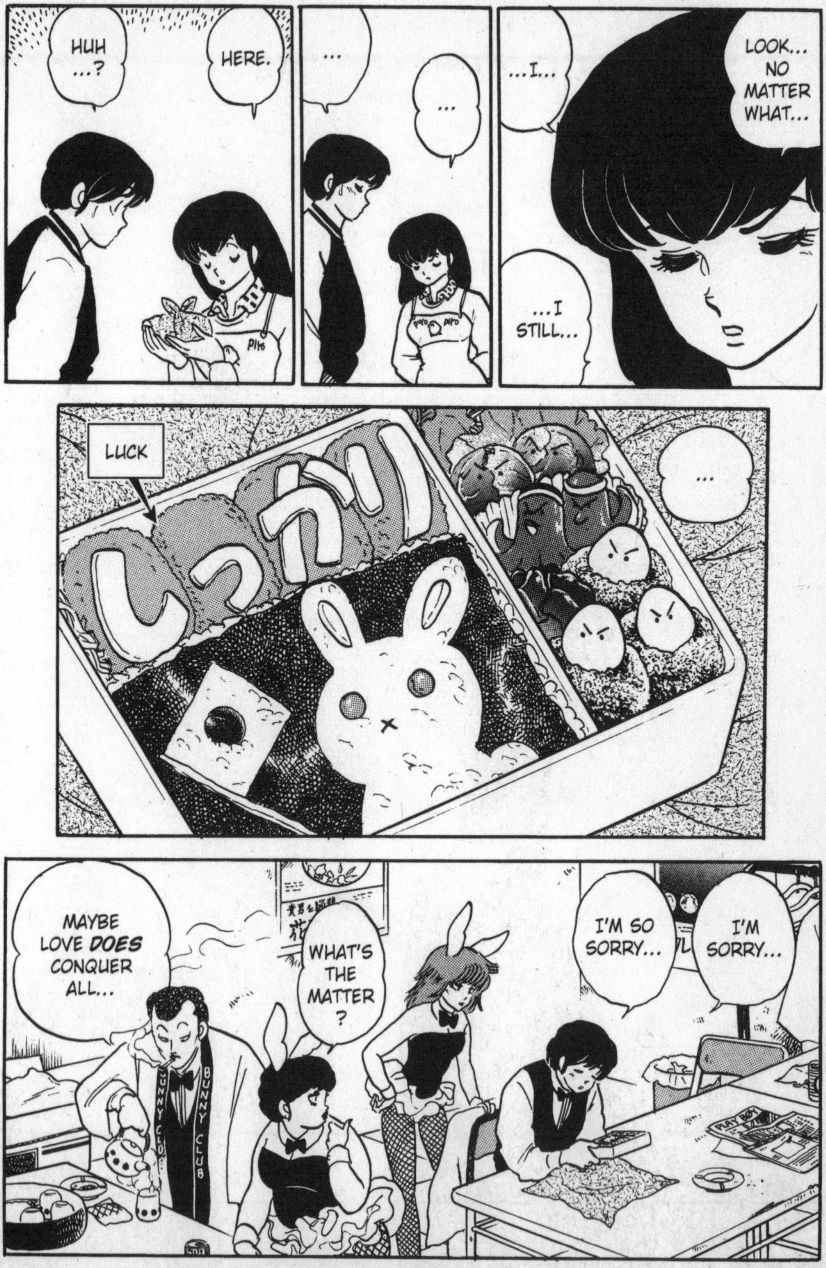
LOOK... NO MATTER WHAT...
...I...
...I STILL...
...
...
HERE.
HUH ...?
...
LUCK
しっかり
I'M SORRY...
I'M SO SORRY...
WHAT'S THE MATTER ?
MAYBE LOVE *DOES* CONQUER ALL...
BUNNY CLUB
BUNNY CLUB
PLAY BOY

PART EIGHT

GOOD MOURNING

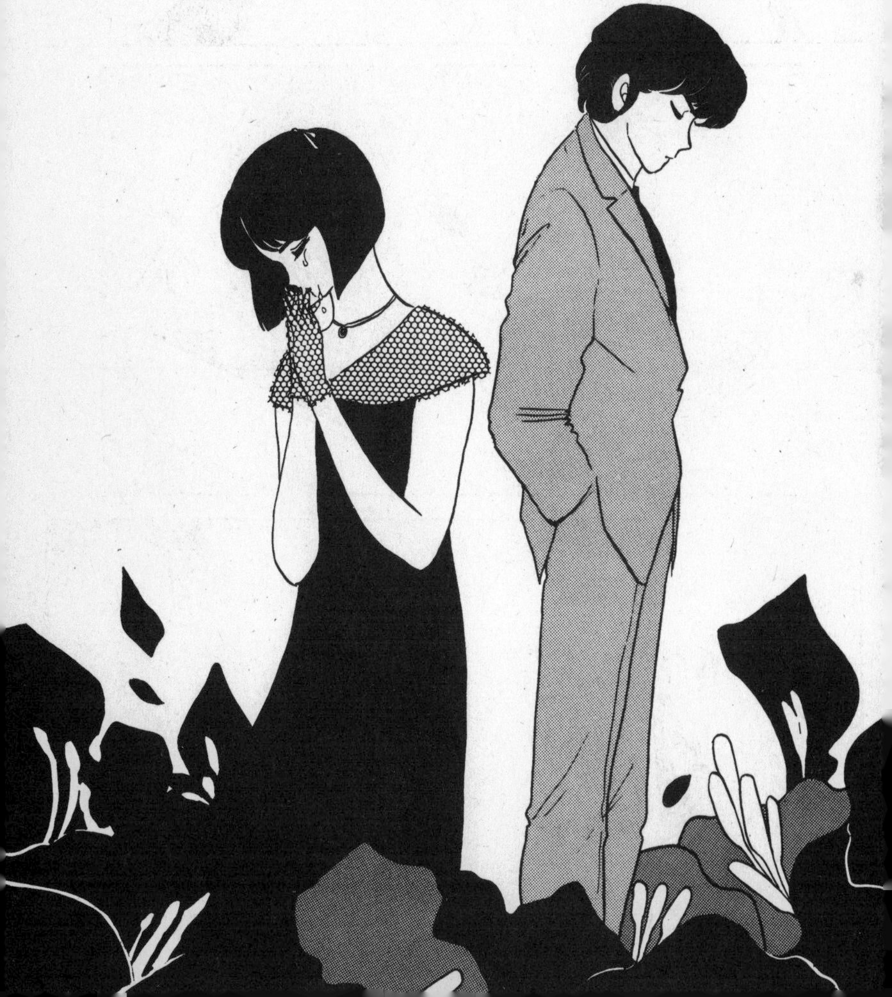

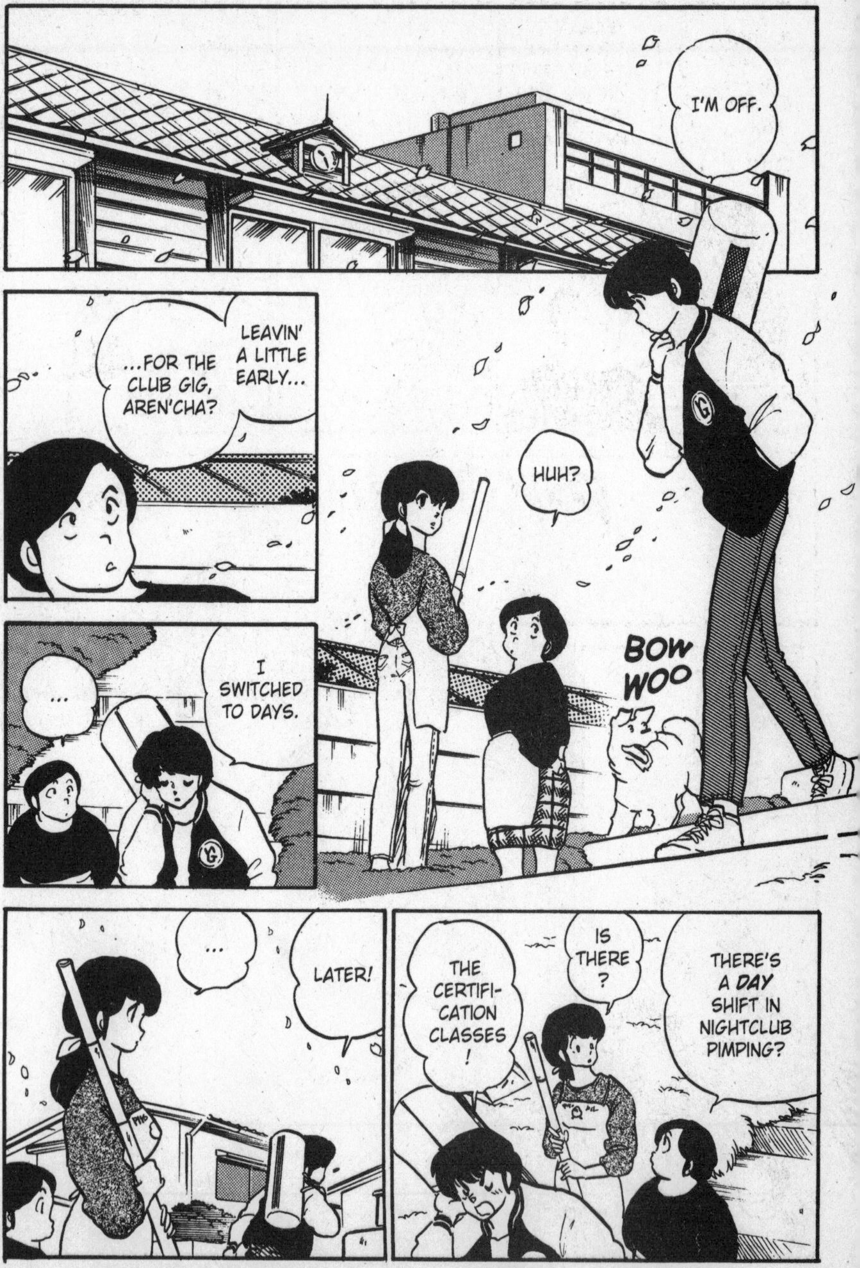
I'M OFF.
HUH?
BOW WOO
LEAVIN' A LITTLE EARLY...
...FOR THE CLUB GIG, AREN'CHA?
I SWITCHED TO DAYS.
...
THERE'S A *DAY* SHIFT IN NIGHTCLUB PIMPING?
IS THERE ?
THE CERTIFICATION CLASSES !
LATER!
...

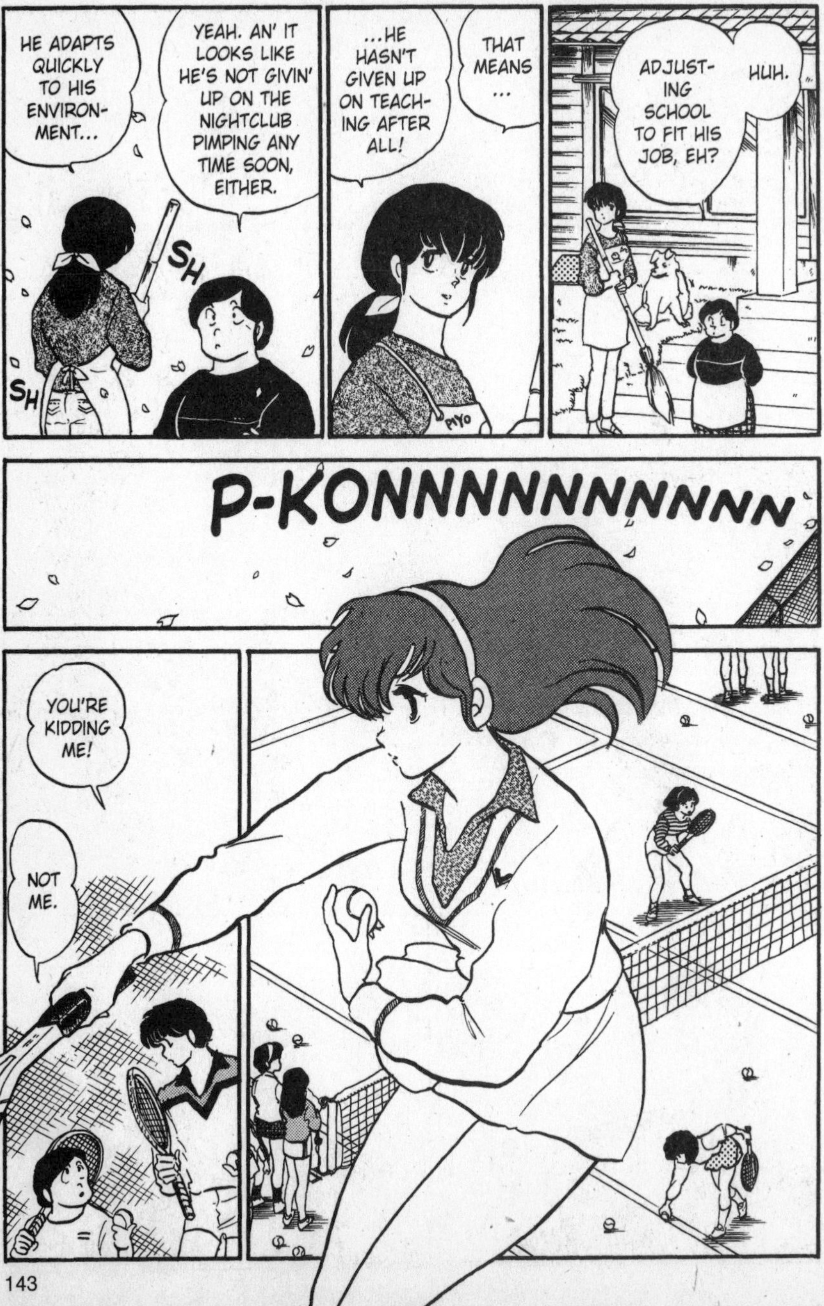
HUH.
ADJUSTING SCHOOL TO FIT HIS JOB, EH?
THAT MEANS ...
...HE HASN'T GIVEN UP ON TEACHING AFTER ALL!
YEAH. AN' IT LOOKS LIKE HE'S NOT GIVIN' UP ON THE NIGHTCLUB PIMPING ANY TIME SOON, EITHER.
HE ADAPTS QUICKLY TO HIS ENVIRONMENT...
SH
SH
P-KONNNNNNNNNN
YOU'RE KIDDING ME!
NOT ME.

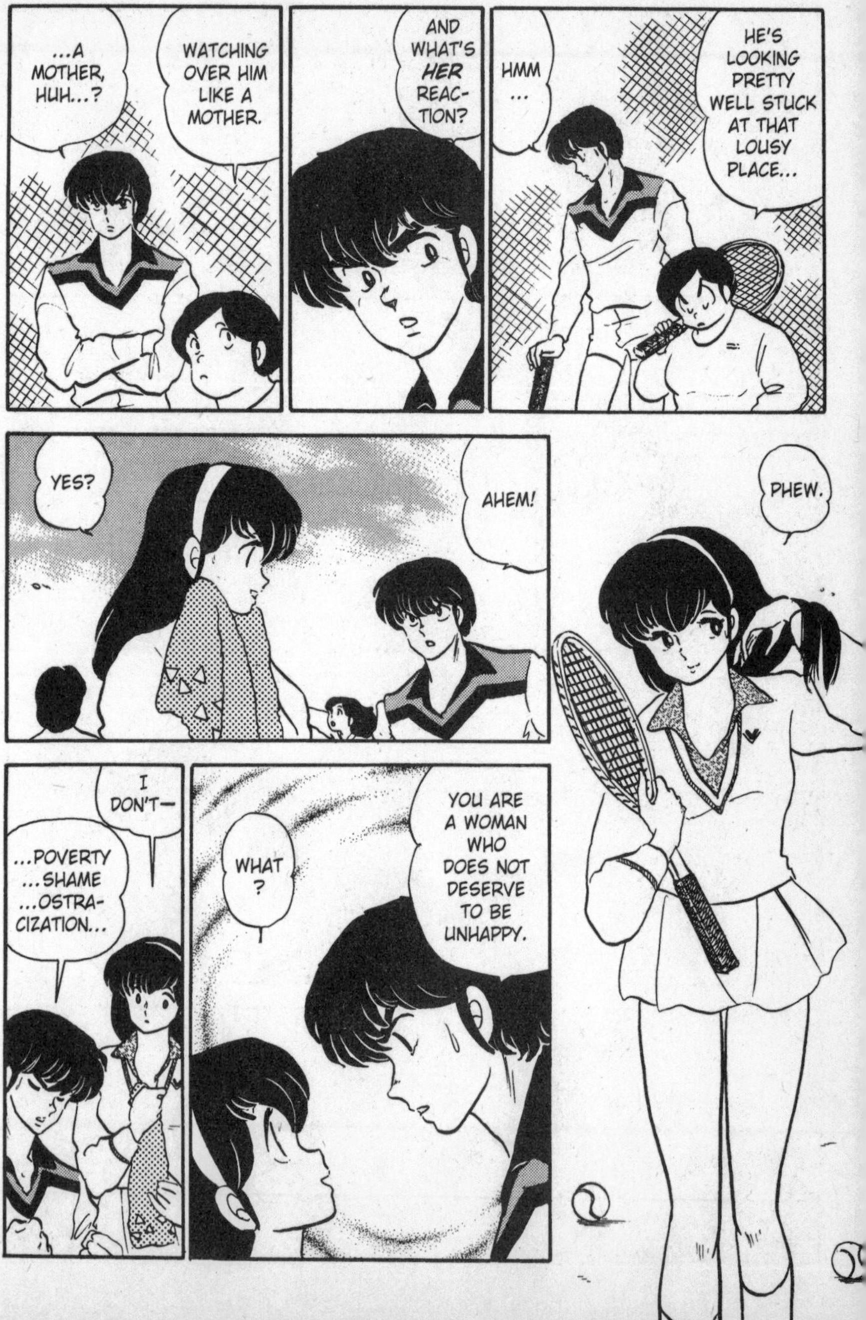
HE'S LOOKING PRETTY WELL STUCK AT THAT LOUSY PLACE...
HMM ...
AND WHAT'S HER REACTION?
WATCHING OVER HIM LIKE A MOTHER.
...A MOTHER, HUH...?
PHEW.
AHEM!
YES?
YOU ARE A WOMAN WHO DOES NOT DESERVE TO BE UNHAPPY.
WHAT ?
I DON'T—
...POVERTY ...SHAME ...OSTRA-CIZATION...

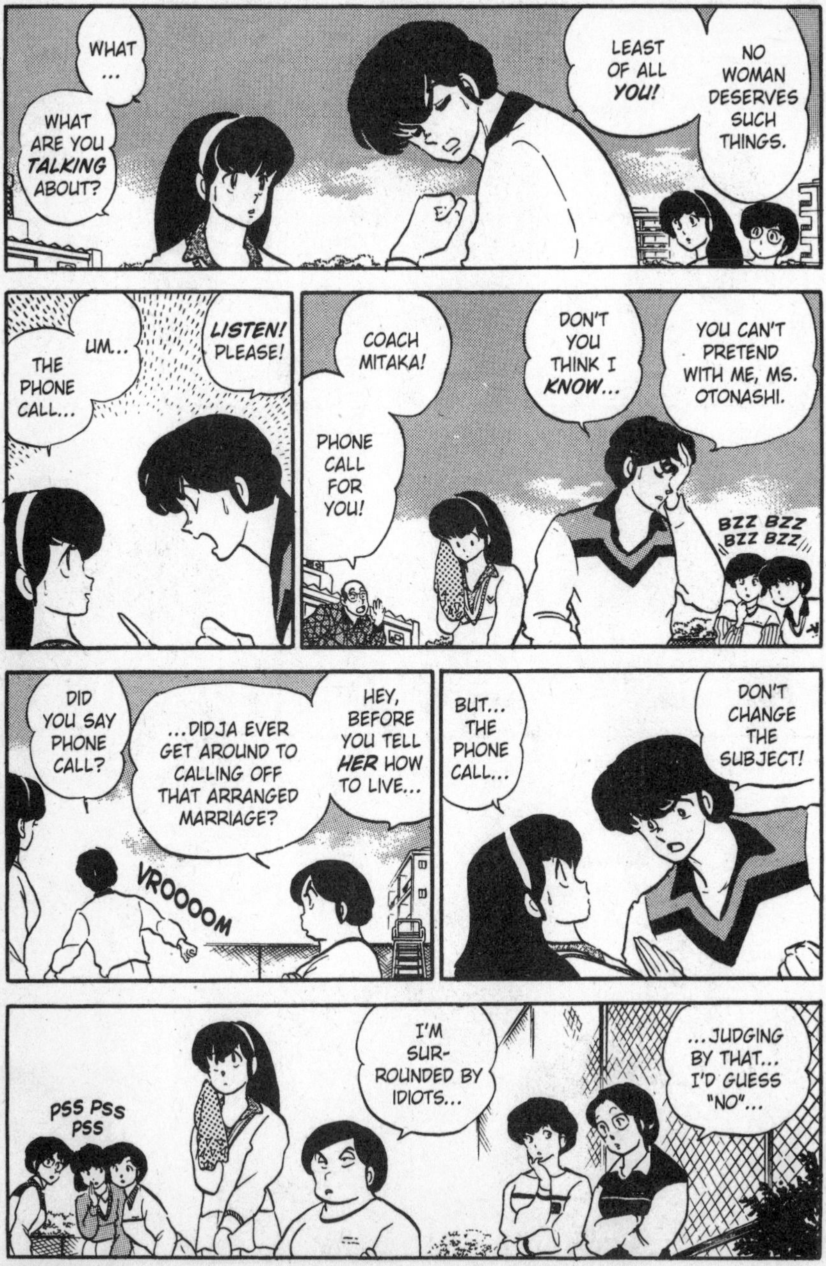
NO WOMAN DESERVES SUCH THINGS.
LEAST OF ALL *YOU!*
WHAT ...
WHAT ARE YOU *TALKING* ABOUT?
YOU CAN'T PRETEND WITH ME, MS. OTONASHI.
DON'T YOU THINK I *KNOW*...
COACH MITAKA!
PHONE CALL FOR YOU!
BZZ BZZ BZZ BZZ
LISTEN! PLEASE!
UM...
THE PHONE CALL...
DON'T CHANGE THE SUBJECT!
BUT... THE PHONE CALL...
HEY, BEFORE YOU TELL *HER* HOW TO LIVE...
...DIDJA EVER GET AROUND TO CALLING OFF THAT ARRANGED MARRIAGE?
DID YOU SAY PHONE CALL?
VROOOOM
...JUDGING BY THAT... I'D GUESS "NO"...
I'M SUR-ROUNDED BY IDIOTS...
PSS PSS PSS

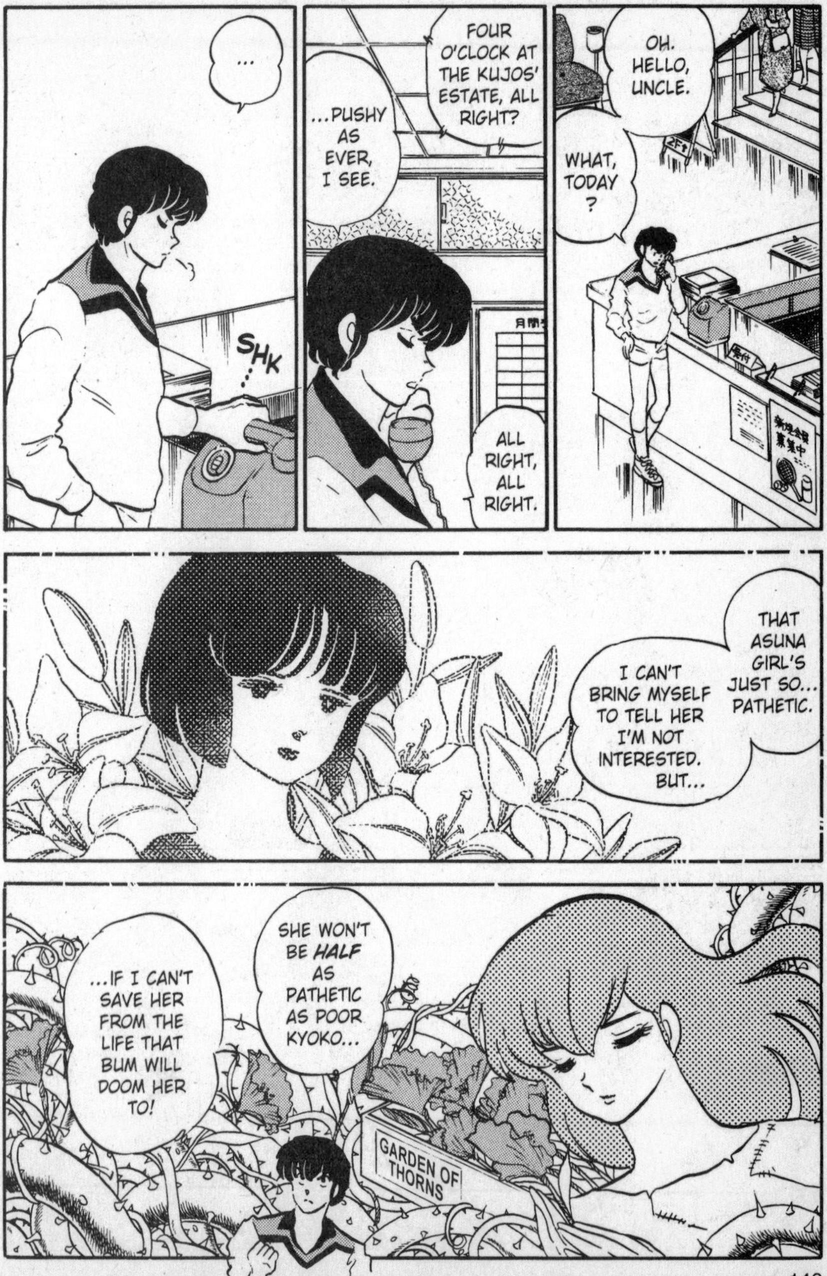
OH. HELLO, UNCLE.
WHAT, TODAY?
FOUR O'CLOCK AT THE KUJOS' ESTATE, ALL RIGHT?
...PUSHY AS EVER, I SEE.
ALL RIGHT, ALL RIGHT.
...
SHK
THAT ASUNA GIRL'S JUST SO... PATHETIC.
I CAN'T BRING MYSELF TO TELL HER I'M NOT INTERESTED. BUT...
SHE WON'T BE *HALF* AS PATHETIC AS POOR KYOKO...
...IF I CAN'T SAVE HER FROM THE LIFE THAT BUM WILL DOOM HER TO!
GARDEN OF THORNS

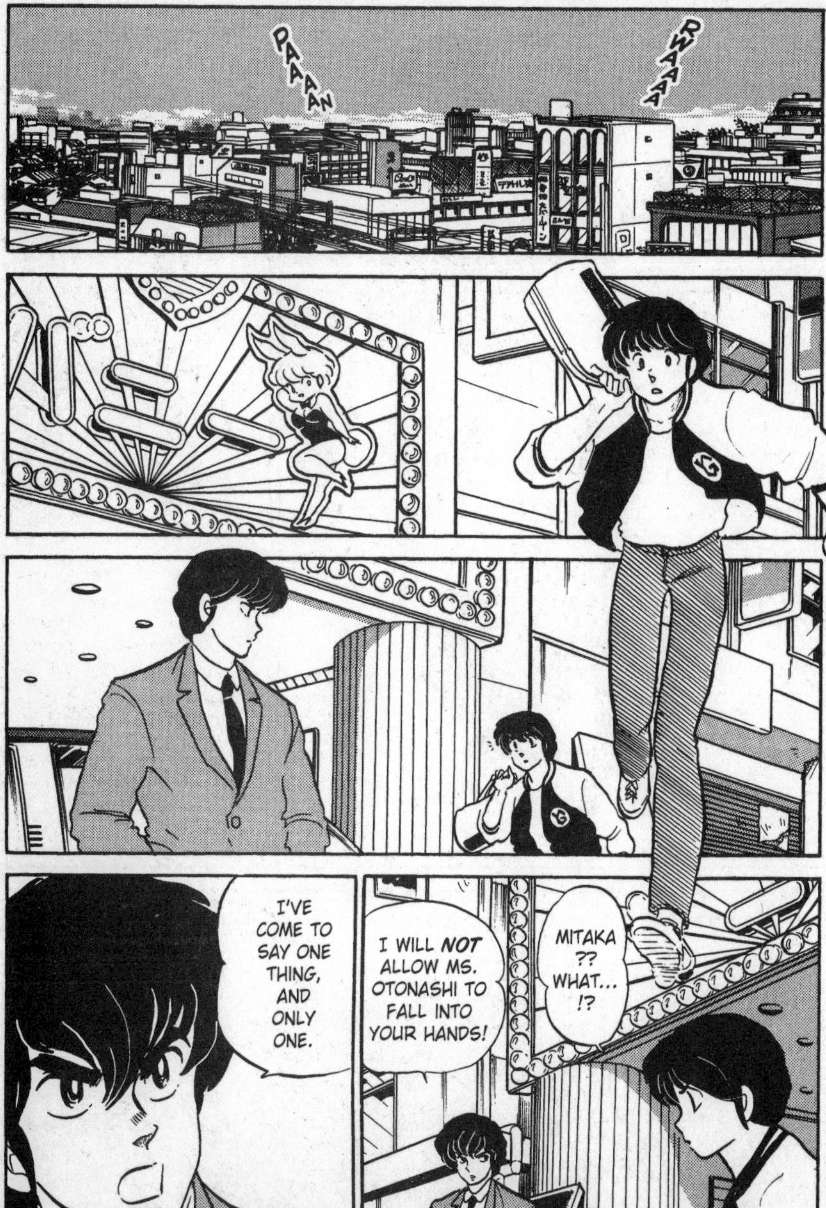
RWAAAA
PAAAAN
MITAKA ?? WHAT... !?
I WILL **NOT** ALLOW MS. OTONASHI TO FALL INTO YOUR HANDS!
I'VE COME TO SAY ONE THING, AND ONLY ONE.

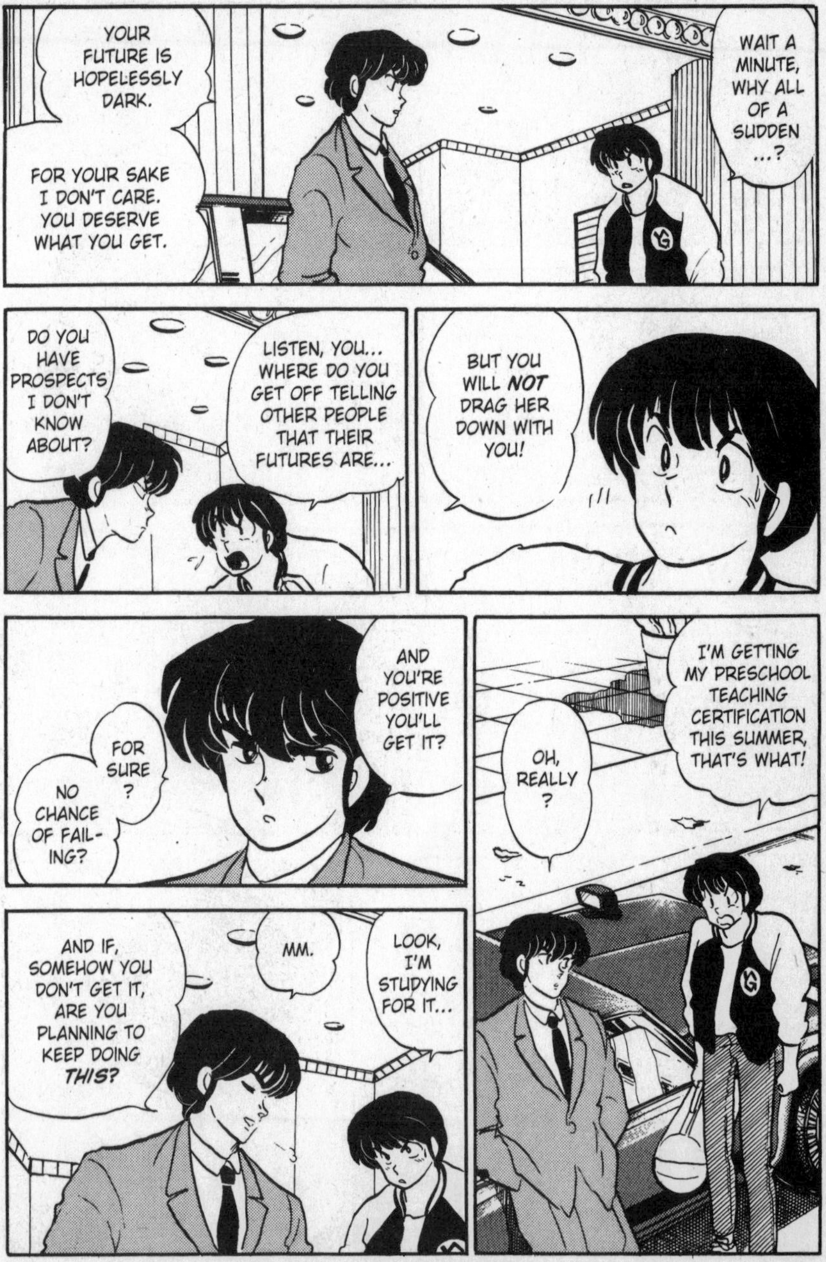
WAIT A MINUTE, WHY ALL OF A SUDDEN ...?
YOUR FUTURE IS HOPELESSLY DARK.
FOR YOUR SAKE I DON'T CARE. YOU DESERVE WHAT YOU GET.
BUT YOU WILL ***NOT*** DRAG HER DOWN WITH YOU!
LISTEN, YOU... WHERE DO YOU GET OFF TELLING OTHER PEOPLE THAT THEIR FUTURES ARE...
DO YOU HAVE PROSPECTS I DON'T KNOW ABOUT?
I'M GETTING MY PRESCHOOL TEACHING CERTIFICATION THIS SUMMER, THAT'S WHAT!
OH, REALLY?
AND YOU'RE POSITIVE YOU'LL GET IT?
FOR SURE?
NO CHANCE OF FAIL-ING?
LOOK, I'M STUDYING FOR IT...
MM.
AND IF, SOMEHOW YOU DON'T GET IT, ARE YOU PLANNING TO KEEP DOING ***THIS?***

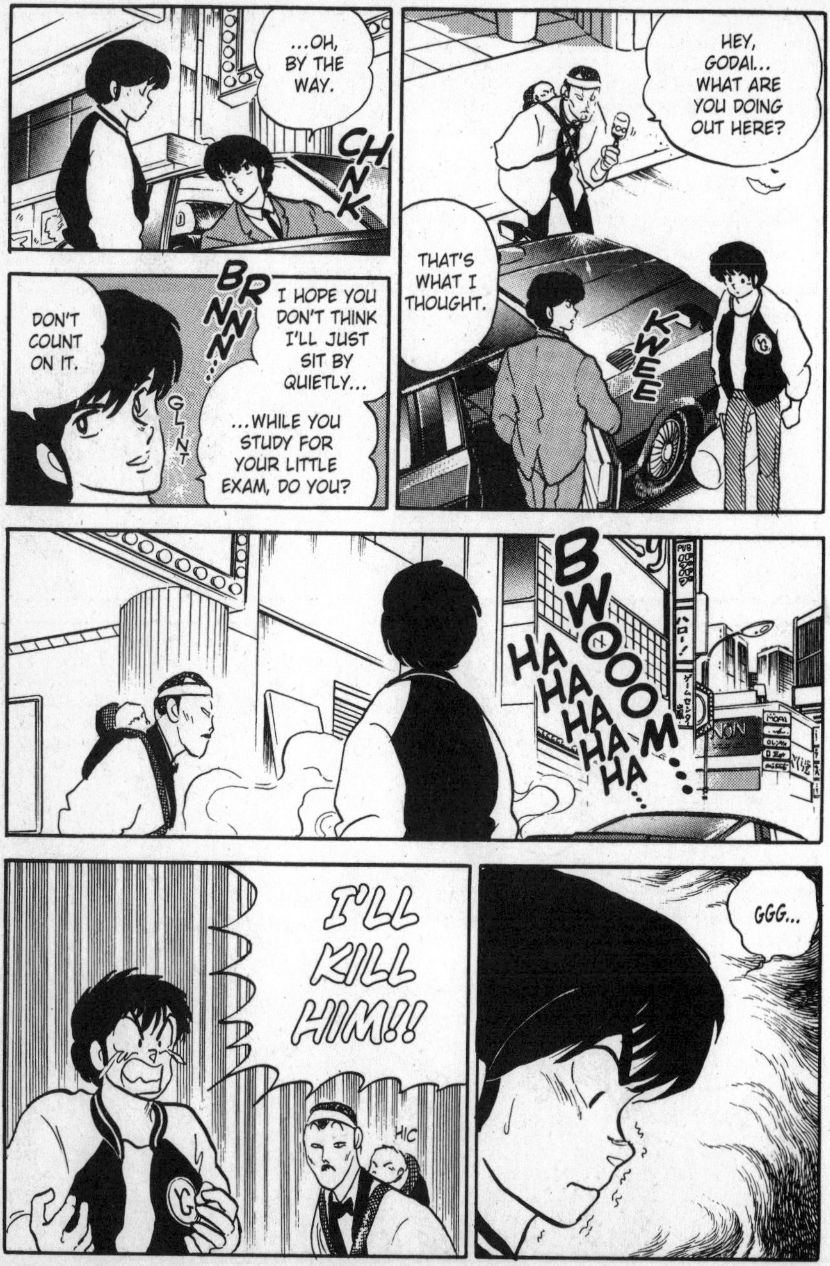
HEY, GODAI... WHAT ARE YOU DOING OUT HERE?
...OH, BY THE WAY.
CHNK
THAT'S WHAT I THOUGHT.
KWEE
BRNNN...
I HOPE YOU DON'T THINK I'LL JUST SIT BY QUIETLY...
...WHILE YOU STUDY FOR YOUR LITTLE EXAM, DO YOU?
GLINT
DON'T COUNT ON IT.
BWOOOM...
HAHAHAHAHA...
GGG...
I'LL KILL HIM!!
HIC

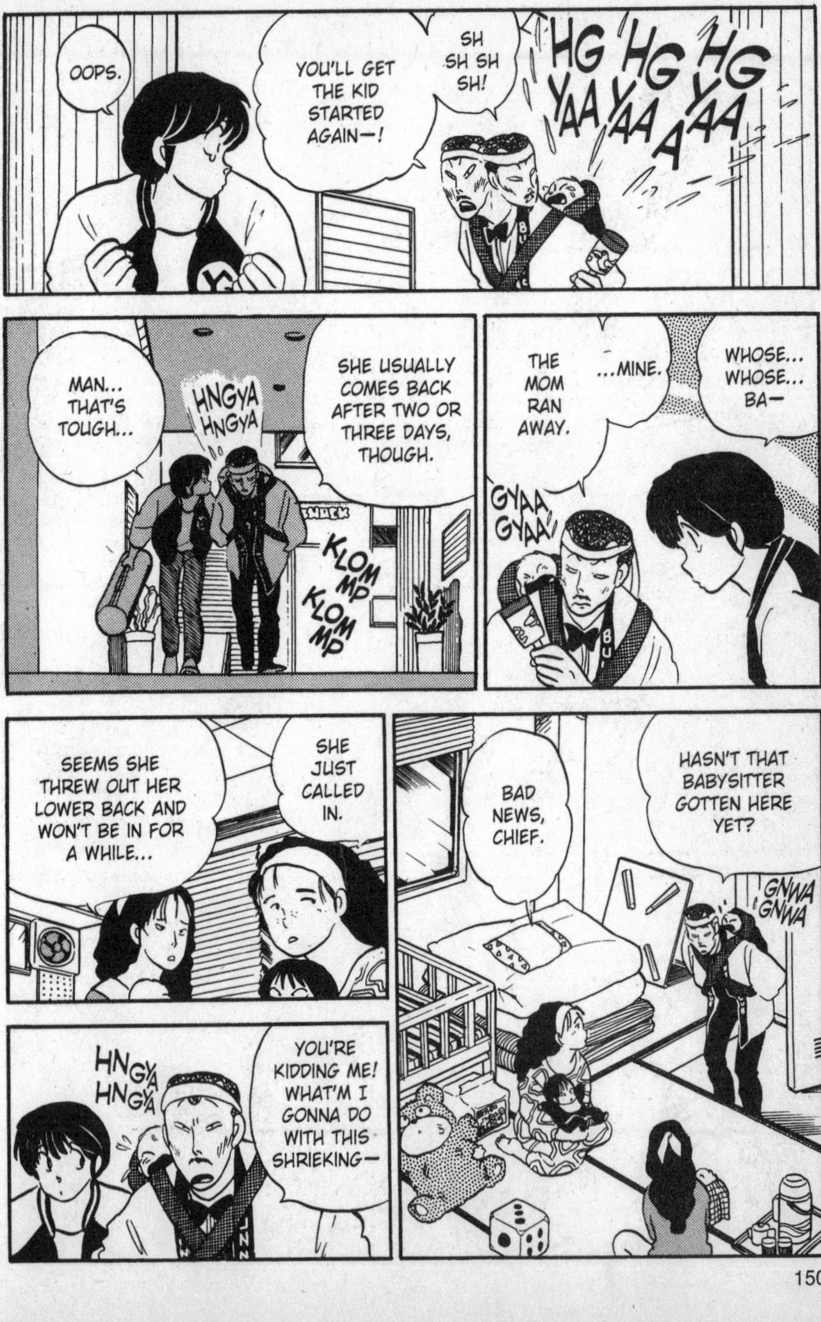
HG HG HG
YAA YAAA YAA
SH SH SH SH!
YOU'LL GET THE KID STARTED AGAIN—!
OOPS.
WHOSE... WHOSE... BA—
...MINE.
THE MOM RAN AWAY.
GYAA GYAA
SHE USUALLY COMES BACK AFTER TWO OR THREE DAYS, THOUGH.
KLOMP KLOMP
HNGYA HNGYA
MAN... THAT'S TOUGH...
HASN'T THAT BABYSITTER GOTTEN HERE YET?
GNWA GNWA
BAD NEWS, CHIEF.
SHE JUST CALLED IN.
SEEMS SHE THREW OUT HER LOWER BACK AND WON'T BE IN FOR A WHILE...
YOU'RE KIDDING ME! WHAT'M I GONNA DO WITH THIS SHRIEKING—
HNGYA HNGYA

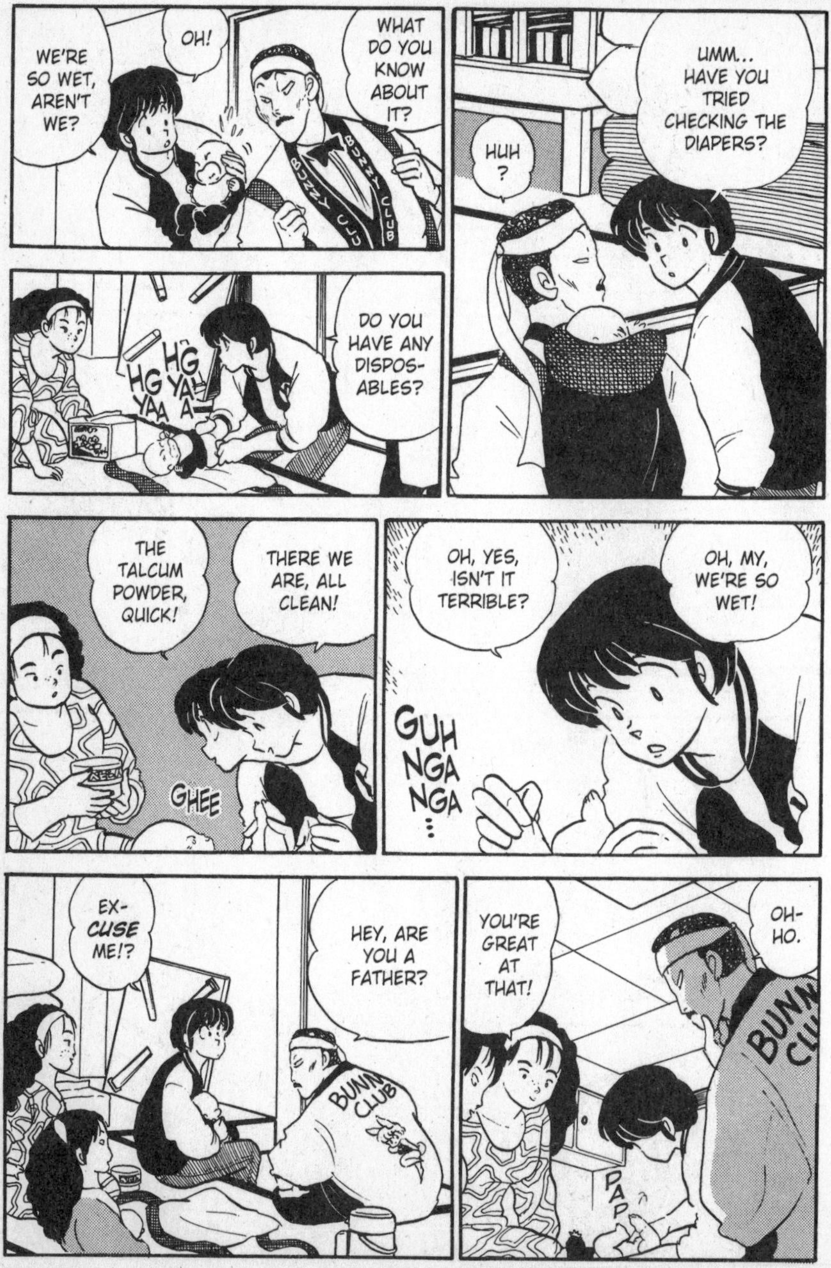
UMM... HAVE YOU TRIED CHECKING THE DIAPERS?
HUH?
WHAT DO YOU KNOW ABOUT IT?
BUNNY CLUB
OH!
WE'RE SO WET, AREN'T WE?
DO YOU HAVE ANY DISPOS-ABLES?
HG YAA
HG YAA
OH, MY, WE'RE SO WET!
OH, YES, ISN'T IT TERRIBLE?
GUH NGA NGA...
THERE WE ARE, ALL CLEAN!
THE TALCUM POWDER, QUICK!
GHEE
OH-HO.
YOU'RE GREAT AT THAT!
BUNN CLUB
PAP
HEY, ARE YOU A FATHER?
EX-CUSE ME!?
BUNN CLUB

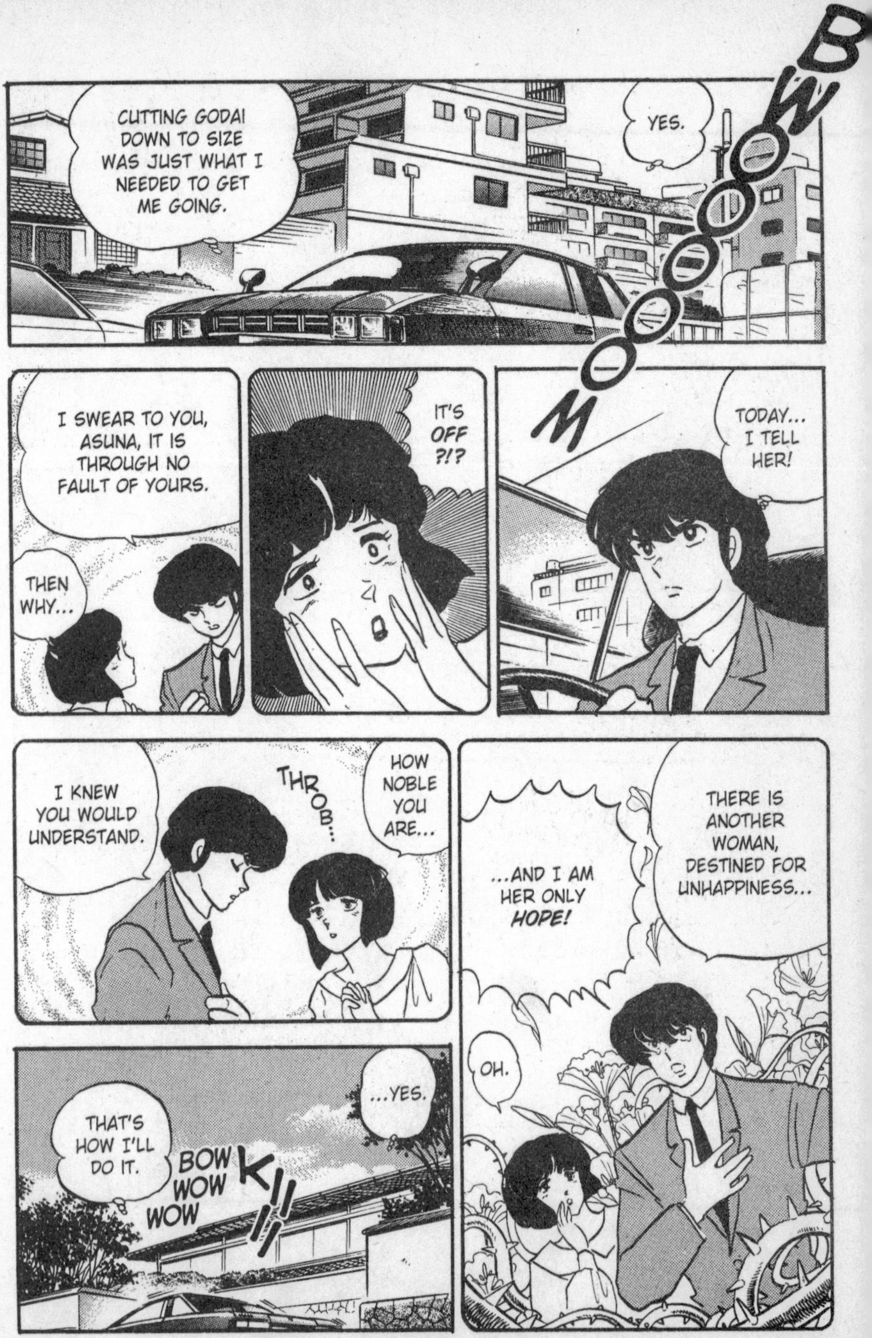
BWOOOOOOOM
YES.
CUTTING GODAI DOWN TO SIZE WAS JUST WHAT I NEEDED TO GET ME GOING.
TODAY... I TELL HER!
IT'S *OFF* ?!?
I SWEAR TO YOU, ASUNA, IT IS THROUGH NO FAULT OF YOURS.
THEN WHY...
THERE IS ANOTHER WOMAN, DESTINED FOR UNHAPPINESS...
...AND I AM HER ONLY *HOPE!*
OH.
HOW NOBLE YOU ARE...
THROB...
I KNEW YOU WOULD UNDERSTAND.
...YES.
THAT'S HOW I'LL DO IT.
KI
BOW WOW WOW

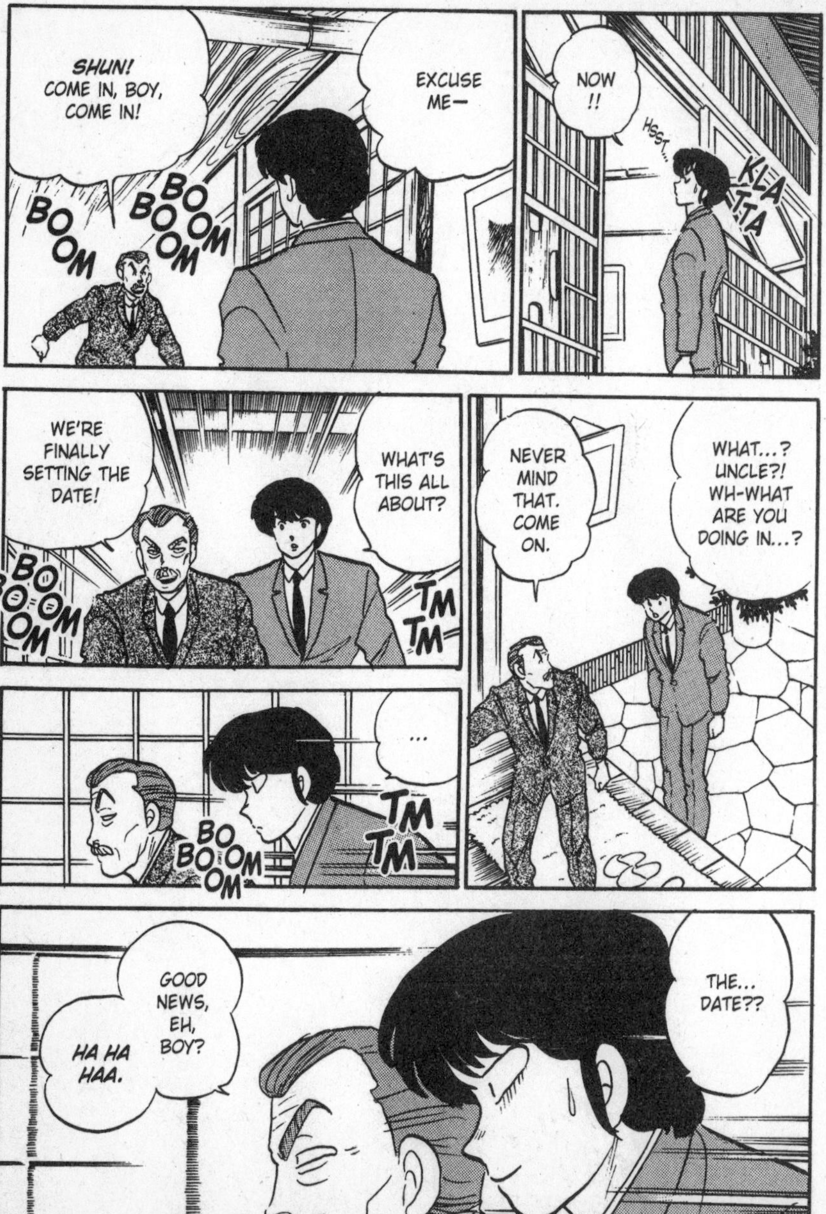
NOW !!
HSST...
KLATTA
EXCUSE ME—
SHUN! COME IN, BOY, COME IN!
BOOM BOOM BOOM
BOOM BOOM
WHAT...? UNCLE?! WH-WHAT ARE YOU DOING IN...?
NEVER MIND THAT. COME ON.
WHAT'S THIS ALL ABOUT?
TM TM
WE'RE FINALLY SETTING THE DATE!
BOOM BOOM BOOM
...
TM TM
BOOM BOOM
THE... DATE??
GOOD NEWS, EH, BOY?
HA HA HAA.

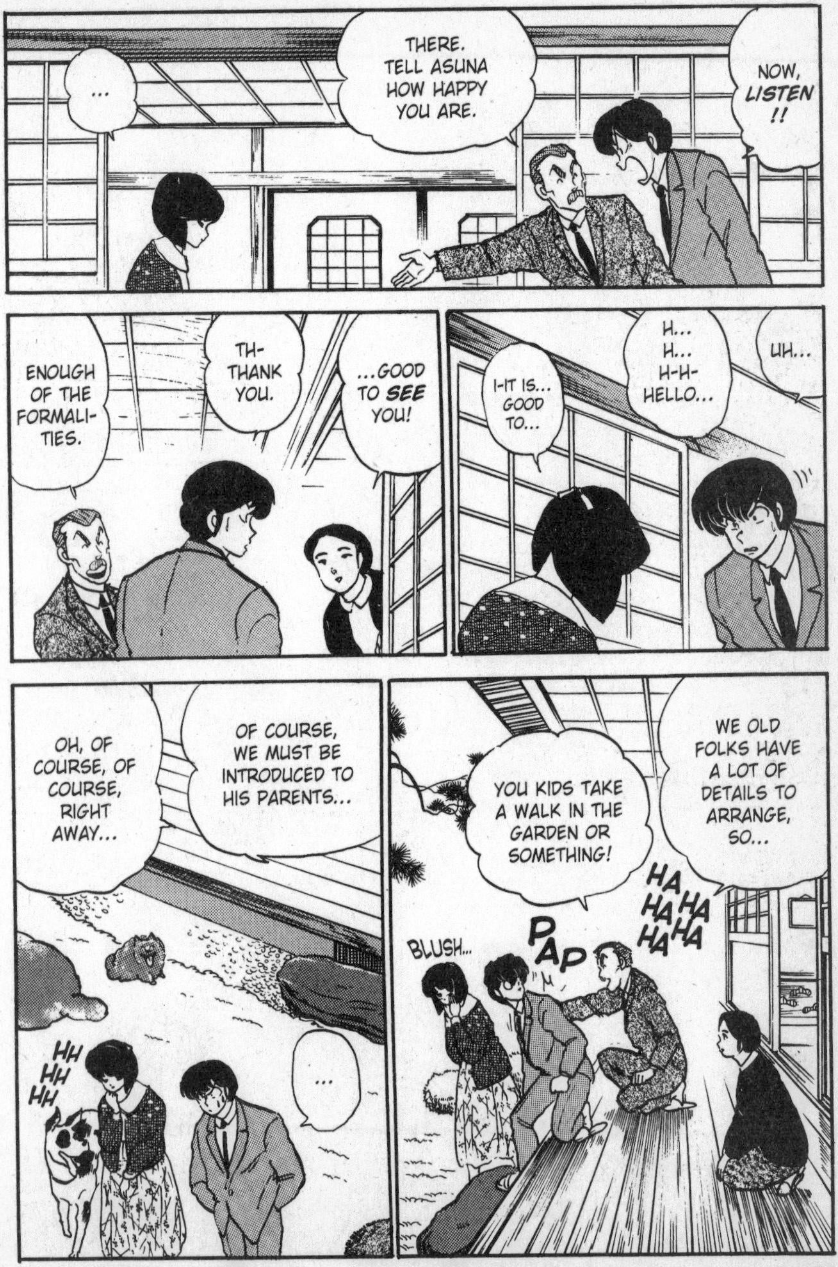
NOW, LISTEN !!
THERE. TELL ASUNA HOW HAPPY YOU ARE.
...
UH...
H... H... H-H-HELLO...
I-IT IS... GOOD TO...
...GOOD TO SEE YOU!
TH- THANK YOU.
ENOUGH OF THE FORMALI-TIES.
WE OLD FOLKS HAVE A LOT OF DETAILS TO ARRANGE, SO...
YOU KIDS TAKE A WALK IN THE GARDEN OR SOMETHING!
HA HA HA HA HA HA
PAP
BLUSH...
OF COURSE, WE MUST BE INTRODUCED TO HIS PARENTS...
OH, OF COURSE, OF COURSE, RIGHT AWAY...
...
HH HH HH

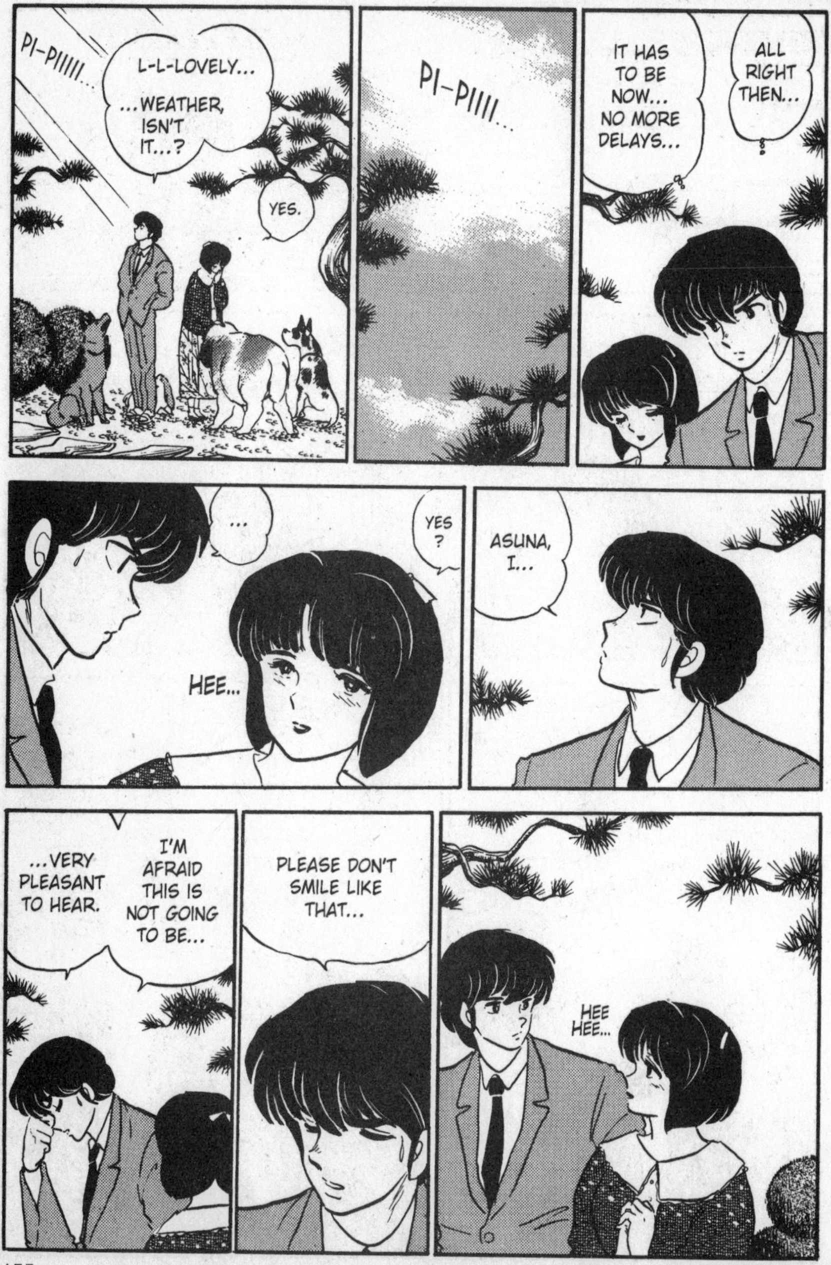
ALL RIGHT THEN...
IT HAS TO BE NOW... NO MORE DELAYS...
PI-PIIII...
PI-PIIIII...
L-L-LOVELY... ...WEATHER, ISN'T IT...?
YES.
ASUNA, I...
YES ?
...
HEE...
HEE HEE...
PLEASE DON'T SMILE LIKE THAT...
I'M AFRAID THIS IS NOT GOING TO BE...
...VERY PLEASANT TO HEAR.

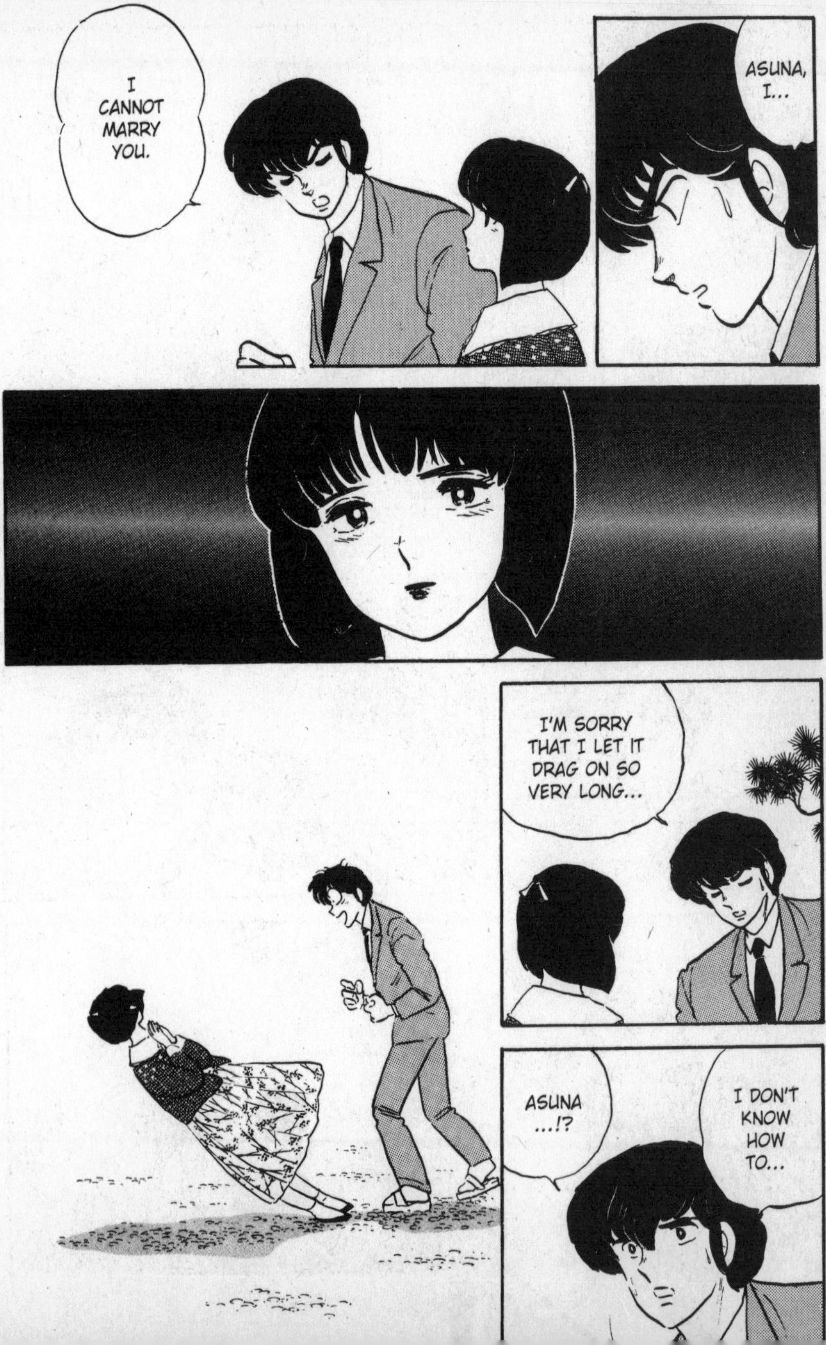
ASUNA, I...
I CANNOT MARRY YOU.
I'M SORRY THAT I LET IT DRAG ON SO VERY LONG...
I DON'T KNOW HOW TO...
ASUNA ...!?

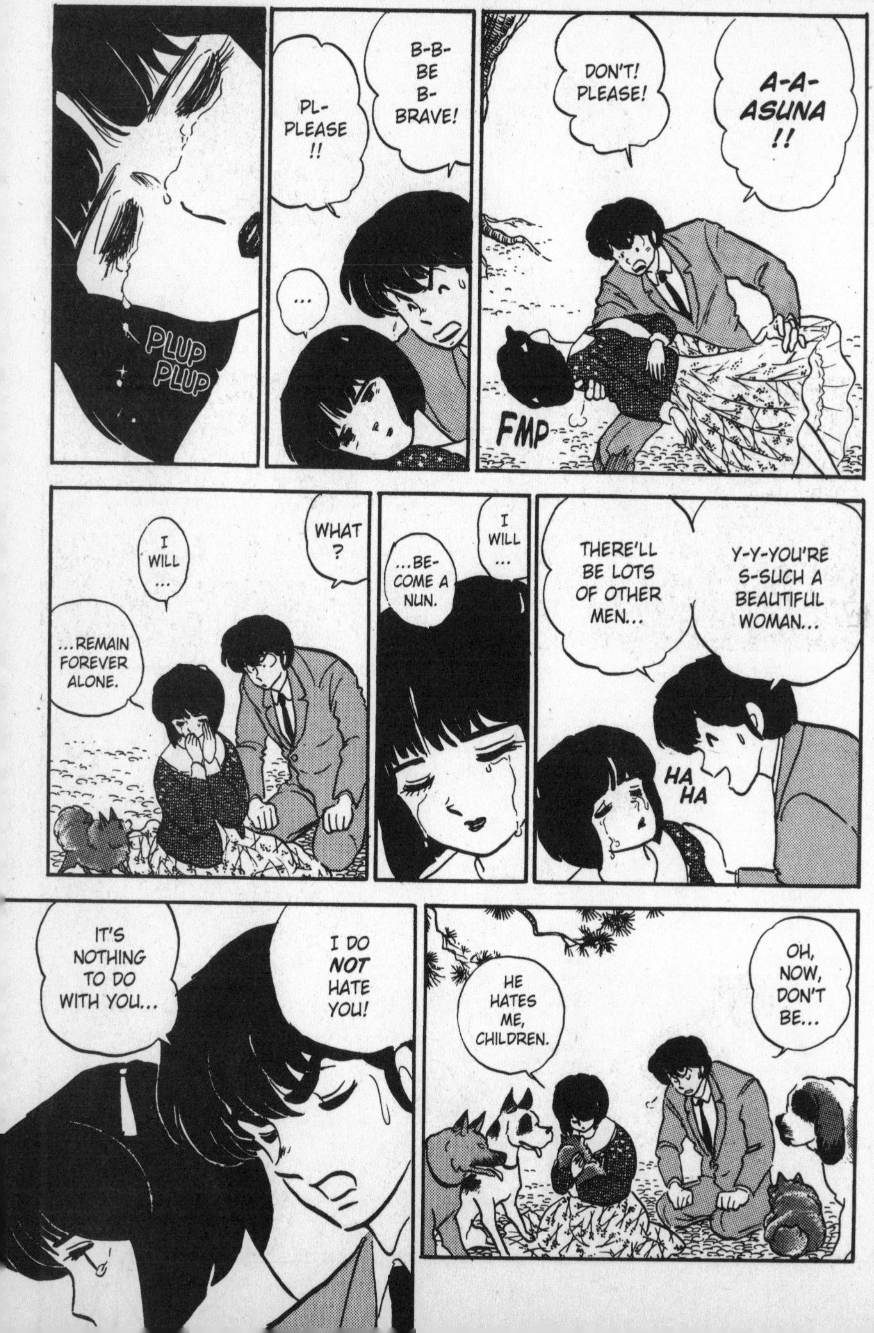
A-A-ASUNA!!
DON'T! PLEASE!
FMP
B-B-BE B-BRAVE!
PL-PLEASE!!
...
PLUP PLUP
Y-Y-YOU'RE S-SUCH A BEAUTIFUL WOMAN...
THERE'LL BE LOTS OF OTHER MEN...
HA HA
I WILL ...
...BE-COME A NUN.
WHAT?
I WILL ...
...REMAIN FOREVER ALONE.
OH, NOW, DON'T BE...
HE HATES ME, CHILDREN.
I DO **NOT** HATE YOU!
IT'S NOTHING TO DO WITH YOU...

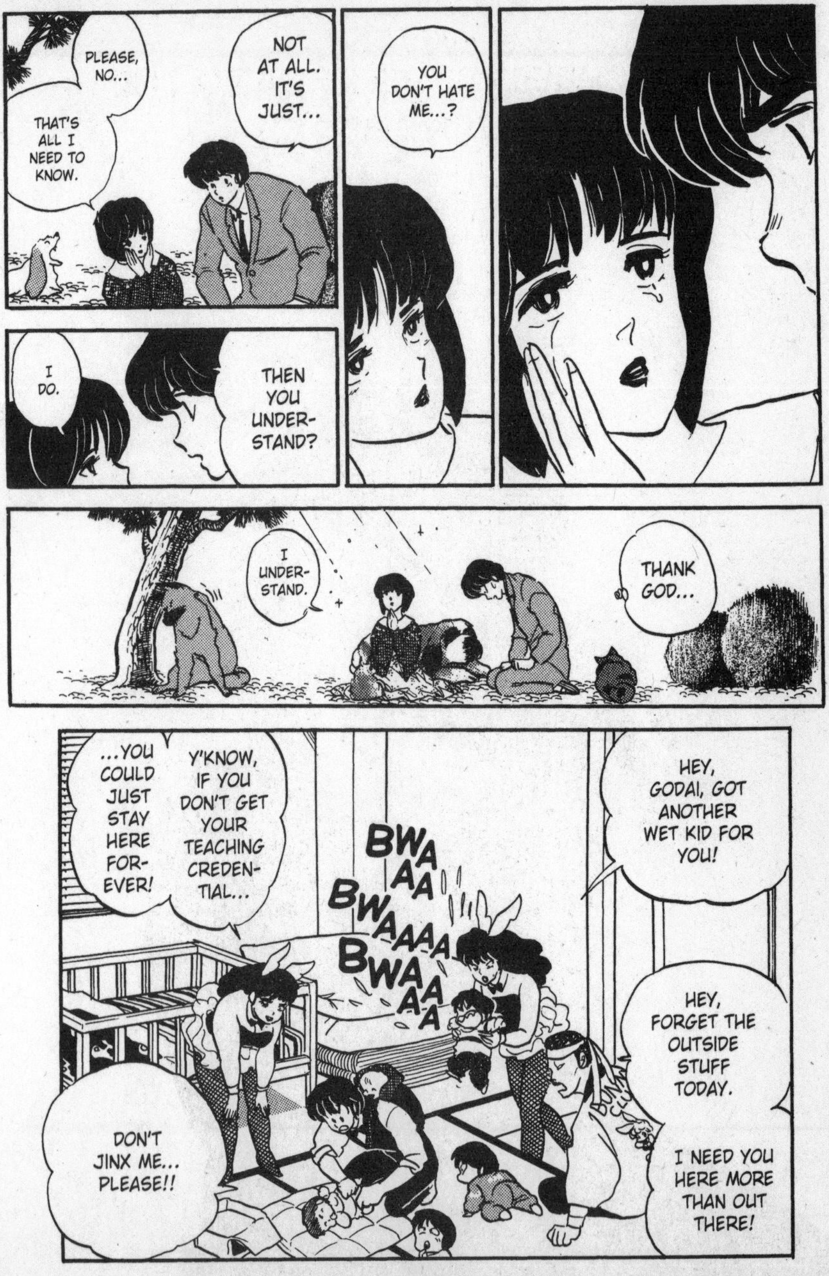
YOU DON'T HATE ME...?
NOT AT ALL. IT'S JUST...
PLEASE, NO...
THAT'S ALL I NEED TO KNOW.
THEN YOU UNDERSTAND?
I DO.
THANK GOD...
I UNDERSTAND.
HEY, GODAI, GOT ANOTHER WET KID FOR YOU!
HEY, FORGET THE OUTSIDE STUFF TODAY.
I NEED YOU HERE MORE THAN OUT THERE!
BWAAA BWAAAAA BWAAAA
Y'KNOW, IF YOU DON'T GET YOUR TEACHING CREDEN-TIAL...
...YOU COULD JUST STAY HERE FOR-EVER!
DON'T JINX ME... PLEASE!!

PART NINE

THE CHRYSANTHEMUM AND THE BUILDING BLOCK

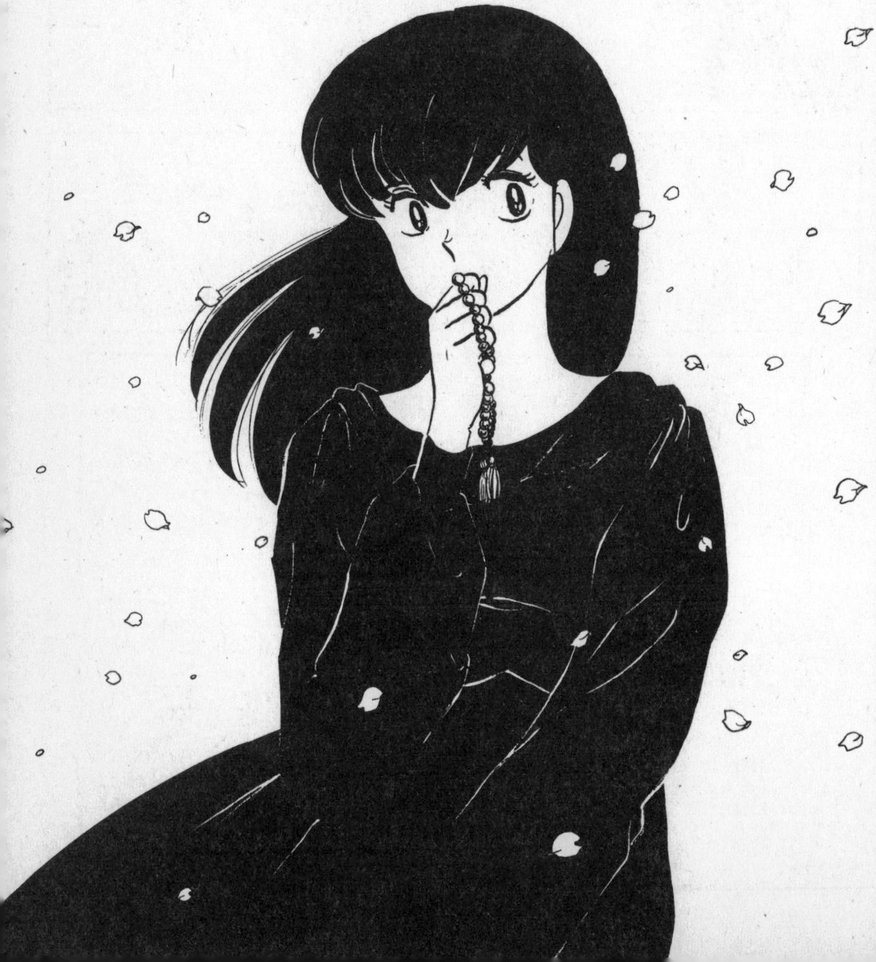

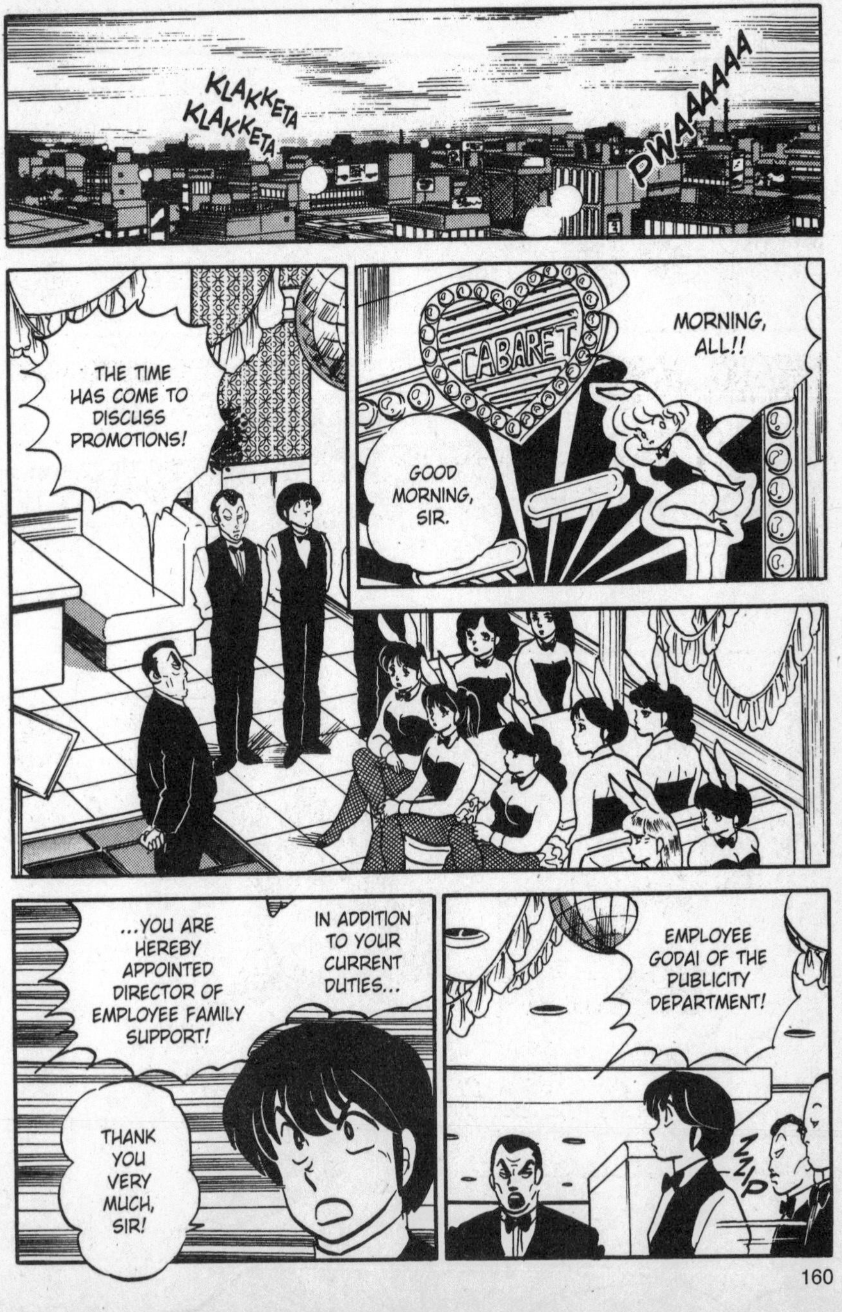
PWAAAAAA
KLAKKETA KLAKKETA
CABARET
MORNING, ALL!!
GOOD MORNING, SIR.
THE TIME HAS COME TO DISCUSS PROMOTIONS!
EMPLOYEE GODAI OF THE PUBLICITY DEPARTMENT!
ZZIP
IN ADDITION TO YOUR CURRENT DUTIES...
...YOU ARE HEREBY APPOINTED DIRECTOR OF EMPLOYEE FAMILY SUPPORT!
THANK YOU VERY MUCH, SIR!

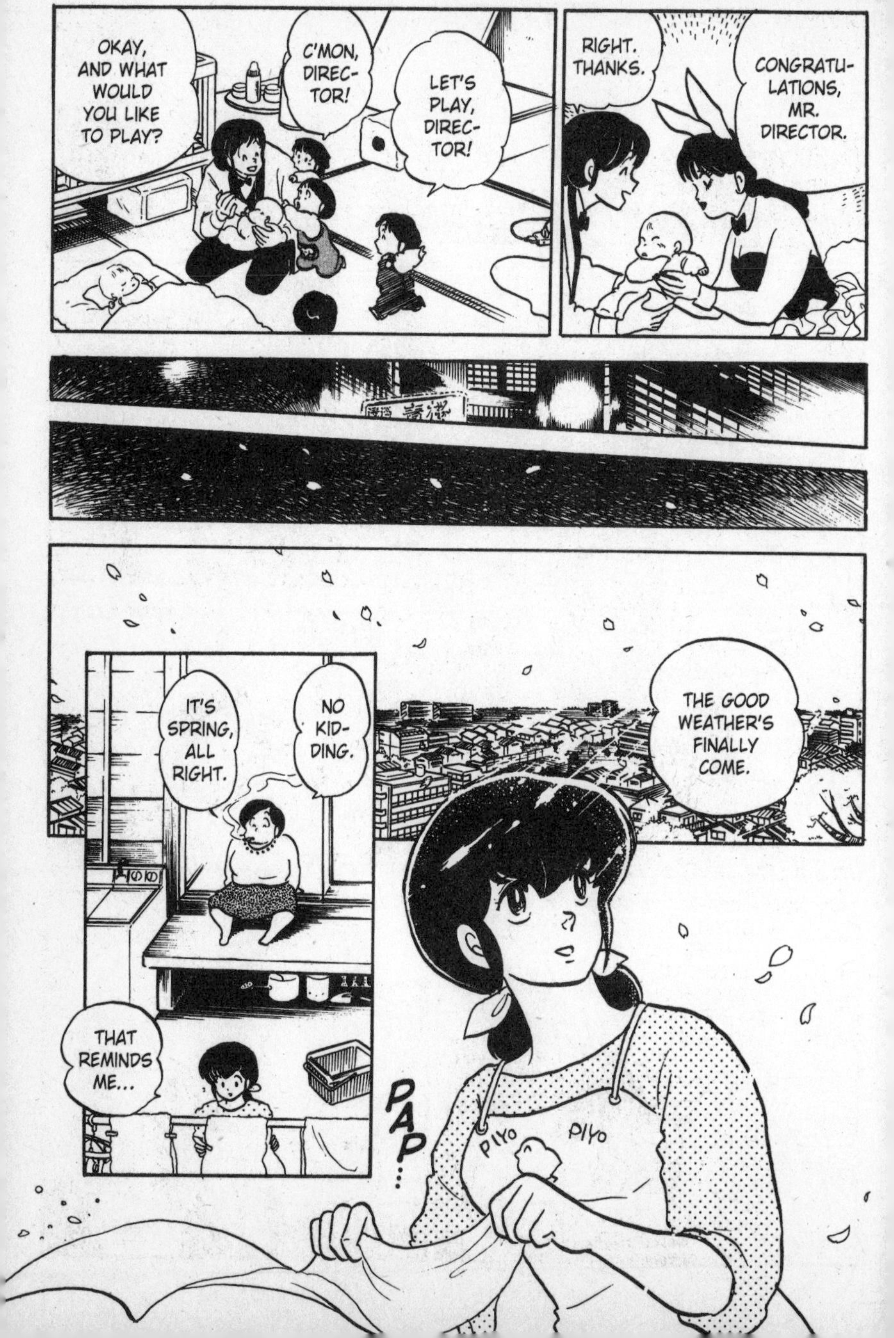
CONGRATULATIONS, MR. DIRECTOR.
RIGHT. THANKS.
LET'S PLAY, DIRECTOR!
C'MON, DIRECTOR!
OKAY, AND WHAT WOULD YOU LIKE TO PLAY?
THE GOOD WEATHER'S FINALLY COME.
NO KIDDING.
IT'S SPRING, ALL RIGHT.
THAT REMINDS ME...
PAP...
PIYO
PIYO

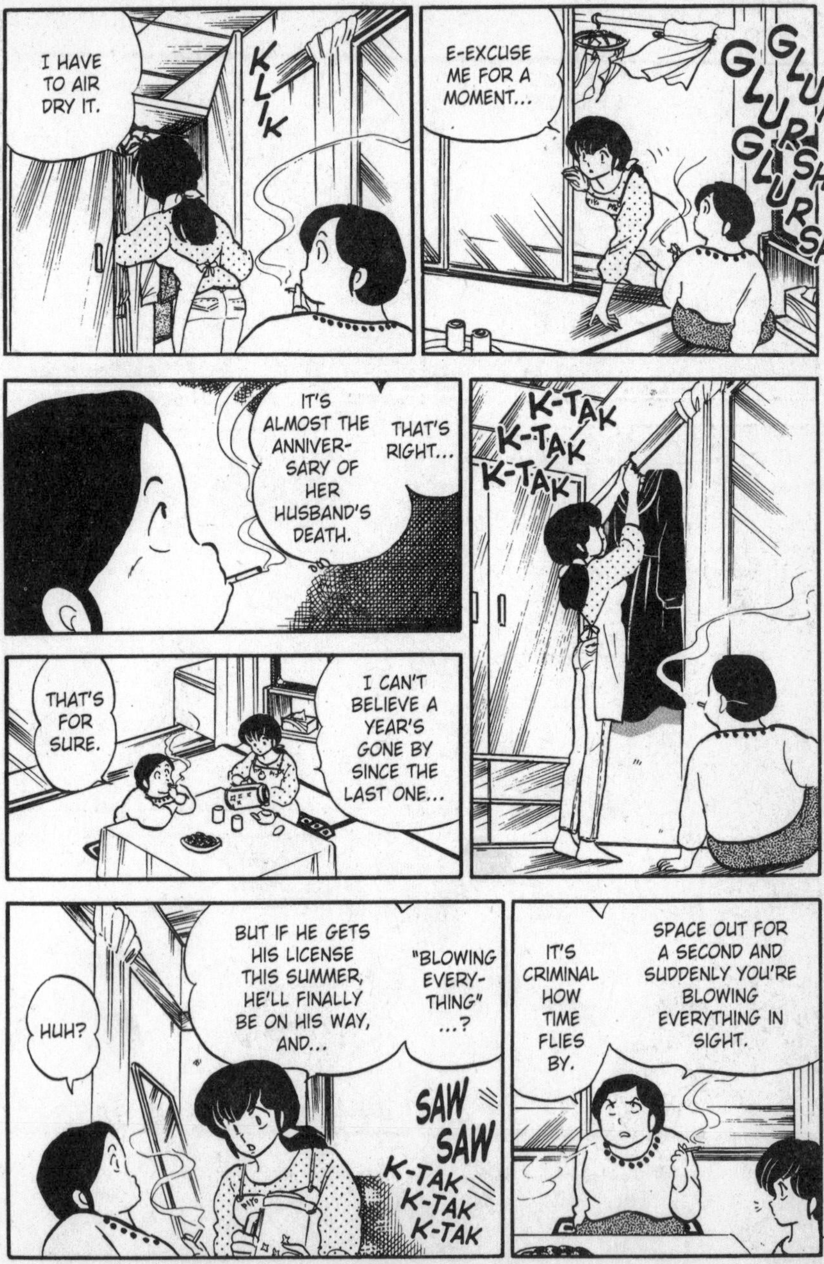
E-EXCUSE ME FOR A MOMENT...
GLURSH GLURSH GLURSH GLURSH
I HAVE TO AIR DRY IT.
KLIK
K-TAK K-TAK K-TAK
THAT'S RIGHT...
IT'S ALMOST THE ANNIVERSARY OF HER HUSBAND'S DEATH.
I CAN'T BELIEVE A YEAR'S GONE BY SINCE THE LAST ONE...
THAT'S FOR SURE.
SPACE OUT FOR A SECOND AND SUDDENLY YOU'RE BLOWING EVERYTHING IN SIGHT.
IT'S CRIMINAL HOW TIME FLIES BY.
"BLOWING EVERYTHING" ...?
BUT IF HE GETS HIS LICENSE THIS SUMMER, HE'LL FINALLY BE ON HIS WAY, AND...
HUH?
SAW SAW
K-TAK K-TAK K-TAK

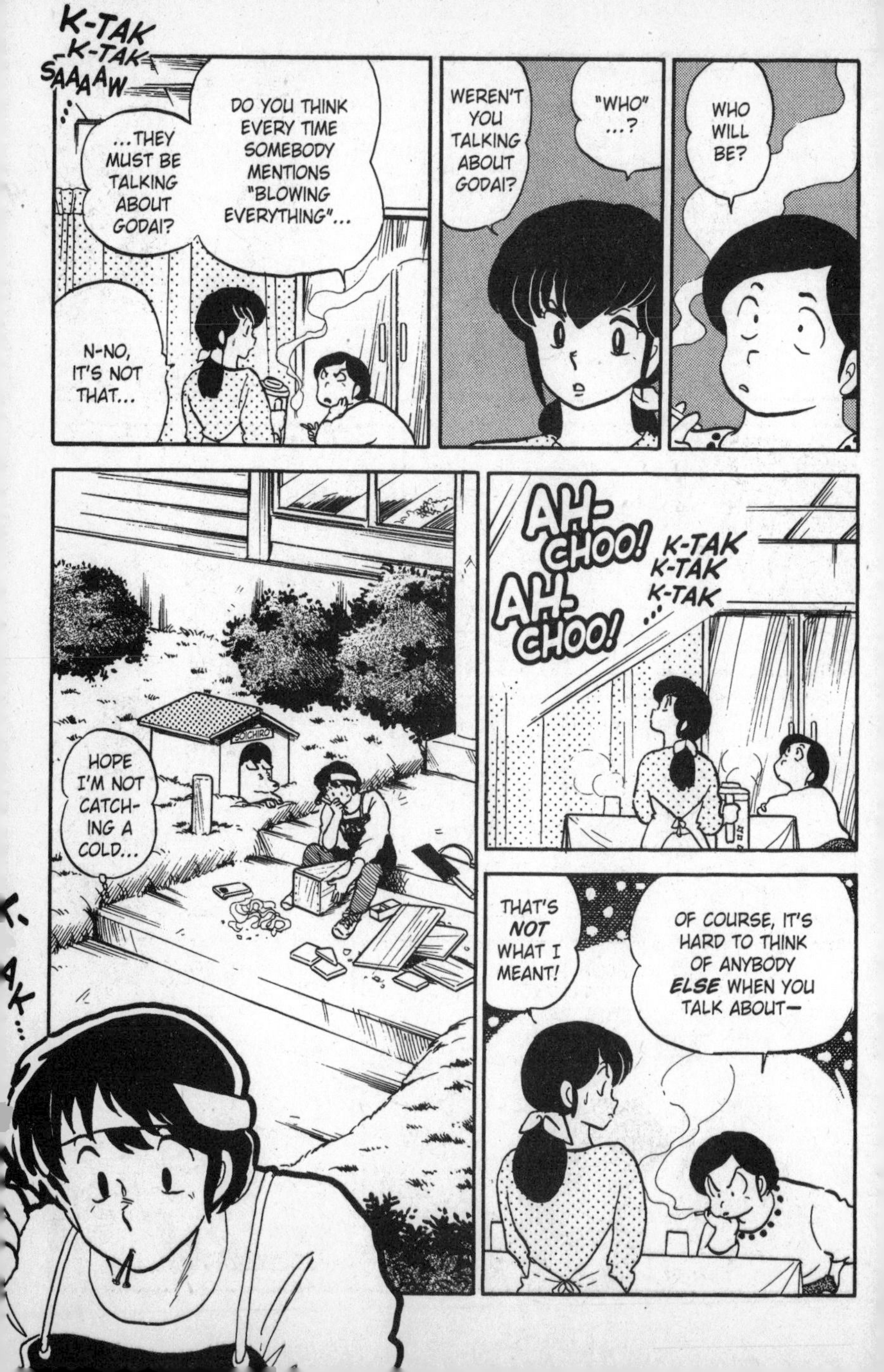
WHO WILL BE?
"WHO" ...?
WEREN'T YOU TALKING ABOUT GODAI?
K-TAK K-TAK SAAAAW
DO YOU THINK EVERY TIME SOMEBODY MENTIONS "BLOWING EVERYTHING"...
...THEY MUST BE TALKING ABOUT GODAI?
N-NO, IT'S NOT THAT...
AH-CHOO! AH-CHOO!
K-TAK K-TAK K-TAK
OF COURSE, IT'S HARD TO THINK OF ANYBODY ELSE WHEN YOU TALK ABOUT—
THAT'S NOT WHAT I MEANT!
SOICHIRO
HOPE I'M NOT CATCHING A COLD...

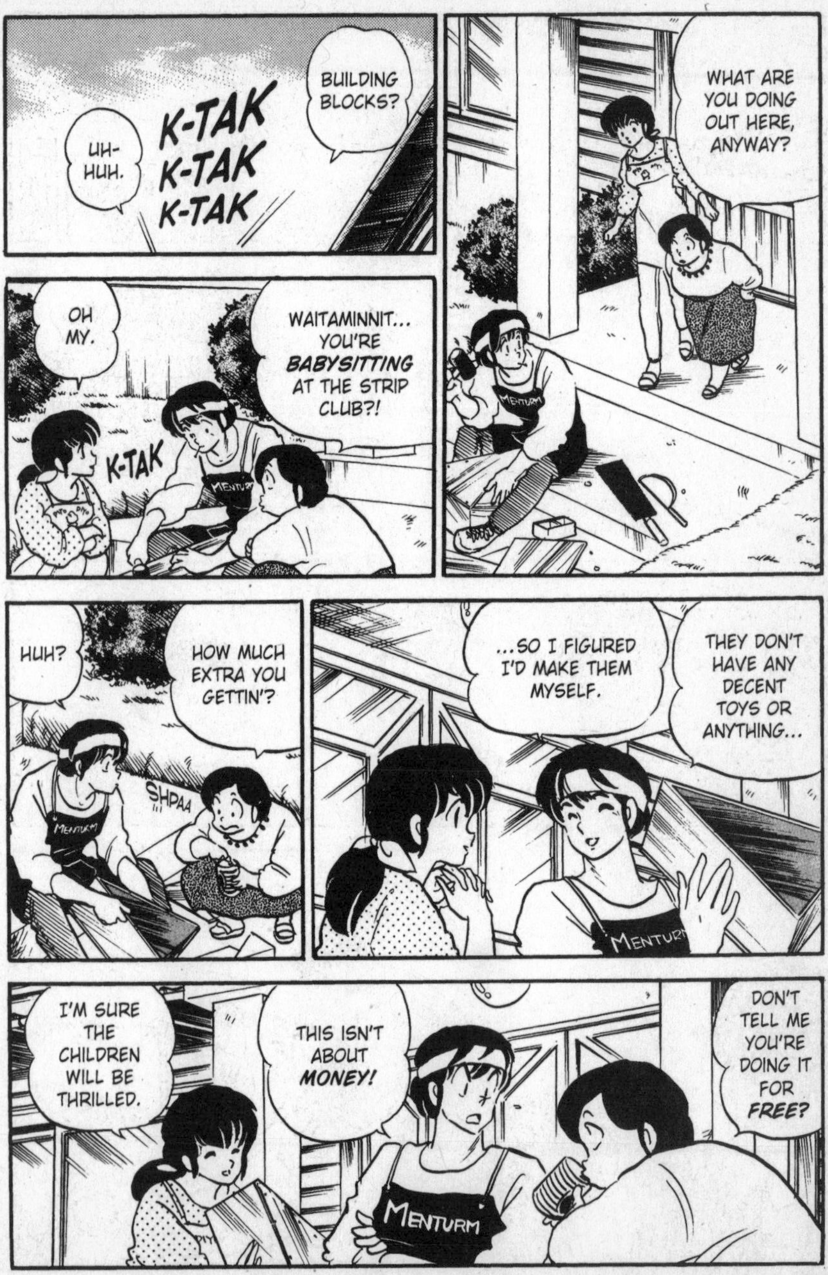
WHAT ARE YOU DOING OUT HERE, ANYWAY?
BUILDING BLOCKS?
K-TAK K-TAK K-TAK
UH-HUH.
WAITAMINNIT... YOU'RE *BABYSITTING* AT THE STRIP CLUB?!
OH MY.
K-TAK
THEY DON'T HAVE ANY DECENT TOYS OR ANYTHING...
...SO I FIGURED I'D MAKE THEM MYSELF.
HOW MUCH EXTRA YOU GETTIN'?
HUH?
SHPAA
DON'T TELL ME YOU'RE DOING IT FOR *FREE?*
THIS ISN'T ABOUT *MONEY!*
I'M SURE THE CHILDREN WILL BE THRILLED.

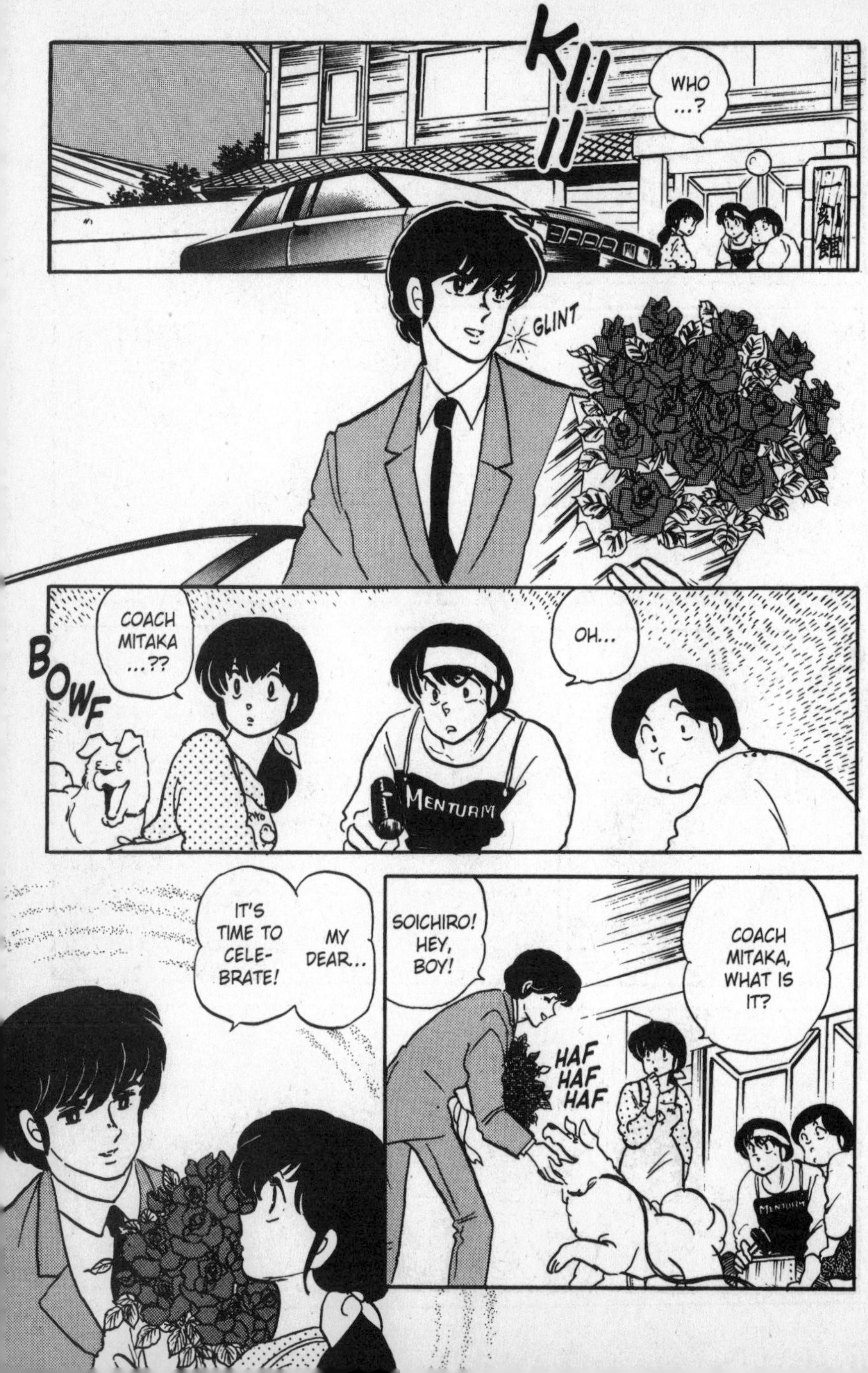
KIIII
WHO ...?
GLINT
OH...
COACH MITAKA ...??
BOWF
COACH MITAKA, WHAT IS IT?
SOICHIRO! HEY, BOY!
HAF HAF HAF
MY DEAR...
IT'S TIME TO CELE-BRATE!

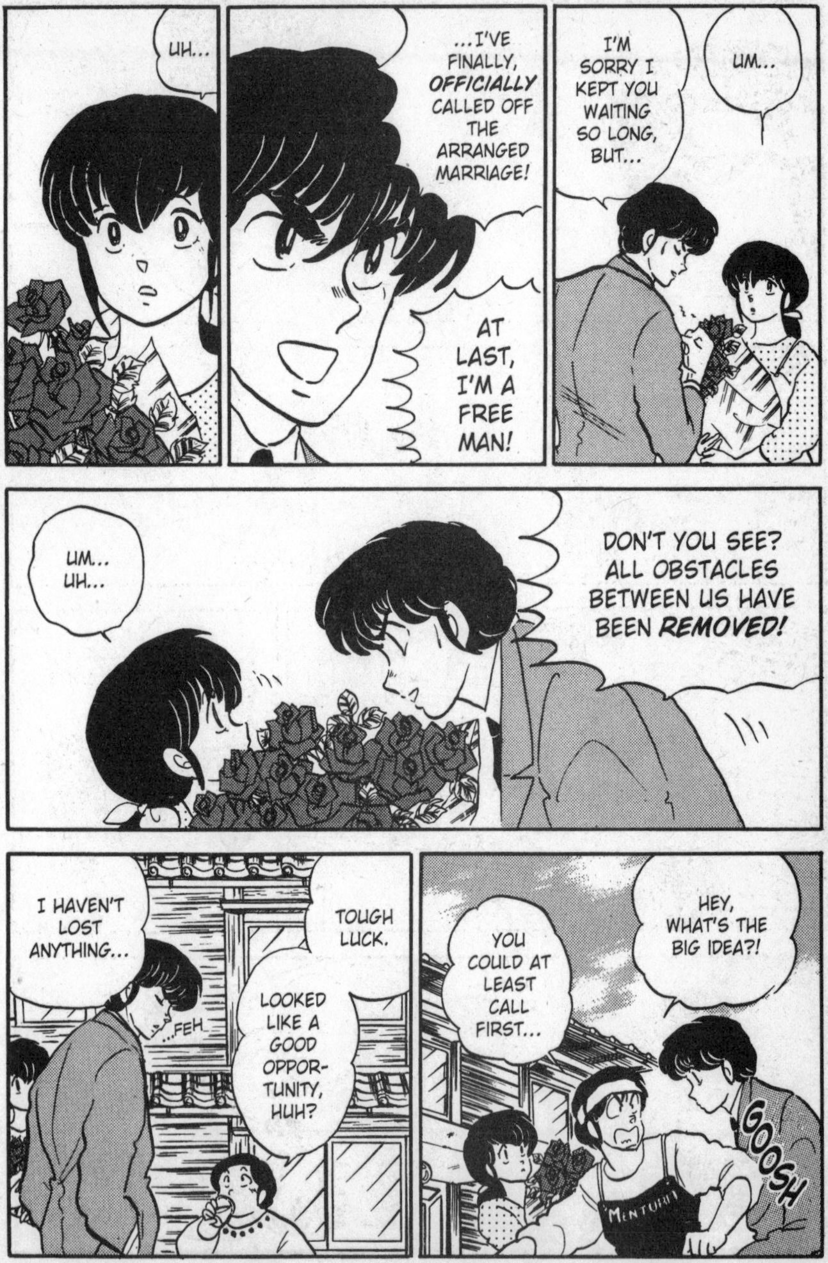
UM...
I'M SORRY I KEPT YOU WAITING SO LONG, BUT...
...I'VE FINALLY, OFFICIALLY CALLED OFF THE ARRANGED MARRIAGE!
AT LAST, I'M A FREE MAN!
UH...
DON'T YOU SEE? ALL OBSTACLES BETWEEN US HAVE BEEN REMOVED!
UM... UH...
HEY, WHAT'S THE BIG IDEA?!
YOU COULD AT LEAST CALL FIRST...
GOOSH
TOUGH LUCK.
I HAVEN'T LOST ANYTHING...
LOOKED LIKE A GOOD OPPOR-TUNITY, HUH?
...FEH

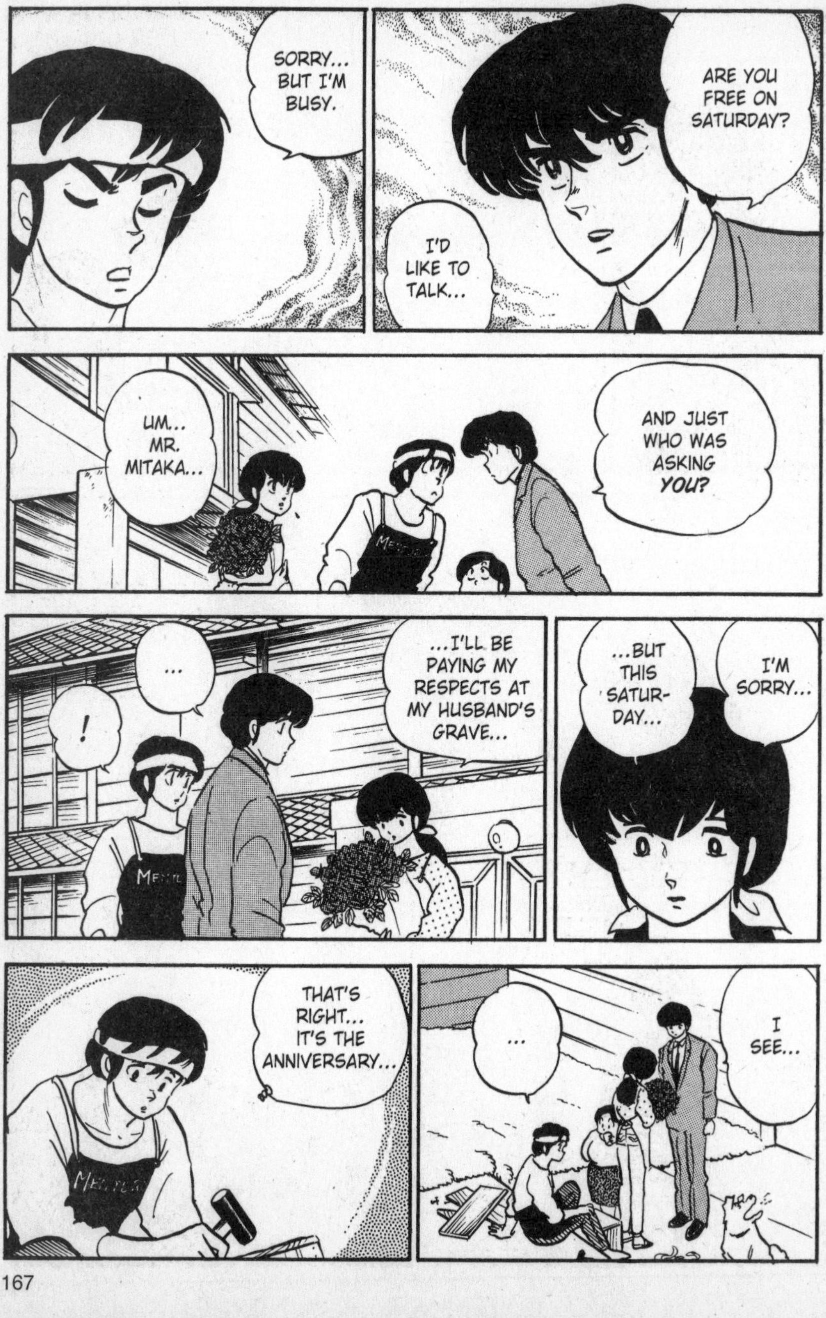
ARE YOU FREE ON SATURDAY?
I'D LIKE TO TALK...
SORRY... BUT I'M BUSY.
AND JUST WHO WAS ASKING *YOU?*
UM... MR. MITAKA...
I'M SORRY...
...BUT THIS SATURDAY...
...I'LL BE PAYING MY RESPECTS AT MY HUSBAND'S GRAVE...
...
!
I SEE...
...
THAT'S RIGHT... IT'S THE ANNIVERSARY...

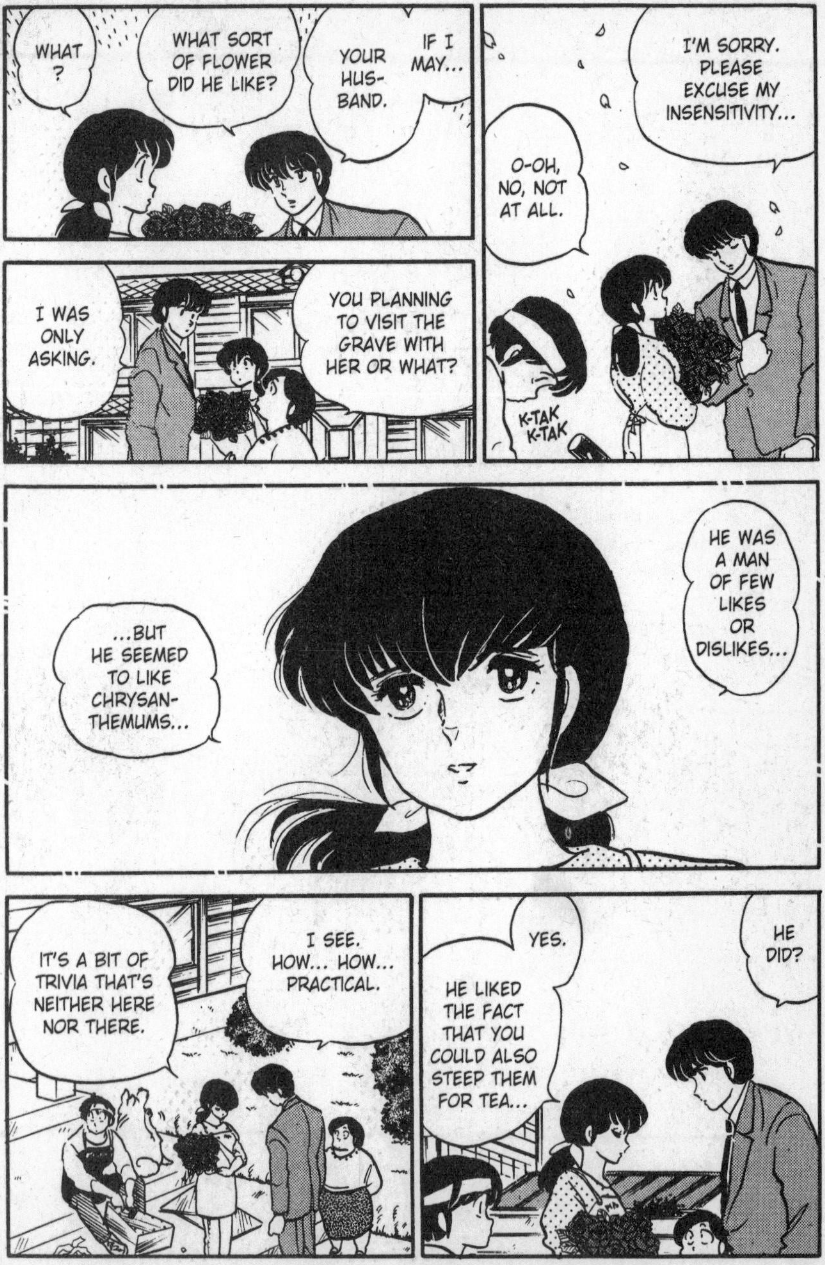
I'M SORRY. PLEASE EXCUSE MY INSENSITIVITY...
O-OH, NO, NOT AT ALL.
K-TAK K-TAK
IF I MAY...
YOUR HUS-BAND.
WHAT SORT OF FLOWER DID HE LIKE?
WHAT ?
YOU PLANNING TO VISIT THE GRAVE WITH HER OR WHAT?
I WAS ONLY ASKING.
HE WAS A MAN OF FEW LIKES OR DISLIKES...
...BUT HE SEEMED TO LIKE CHRYSAN-THEMUMS...
HE DID?
YES.
HE LIKED THE FACT THAT YOU COULD ALSO STEEP THEM FOR TEA...
I SEE. HOW... HOW... PRACTICAL.
IT'S A BIT OF TRIVIA THAT'S NEITHER HERE NOR THERE.

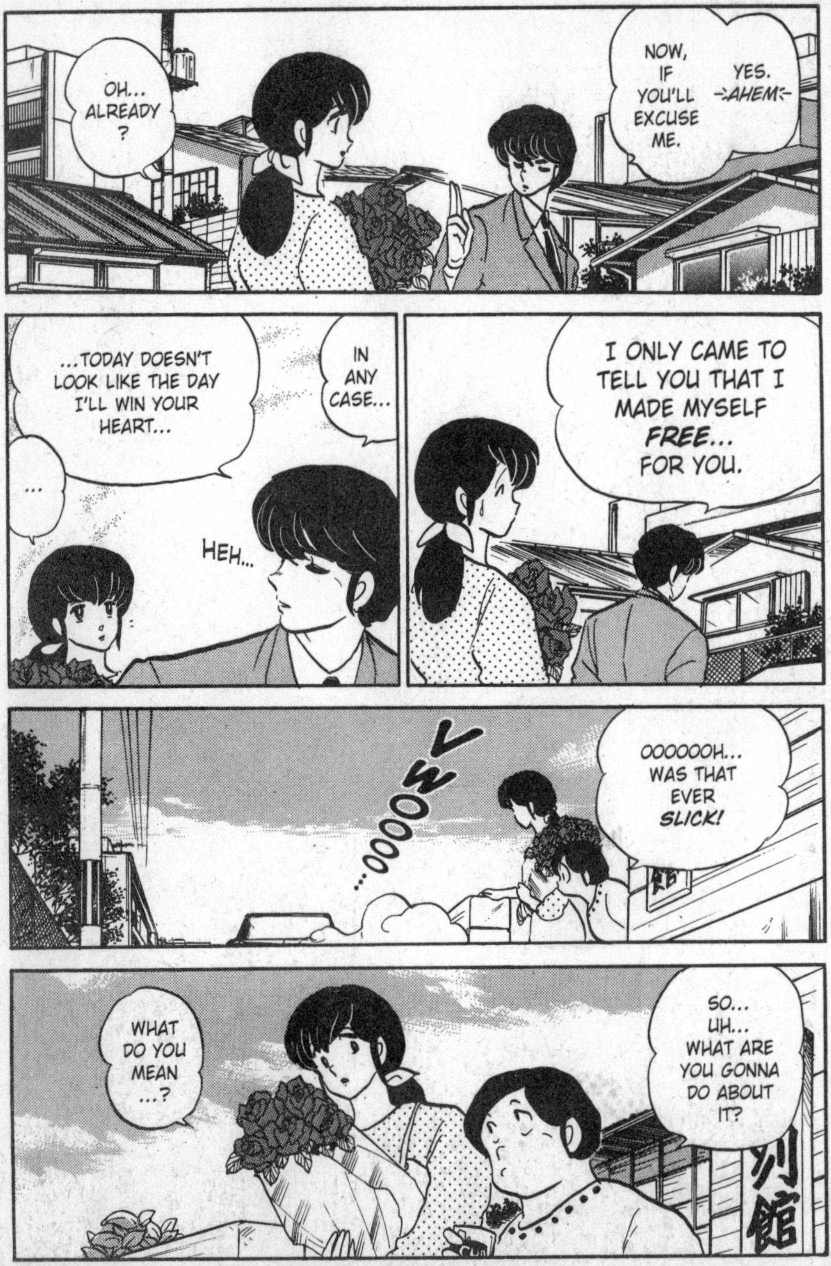
YES. -AHEM-
NOW, IF YOU'LL EXCUSE ME.
OH... ALREADY?
I ONLY CAME TO TELL YOU THAT I MADE MYSELF **FREE**... FOR YOU.
IN ANY CASE...
...TODAY DOESN'T LOOK LIKE THE DAY I'LL WIN YOUR HEART...
...
HEH...
OOOOOOH... WAS THAT EVER **SLICK!**
VWOOOOO...
SO... UH... WHAT ARE YOU GONNA DO ABOUT IT?
WHAT DO YOU MEAN ...?

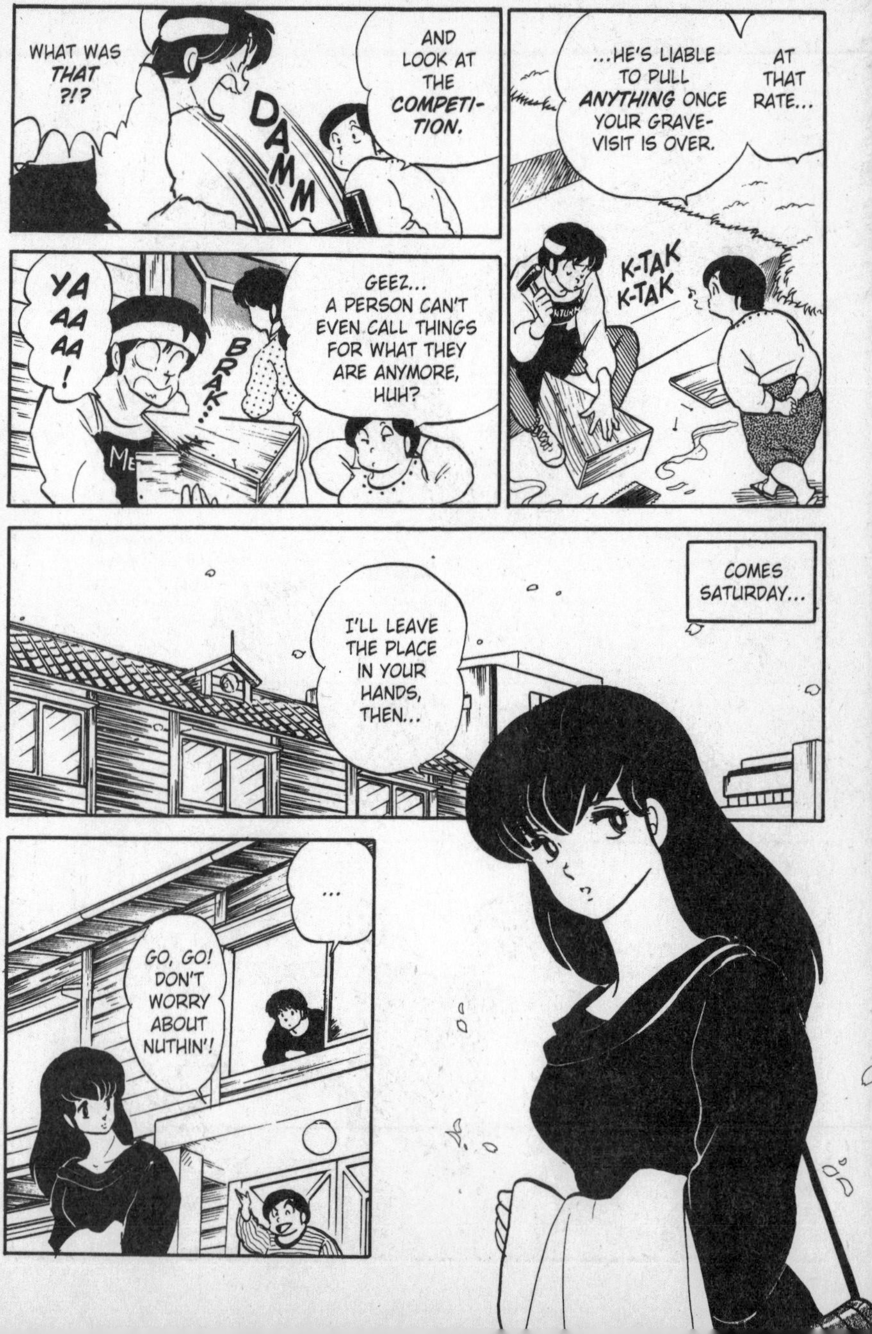
AT THAT RATE...
...HE'S LIABLE TO PULL ANYTHING ONCE YOUR GRAVE-VISIT IS OVER.
AND LOOK AT THE COMPETITION.
DAMM
WHAT WAS THAT ?!?
K-TAK K-TAK
GEEZ... A PERSON CAN'T EVEN CALL THINGS FOR WHAT THEY ARE ANYMORE, HUH?
BRAK...
YAAAAA!
COMES SATURDAY...
I'LL LEAVE THE PLACE IN YOUR HANDS, THEN...
...
GO, GO! DON'T WORRY ABOUT NUTHIN'!

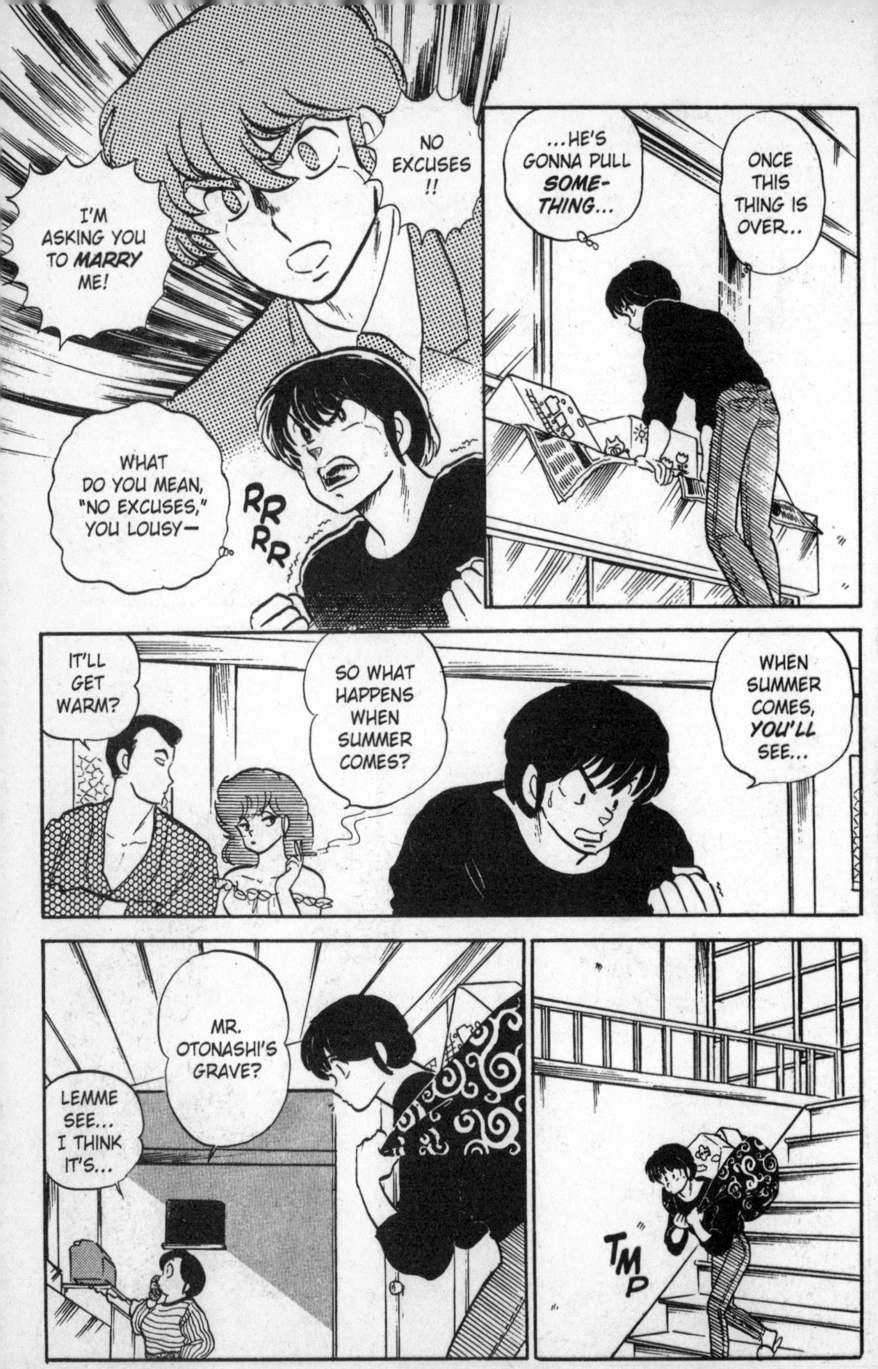
ONCE THIS THING IS OVER...
...HE'S GONNA PULL SOMETHING...
NO EXCUSES !!
I'M ASKING YOU TO MARRY ME!
WHAT DO YOU MEAN, "NO EXCUSES," YOU LOUSY—
RRRR
WHEN SUMMER COMES, YOU'LL SEE...
SO WHAT HAPPENS WHEN SUMMER COMES?
IT'LL GET WARM?
TMP
MR. OTONASHI'S GRAVE?
LEMME SEE... I THINK IT'S...

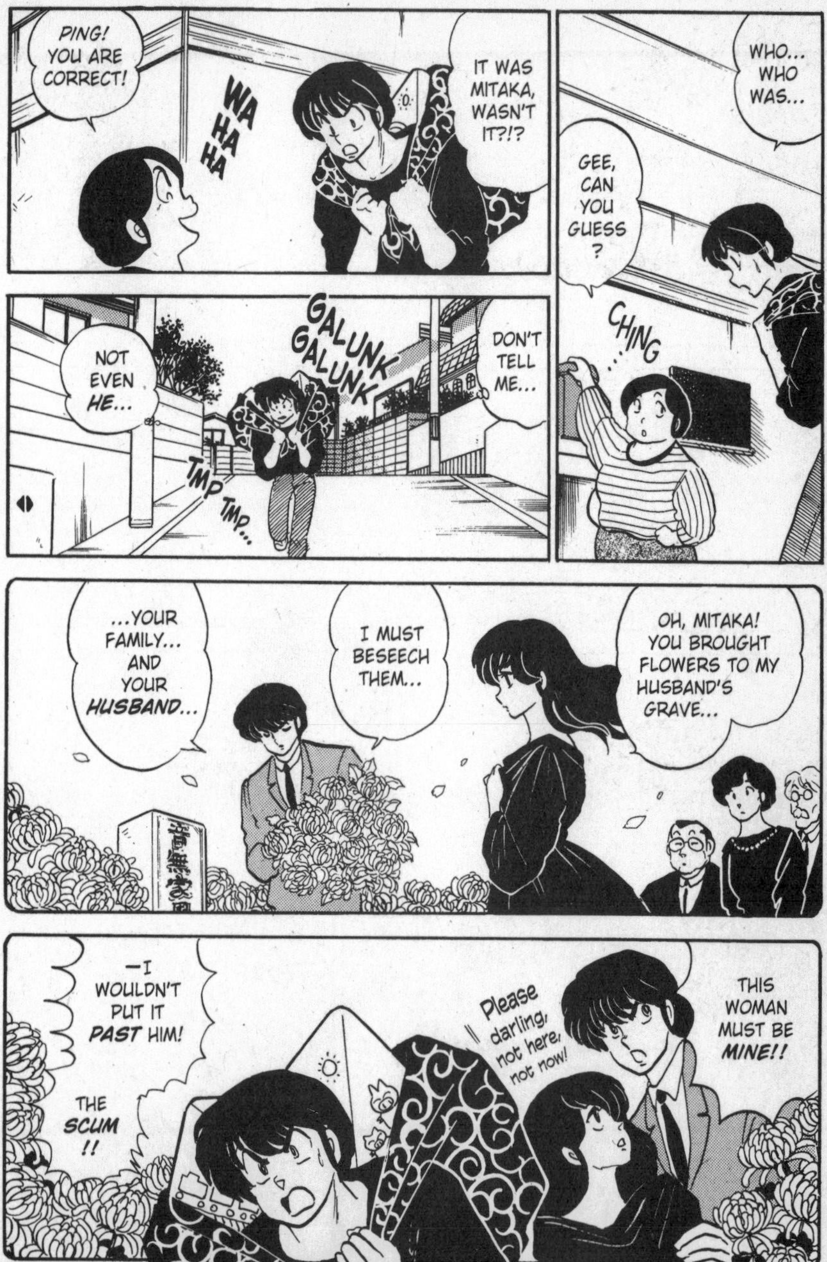
WHO... WHO WAS...
GEE, CAN YOU GUESS?
CHING
IT WAS MITAKA, WASN'T IT?!?
WA HA HA HA
PING! YOU ARE CORRECT!
DON'T TELL ME...
GALUNK GALUNK
NOT EVEN HE...
TMP TMP...
OH, MITAKA! YOU BROUGHT FLOWERS TO MY HUSBAND'S GRAVE...
I MUST BESEECH THEM...
...YOUR FAMILY... AND YOUR HUSBAND...
THIS WOMAN MUST BE MINE!!
Please darling, not here, not now!
—I WOULDN'T PUT IT PAST HIM!
THE SCUM!!

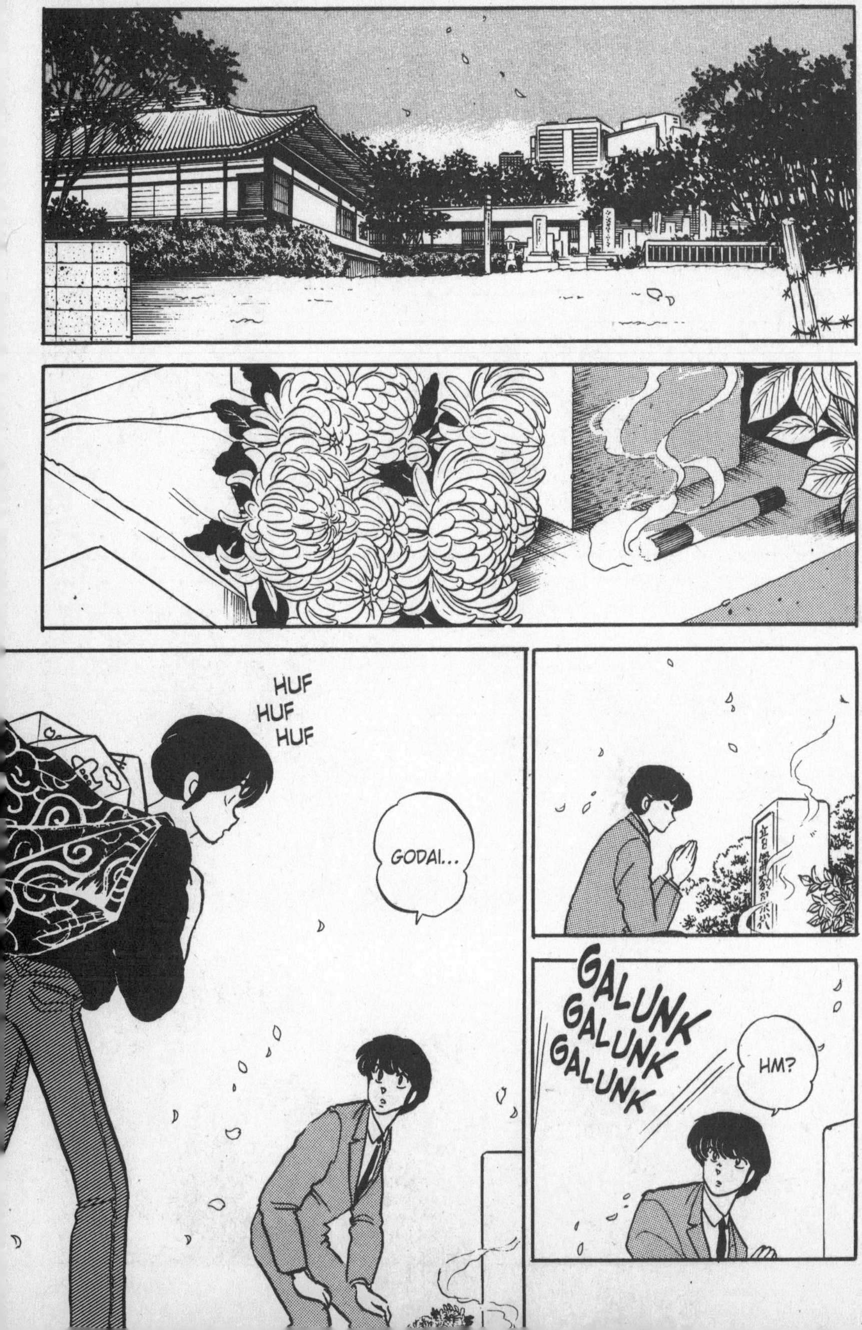
GALUNK
GALUNK
GALUNK
HM?
HUF
HUF
HUF
GODAI...

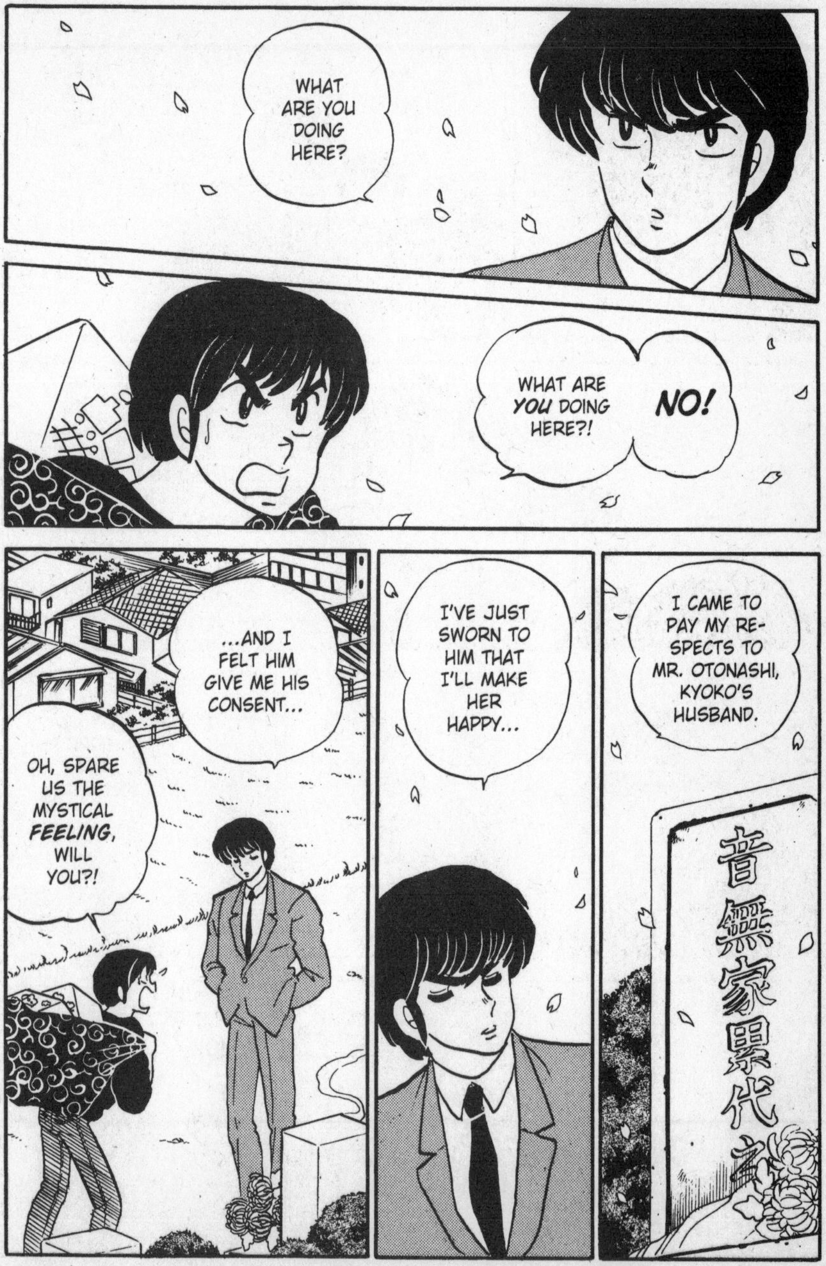
WHAT ARE YOU DOING HERE?
NO!
WHAT ARE *YOU* DOING HERE?!
I CAME TO PAY MY RE-SPECTS TO MR. OTONASHI, KYOKO'S HUSBAND.
音無家累代之
I'VE JUST SWORN TO HIM THAT I'LL MAKE HER HAPPY...
...AND I FELT HIM GIVE ME HIS CONSENT...
OH, SPARE US THE MYSTICAL **FEELING**, WILL YOU?!

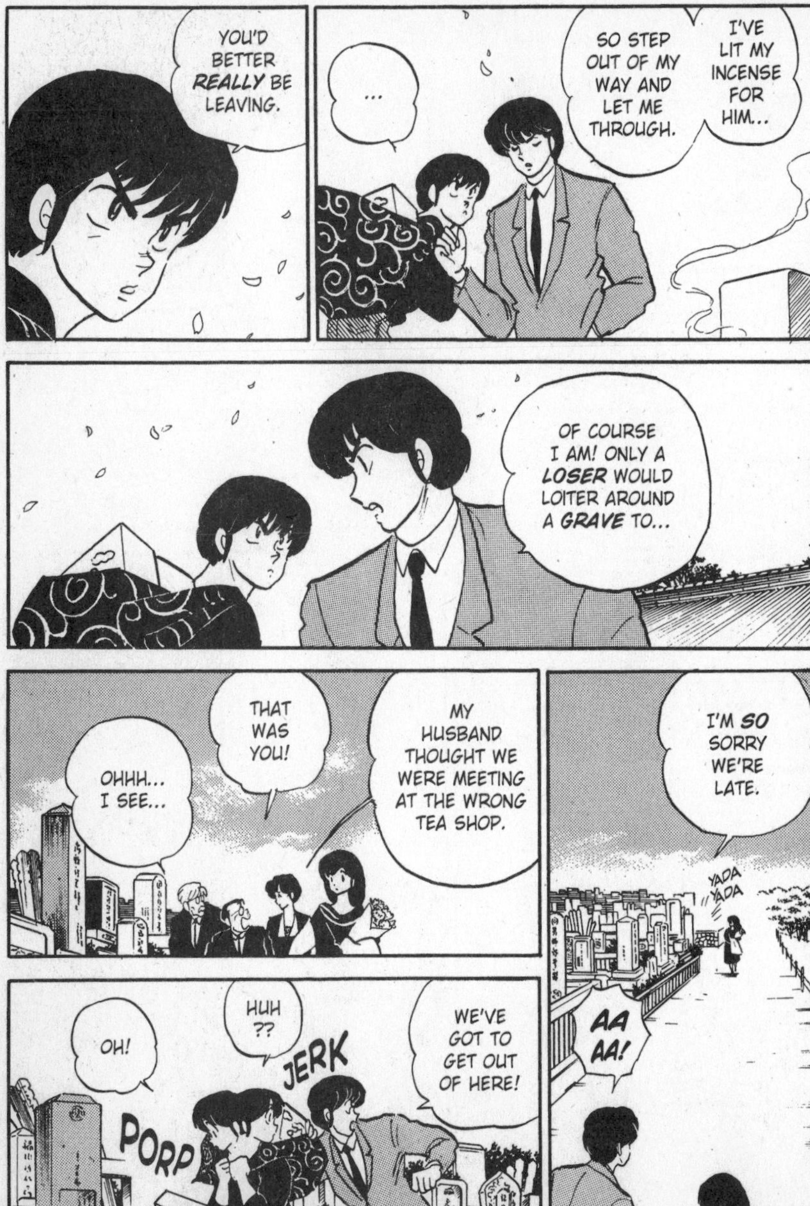
I'VE LIT MY INCENSE FOR HIM...
SO STEP OUT OF MY WAY AND LET ME THROUGH.
...
YOU'D BETTER *REALLY* BE LEAVING.
OF COURSE I AM! ONLY A *LOSER* WOULD LOITER AROUND A *GRAVE* TO...
I'M *SO* SORRY WE'RE LATE.
YADA YADA
AA AA!
MY HUSBAND THOUGHT WE WERE MEETING AT THE WRONG TEA SHOP.
THAT WAS YOU!
OHHH... I SEE...
WE'VE GOT TO GET OUT OF HERE!
JERK
HUH ??
OH!
PORP

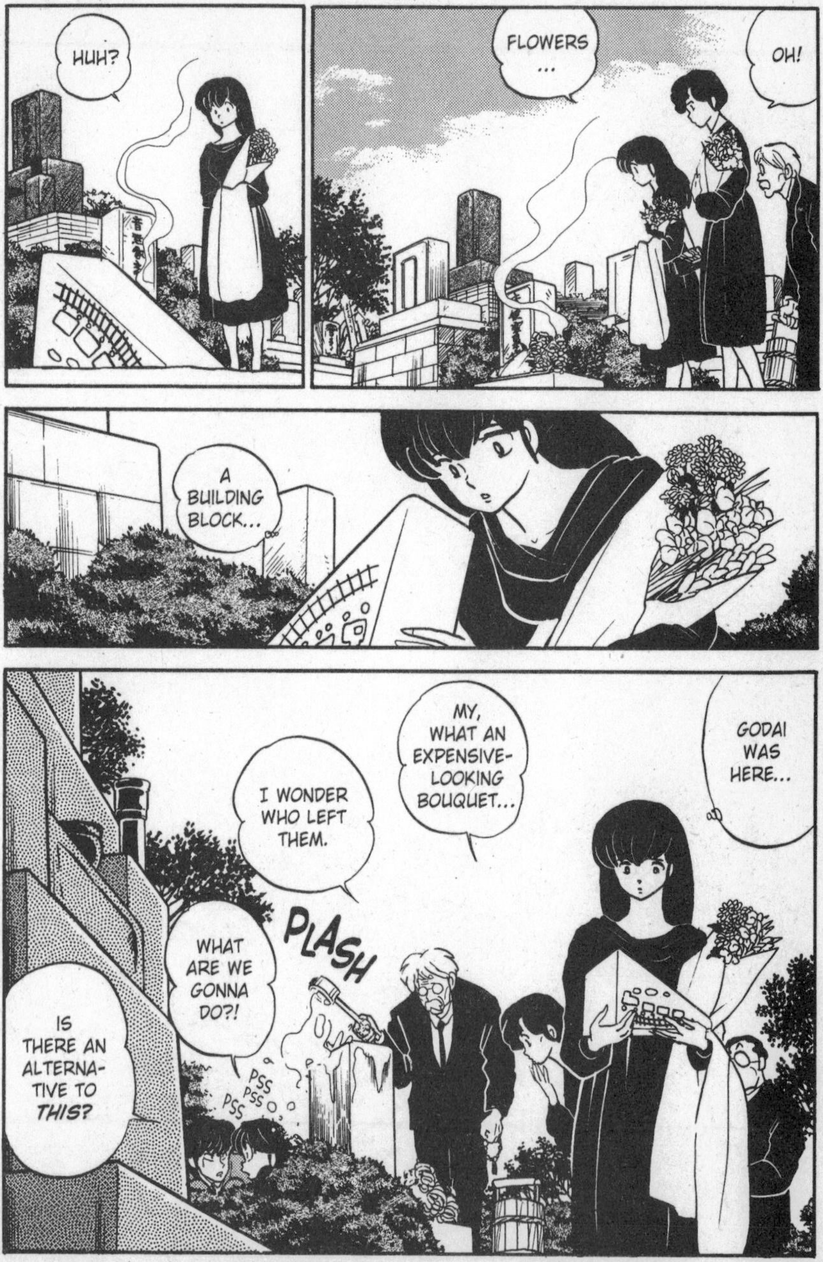
HUH?
FLOWERS ...
OH!
A BUILDING BLOCK...
MY, WHAT AN EXPENSIVE-LOOKING BOUQUET...
I WONDER WHO LEFT THEM.
GODAI WAS HERE...
PLASH
WHAT ARE WE GONNA DO?!
IS THERE AN ALTERNATIVE TO *THIS?*
PSS PSS PSS

PART TEN
BACK FROM THE GRAVE

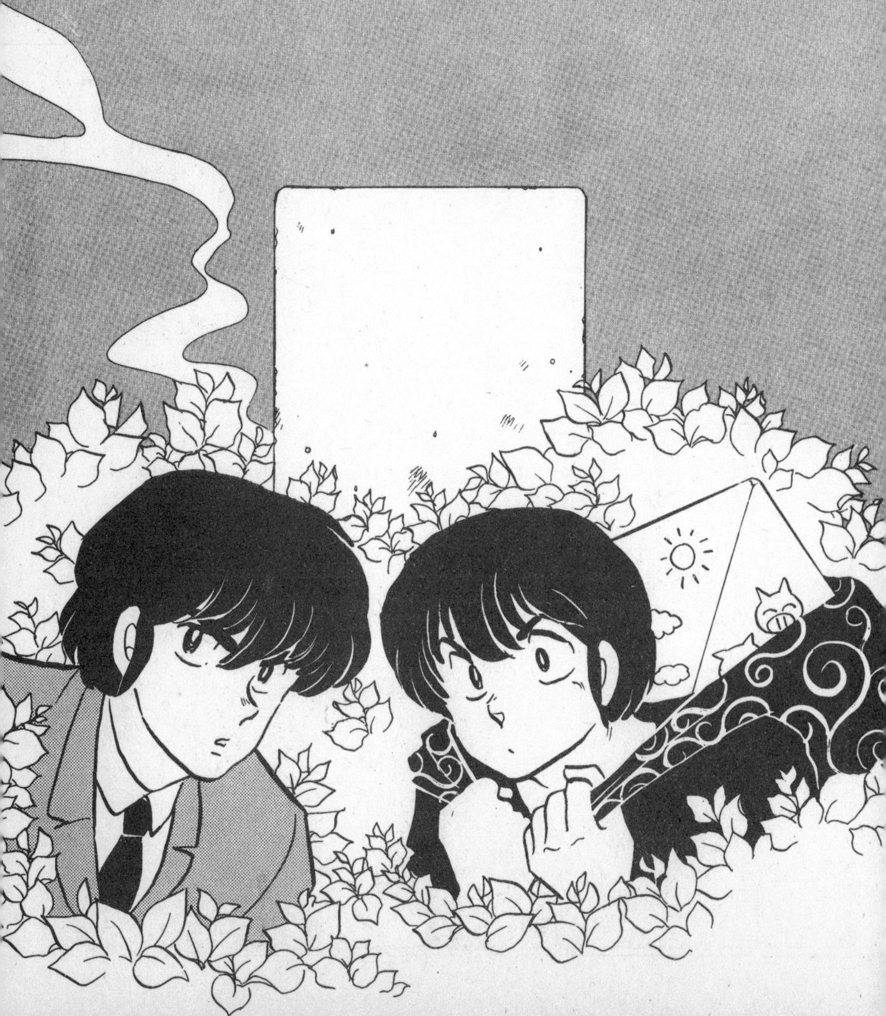

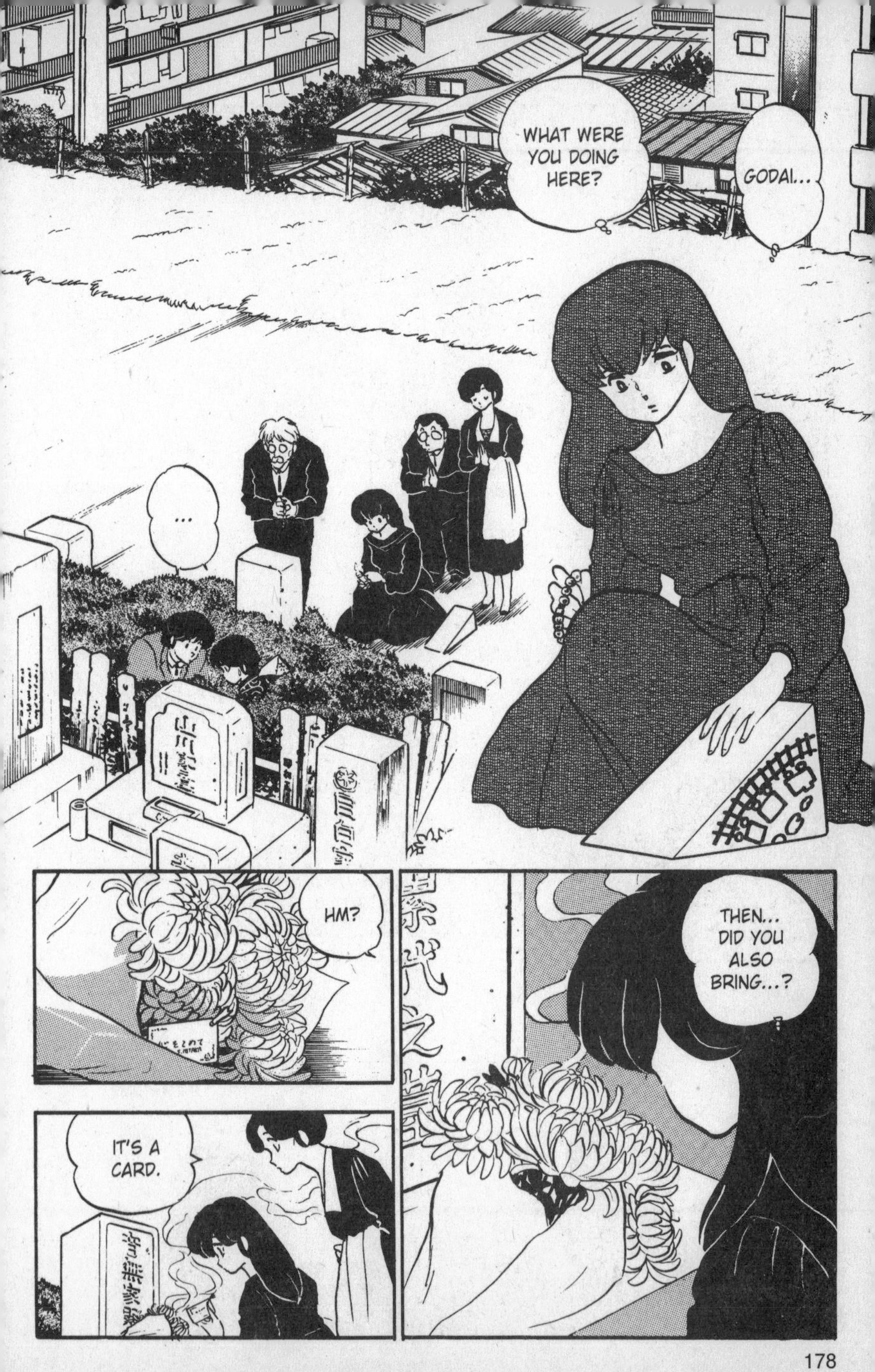
GODAI...
WHAT WERE YOU DOING HERE?
...
THEN... DID YOU ALSO BRING...?
HM?
IT'S A CARD.

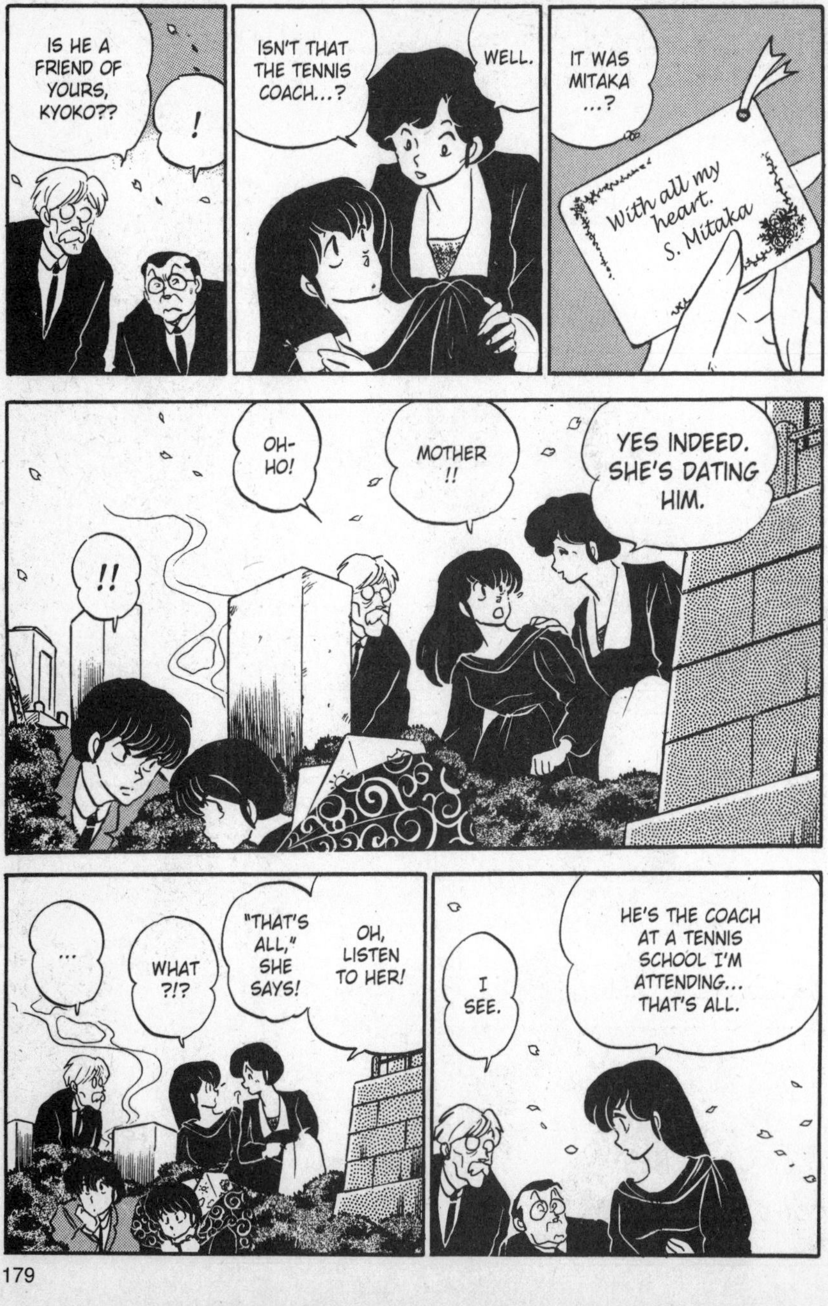
IT WAS MITAKA ...?
With all my heart. S. Mitaka
WELL.
ISN'T THAT THE TENNIS COACH...?
IS HE A FRIEND OF YOURS, KYOKO??
!
YES INDEED. SHE'S DATING HIM.
MOTHER !!
OH-HO!
!!
HE'S THE COACH AT A TENNIS SCHOOL I'M ATTENDING... THAT'S ALL.
I SEE.
OH, LISTEN TO HER!
"THAT'S ALL," SHE SAYS!
WHAT ?!?
...

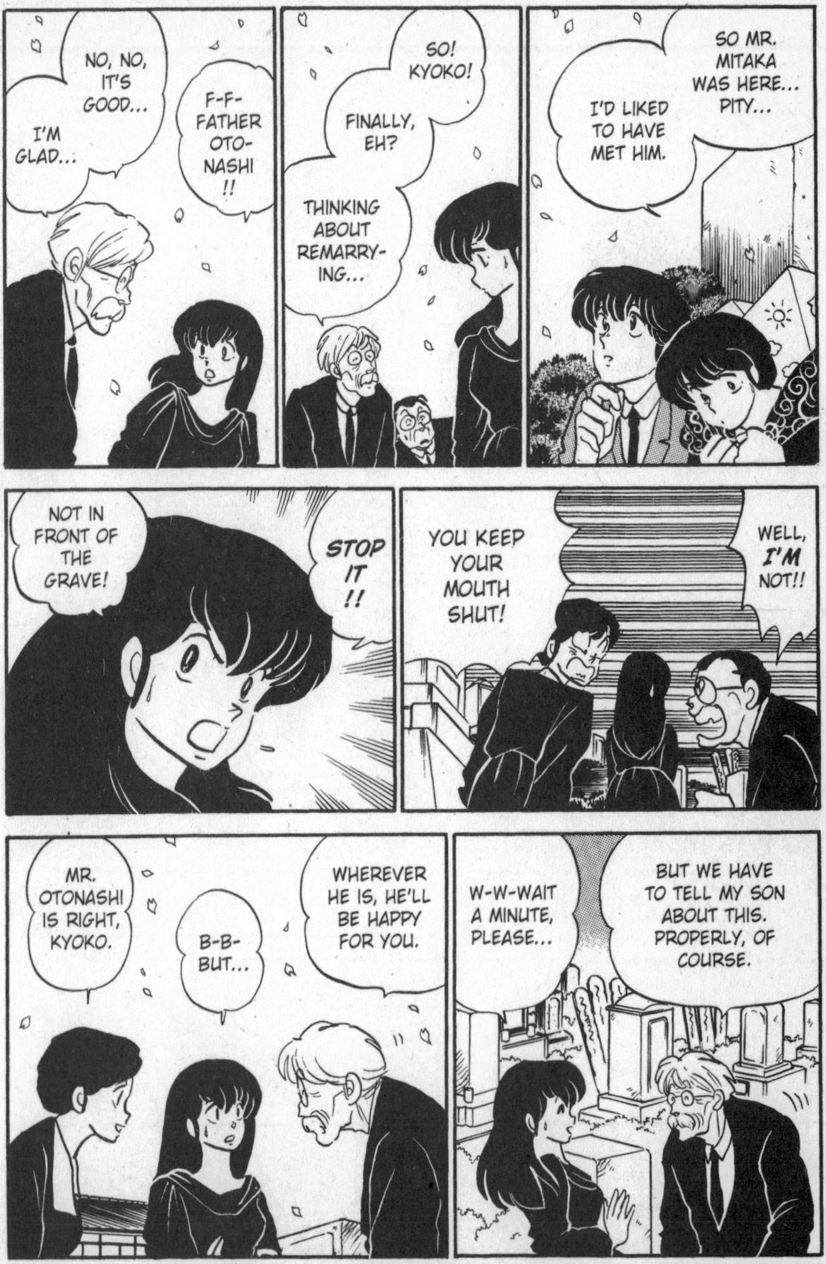
SO MR. MITAKA WAS HERE... PITY...
I'D LIKED TO HAVE MET HIM.
SO! KYOKO!
FINALLY, EH?
THINKING ABOUT REMARRY-ING...
F-F-FATHER OTO-NASHI !!
NO, NO, IT'S GOOD...
I'M GLAD...
WELL, ***I'M*** NOT!!
YOU KEEP YOUR MOUTH SHUT!
STOP IT !!
NOT IN FRONT OF THE GRAVE!
BUT WE HAVE TO TELL MY SON ABOUT THIS. PROPERLY, OF COURSE.
W-W-WAIT A MINUTE, PLEASE...
WHEREVER HE IS, HE'LL BE HAPPY FOR YOU.
B-B-BUT...
MR. OTONASHI IS RIGHT, KYOKO.

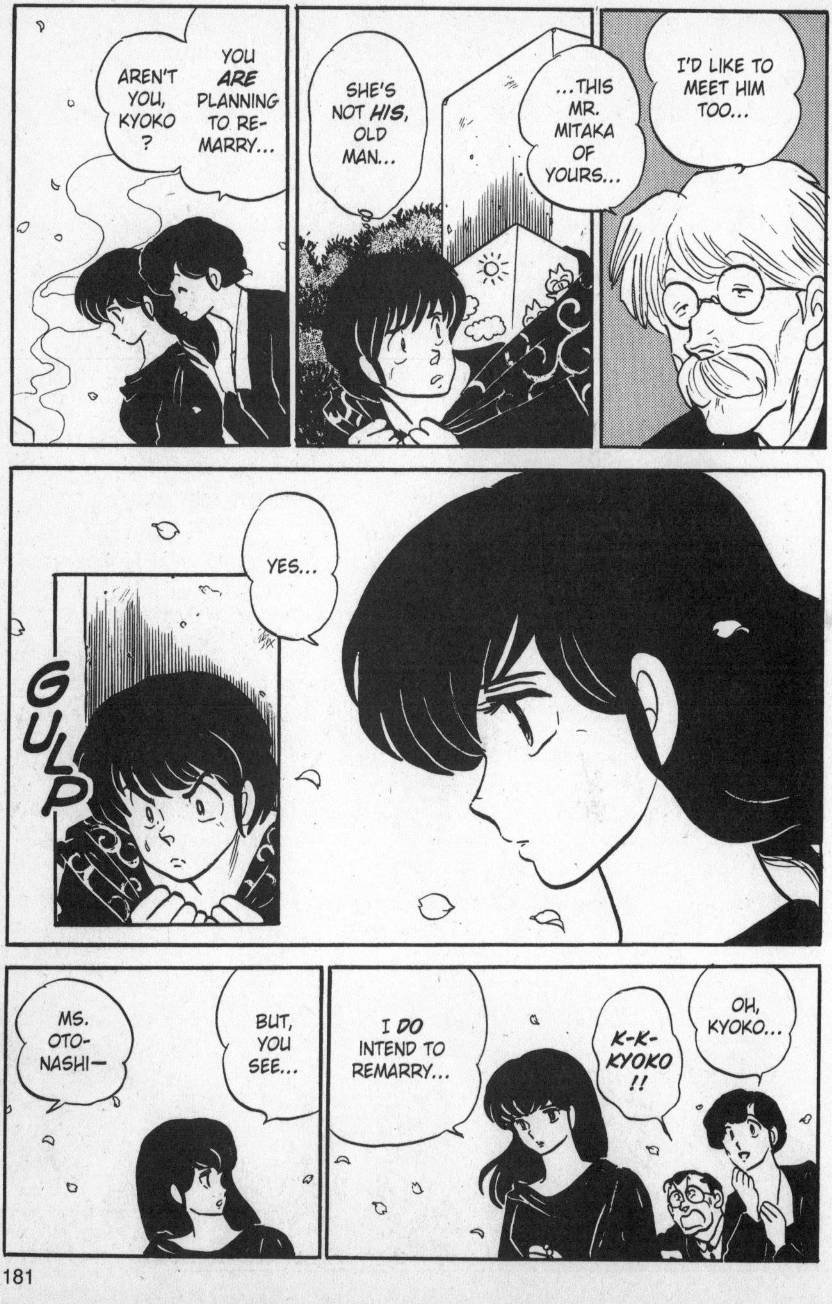
I'D LIKE TO MEET HIM TOO...
...THIS MR. MITAKA OF YOURS...
SHE'S NOT *HIS*, OLD MAN...
YOU *ARE* PLANNING TO RE-MARRY...
AREN'T YOU, KYOKO?
YES...
GULP
OH, KYOKO...
K-K-KYOKO!!
I *DO* INTEND TO REMARRY...
BUT, YOU SEE...
MS. OTO-NASHI—

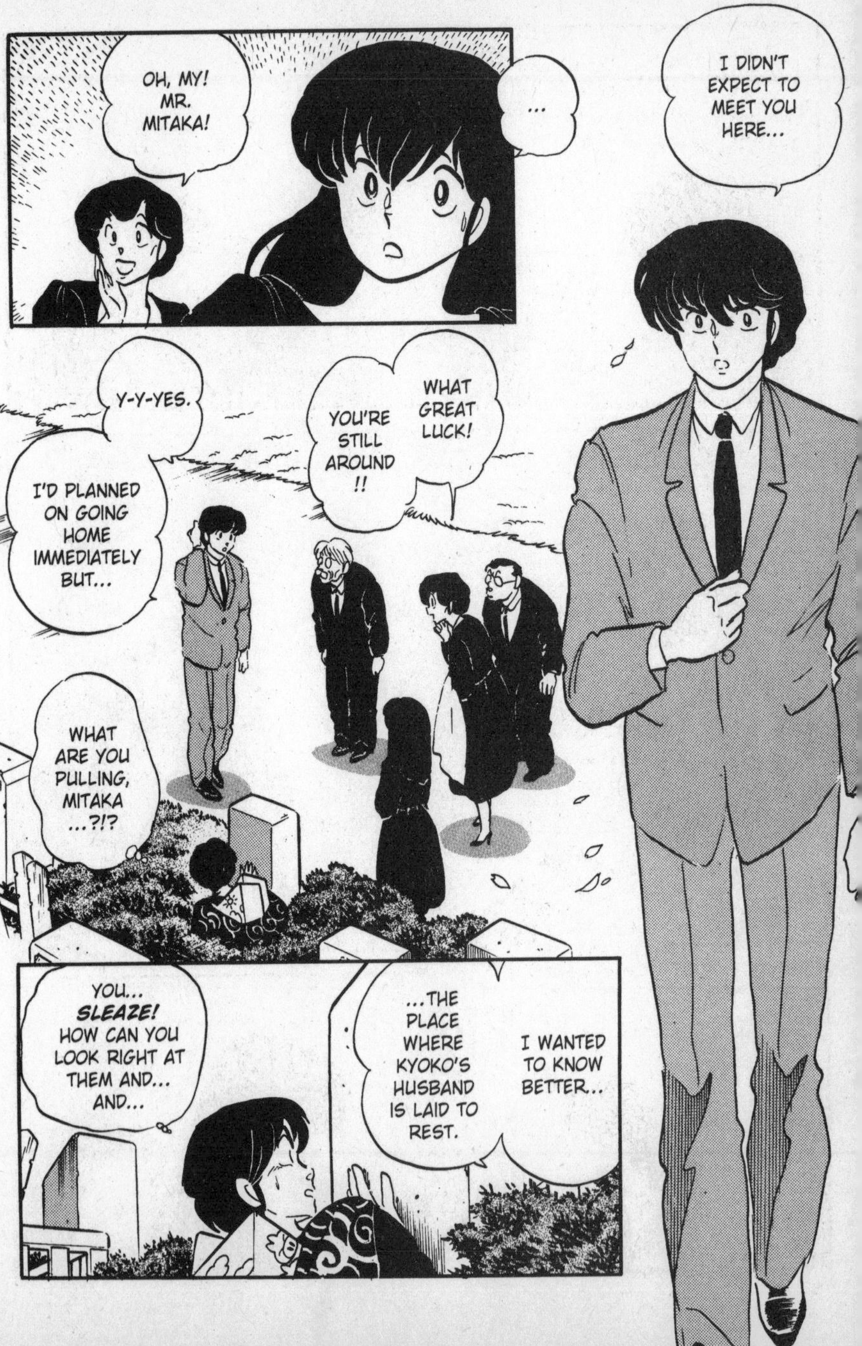
I DIDN'T EXPECT TO MEET YOU HERE...
...
OH, MY! MR. MITAKA!
WHAT GREAT LUCK! YOU'RE STILL AROUND!!
Y-Y-YES.
I'D PLANNED ON GOING HOME IMMEDIATELY BUT...
WHAT ARE YOU PULLING, MITAKA ...?!?
I WANTED TO KNOW BETTER...
...THE PLACE WHERE KYOKO'S HUSBAND IS LAID TO REST.
YOU... SLEAZE! HOW CAN YOU LOOK RIGHT AT THEM AND... AND...

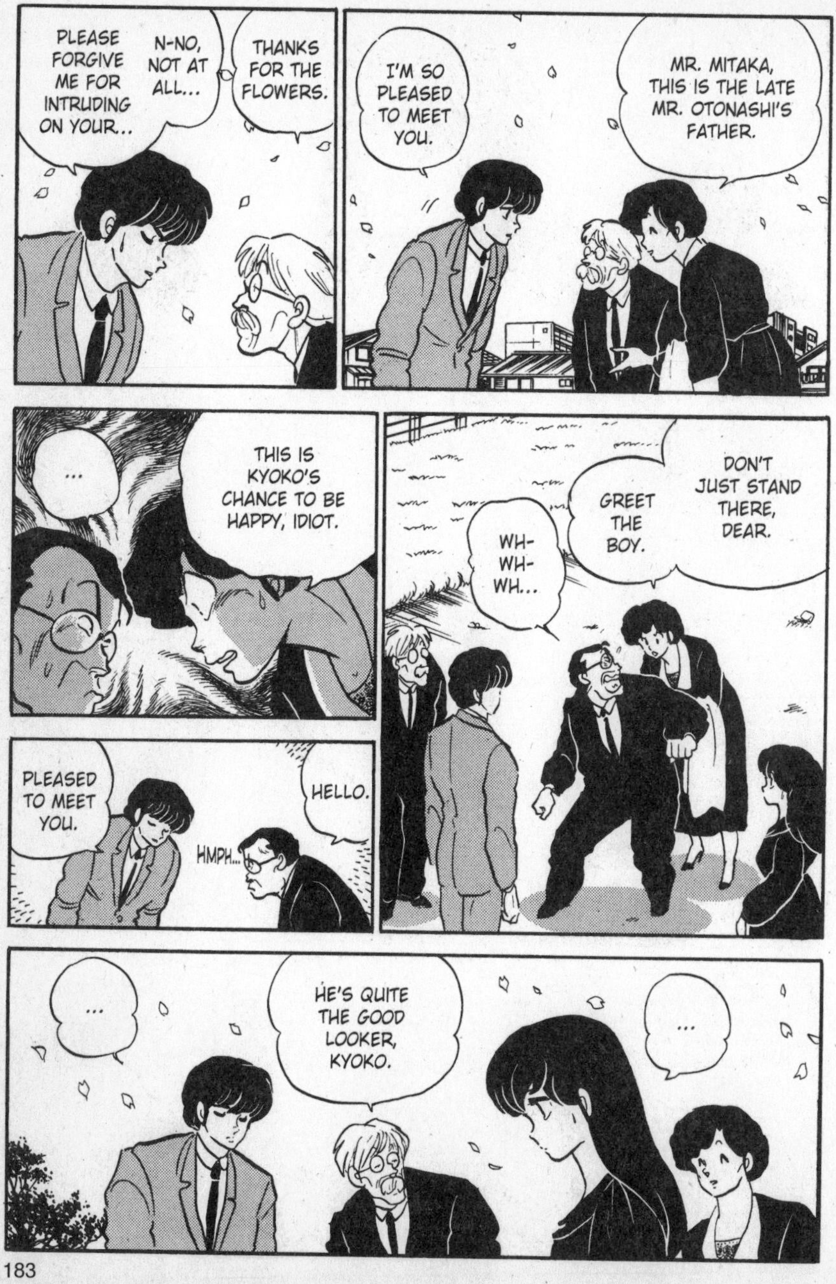
MR. MITAKA, THIS IS THE LATE MR. OTONASHI'S FATHER.
I'M SO PLEASED TO MEET YOU.
THANKS FOR THE FLOWERS.
N-NO, NOT AT ALL...
PLEASE FORGIVE ME FOR INTRUDING ON YOUR...
DON'T JUST STAND THERE, DEAR.
GREET THE BOY.
WH-WH-WH...
THIS IS KYOKO'S CHANCE TO BE HAPPY, IDIOT.
...
HELLO.
HMPH...
PLEASED TO MEET YOU.
...
HE'S QUITE THE GOOD LOOKER, KYOKO.
...

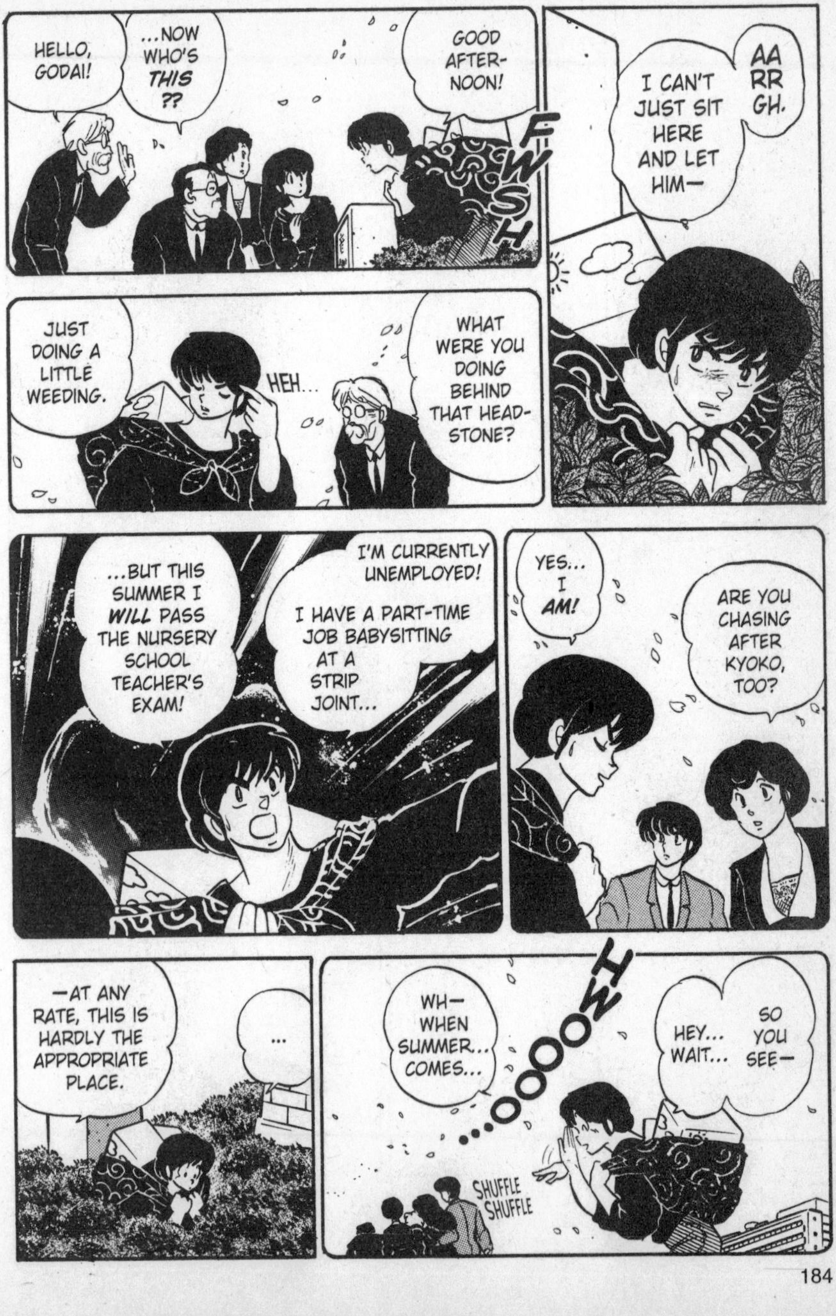
AARRGH.
I CAN'T JUST SIT HERE AND LET HIM—
GOOD AFTERNOON!
FWSH
...NOW WHO'S THIS ??
HELLO, GODAI!
WHAT WERE YOU DOING BEHIND THAT HEADSTONE?
HEH...
JUST DOING A LITTLE WEEDING.
ARE YOU CHASING AFTER KYOKO, TOO?
YES... I AM!
I'M CURRENTLY UNEMPLOYED!
I HAVE A PART-TIME JOB BABYSITTING AT A STRIP JOINT...
...BUT THIS SUMMER I WILL PASS THE NURSERY SCHOOL TEACHER'S EXAM!
SO YOU SEE—
HEY... WAIT...
...OOOOWH
WH— WHEN SUMMER... COMES...
SHUFFLE SHUFFLE
...
—AT ANY RATE, THIS IS HARDLY THE APPROPRIATE PLACE.

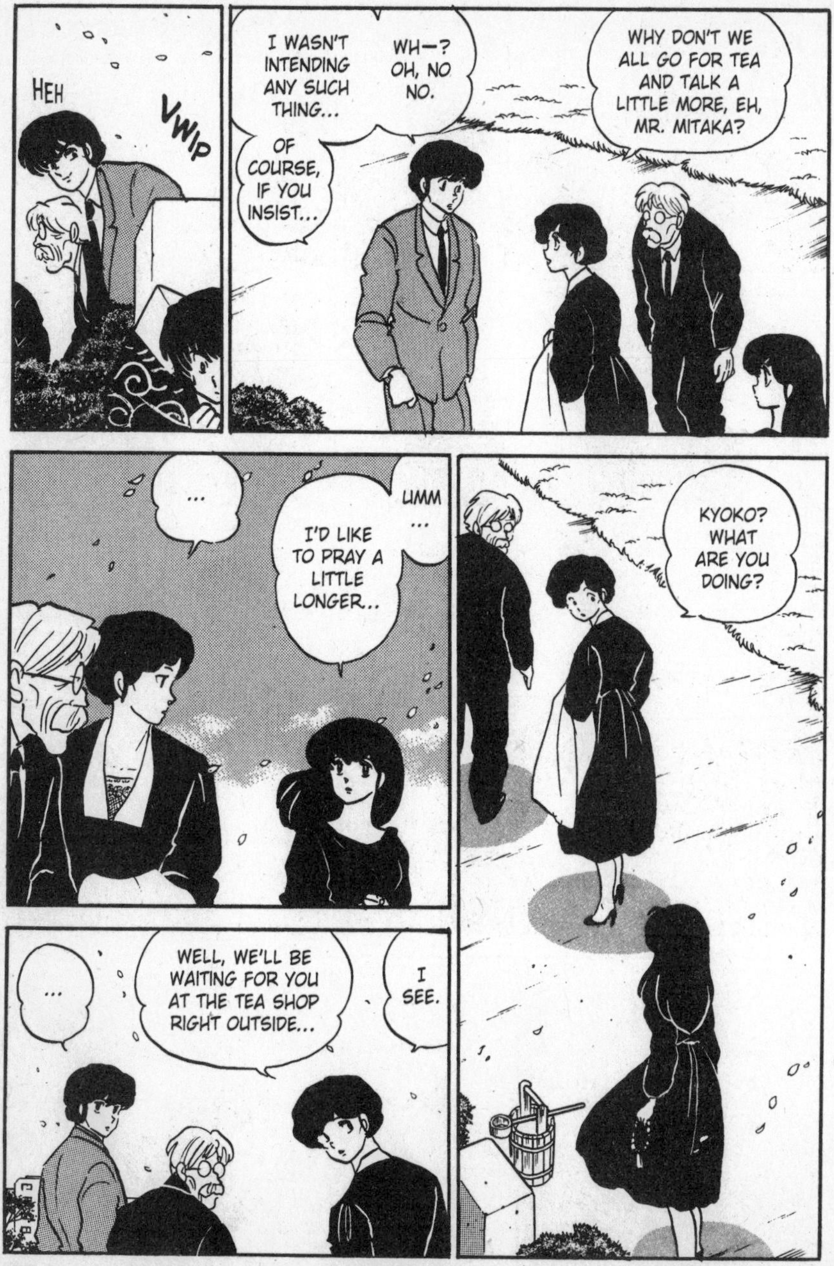

WHY DON'T WE ALL GO FOR TEA AND TALK A LITTLE MORE, EH, MR. MITAKA?
WH—? OH, NO NO.
I WASN'T INTENDING ANY SUCH THING...
OF COURSE, IF YOU INSIST...
VWIP
HEH
KYOKO? WHAT ARE YOU DOING?
UMM ...
I'D LIKE TO PRAY A LITTLE LONGER...
...
I SEE.
WELL, WE'LL BE WAITING FOR YOU AT THE TEA SHOP RIGHT OUTSIDE...
...

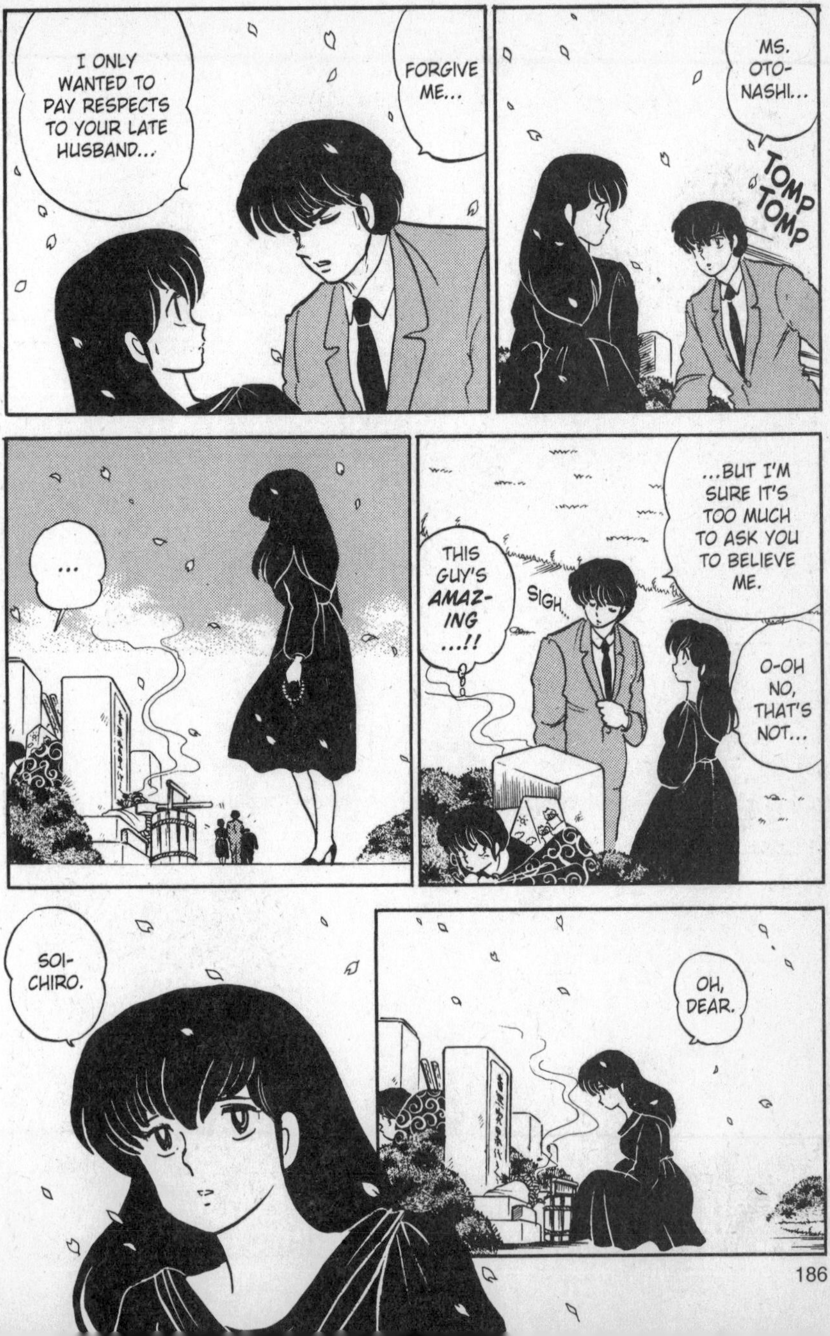
MS. OTO-NASHI...
TOMP TOMP
FORGIVE ME...
I ONLY WANTED TO PAY RESPECTS TO YOUR LATE HUSBAND...
...BUT I'M SURE IT'S TOO MUCH TO ASK YOU TO BELIEVE ME.
THIS GUY'S *AMAZING*...!!
SIGH...
O-OH NO, THAT'S NOT...
...
OH, DEAR.
SOI-CHIRO.

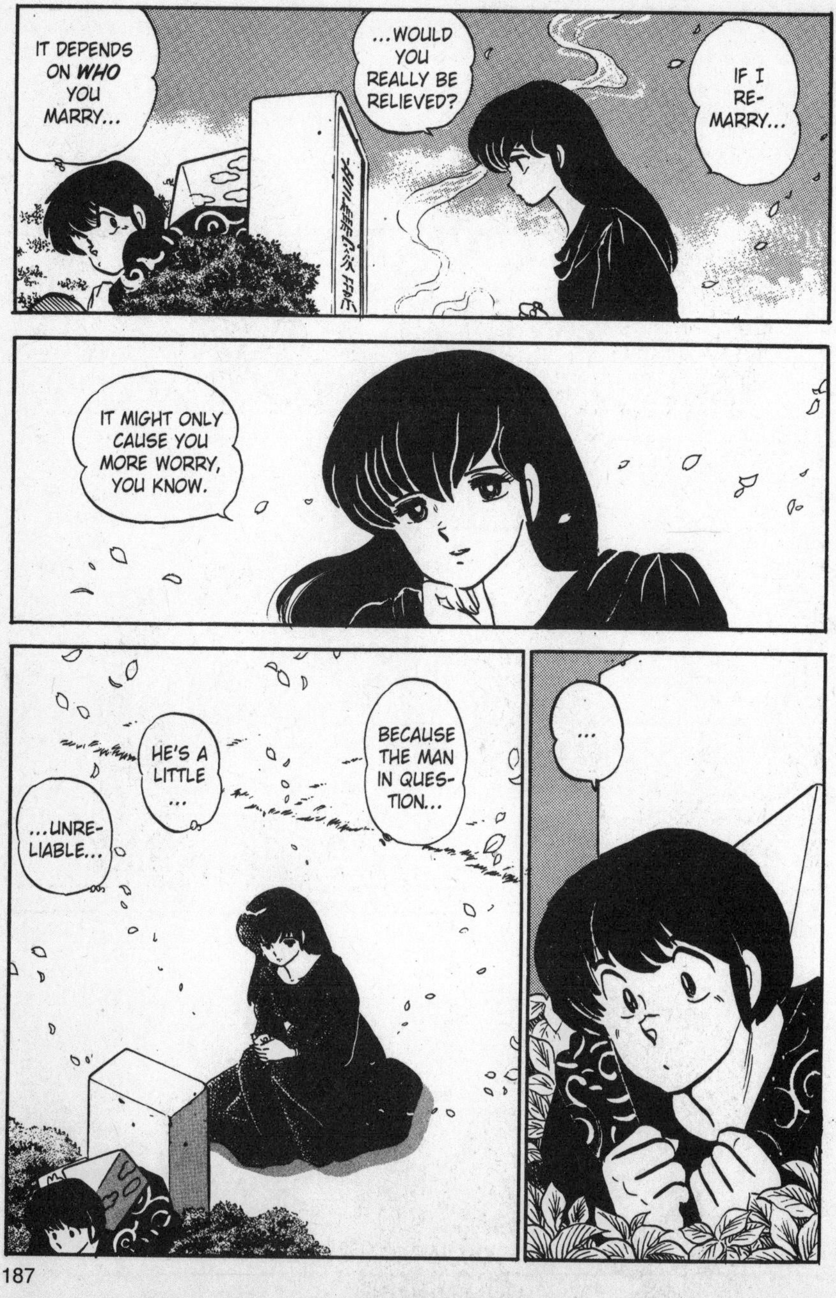
IF I RE-MARRY...
...WOULD YOU REALLY BE RELIEVED?
IT DEPENDS ON ***WHO*** YOU MARRY...
IT MIGHT ONLY CAUSE YOU MORE WORRY, YOU KNOW.
...
BECAUSE THE MAN IN QUES-TION...
HE'S A LITTLE ...
...UNRE-LIABLE...

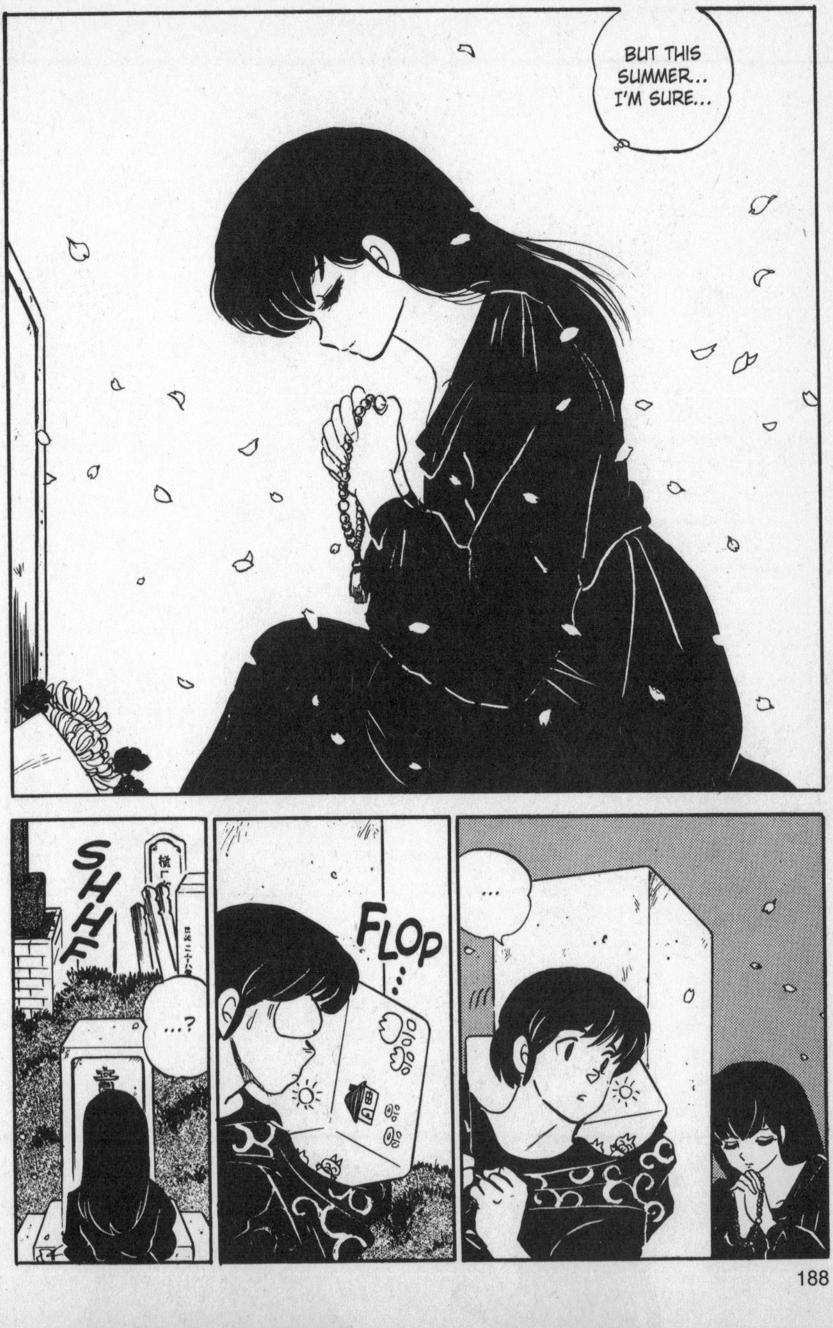
BUT THIS SUMMER... I'M SURE...
...
FLOP
...
SHHF
...?

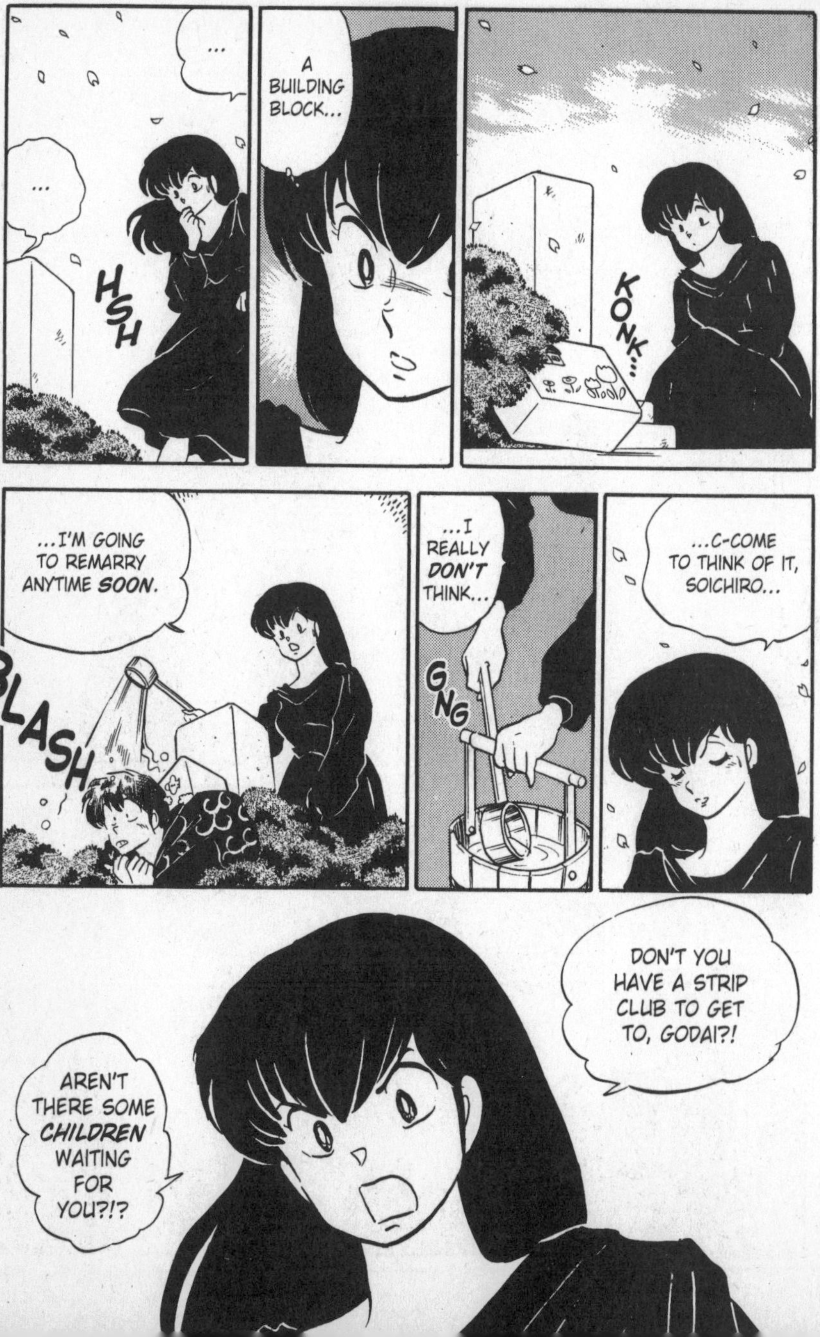
KONK...
A BUILDING BLOCK...
...
...
HSH
...C-COME TO THINK OF IT, SOICHIRO...
...I REALLY DON'T THINK...
GNG
...I'M GOING TO REMARRY ANYTIME SOON.
BLASH
DON'T YOU HAVE A STRIP CLUB TO GET TO, GODAI?!
AREN'T THERE SOME CHILDREN WAITING FOR YOU?!?

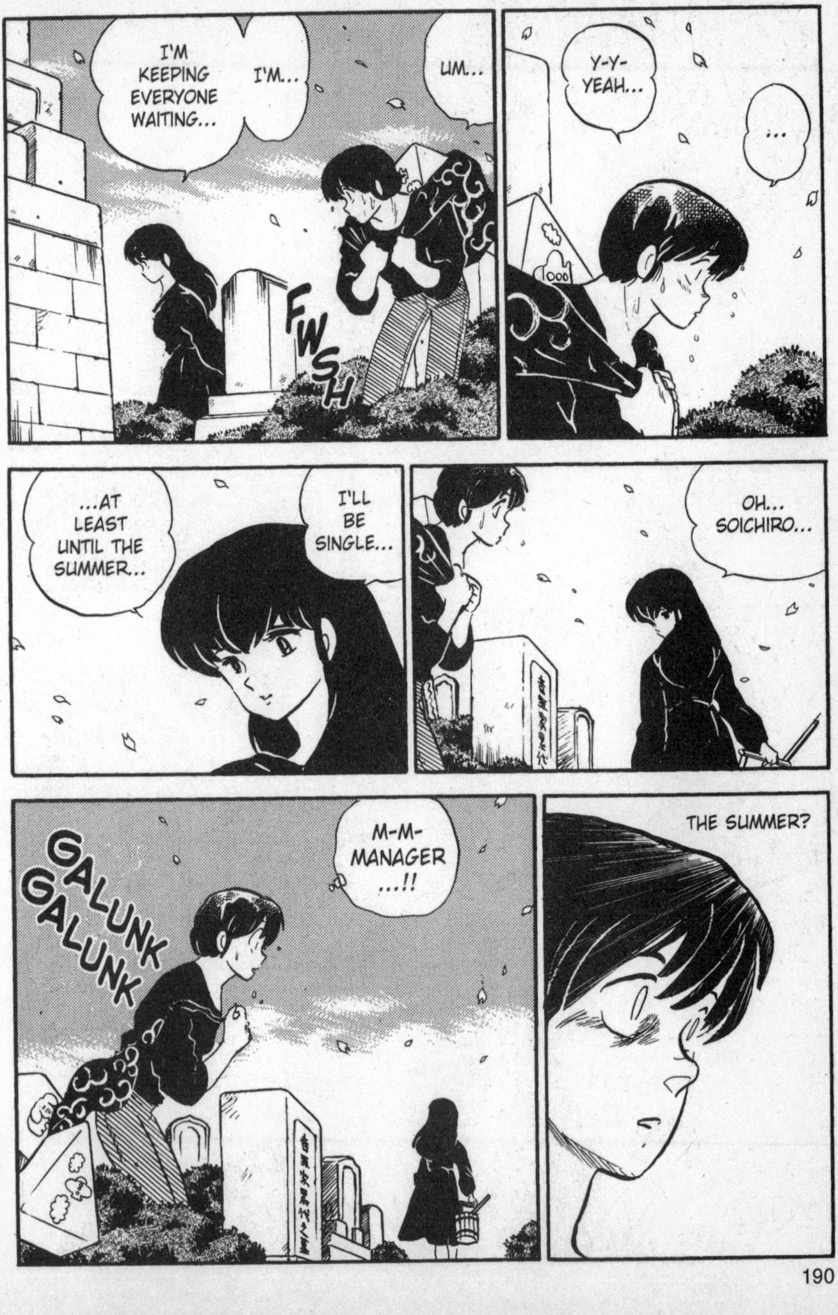
Y-Y-YEAH...
...
UM...
I'M...
I'M KEEPING EVERYONE WAITING...
FWSH
OH... SOICHIRO...
I'LL BE SINGLE...
...AT LEAST UNTIL THE SUMMER...
THE SUMMER?
M-M-MANAGER ...!!
GALUNK GALUNK

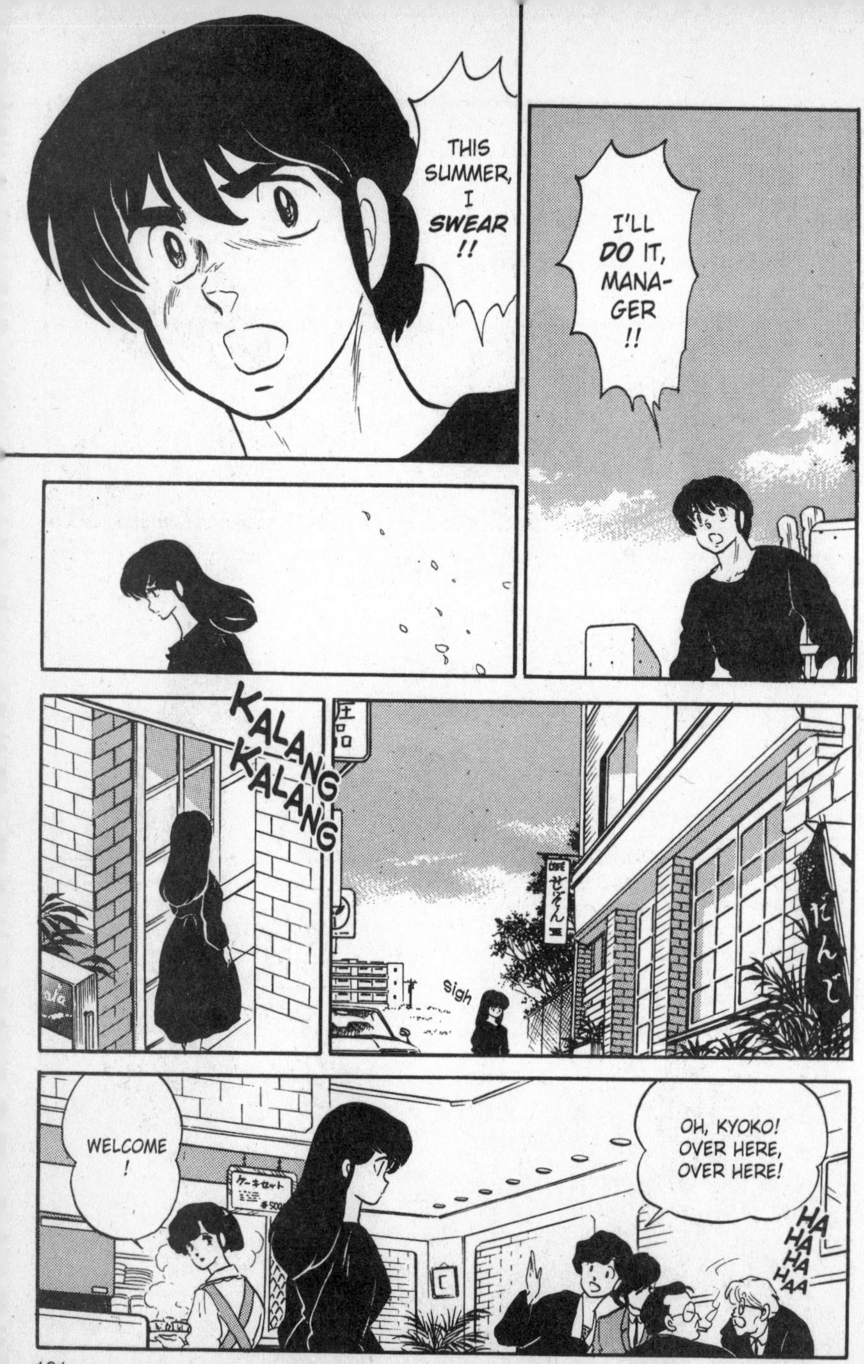
I'LL DO IT, MANAGER !!
THIS SUMMER, I SWEAR !!
sigh
KALANG KALANG
OH, KYOKO! OVER HERE, OVER HERE!
HA HA HA HA HAA
WELCOME !

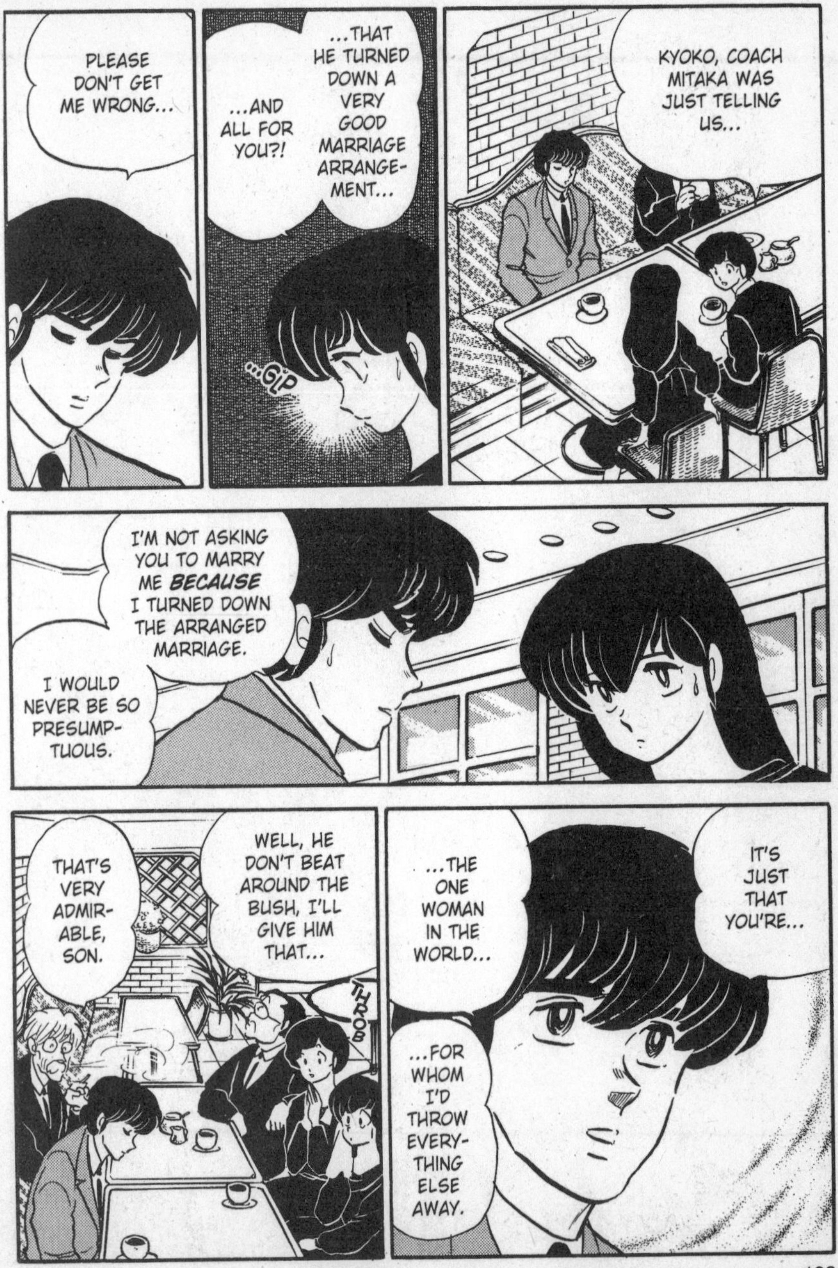
KYOKO, COACH MITAKA WAS JUST TELLING US...
...THAT HE TURNED DOWN A VERY GOOD MARRIAGE ARRANGEMENT...
...AND ALL FOR YOU?!
PLEASE DON'T GET ME WRONG...
I'M NOT ASKING YOU TO MARRY ME BECAUSE I TURNED DOWN THE ARRANGED MARRIAGE.
I WOULD NEVER BE SO PRESUMPTUOUS.
IT'S JUST THAT YOU'RE...
...THE ONE WOMAN IN THE WORLD...
...FOR WHOM I'D THROW EVERYTHING ELSE AWAY.
WELL, HE DON'T BEAT AROUND THE BUSH, I'LL GIVE HIM THAT...
THROB
THAT'S VERY ADMIRABLE, SON.

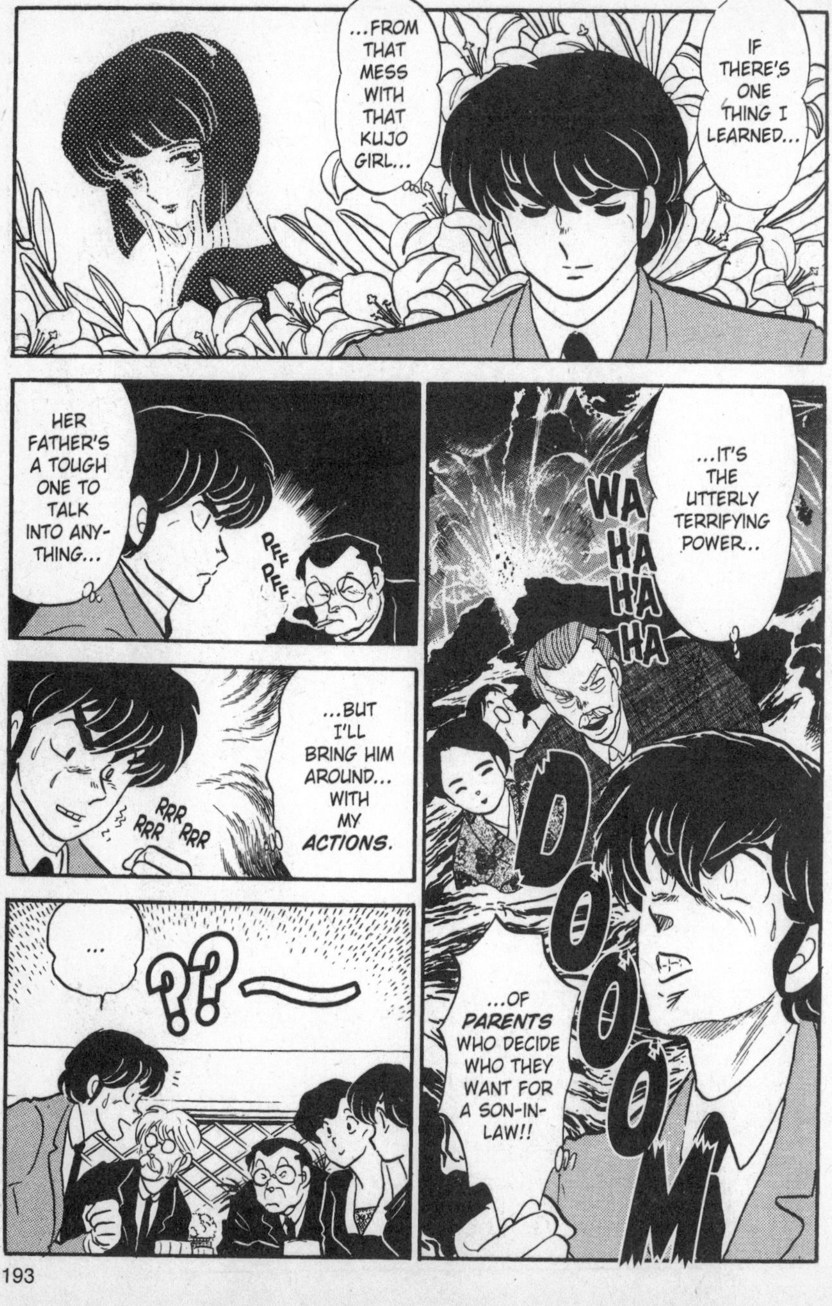
IF THERE'S ONE THING I LEARNED...
...FROM THAT MESS WITH THAT KUJO GIRL...
...IT'S THE UTTERLY TERRIFYING POWER...
WA HA HA HA HA HA
DOOOOM
...OF PARENTS WHO DECIDE WHO THEY WANT FOR A SON-IN-LAW!!
HER FATHER'S A TOUGH ONE TO TALK INTO ANY-THING...
PFF PFF
...BUT I'LL BRING HIM AROUND... WITH MY ACTIONS.
RRR RRR RRR
...
??—

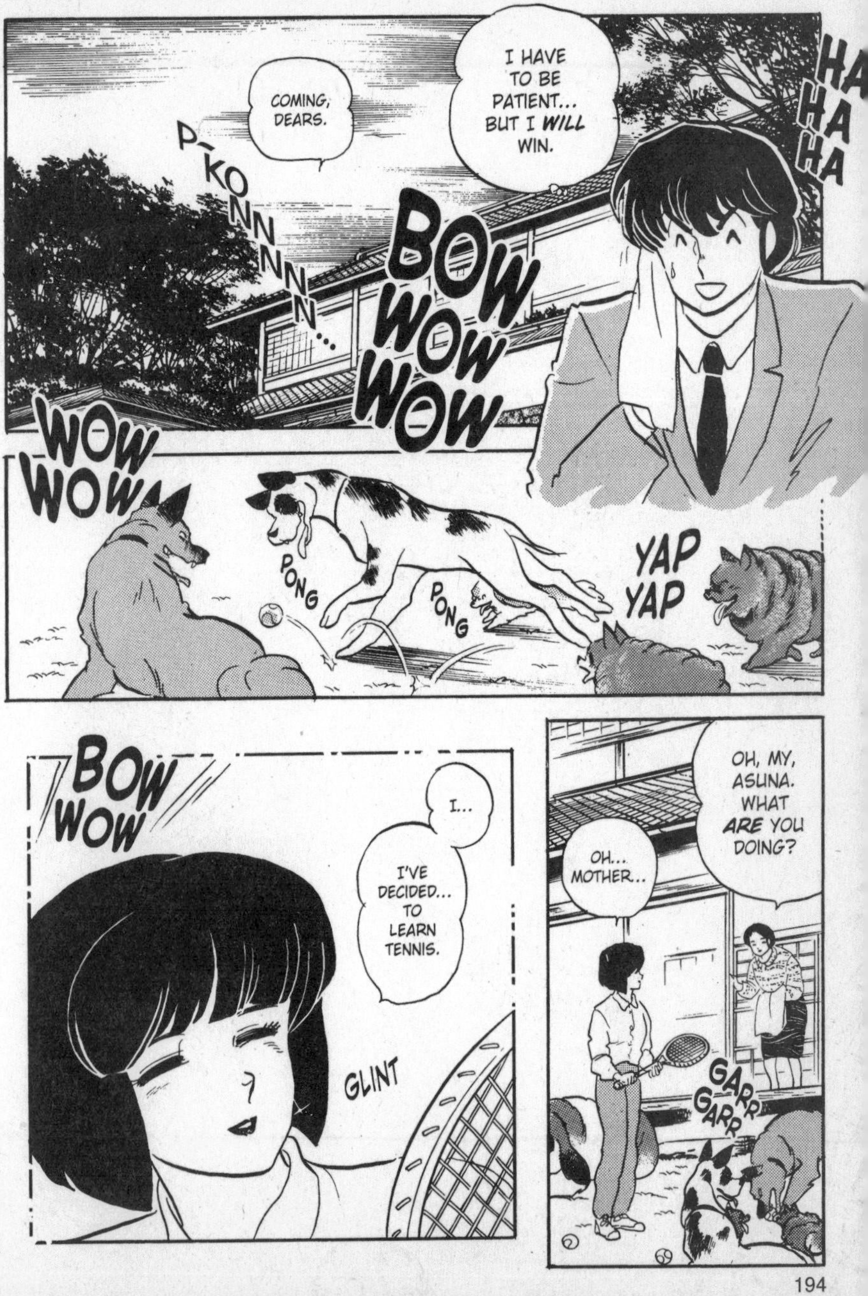
HA HA HA
I HAVE TO BE PATIENT... BUT I WILL WIN.
COMING, DEARS.
P-KONNNNNNN...
BOW WOW WOW WOW
YAP YAP
PONG
PONG
WOW WOW
OH, MY, ASUNA. WHAT ARE YOU DOING?
OH... MOTHER...
GARR GARR
BOW WOW
I...
I'VE DECIDED... TO LEARN TENNIS.
GLINT

PART ELEVEN

NEVER LET YOU GO

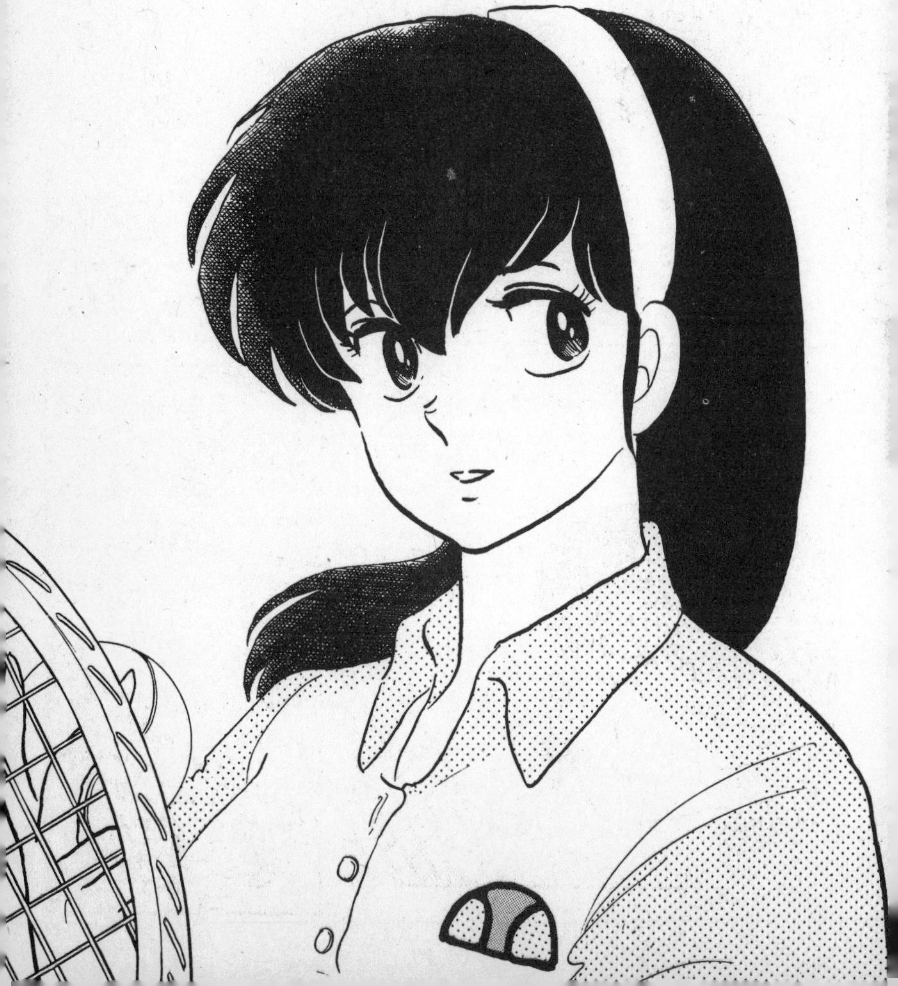

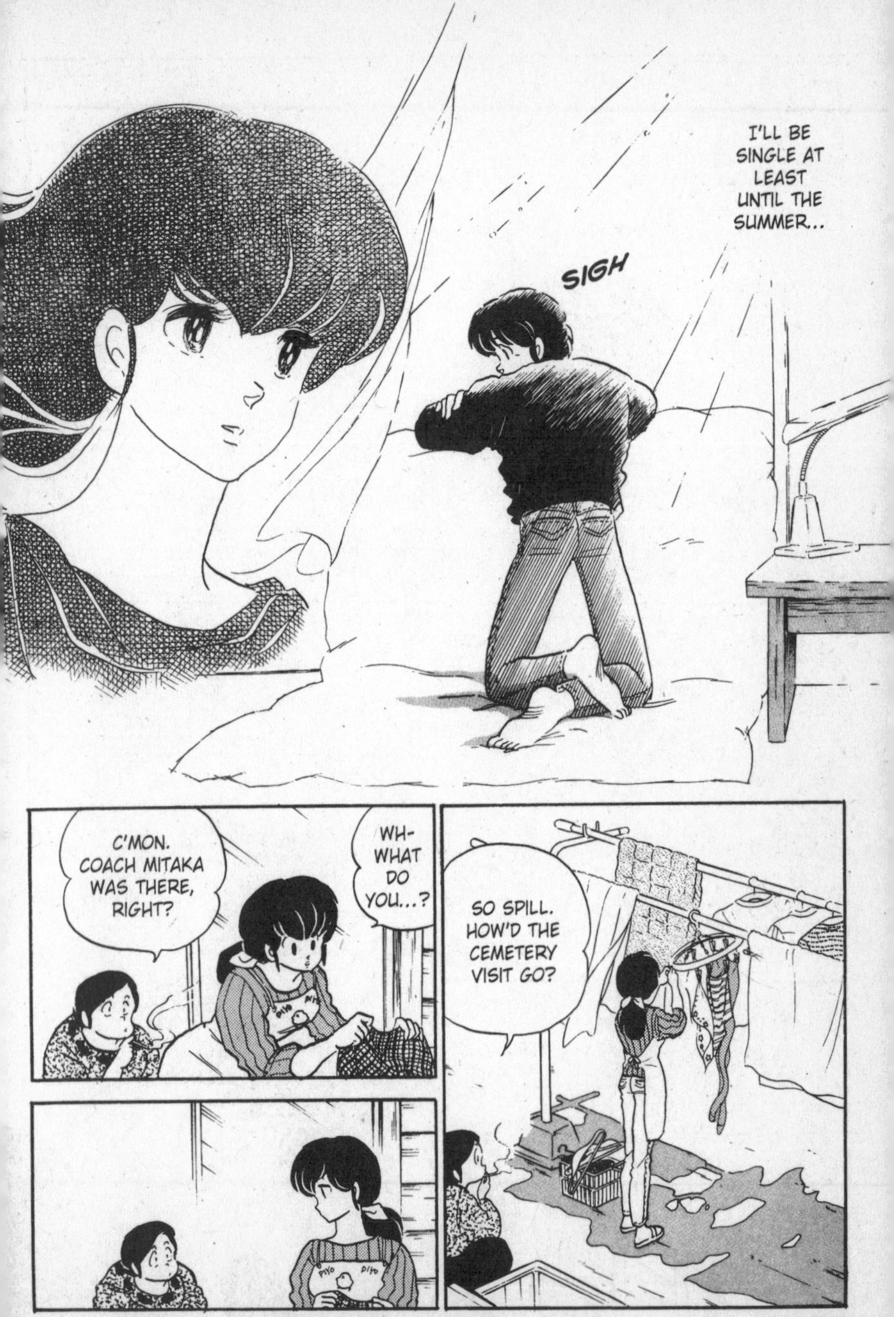
I'LL BE SINGLE AT LEAST UNTIL THE SUMMER...
SIGH
SO SPILL. HOW'D THE CEMETERY VISIT GO?
WH-WHAT DO YOU...?
C'MON. COACH MITAKA WAS THERE, RIGHT?

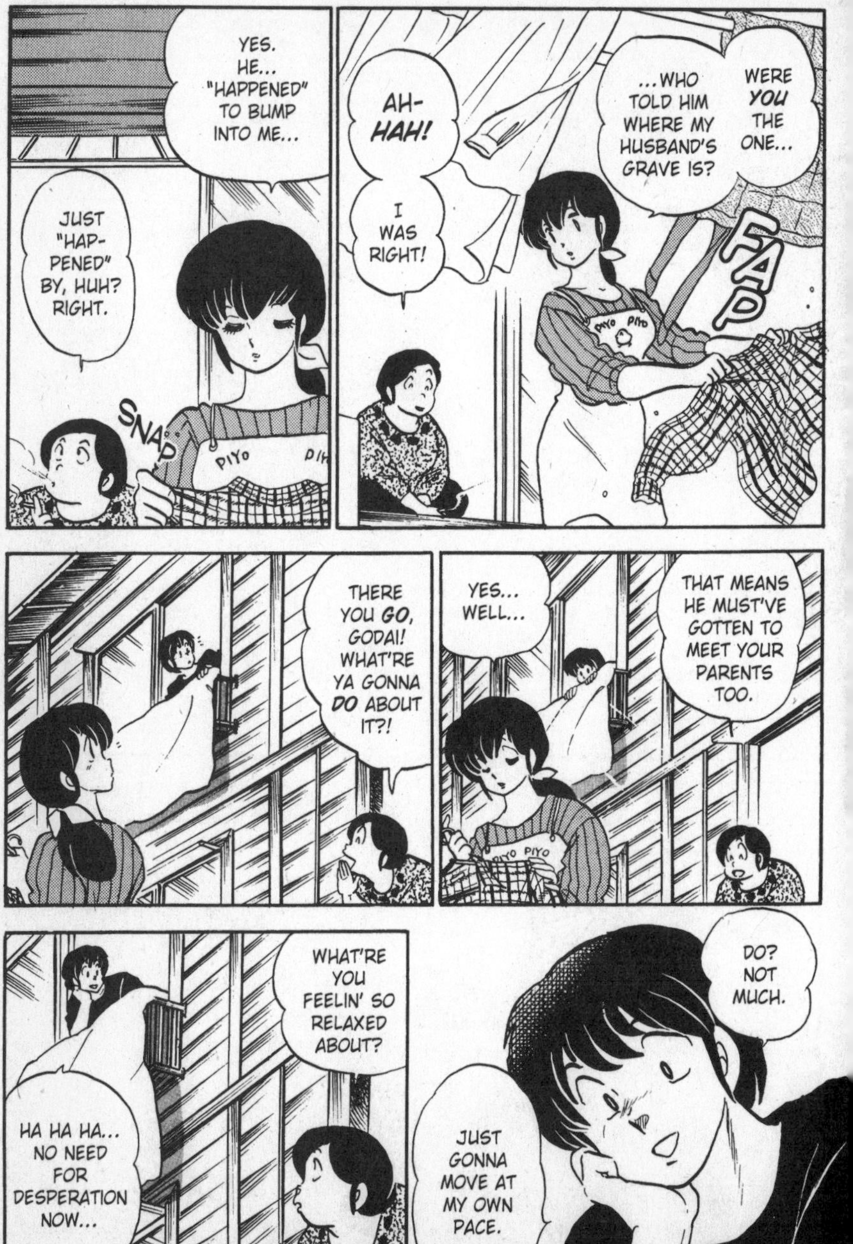
WERE YOU THE ONE...
...WHO TOLD HIM WHERE MY HUSBAND'S GRAVE IS?
FAP
AH-HAH!
I WAS RIGHT!
YES. HE... "HAPPENED" TO BUMP INTO ME...
JUST "HAP-PENED" BY, HUH? RIGHT.
SNAP
THAT MEANS HE MUST'VE GOTTEN TO MEET YOUR PARENTS TOO.
YES... WELL...
THERE YOU GO, GODAI! WHAT'RE YA GONNA DO ABOUT IT?!
DO? NOT MUCH.
JUST GONNA MOVE AT MY OWN PACE.
WHAT'RE YOU FEELIN' SO RELAXED ABOUT?
HA HA HA... NO NEED FOR DESPERATION NOW...

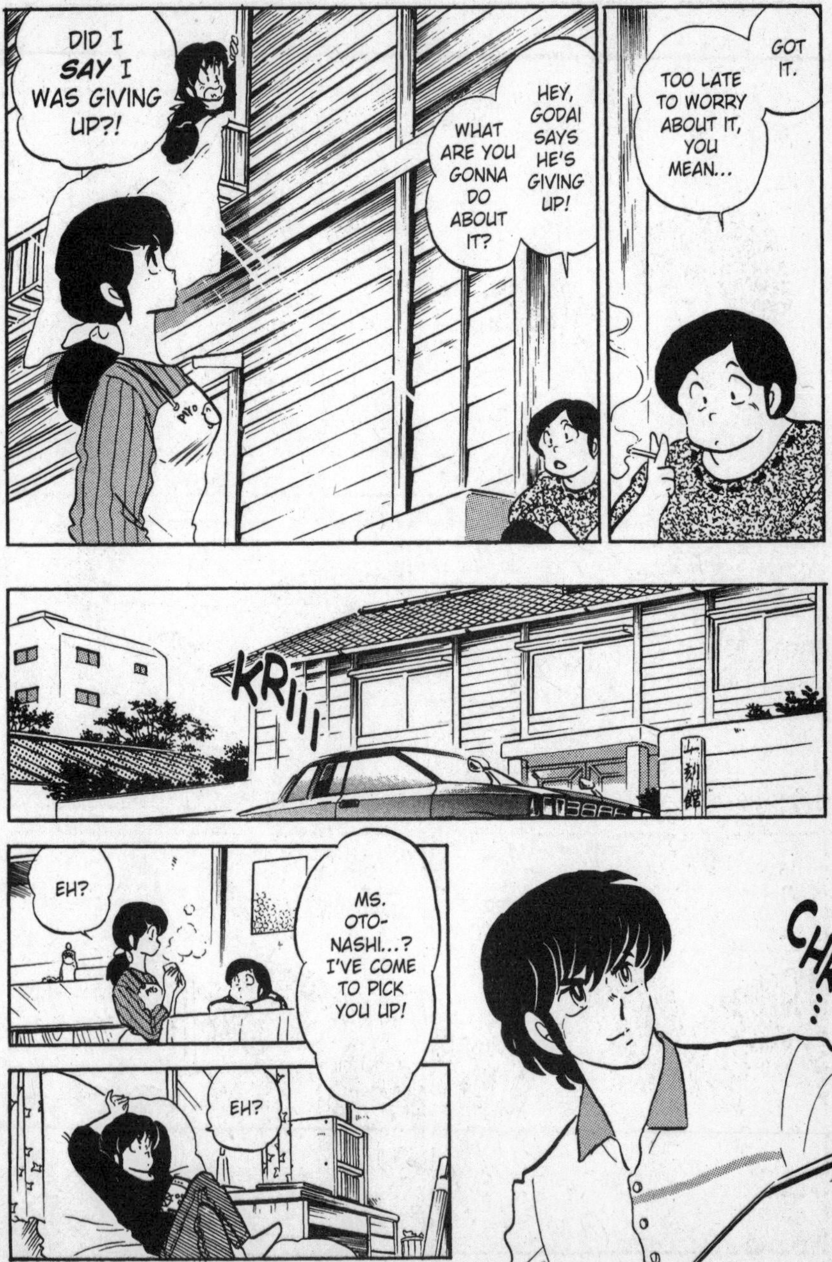
GOT IT.
TOO LATE TO WORRY ABOUT IT, YOU MEAN...
HEY, GODAI SAYS HE'S GIVING UP!
WHAT ARE YOU GONNA DO ABOUT IT?
DID I SAY I WAS GIVING UP?!
KRIII
CHK...
MS. OTO-NASHI...? I'VE COME TO PICK YOU UP!
EH?
EH?

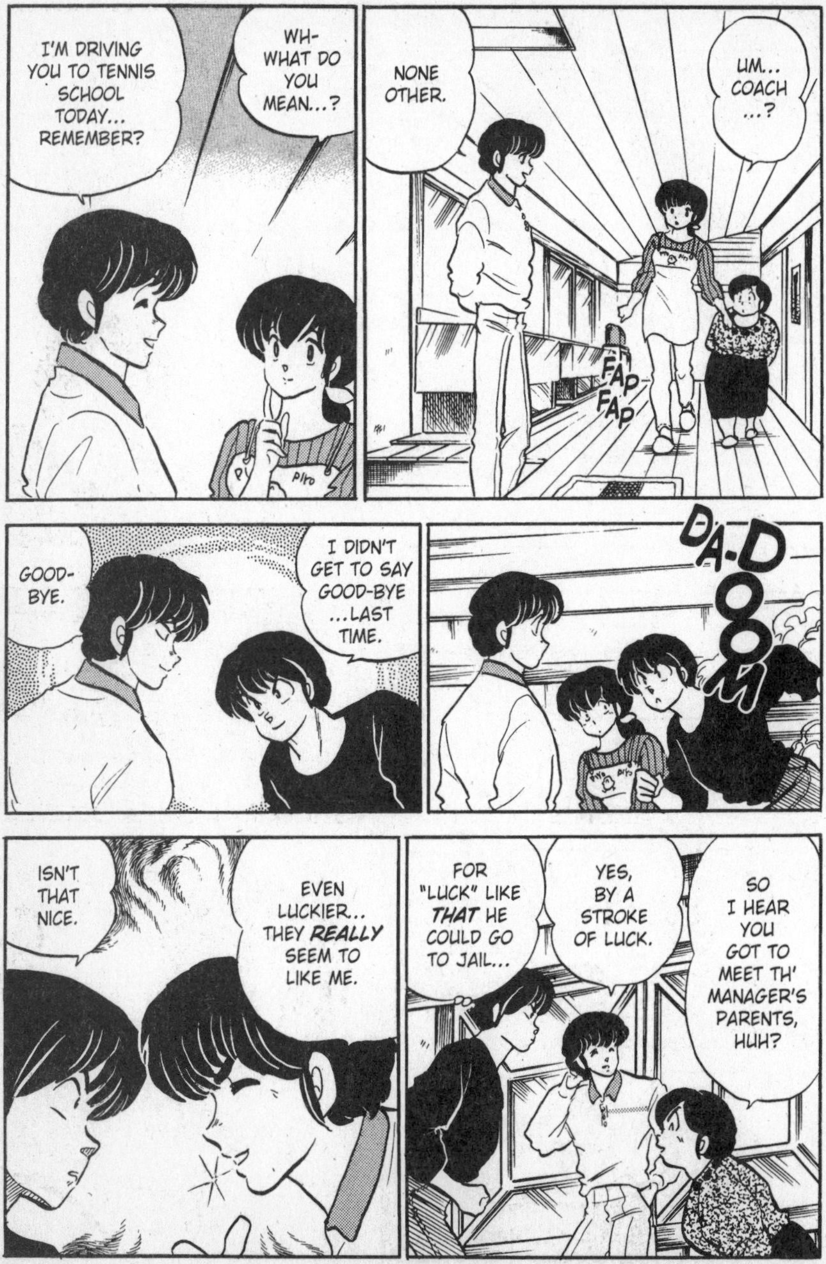
UM... COACH ...?
NONE OTHER.
FAP FAP
WH- WHAT DO YOU MEAN...?
I'M DRIVING YOU TO TENNIS SCHOOL TODAY... REMEMBER?
DA-DOOOM
I DIDN'T GET TO SAY GOOD-BYE ...LAST TIME.
GOOD-BYE.
SO I HEAR YOU GOT TO MEET TH' MANAGER'S PARENTS, HUH?
YES, BY A STROKE OF LUCK.
FOR "LUCK" LIKE *THAT* HE COULD GO TO JAIL...
EVEN LUCKIER... THEY *REALLY* SEEM TO LIKE ME.
ISN'T THAT NICE.

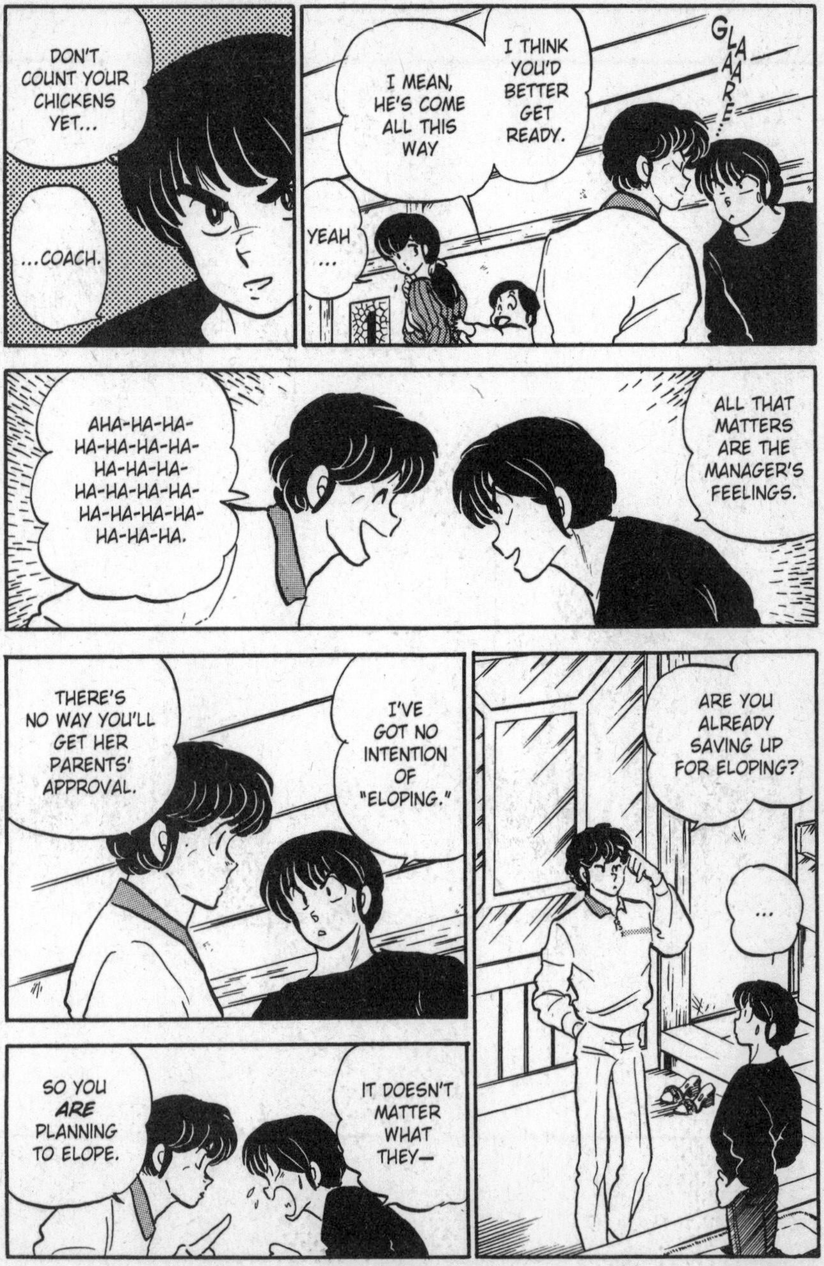
GLAAARE...
I THINK YOU'D BETTER GET READY.
I MEAN, HE'S COME ALL THIS WAY
YEAH...
DON'T COUNT YOUR CHICKENS YET...
...COACH.
ALL THAT MATTERS ARE THE MANAGER'S FEELINGS.
AHA-HA-HA-HA-HA-HA-HA-HA-HA-HA-HA-HA-HA-HA-HA-HA-HA-HA-HA-HA-HA-HA.
ARE YOU ALREADY SAVING UP FOR ELOPING?
...
I'VE GOT NO INTENTION OF "ELOPING."
THERE'S NO WAY YOU'LL GET HER PARENTS' APPROVAL.
IT DOESN'T MATTER WHAT THEY—
SO YOU *ARE* PLANNING TO ELOPE.

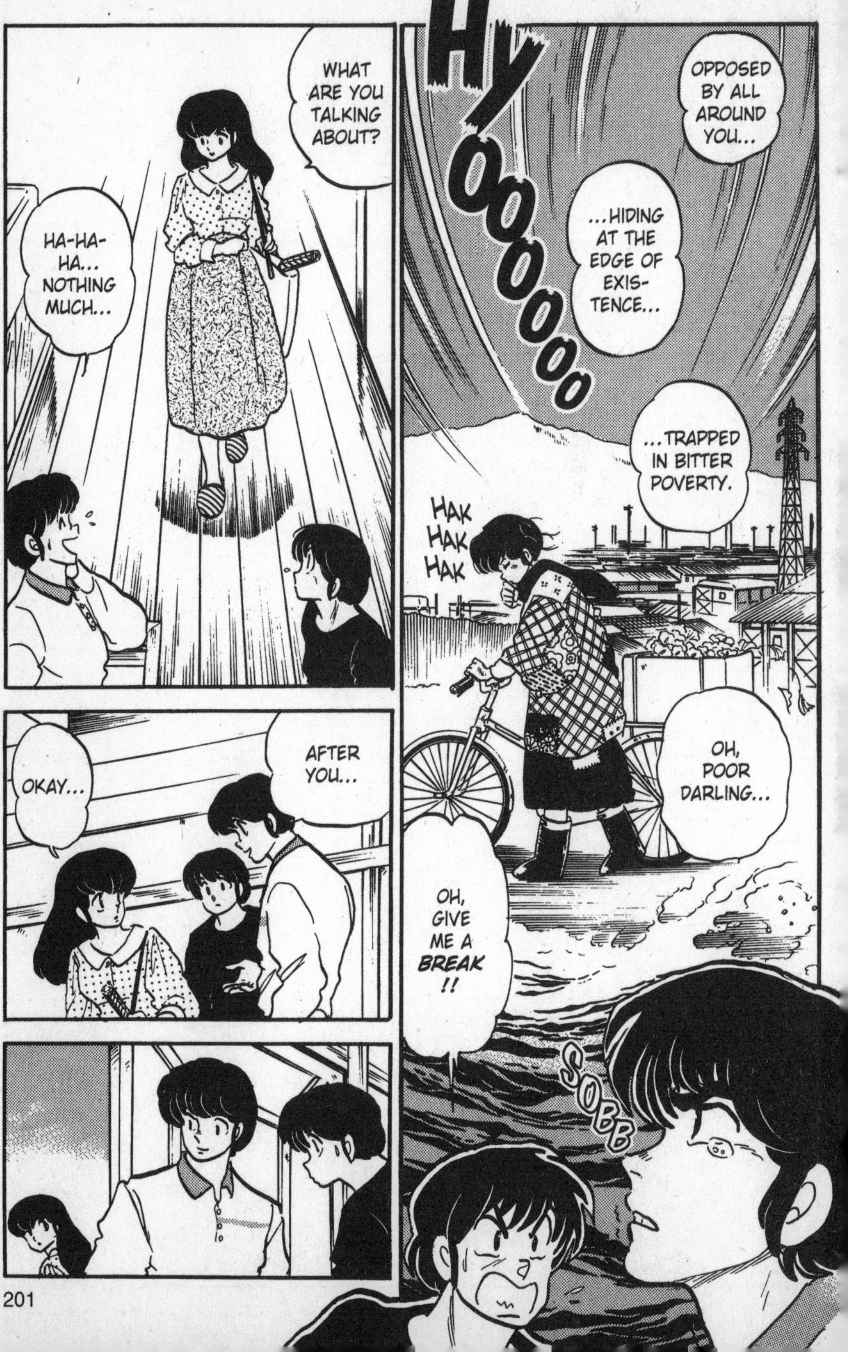
HYOOOOOOO
OPPOSED BY ALL AROUND YOU...
...HIDING AT THE EDGE OF EXIS-TENCE...
...TRAPPED IN BITTER POVERTY.
HAK HAK HAK
OH, POOR DARLING...
OH, GIVE ME A BREAK !!
SOBB
WHAT ARE YOU TALKING ABOUT?
HA-HA-HA... NOTHING MUCH...
AFTER YOU...
OKAY...

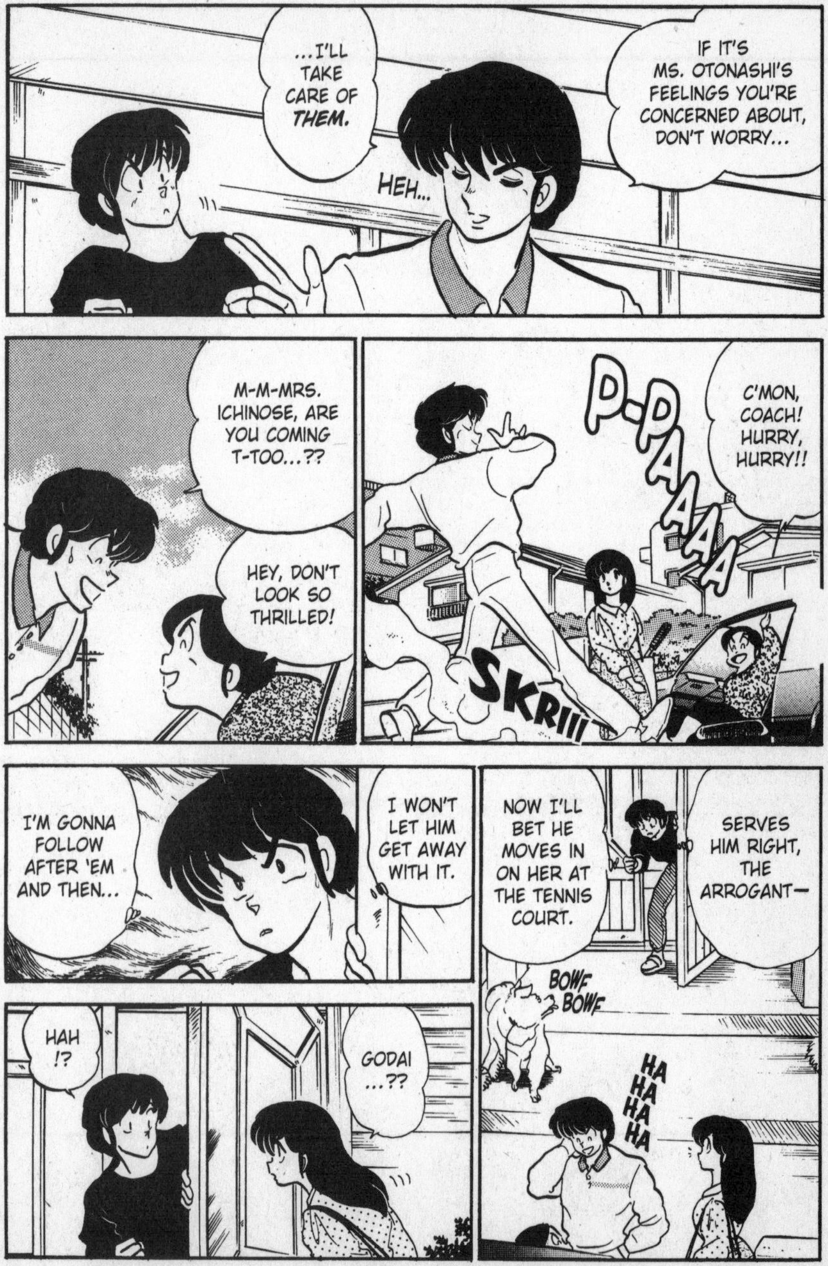
IF IT'S MS. OTONASHI'S FEELINGS YOU'RE CONCERNED ABOUT, DON'T WORRY...
HEH...
...I'LL TAKE CARE OF *THEM.*
C'MON, COACH! HURRY, HURRY!!
P-PAAAAA
SKRIII
M-M-MRS. ICHINOSE, ARE YOU COMING T-TOO...??
HEY, DON'T LOOK SO THRILLED!
SERVES HIM RIGHT, THE ARROGANT—
NOW I'LL BET HE MOVES IN ON HER AT THE TENNIS COURT.
BOWF BOWF
HA HA HA HA HA
I WON'T LET HIM GET AWAY WITH IT.
I'M GONNA FOLLOW AFTER 'EM AND THEN...
GODAI ...??
HAH !?

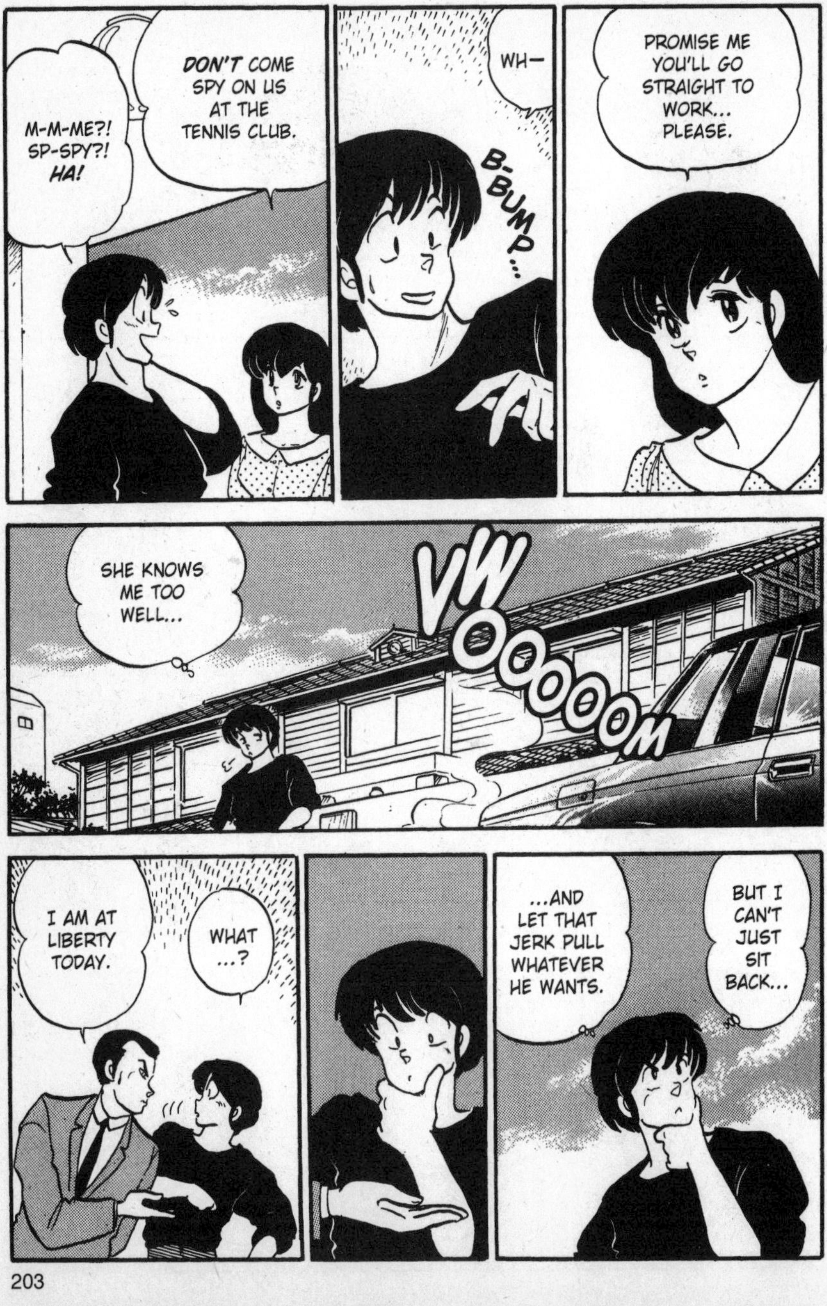
PROMISE ME YOU'LL GO STRAIGHT TO WORK... PLEASE.
WH—
B-BUMP...
DON'T COME SPY ON US AT THE TENNIS CLUB.
M-M-ME?! SP-SPY?! HA!
VWOOOOOM
SHE KNOWS ME TOO WELL...
BUT I CAN'T JUST SIT BACK...
...AND LET THAT JERK PULL WHATEVER HE WANTS.
WHAT ...?
I AM AT LIBERTY TODAY.

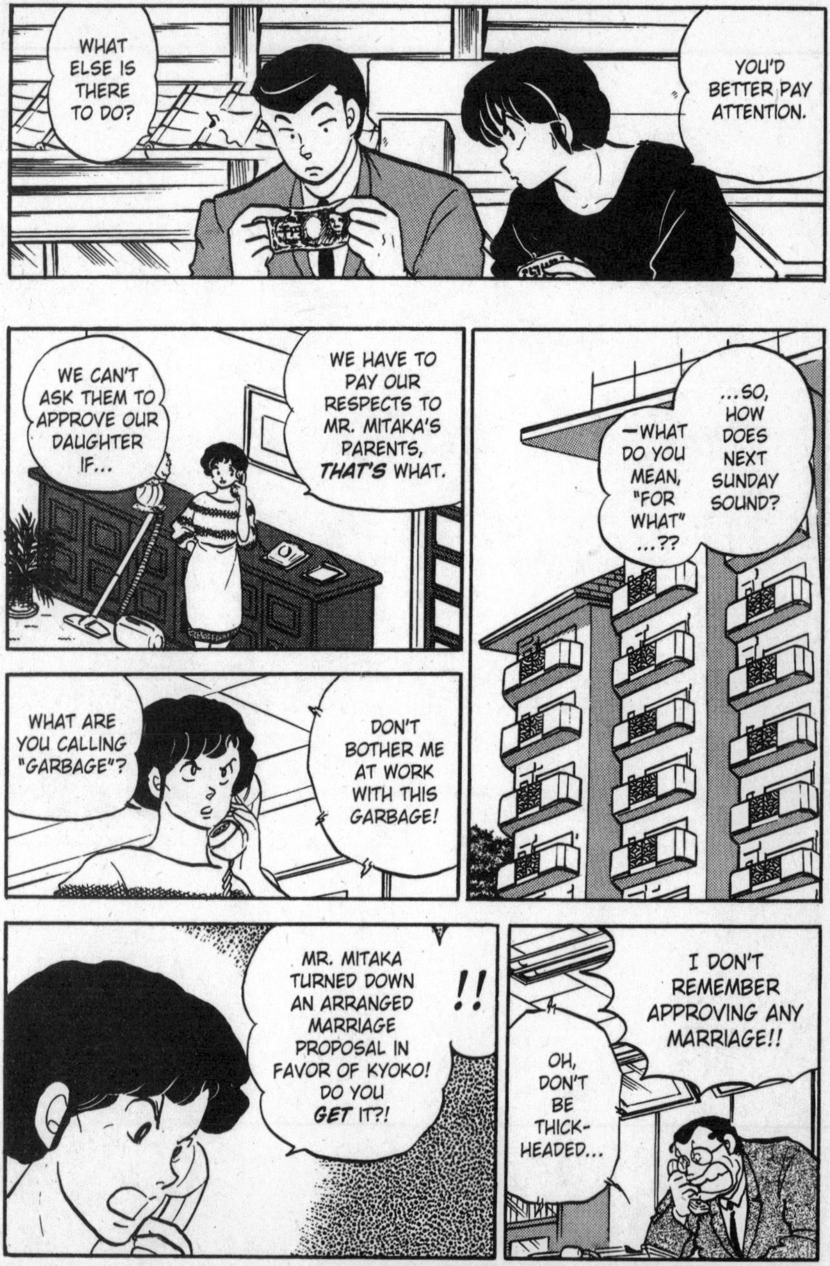
YOU'D BETTER PAY ATTENTION.
WHAT ELSE IS THERE TO DO?
...SO, HOW DOES NEXT SUNDAY SOUND?
—WHAT DO YOU MEAN, "FOR WHAT" ...??
WE HAVE TO PAY OUR RESPECTS TO MR. MITAKA'S PARENTS, ***THAT'S*** WHAT.
WE CAN'T ASK THEM TO APPROVE OUR DAUGHTER IF...
DON'T BOTHER ME AT WORK WITH THIS GARBAGE!
WHAT ARE YOU CALLING "GARBAGE"?
I DON'T REMEMBER APPROVING ANY MARRIAGE!!
OH, DON'T BE THICK-HEADED...
MR. MITAKA TURNED DOWN AN ARRANGED MARRIAGE PROPOSAL IN FAVOR OF KYOKO! DO YOU ***GET*** IT?!
!!

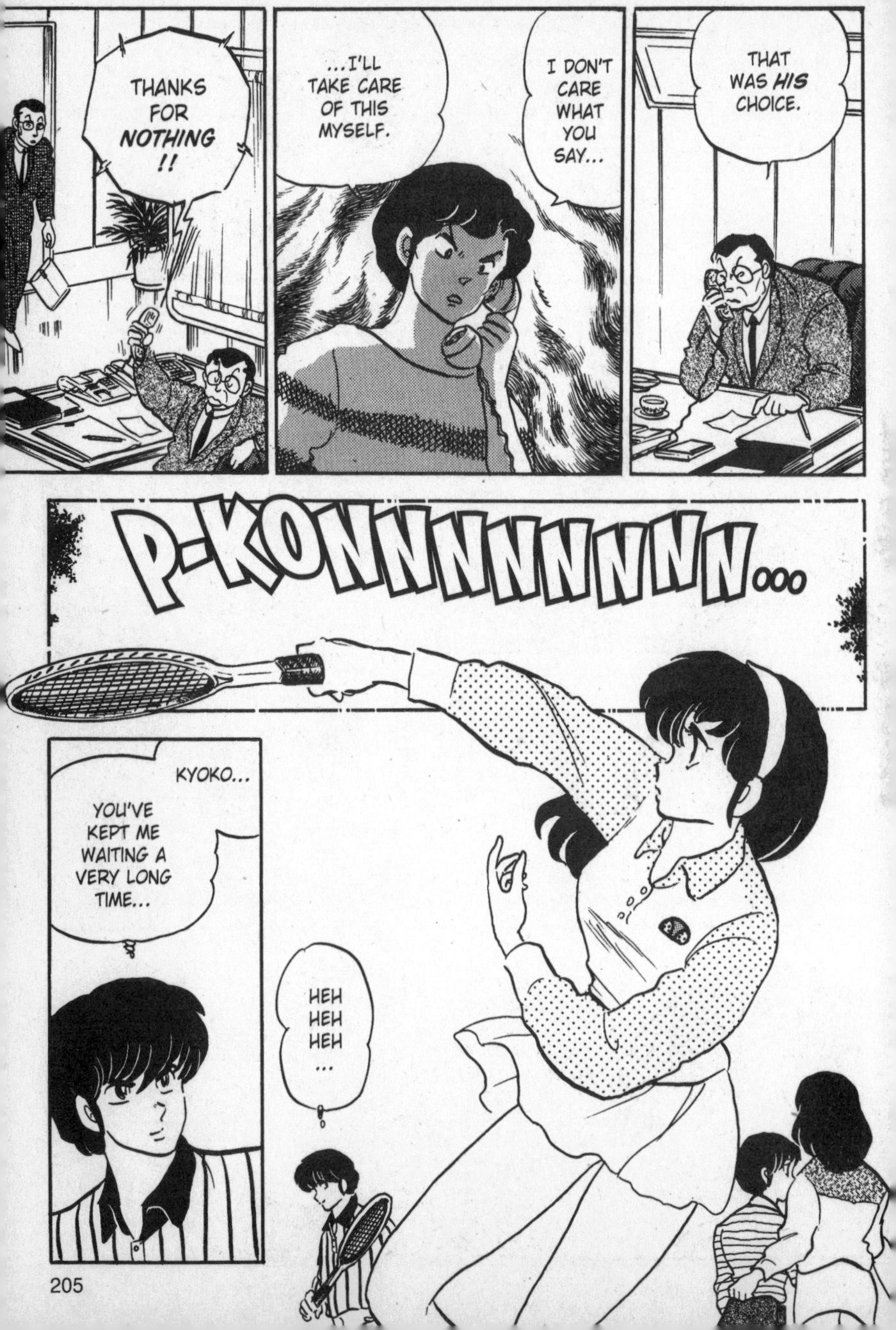
THAT WAS *HIS* CHOICE.
I DON'T CARE WHAT YOU SAY...
...I'LL TAKE CARE OF THIS MYSELF.
THANKS FOR *NOTHING* !!
P-KONNNNNNNNN...
HEH HEH HEH ...
KYOKO...
YOU'VE KEPT ME WAITING A VERY LONG TIME...

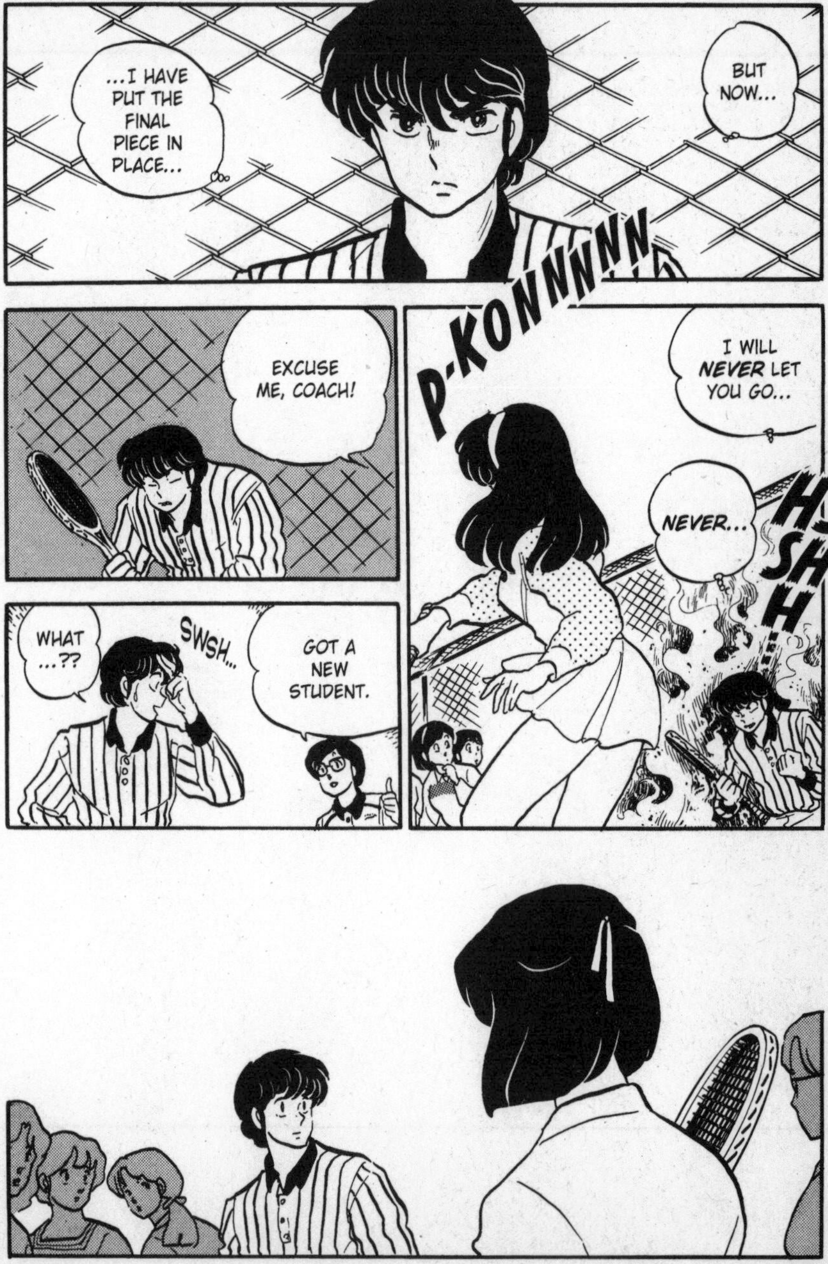
BUT NOW...
...I HAVE PUT THE FINAL PIECE IN PLACE...
P-KONNNNN
I WILL NEVER LET YOU GO...
NEVER...
HSSHH...
EXCUSE ME, COACH!
GOT A NEW STUDENT.
SWSH...
WHAT ...??

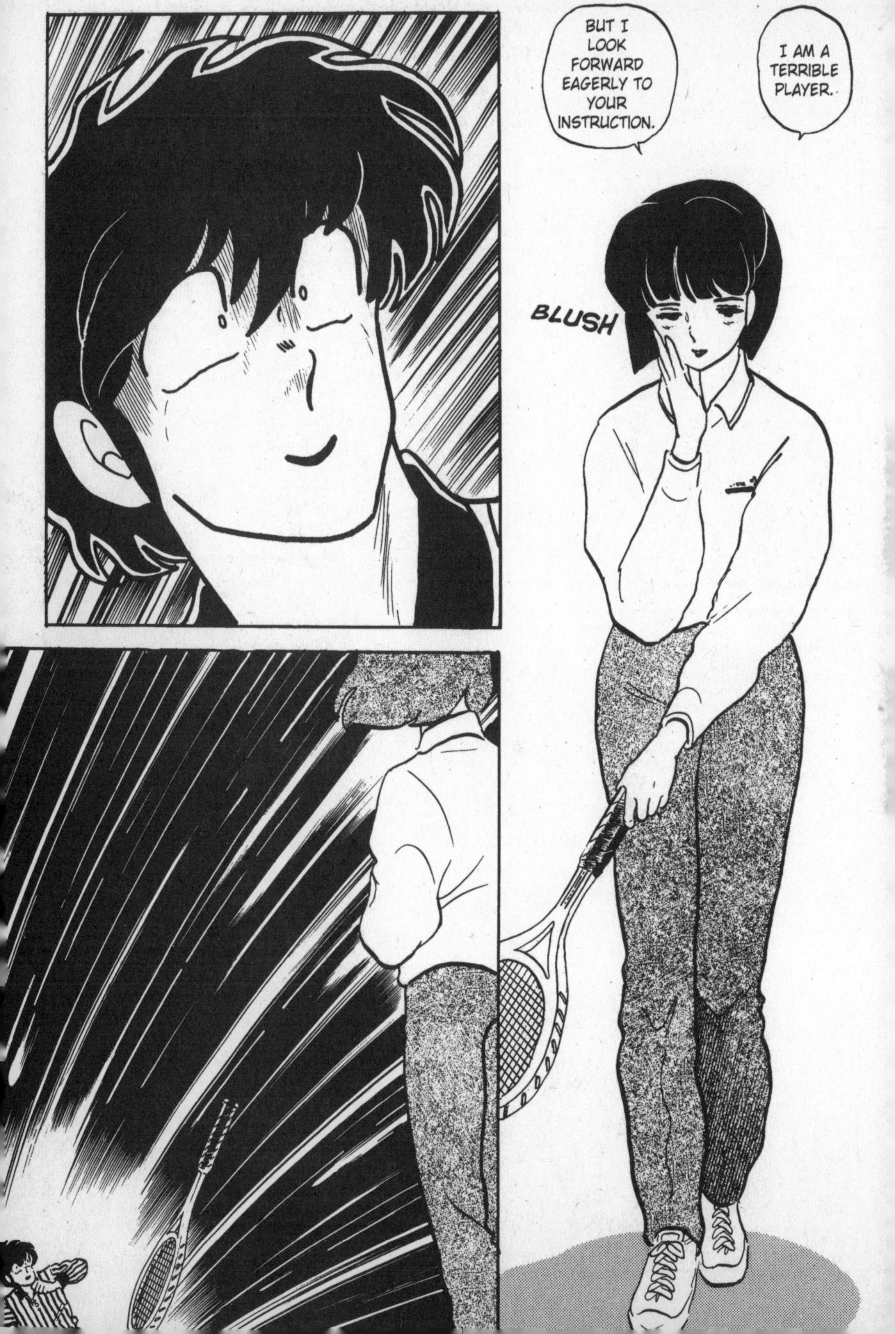
I AM A TERRIBLE PLAYER..
BUT I LOOK FORWARD EAGERLY TO YOUR INSTRUCTION.
BLUSH

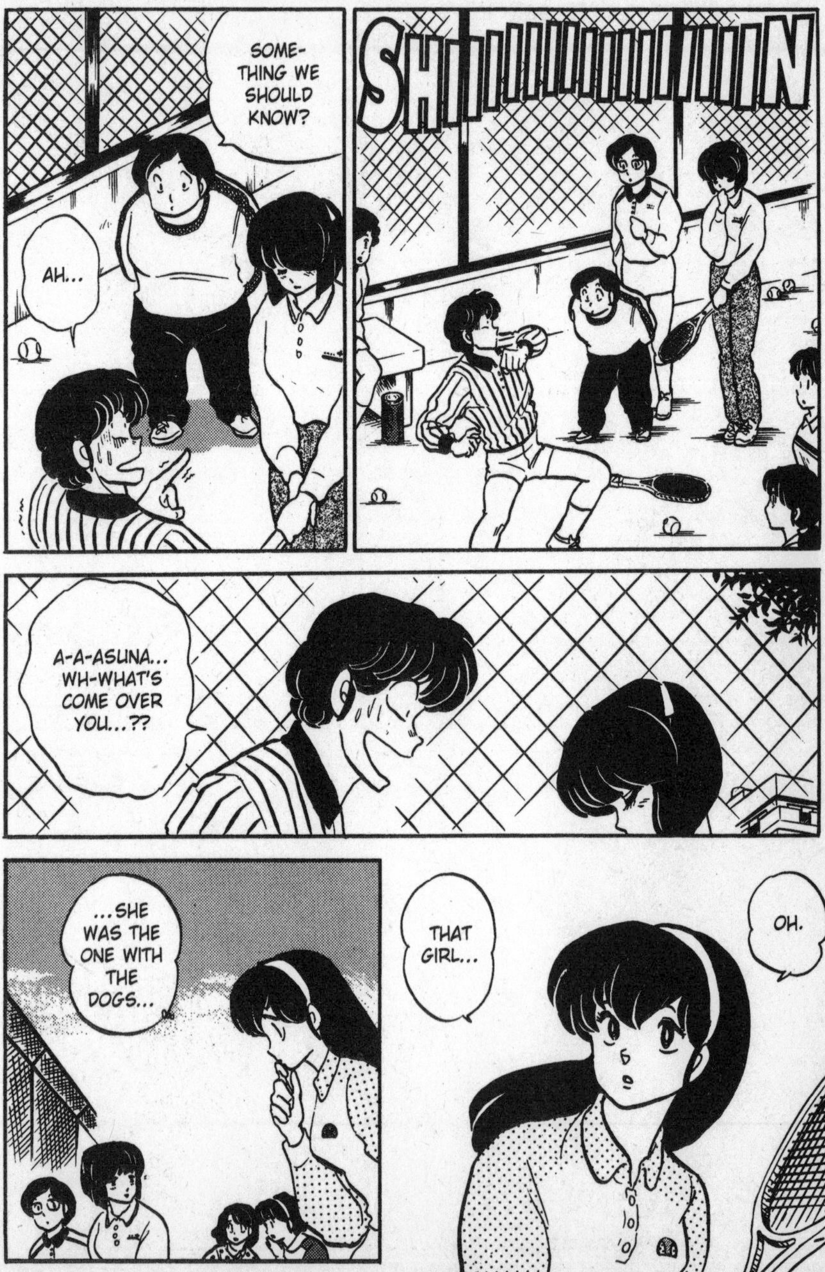
SHIIIIIIIIIIIIIIN
SOME-THING WE SHOULD KNOW?
AH...
A-A-ASUNA... WH-WHAT'S COME OVER YOU...??
OH.
THAT GIRL...
...SHE WAS THE ONE WITH THE DOGS...

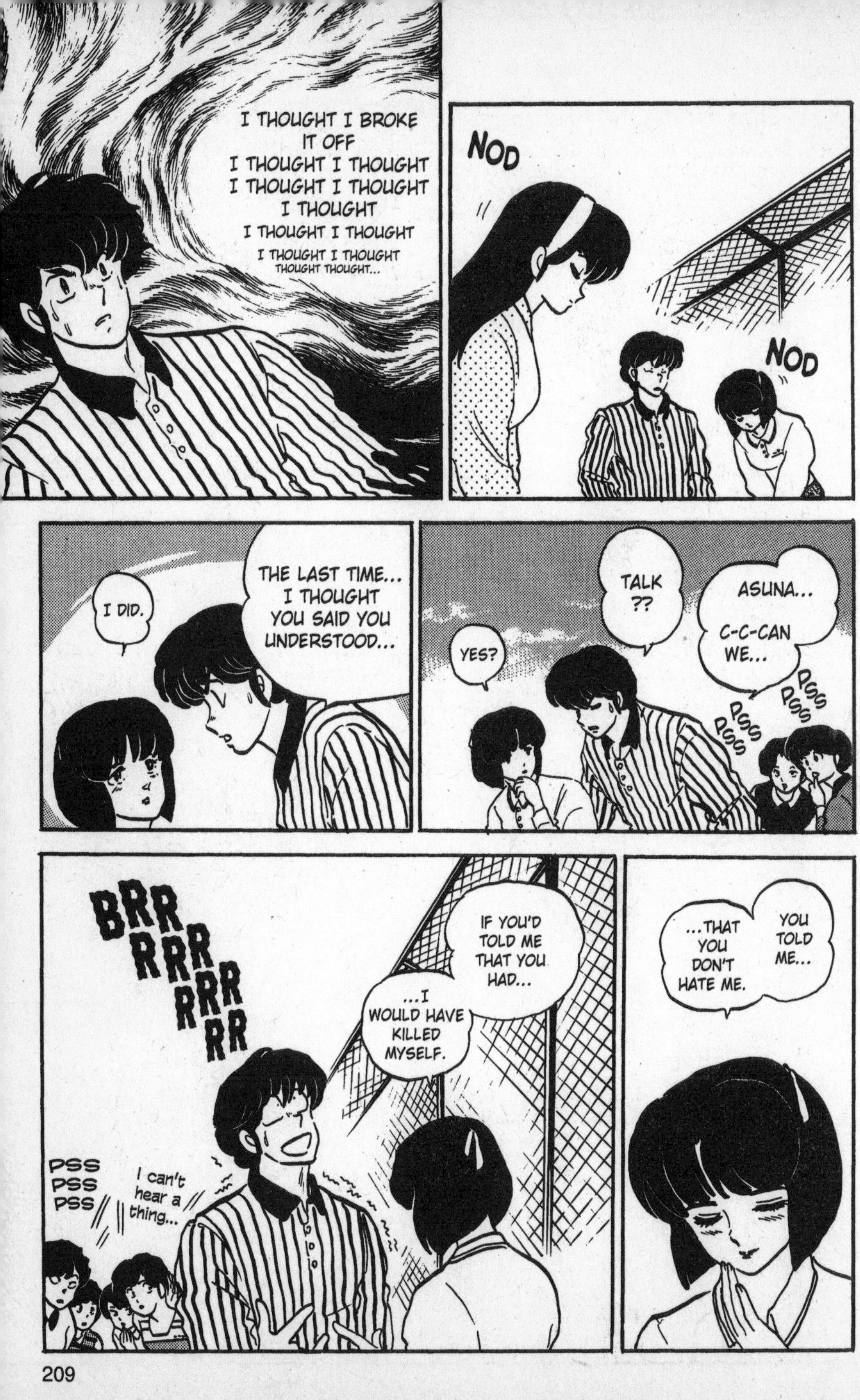
NOD
NOD
I THOUGHT I BROKE IT OFF
I THOUGHT I THOUGHT
I THOUGHT I THOUGHT
I THOUGHT
I THOUGHT I THOUGHT
I THOUGHT I THOUGHT THOUGHT THOUGHT...
ASUNA...
C-C-CAN WE...
TALK ??
YES?
PSSS PSSS PSSS PSSS
THE LAST TIME... I THOUGHT YOU SAID YOU UNDERSTOOD...
I DID.
YOU TOLD ME...
...THAT YOU DON'T HATE ME.
BRRRRRRRRRRR
IF YOU'D TOLD ME THAT YOU HAD...
...I WOULD HAVE KILLED MYSELF.
I can't hear a thing...
PSS PSS PSS

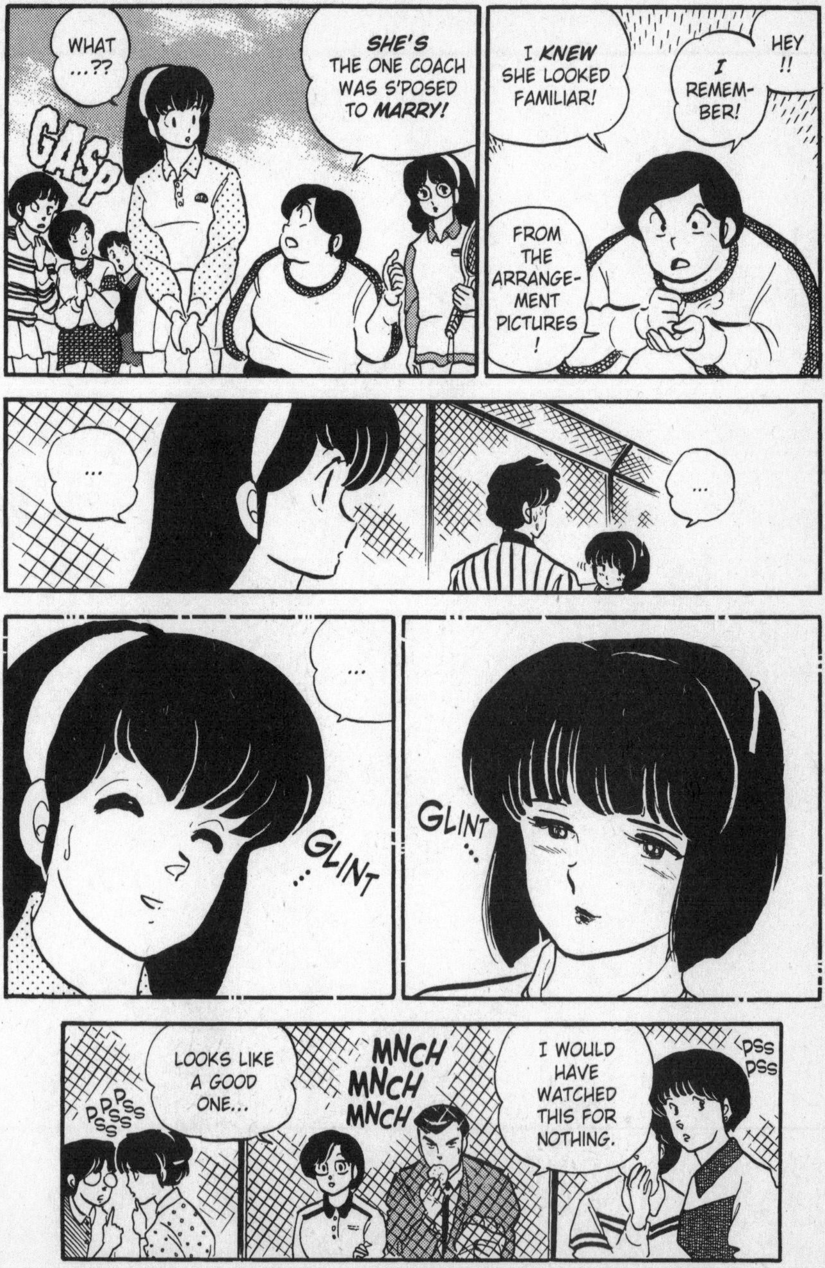
HEY !!
I REMEMBER!
I KNEW SHE LOOKED FAMILIAR!
FROM THE ARRANGEMENT PICTURES!
SHE'S THE ONE COACH WAS S'POSED TO MARRY!
WHAT ...??
GASP
...
...
GLINT ...
...
... GLINT
PSS PSS
I WOULD HAVE WATCHED THIS FOR NOTHING.
MNCH MNCH MNCH
LOOKS LIKE A GOOD ONE...
PSSS PSSS

PART TWELVE

THE AGE OF INNOCENCE

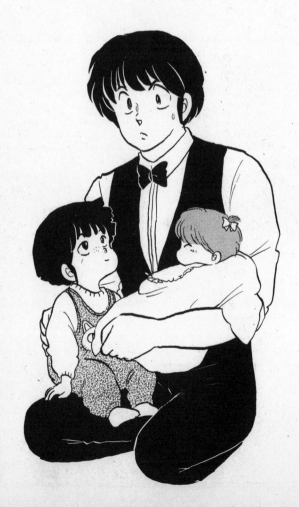

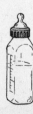

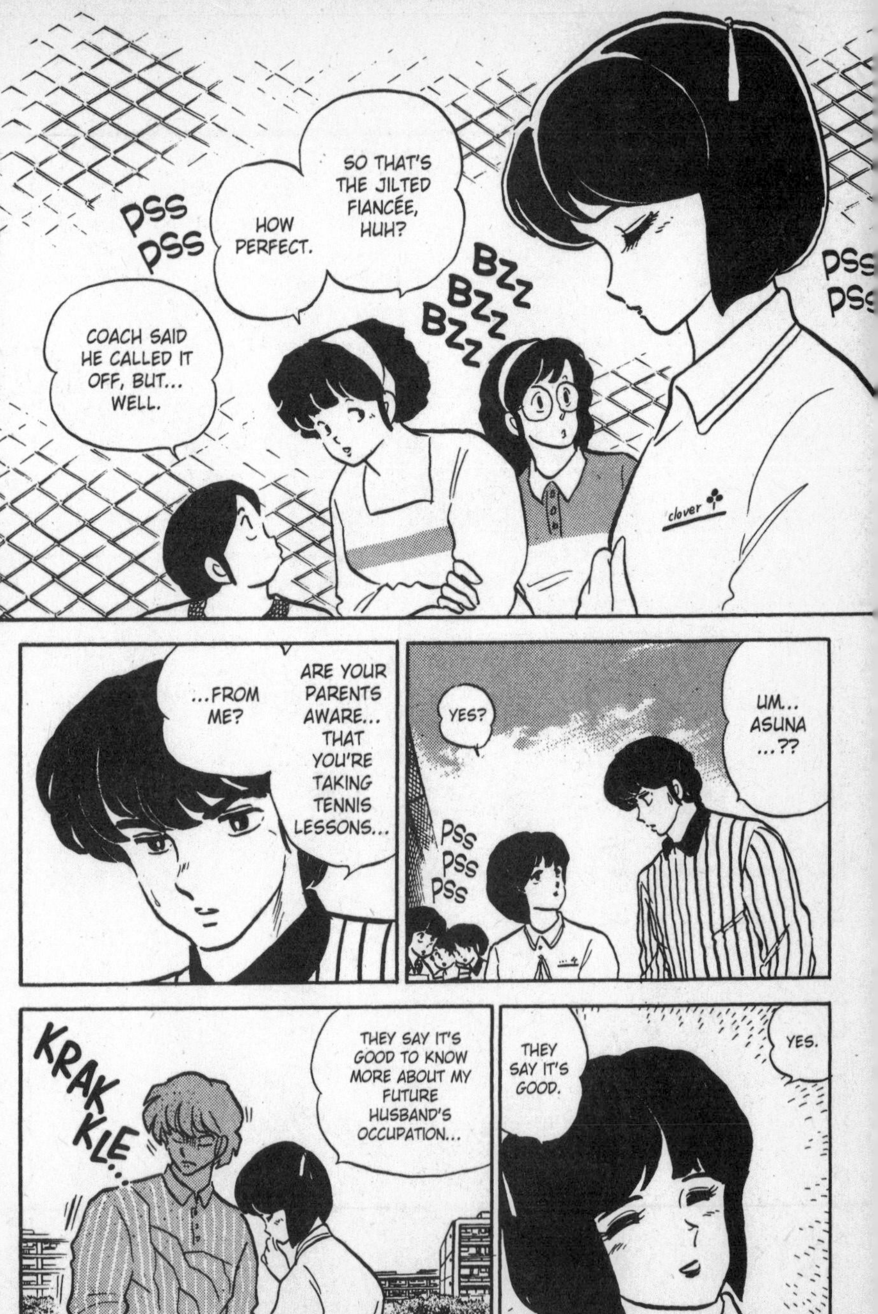
PSS PSS
SO THAT'S THE JILTED FIANCÉE, HUH?
HOW PERFECT.
PSS PSS
BZZ BZZ BZZ
COACH SAID HE CALLED IT OFF, BUT... WELL.
UM... ASUNA ...??
YES?
PSS PSS PSS
ARE YOUR PARENTS AWARE... THAT YOU'RE TAKING TENNIS LESSONS...
...FROM ME?
YES.
THEY SAY IT'S GOOD.
THEY SAY IT'S GOOD TO KNOW MORE ABOUT MY FUTURE HUSBAND'S OCCUPATION...
KRAKKLE...

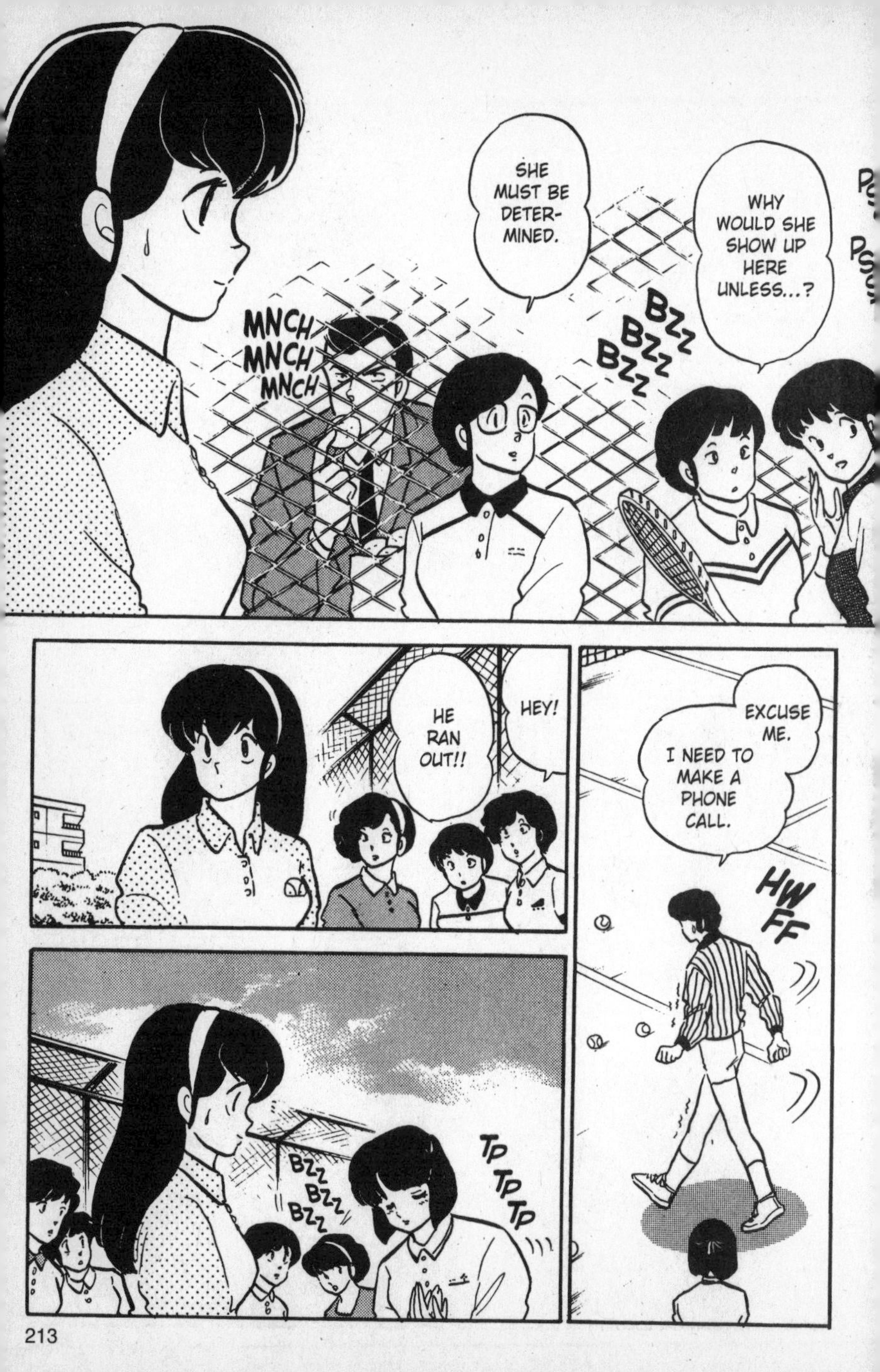
WHY WOULD SHE SHOW UP HERE UNLESS...?
BZZ BZZ BZZ
SHE MUST BE DETER-MINED.
MNCH MNCH MNCH
EXCUSE ME. I NEED TO MAKE A PHONE CALL.
HWFF
HEY!
HE RAN OUT!!
TP TP TP
BZZ BZZ BZZ

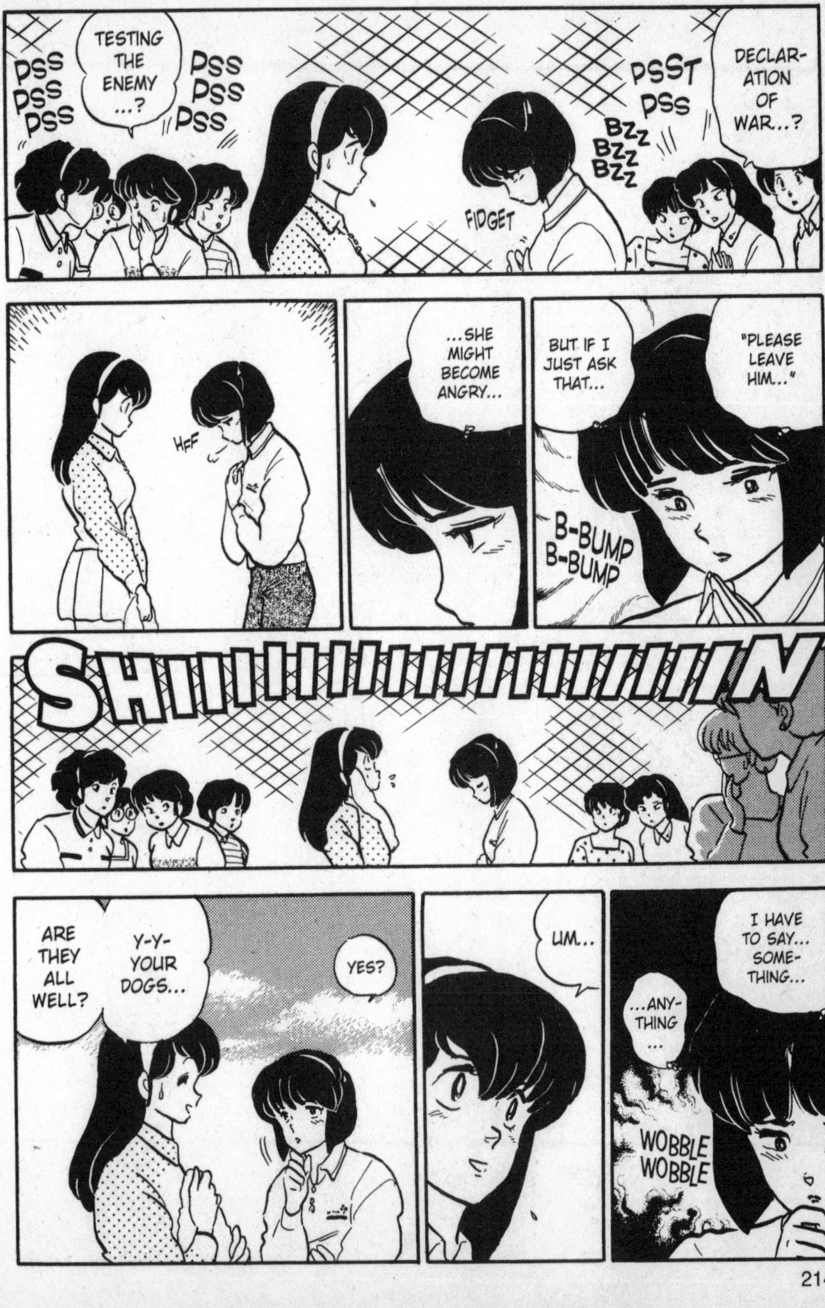
DECLARATION OF WAR...?
PSST PSS
BZZ BZZ BZZ
FIDGET
PSS PSS PSS
TESTING THE ENEMY ...?
PSS PSS PSS
"PLEASE LEAVE HIM..."
BUT IF I JUST ASK THAT...
B-BUMP B-BUMP
...SHE MIGHT BECOME ANGRY...
HFF
SHIIIIIIIIIIIIIIIIIIIIIN
I HAVE TO SAY... SOMETHING...
...ANYTHING ...
WOBBLE WOBBLE
UM...
YES?
Y-Y-YOUR DOGS...
ARE THEY ALL WELL?

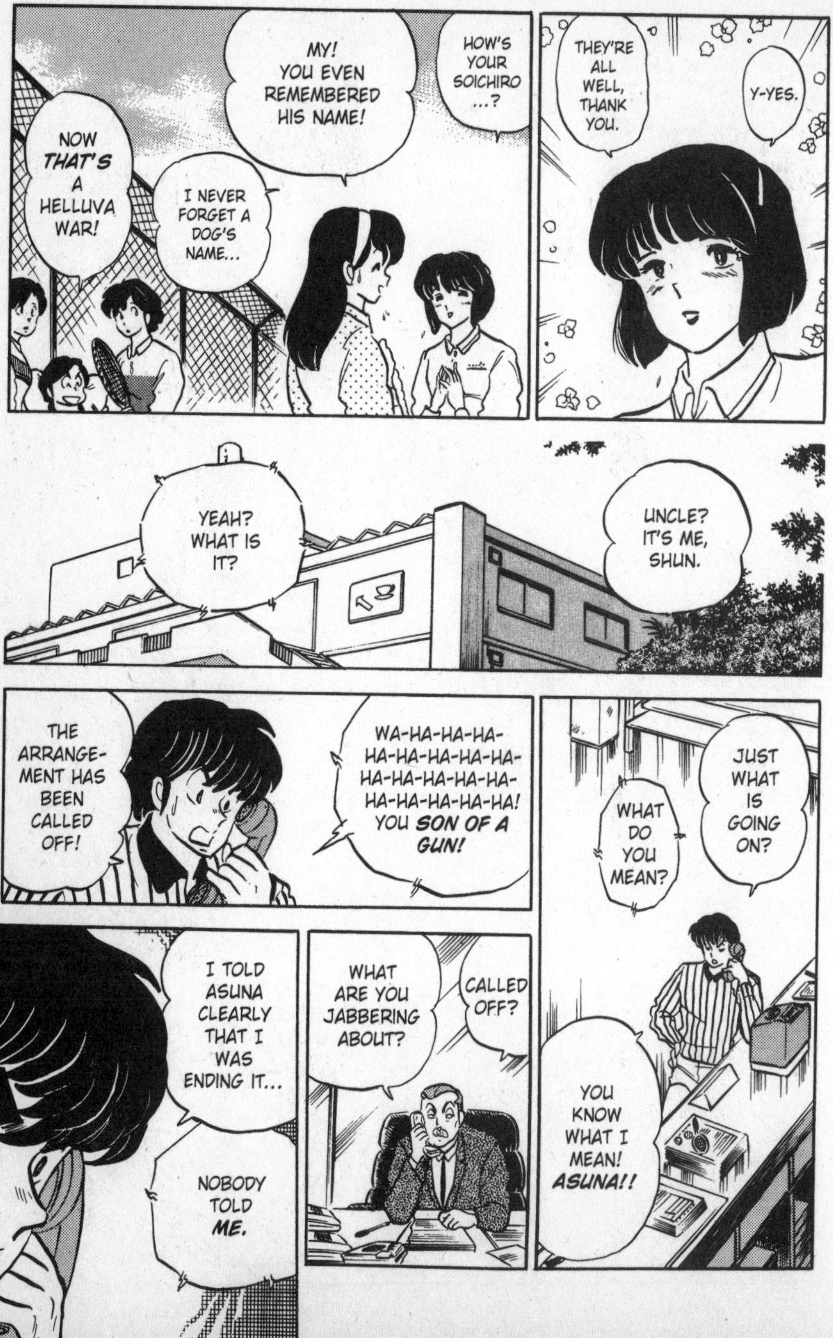
Y-YES.
THEY'RE ALL WELL, THANK YOU.
HOW'S YOUR SOICHIRO ...?
MY! YOU EVEN REMEMBERED HIS NAME!
I NEVER FORGET A DOG'S NAME...
NOW *THAT'S* A HELLUVA WAR!
UNCLE? IT'S ME, SHUN.
YEAH? WHAT IS IT?
JUST WHAT IS GOING ON?
WHAT DO YOU MEAN?
YOU KNOW WHAT I MEAN! ***ASUNA!!***
WA-HA-HA-HA-HA-HA-HA-HA-HA-HA-HA-HA-HA-HA-HA-HA-HA-HA-HA! YOU ***SON OF A GUN!***
THE ARRANGEMENT HAS BEEN CALLED OFF!
CALLED OFF?
WHAT ARE YOU JABBERING ABOUT?
I TOLD ASUNA CLEARLY THAT I WAS ENDING IT...
NOBODY TOLD ***ME.***

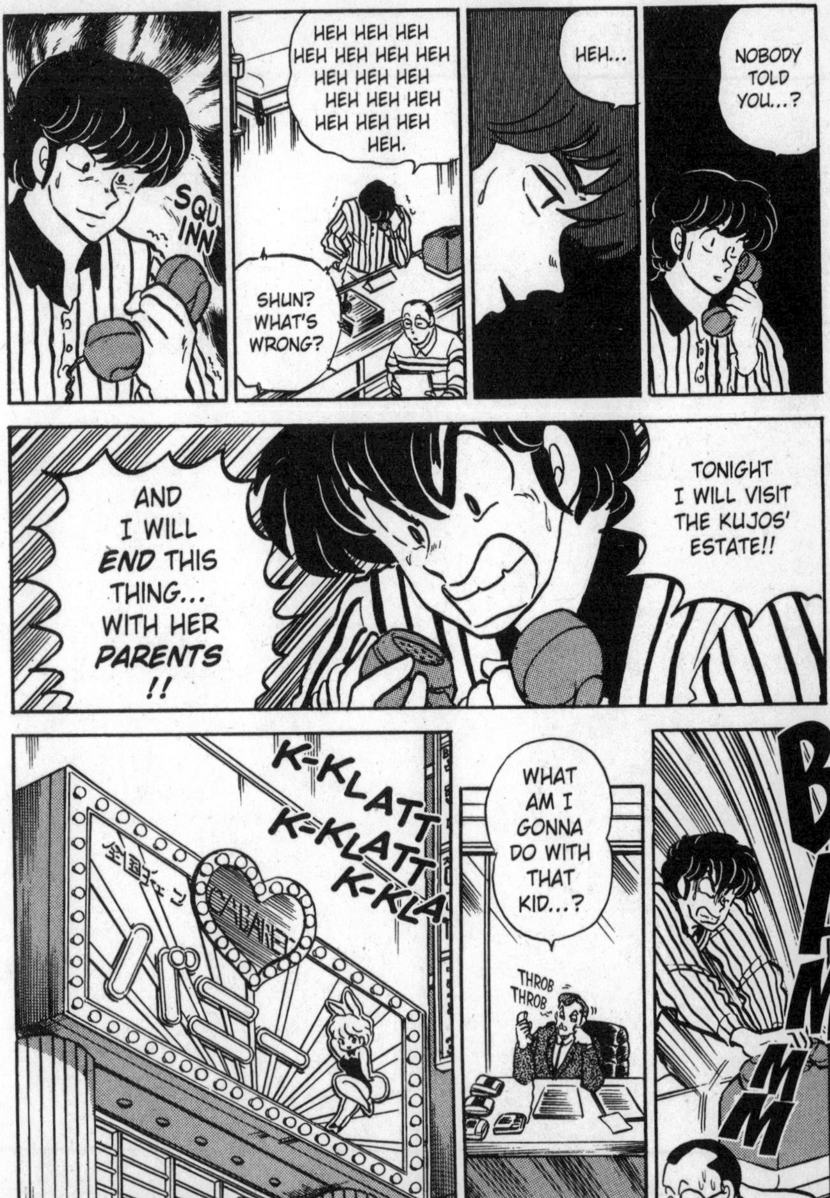
NOBODY TOLD YOU...?
HEH...
HEH HEH HEH HEH HEH HEH HEH HEH HEH HEH HEH HEH HEH HEH HEH HEH HEH.
SHUN? WHAT'S WRONG?
SQU INN
TONIGHT I WILL VISIT THE KUJOS' ESTATE!!
AND I WILL END THIS THING... WITH HER PARENTS !!
BAMMMM
WHAT AM I GONNA DO WITH THAT KID...?
THROB THROB
K-KLATT K-KLATT K-KLA
CABARET

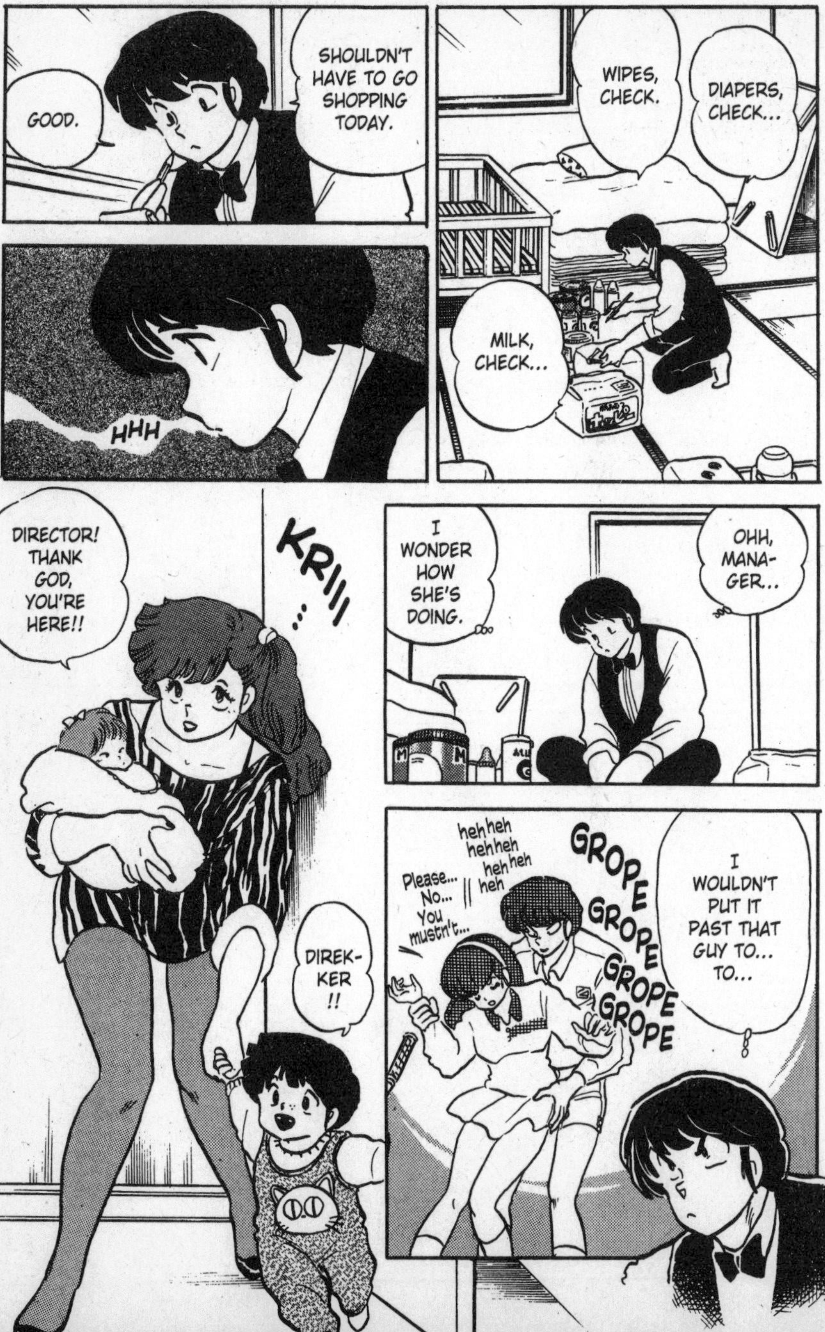
DIAPERS, CHECK...
WIPES, CHECK.
MILK, CHECK...
SHOULDN'T HAVE TO GO SHOPPING TODAY.
GOOD.
HHH
OHH, MANAGER...
I WONDER HOW SHE'S DOING.
I WOULDN'T PUT IT PAST THAT GUY TO... TO...
GROPE GROPE GROPE GROPE GROPE
heh heh heh heh heh heh heh
Please... No... You mustn't...
KRIII
...
DIRECTOR! THANK GOD, YOU'RE HERE!!
DIREK-KER!!

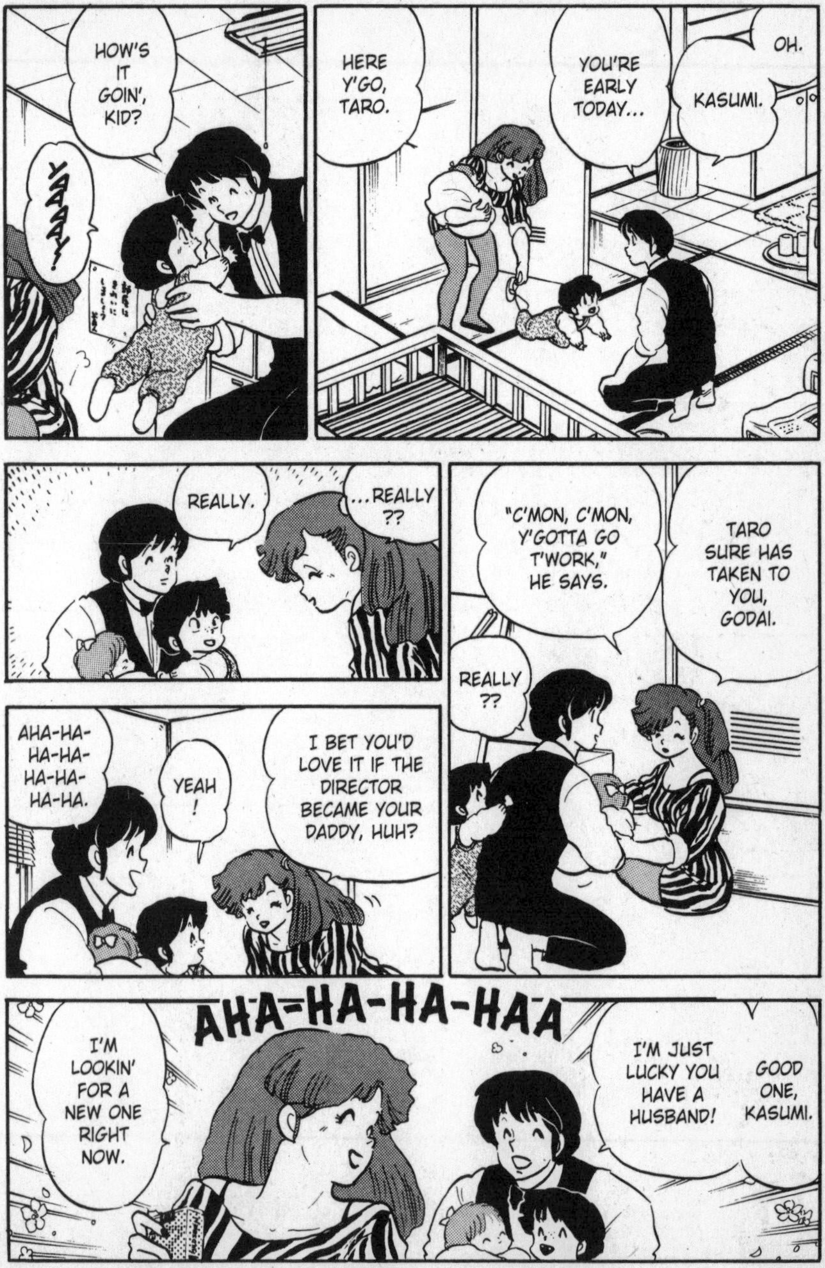
OH.
KASUMI.
YOU'RE EARLY TODAY...
HERE Y'GO, TARO.
HOW'S IT GOIN', KID?
YAAAAY!
TARO SURE HAS TAKEN TO YOU, GODAI.
"C'MON, C'MON, Y'GOTTA GO T'WORK," HE SAYS.
REALLY ??
...REALLY ??
REALLY.
I BET YOU'D LOVE IT IF THE DIRECTOR BECAME YOUR DADDY, HUH?
YEAH !
AHA-HA-HA-HA-HA-HA-HA-HA.
GOOD ONE, KASUMI.
I'M JUST LUCKY YOU HAVE A HUSBAND!
AHA-HA-HA-HAA
I'M LOOKIN' FOR A NEW ONE RIGHT NOW.

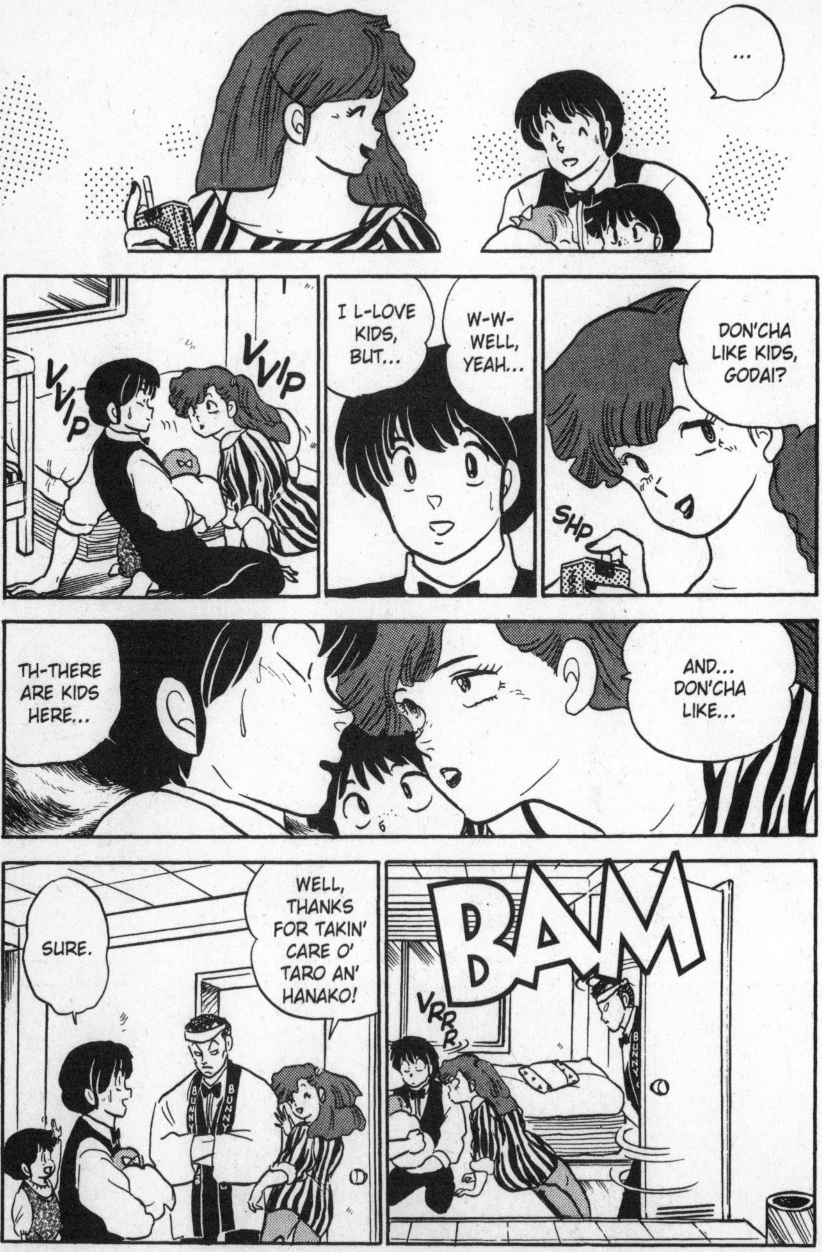
...
DON'CHA LIKE KIDS, GODAI?
SHP
W-W-WELL, YEAH...
I L-LOVE KIDS, BUT...
VVIP
VVIP
AND... DON'CHA LIKE...
TH-THERE ARE KIDS HERE...
BAM
VRRR
WELL, THANKS FOR TAKIN' CARE O' TARO AN' HANAKO!
SURE.

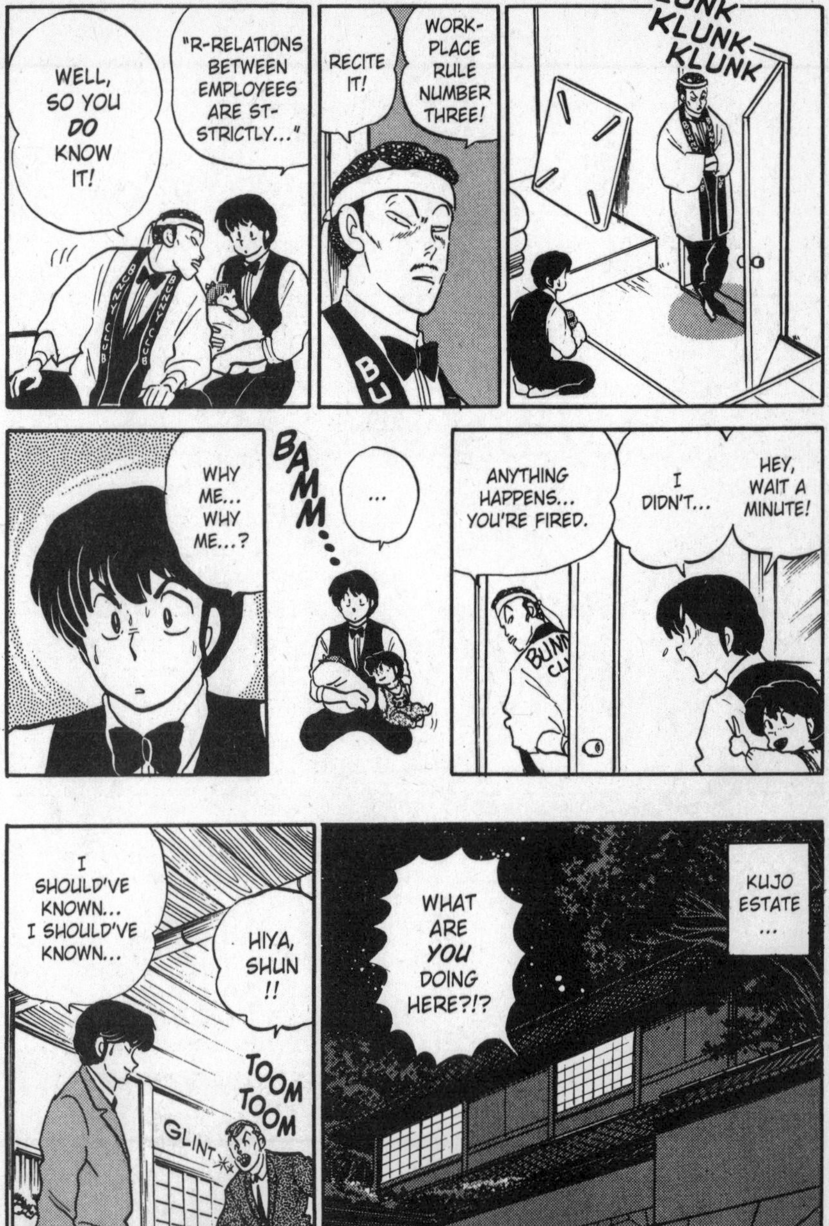
KLUNK KLUNK KLUNK
WORK-PLACE RULE NUMBER THREE!
RECITE IT!
"R-RELATIONS BETWEEN EMPLOYEES ARE ST-STRICTLY..."
WELL, SO YOU DO KNOW IT!
HEY, WAIT A MINUTE!
I DIDN'T...
ANYTHING HAPPENS... YOU'RE FIRED.
BAMM...
...
WHY ME... WHY ME...?
KUJO ESTATE ...
WHAT ARE YOU DOING HERE?!?
HIYA, SHUN !!
I SHOULD'VE KNOWN... I SHOULD'VE KNOWN...
TOOM TOOM
GLINT

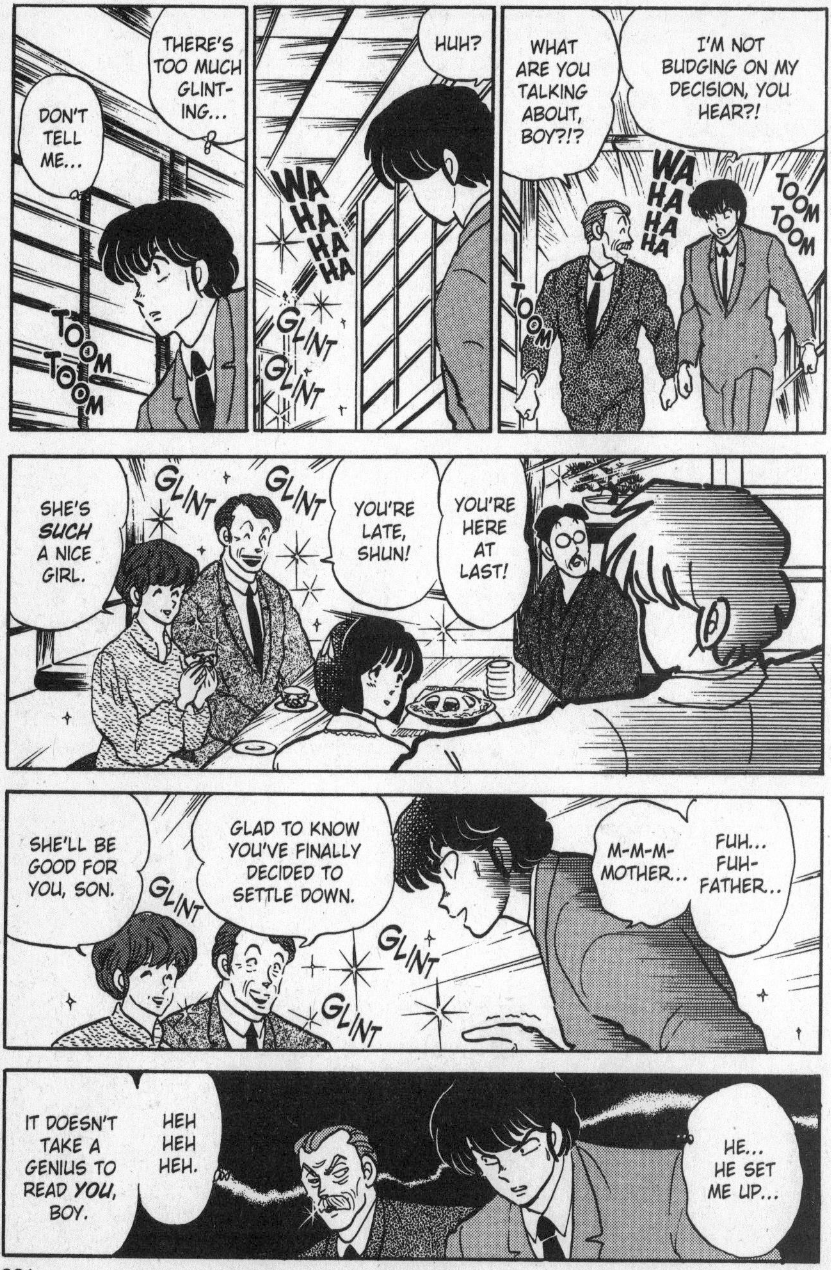
I'M NOT BUDGING ON MY DECISION, YOU HEAR?!
WHAT ARE YOU TALKING ABOUT, BOY?!?
WA HA HA HA HA
TOOM TOOM
TOOM
HUH?
WA HA HA HA HA
GLINT
GLINT
THERE'S TOO MUCH GLINT-ING...
DON'T TELL ME...
TOOM TOOM
YOU'RE HERE AT LAST!
YOU'RE LATE, SHUN!
GLINT
GLINT
SHE'S *SUCH* A NICE GIRL.
FUH... FUH-FATHER...
M-M-M-MOTHER...
GLINT
GLINT
GLAD TO KNOW YOU'VE FINALLY DECIDED TO SETTLE DOWN.
GLINT
SHE'LL BE GOOD FOR YOU, SON.
HE... HE SET ME UP...
HEH HEH HEH.
IT DOESN'T TAKE A GENIUS TO READ *YOU*, BOY.

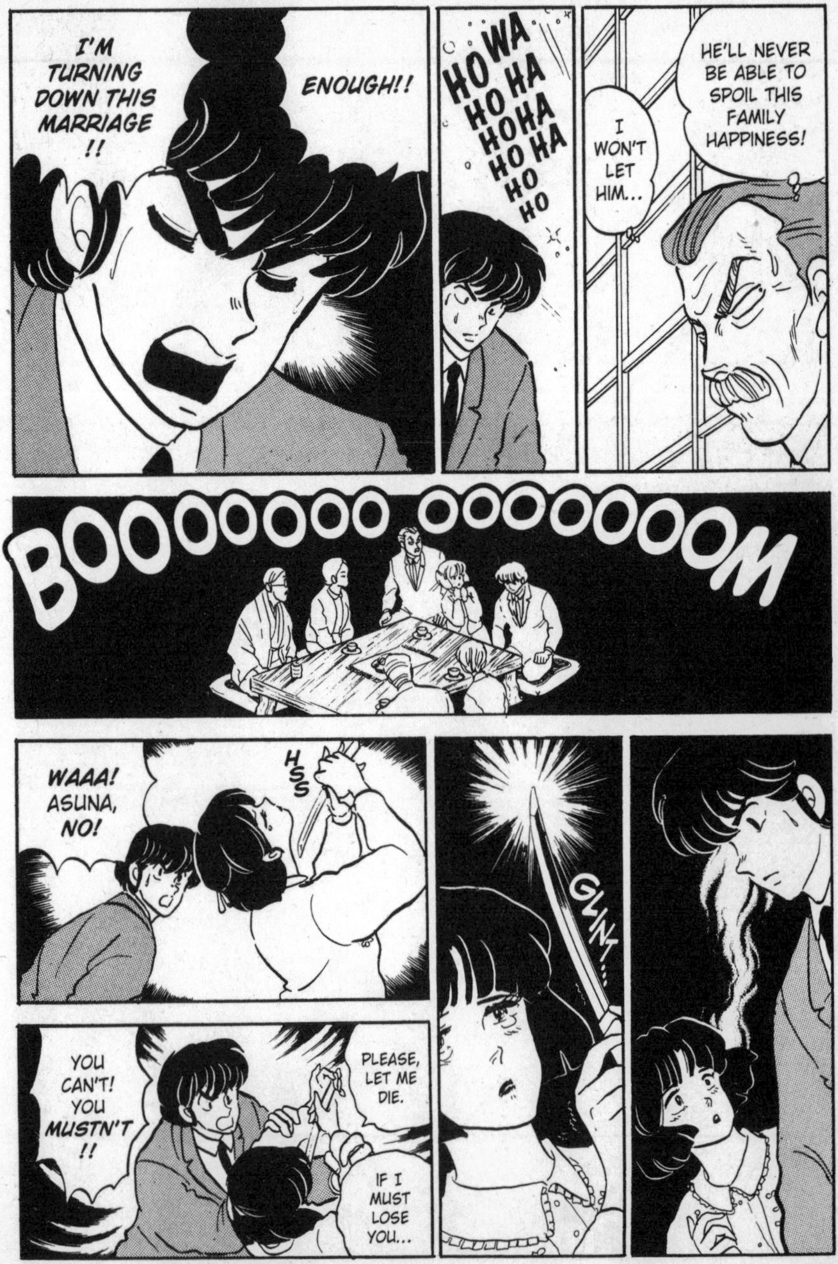
HE'LL NEVER BE ABLE TO SPOIL THIS FAMILY HAPPINESS!
I WON'T LET HIM...
HO WA HO HA HO HA HO HA HO HA HO HO
ENOUGH!!
I'M TURNING DOWN THIS MARRIAGE!!
BOOOOOOO OOOOOOOM
GLINK...
HSS
WAAA! ASUNA, NO!
PLEASE, LET ME DIE.
IF I MUST LOSE YOU...
YOU CAN'T! YOU MUSTN'T!!

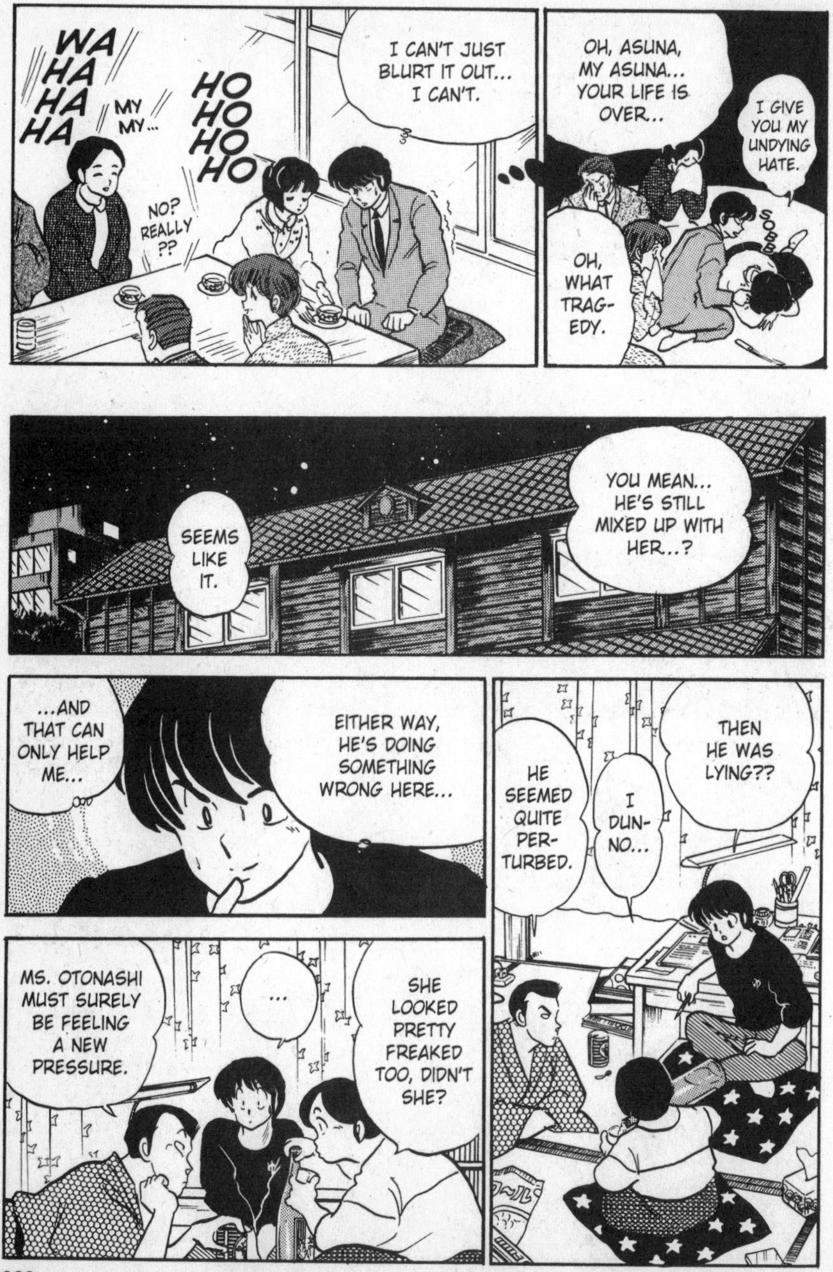
OH, ASUNA, MY ASUNA... YOUR LIFE IS OVER...
I GIVE YOU MY UNDYING HATE.
SOBB
OH, WHAT TRAG-EDY.
I CAN'T JUST BLURT IT OUT... I CAN'T.
HO HO HO HO HO
NO? REALLY ??
MY MY...
WA HA HA HA HA
YOU MEAN... HE'S STILL MIXED UP WITH HER...?
SEEMS LIKE IT.
THEN HE WAS LYING??
I DUN-NO...
HE SEEMED QUITE PER-TURBED.
EITHER WAY, HE'S DOING SOMETHING WRONG HERE...
...AND THAT CAN ONLY HELP ME...
SHE LOOKED PRETTY FREAKED TOO, DIDN'T SHE?
...
MS. OTONASHI MUST SURELY BE FEELING A NEW PRESSURE.

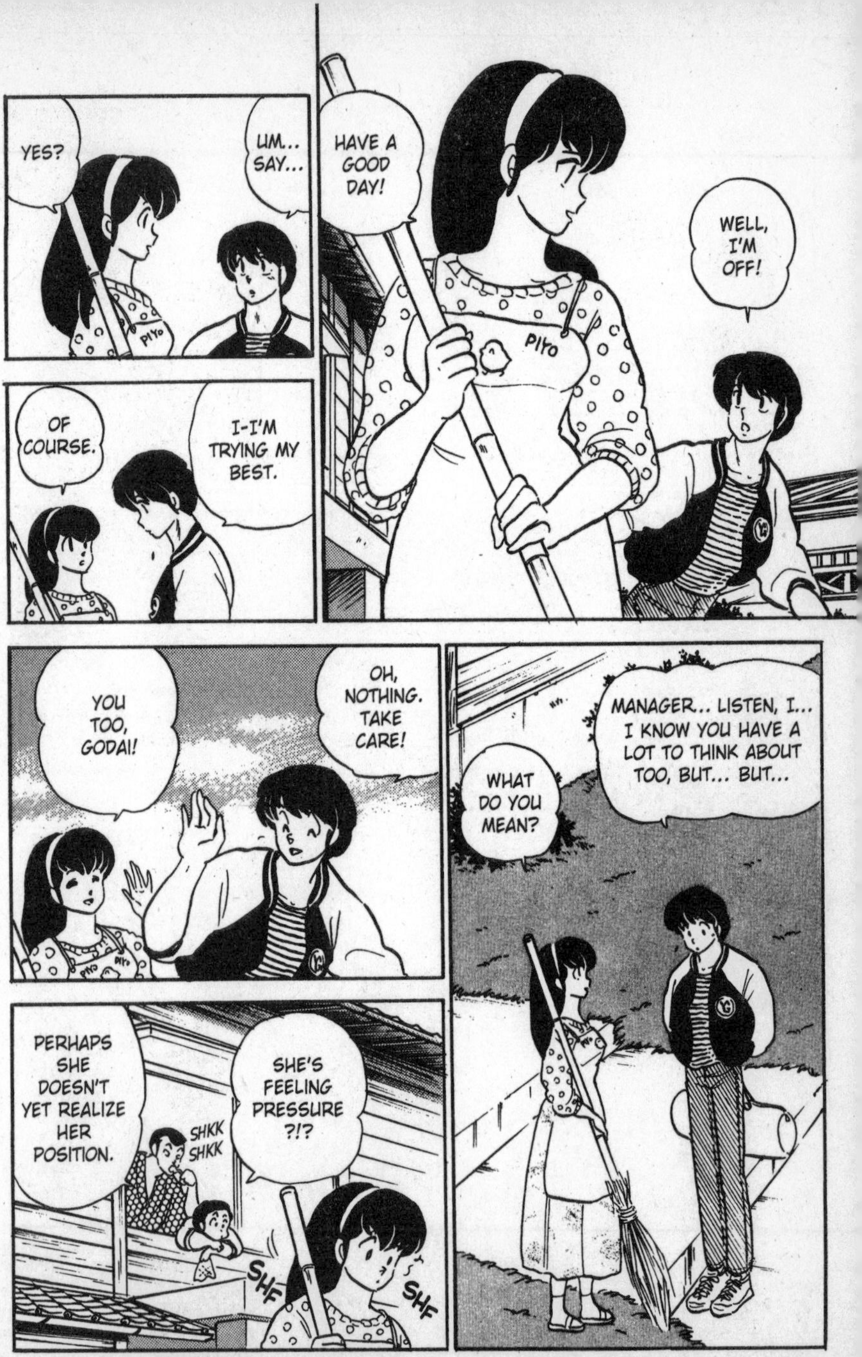
WELL, I'M OFF!
HAVE A GOOD DAY!
UM... SAY...
YES?
I-I'M TRYING MY BEST.
OF COURSE.
MANAGER... LISTEN, I... I KNOW YOU HAVE A LOT TO THINK ABOUT TOO, BUT... BUT...
WHAT DO YOU MEAN?
OH, NOTHING. TAKE CARE!
YOU TOO, GODAI!
SHE'S FEELING PRESSURE ?!?
SHKK SHKK
PERHAPS SHE DOESN'T YET REALIZE HER POSITION.
SHF
SHF

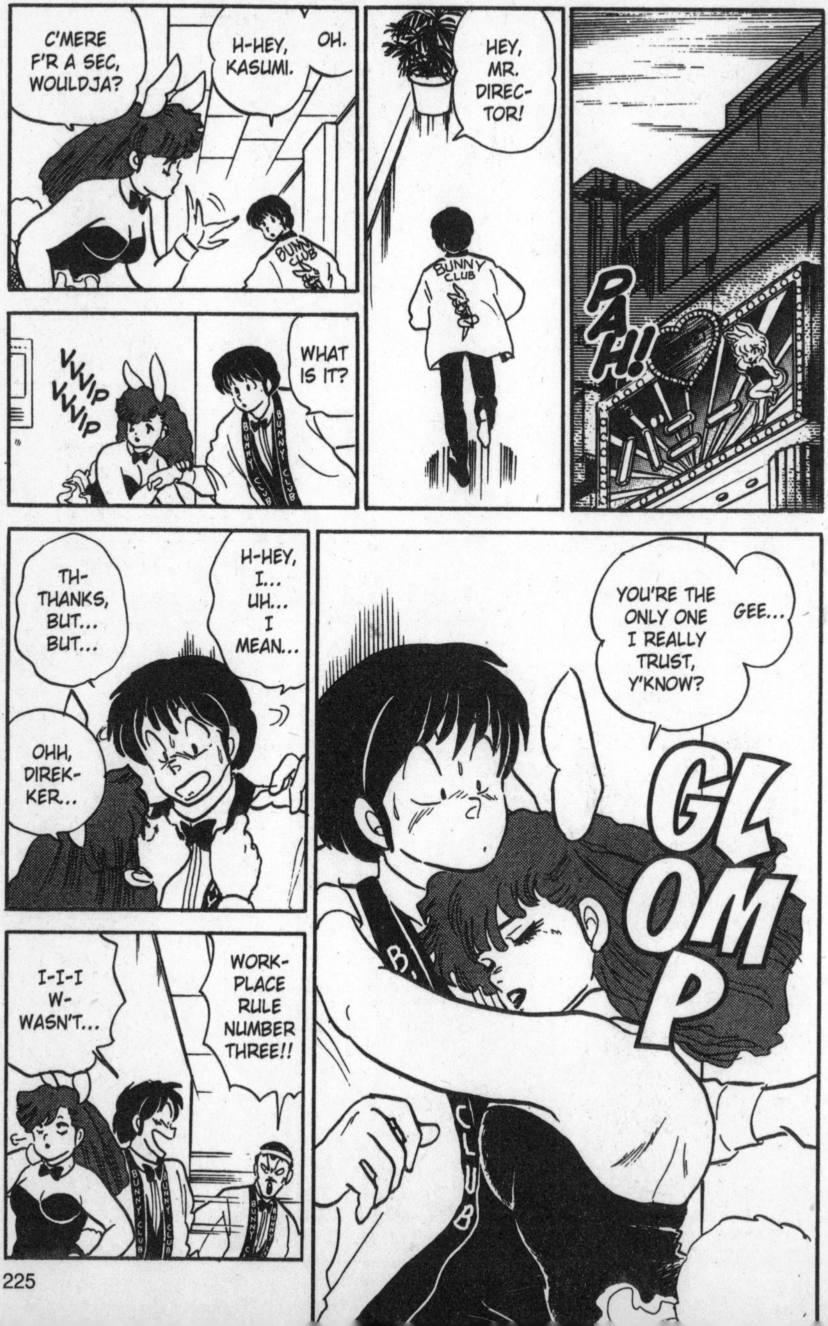
PAH!
HEY, MR. DIRECTOR!
OH.
H-HEY, KASUMI.
C'MERE F'R A SEC, WOULDJA?
WHAT IS IT?
VVVIP VVVIP
GEE...
YOU'RE THE ONLY ONE I REALLY TRUST, Y'KNOW?
GLOMP
H-HEY, I... UH... I MEAN...
TH-THANKS, BUT... BUT...
OHH, DIREK-KER...
WORK-PLACE RULE NUMBER THREE!!
I-I-I W-WASN'T...

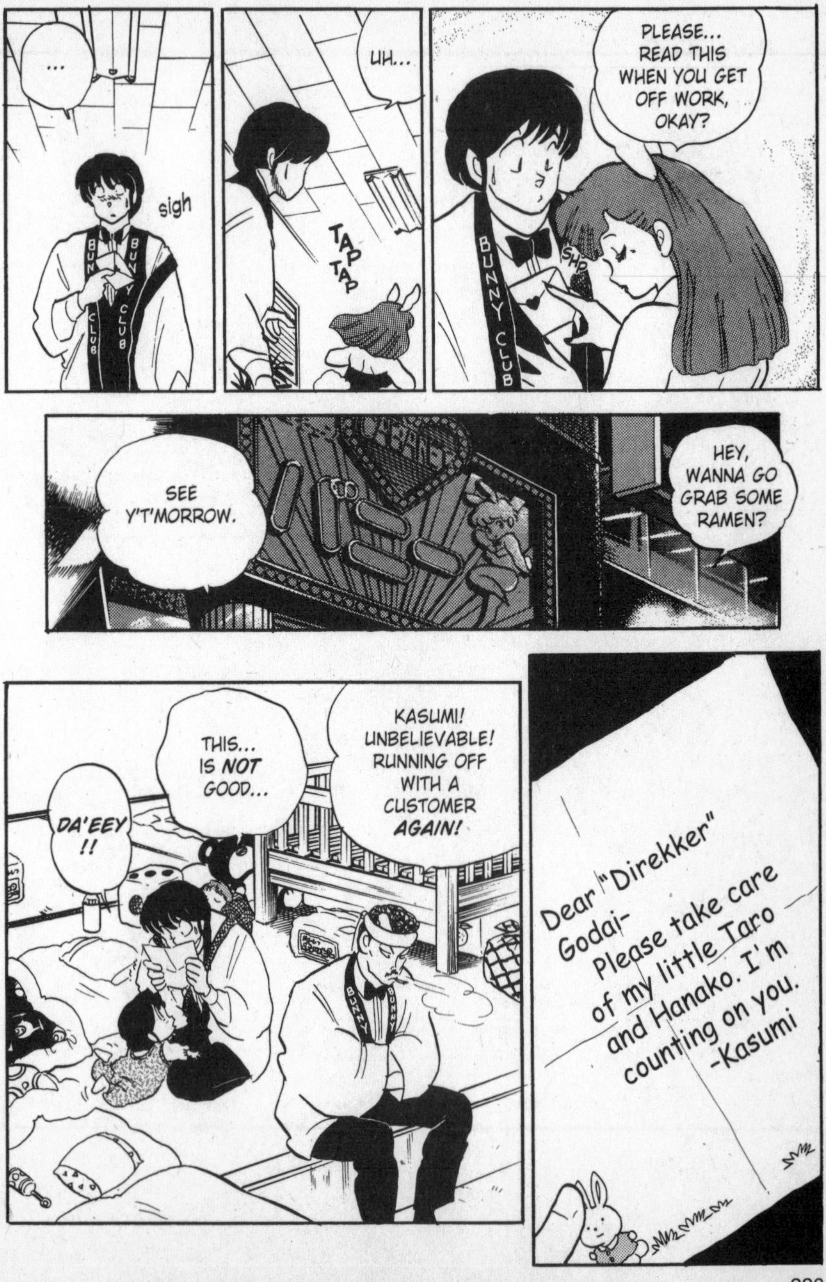
PLEASE... READ THIS WHEN YOU GET OFF WORK, OKAY?
SHP
BUNNY CLUB
UH...
TAP TAP
...
sigh
BUNNY CLUB
HEY, WANNA GO GRAB SOME RAMEN?
SEE Y'T'MORROW.
Dear "Direkker" Godai-
Please take care of my little Taro and Hanako. I'm counting on you.
-Kasumi
KASUMI! UNBELIEVABLE! RUNNING OFF WITH A CUSTOMER AGAIN!
THIS... IS NOT GOOD...
DA'EEY!!
BUNNY

MAISON IKKOKU

VOLUME 12
Story and Art by Rumiko Takahashi

Translation/Gerard Jones & Mari Morimoto
Touch-Up Art & Lettering/Susan Daigle-Leach
Design/Nozomi Akashi
Editor – 1st Edition/Trish Ledoux
Editor – Editor's Choice Edition/Kit Fox

Managing Editor/Annette Roman
Director of Production/Noboru Watanabe
Vice President of Publishing/Alvin Lu
Sr. Director of Acquisitions/Rika Inouye
Vice President of Sales & Marketing/Liza Coppola
Publisher/Hyoe Narita

Published by VIZ, LLC
P.O. Box 77010
San Francisco, CA 94107

Editor's Choice Edition
10 9 8 7 6 5 4 3 2 1
First printing, July 2005
First English edition published 1998

www.viz.com

ABOUT THE ARTIST

Rumiko Takahashi, born in 1957 in Niigata, Japan, is the acclaimed creator and artist of *Maison Ikkoku, InuYasha, Ranma 1/2* and *Lum * Urusei Yatsura*.

She lived in a small student apartment in Nakano, Japan, which was the basis for the *Maison Ikkoku* series, while she attended the prestigious Nihon Joseidai (Japan Women's University). At the same time, Takahashi also began studying comics at Gekiga Sonjuku, a famous school for manga artists run by Kazuo Koike, author of *Crying Freeman* and *Lone Wolf and Cub*. In 1978, Takahashi won a prize in Shogakukan's annual New Comic Artist Contest and her boy-meets-alien comedy *Lum * Urusei Yatsura* began appearing in the weekly manga magazine *Shonen Sunday*.

Takahashi's success and critical acclaim continues to grow, with popular titles including *Ranma 1/2* and *InuYasha*. Many of her graphic novel series have also been animated, and are widely available in several languages.

DATIONS

Fans of

maison ikkoku

should also read:

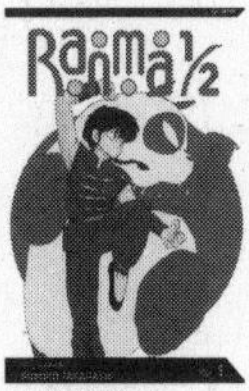
Ranma 1/2

©1988 Rumiko Takahashi/Shogakukan, Inc.

RANMA 1/2

Rumiko Takahashi's gender-bending comedy series is the tale of a father and son who fall into cursed springs in China, and their lives are transformed, literally. When they get wet, the father turns into a panda and the son, Ranma, turns into a girl. Comic situations ensue as they try and keep their friends and family, especially Ranma's fiancée and her family, from finding out their secret.

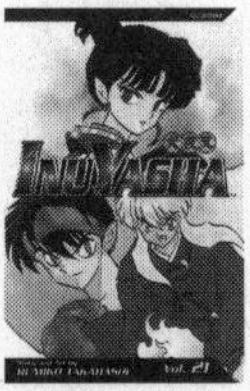
InuYasha

© 1997 Rumiko Takahashi/Shogakukan, Inc.

INUYASHA

Takahashi returned to her fantasy roots with this exciting manga that combines elements of historical action, exciting horror, touching romance, and ridiculous physical comedy. Modern schoolgirl Kagome is pulled into Japan's mystical past and must join forces with a scabrous half-demon named Inu-Yasha. This series has also spawned an immensely popular TV series as well!

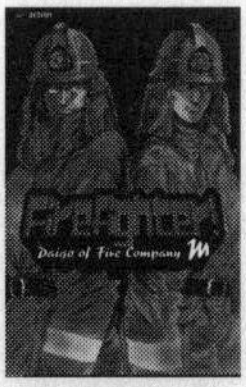
Daigo of Fire Company M

© 1996 Masahito Soda/Shogakukan, Inc.

FIREFIGHTER!: Daigo of Fire Company M

Tired of magical girls and romantic misunderstandings? Would you sooner take a long walk off a short pier than slog through another tale of a prepubescent-boy-coming-into-his-own-thanks-to-his-father's-giant-robot? Then look no further than *FIREFIGHTER!*, an immensely readable and entertaining manga about a cocky young man who, despite the feelings of his superior officers (and the public at large), has been earmarked for fire-fighting greatness. Daigo takes "going over the top" to new, heretofore unheard of, levels.

LOVE MANGA? LET US KNOW!

☐ Please do NOT send me information about VIZ Media products, news and events, special offers, or other information.

☐ Please do NOT send me information from VIZ Media's trusted business partners.

Name: _____

Address: _____

City: _____ **State:** _____ **Zip:** _____

E-mail: _____

☐ Male ☐ Female **Date of Birth** (mm/dd/yyyy): ____/____/_____ (Under 13? Parental consent required)

What race/ethnicity do you consider yourself? (check all that apply)

☐ White/Caucasian ☐ Black/African American ☐ Hispanic/Latino

☐ Asian/Pacific Islander ☐ Native American/Alaskan Native ☐ Other: _____

What VIZ title(s) did you purchase? (indicate title(s) purchased) _____

_____

What other VIZ titles do you own? _____

_____

Reason for purchase: (check all that apply)

☐ Special offer ☐ Favorite title / author / artist / genre

☐ Gift ☐ Recommendation ☐ Collection

☐ Read excerpt in VIZ manga sampler ☐ Other _____

Where did you make your purchase? (please check one)

☐ Comic store ☐ Bookstore ☐ Grocery Store

☐ Convention ☐ Newsstand ☐ Video Game Store

☐ Online (site:_____) ☐ Other _____

How many manga titles have you purchased in the last year? How many were VIZ titles?
(please check one from each column)

MANGA
☐ None
☐ 1 – 4
☐ 5 – 10
☐ 11+

VIZ
☐ None
☐ 1 – 4
☐ 5 – 10
☐ 11+

How much influence do special promotions and gifts-with-purchase have on the titles you buy?
(please circle, with 5 being great influence and 1 being none)

1 2 3 4 5

Do you purchase every volume of your favorite series?

☐ Yes! Gotta have 'em as my own ☐ No. Please explain: ____________

What kind of manga storylines do you most enjoy? **(check all that apply)**

☐ Action / Adventure
☐ Comedy
☐ Fighting
☐ Artistic / Alternative
☐ Science Fiction
☐ Romance (shojo)
☐ Sports
☐ Other ____________
☐ Horror
☐ Fantasy (shojo)
☐ Historical

If you watch the anime or play a video or TCG game from a series, how likely are you to buy the manga? **(please circle, with 5 being very likely and 1 being unlikely)**

1 2 3 4 5

If unlikely, please explain: ____________

Who are your favorite authors / artists? ____________

____

What titles would like you translated and sold in English? ____________

____

THANK YOU! Please send the completed form to:

NJW Research
42 Catharine Street
Poughkeepsie, NY 12601

Your privacy is very important to us. All information provided will be used for internal purposes only and will not be sold or otherwise divulged.